ARCHITECTS OF AFFLUENCE

D1189908

Subseries on the History of Japanese Business and Industry
Harvard East Asian Monographs, 166

Nishi Amane and Modern Japanese Thought

Farm and Nation in Modern Japan: Agrarian Nationalism, 1870–1940

Valley of Darkness: The Japanese People and World War Two

The Historical Encylopedia of World War II (coauthor)

Artist and Patron in Postwar Japan: Dance, Music, Theater, and the Visual Arts, 1955–1980

Fire Across the Sea: The Vietnam War and Japan, 1965–1975

The Ambivalence of Nationalism: Modern Japan between East and West (coeditor)

ARCHITECTS OF AFFLUENCE

*THE TSUTSUMI FAMILY
AND THE SEIBU-SAISON ENTERPRISES
IN TWENTIETH-CENTURY JAPAN*

THOMAS R. H. HAVENS

Published by the COUNCIL ON EAST ASIAN STUDIES, HARVARD UNIVERSITY, and distributed by HARVARD UNIVERSITY PRESS, Cambridge (Massachusetts) and London   1994

The Council on East Asian Studies at Harvard University publishes a monograph series and, through the Fairbank Center for East Asian Research and the Reischauer Institute of Japanese Studies, administers research projects designed to further scholarly understanding of China, Japan, Korea, Vietnam, Inner Asia, and adjacent areas.

Havens, Thomas R. H.
    Architects of affluence : the Tsutsumi family and the Seibu-Saison Enterprises in twentieth-century Japan / Thomas R. H. Havens.
        p. cm. – (Harvard East Asian monographs ; 166. Subseries on the history of Japanese business and industry)
    Includes bibliographical references and index.
    ISBN 0-674-04360-X
    1. Seibu Group–History.   2. Conglomerate corporations–Japan–History.
3. Tsutsumi family. I. Title. II. Series: Harvard East Asian monographs ; 166.
III. Series: Harvard East Asian monographs. Subseries on the history of Japanese business and industry.
HD2756.2.J3H38 1994
338.8'3'0952–dc20   94-9723
                                                                CIP

Index by Thomas R. H. Havens

Subseries on the History of Japanese Business and Industry

Japan's rise from the destruction and bitter defeat of World War II to its present eminence in world business and industry is perhaps the most striking development in recent world history. This did not occur in a vacuum. It was linked organically to at least a century of prior growth and transformation. To illuminate this growth, a new kind of scholarship on Japan is needed: historical study *in the context of a company or industry* of the interrelations among entrepreneurs, managers, engineers, workers, stockholders, bankers, and bureaucrats, and of the institutions and policies they created. Only in such a context can the contribution of particular factors be weighed and understood. It is to promote and encourage such scholarship that this subseries is established, supported by the Reischauer Institute of Japanese Studies and published by the Council on East Asian Studies at Harvard.

Albert M. Craig
Cambridge, Massachusetts

Preface

Most Japanese old enough to enjoy it seem uneasy with the idea of affluence. Ever since the Edo period (1600–1868), Japanese writers have compared Japan with other countries in humble, if formulaic, terms: "although ours is a small and poor country" are the opening words of countless treatises on China, western Europe, or more recently the United States. Today only the United States exceeds Japan's $3 trillion Gross National Product, and only Switzerland and Iceland have higher per-capita incomes. Three-quarters of all Japanese households have VCRs and microwaves, four-fifths own cars, and nearly everybody has a color television (the average family has two). One in ten Japanese takes an overseas trip each year, a sign of the true affluence that began to supersede simple material abundance for many families in the 1980s.

Yet most persons over age thirty remember when times were less flush, when employees worked long hours for modest pay, when Japan was still playing catch-up to the West—and many of them feel slightly awkward about the leisure time that has become part of their weekly routines during the past decade or more. Government exhortations to tighten belts and curb consumption during the 1992–1993 business recession resonated with this mature generation. Not so for the young—known as *shinjinrui*, the New Breed—who take affluence for granted and seek lifestyles of studied casualness or almost mannered self-indulgence.

No businesses have taken fuller advantage of Japan's consumer prosperity during the past thirty years than the interconnected enterprise groups known as Seibu and Saison. These sizable conglomerates, centered in transportation, retailing, travel, and leisure, are the subject of the narrative that follows. Readers of history are invited to consider how and why the Tsutsumi family turned the Seibu and Saison companies into powerhouses that designed much of the architecture of middle-class consumption and material well-being in a country where the interface of business and society is widely acknowledged but incompletely understood.

In preparing this account, I have benefited from the help of many persons. Without exception the individuals listed among the sources at the back of the book answered my questions with courtesy and candor. I am especially grateful to Kawahara Hiroshi and Kawahara Miyako for generous hospitality during 1990–1991 when I was a visiting fellow at Waseda University. The following persons in Japan also aided my studies: Akimoto Ritsuo, Isamu Amemiya, Kazuko Amemiya, Hashimoto Minoru, Hashimoto Seiko, Katō Mikio, Amy S. Katoh, Yūichi Katoh, Nagai Michio, Ozaki Katsuhiko, Tasaka Hiroshi, Tracey F. Watanabe, and Yui Tsunehiko. I am also grateful to many colleagues in correspondence and conversation, especially Beverly J. Bossler, Delmer M. Brown, Edward I. Brodkin, Marius B. Jansen, Bruce H. Kirmmse, Karen I. Mavec, Ronald Napier, Susan Napier, Henry DeW. Smith II, Jacqueline Soteropoulos, Valdo H. Viglielmo, Dennis C. Washburn, and Ikuko Watanabe. I am indebted to Katherine Keenum and the staff of the Council on East Asian Studies Publications of Harvard University for expert editorial care.

Funds from the National Endowment for the Humanities and a Fulbright-Hays Fellowship through the U.S. Department of Education speeded my studies, and I am grateful to these sources for indispensable assistance.

Except in citations to Western-language publications, the personal names of Japanese nationals are given in the customary Japanese manner, with the family name first. Abbreviations used in the text, as well as Japanese-language titles of companies and organizations, are cited in the index. Whenever possible, changes across time in sales, profits, and borrowings by Japanese businesses are expressed as percentage changes in yen terms, to eliminate the effects of differing currency-conversion rates. In principle, the narrative treats the history of the Seibu and Saison enterprises from 1915 to 1990. From 1915 to 1932, one

U.S. dollar is considered equivalent to 2 yen; then the exchange rate fluctuated around 3 yen to the dollar until 1939 and 4 yen to the dollar thereafter. Following Japan's surrender in August 1945, the yen was greatly debased by inflation until a fixed ratio of 360 to the dollar was established in 1949. The following Bank of Japan rates have been used for converting yen to dollars:

Yen per U.S. Dollar

1949–1971	360	1983–1984	238
1972–1974	300	1985	239
1975–1976	297	1986	169
1977	269	1987	145
1978	211	1988	128
1979	219	1989	138
1980	227	1990	145
1981	220	1991	138
1982	249	1992	125

Contents

Figures

ARCHITECTS OF AFFLUENCE

INTRODUCTION

"Thanks and Service"—
At a Price

CERTIFICATE OF APPRECIATION

Your company cooperated in railway transport to carry out sanitation work for this prefecture for more than eight years starting June 1944. You resolved various difficulties and brought stability to this work, contributing to increased food production. For this success I express profound thanks.

Yasui Seiichirō
Governor of Tokyo Prefecture
August 12, 1953

To Seibu Railway Company, Ltd.[1]

This testimonial, found in the somber headquarters fortress of the Seibu Railway (Seibu Tetsudō) in suburban Tokorozawa, succinctly states the city's gratitude for the company's hauling as much as 3.6 million liters of raw sewage a day from central Tokyo to nearby truck farms, to be used as fertilizer when food was scarce at the end of World War II and shortly after. Seibu's "golden trains" (*ōgon densha*), which helped to make up for depleted chemical fertilizers in reclaiming 2,000 hectares of farmland, replaced a fleet of sanitation trucks idled by gasoline shortages from their usual task of dumping the city's human waste, untreated, into Tokyo Bay. For this civic service the rail-

3

way earned a substantial ¥30 million—and the ire of many Tokyoites for its smelly cargoes.[2] Remarkably, in the half-century since this humble undertaking the same company has transformed itself, like a bird of paradise, into the sleekest retailing, recreation, and leisure enterprises in the country—Japan's postwar history in cameo.

The Seibu Railway Group traces its origins to a resort-development firm founded in 1920 and a private commuter railroad formed in 1945 when two struggling suburban lines in northwestern Tokyo merged. Today the railway group enjoys annual sales of about $7.2 billion from transporting nearly 2 million passengers and thousands of tons of freight each day, operating the country's most extensive network of luxury hotels, and developing Japan's largest chain of ski, golf, and vacation resorts. Its chieftain, Tsutsumi Yoshiaki, is sometimes considered the world's richest private citizen because he controls companies with hidden assets, mainly in land, estimated in 1990 to be worth the astonishing sum of $280 billion.[3]

A related cluster of retailing businesses now known as the Saison Group evolved from a rustic dry-goods store on the fringes of Tokyo purchased in 1940 by the founder of the Seibu enterprises, Tsutsumi Yasujirō (1889–1964), who was Yoshiaki's father. From modest beginnings as merchants to muddy-soled shoppers from rural areas near the capital, the Seibu Department Stores, Ltd. (Seibu Hyakkaten), has catapulted to the top of the industry in both revenues and repute—the sales leader in Japan's most populous market and the unquestioned arbiter of fashion and urban culture among the giant merchant houses. Anchored by the department-store company and a major supermarket chain, the Saison Group rings up net sales at the rate of $35.21 billion a year, largest among Japanese retailers and comparable to Nissan ($42.91 billion) or Tōshiba ($33.23 billion).[4] Saison's chief executive since 1955 has been Tsutsumi Seiji, another son of the founder and a serious poet as well as the doyen of postwar merchandising in Japan.

Collectively the Seibu and Saison enterprises now generate almost as much cash flow as the Matsushita Panasonic empire, yet for the first half of their seventy-year history these businesses scarcely made their founder any money at all. Only after 1955 did Tsutsumi Yasujirō start earning a sizable return on his lifelong investments in land, transit, and housing for middle-class customers. His sons Yoshiaki and Seiji have likewise spent much of their careers investing in future assets—in businesses related to recreation, sports, travel, and leisure—that began to pay rich dividends only when true household affluence spread widely in the 1980s. The record of the Seibu and Saison organizations connects very directly with the rise of middle-class consumer culture in Japan since the mid-1950s: the growth of these enterprises is a prism for refracting the historical experience of millions of Japanese families as they dealt with institutions of commerce offering retail services beyond the means, even the dreams, of their immediate forebears.

"After 1917 there were two models of development, the American capitalist one and the communist system of the Soviet Union. America had many entrepreneurs like Carnegie and Rockefeller, but in Japan at that time there were very few pioneers of the free-enterprise system. The best examples were Gotō of Tōkyū, Nezu of Tōbu, Kobayashi of Hankyū, and Tsutsumi of Seibu."[5] These words from Nagai Michio, a former minister of education and longtime intimate of the Tsutsumis, aptly place Tsutsumi Yasujirō in the history of modern Japanese business—outside the elite of family-dominated trusts and banks known before World War II as *zaibatsu*. Tsutsumi was much affected by the rise of Taishō democracy during 1912–1926, when Japan experienced its first cabinets responsible to the majority party in the lower house of the national Diet, universal male suffrage was achieved, and much urban prosperity resulted from World War I. He foresaw a huge increase in the number of middle-class consumers and invested in tertiary-sector businesses in the 1920s to cater to them: railways, suburban housing, and mountain resorts. Of these only housing earned him much money before World War II; otherwise he was too far ahead of his time. As Nagai has observed, "He felt remuneration for his work only after 1955, with the rise of mass consumerism in Japan."[6]

"Thanks and service" became the corporate shibboleth as soon as Tsutsumi formed the Hakone Land Company, Ltd. (Hakone Tochi), in March 1920. He adopted this motto, which may trace to Pure Land Buddhist teachings popular since the thirteenth century in his home region of Ōmi, after a series of business failures that he himself later attributed to his greediness as a youth. An official biography quotes Tsutsumi in the late 1950s: "In the world of profits there is competition, but there is none in the world of service. I think the spirit of scr-vice is the deciding factor in business."[7] An attitude of thanks and service to customers would lead to profits more surely than pell-mell jousts with competitors for advantage. Indeed Tsutsumi was fond of saying, "It's wrong to think that a company is intended to make money. If you don't think in terms of serving society, your enterprise will not succeed."[8]

Japanese firms have probably disregarded such corporate catechisms as regularly as European nobles ignored the Latin inscriptions on their medieval coats of arms, yet phrases like "thanks and service" possess much allure in Japanese business culture. Tsutsumi undertook too many Machiavellian schemes and engaged in too many brutal struggles to be a real disciple of his own teachings, but his motto remains a powerful ideal for both the railway and Saison groups to this day. Even when they seemed to agree on little else, both Tsutsumi Yoshiaki and Tsutsumi Seiji have regularly invoked "thanks and service" to inspirit their respective organizations.[9] Still it would be naive to ignore that the ultimate purpose has always been commercial gain, whether in building resorts in Karuizawa in the 1920s or golf courses in Kyushu today.

The paradoxes surrounding these twin themes—commercial success from modest beginnings and pieties about service that seem self-serving—help to explain the ambivalence many Japanese feel about the Tsutsumis, both father and sons. Some even dismiss the Tsutsumi wealth as the product of good fortune, forgetting that luck in business is usually the residue of design. The founder's reputation is based almost exclusively on his corporate career, not on the thirteen terms he served in the lower house of the Diet. One admirer was Kobayashi Ichizō, the Hankyū czar, who noted that "Mr. Tsutsumi and I were active in both railways and land. In railways I was not outdone, but I was no match for him in land."[10] Nonetheless, respected as he may be for his self-made prosperity, Tsutsumi Yasujirō is most often remembered as "Pistol Tsutsumi," from a threat on his life with firearms in 1924, and as a brusque dealmaker with a flamboyant personal life. Even though he was born to an owner-farmer household in Shiga Prefecture, Tsutsumi is sometimes scorned as an "Ōmi merchant" (*Ōmi shōnin*) interested only in making money. Shiga omitted him from its honor roll of illustrious natives when it celebrated one hundred years as a prefecture in 1972 because he was deemed too self-interested and too little concerned with the livelihoods of others in the region, where he owned various companies. More subtly, the novelists Ishikawa Tatsuzō and Kajiyama Toshiyuki have satirized Tsutsumi's romantic liaisons and business methods in vigorous and amusing prose.[11]

Nearly everyone in Japan has opinions about Tsutsumi's sons Seiji and Yoshiaki, because the groups they head (Saison and Seibu Railway, respectively) were the most publicized conglomerates in Japan during the 1980s.[12] Much of the attention has centered on the extraordinary marketing and cultural impact of Seiji's Seibu department store and on the success of Yoshiaki's Seibu Lions baseball team. Tsutsumi Seiji, who was born in 1927 and reared by the woman who in 1955 became Yasujirō's third wife, started off like his father with almost nothing. Today he symbolizes the enormous Saison Group, which college seniors perennially rank one of the most desirable to join after graduation. Consumers rate Seiji's department stores as freshest, most inviting, cleverest in advertising, and most cultured in the industry—in good part because of his own eminence as a poet and novelist.[13] His image of pensive individuality contrasts with the blandness of most corporate leaders; he is something of a contemporary hero who invites creativity and offers meaning to the young.[14] Yet Seiji is widely known to be a demanding boss, at times almost impossible to please; and securities analysts warn of Saison's low profits and highly leveraged financing.

Nonetheless Japan's corporate managers and opinion makers continue to give high marks to both Seiji and his half-brother Yoshiaki, who was born in 1934 to the woman who was Tsutsumi Yasujirō's mistress for the final three decades of his life. In a survey of 850 executives published in 1990, the respected financial weekly *Diamond* found that Yoshiaki's railway ranked third and Seiji's department store twentieth among Japanese businesses in the effectiveness of top management.[15] Another poll the previous autumn rated Tsutsumi Yoshiaki, Morita Akio of Sony, Toyoda Eiji of Toyota, and Tsutsumi Seiji as the four most influential business sultans in the country. Yoshiaki is also regularly deemed one of the most politically powerful figures in Japan, even though he has never held public or party office at any level.[16] *Diamond* reported on August 26, 1990, that Yoshiaki had been chosen by his peers as the most active businessperson of the year, although they ranked the rather stodgy Seibu Railway Company just fiftieth. The

7

reason for the gap is the vast hidden assets at his disposal in the form of land bequeathed by his father. The general public's opinion of Yoshiaki is more guarded. The Seibu Lions have won him the championship of Japanese pro baseball seven times in the past decade, and much popular acclaim besides. Yet his high-handed treatment of the team manager in 1989, his clumsy attempt early the next year to manipulate the winter Olympics of 1998 to his evident advantage, and his efforts to build golf courses despite outcries from environmentalists have cost Yoshiaki a great deal of public favor. Perhaps most resented by ordinary citizens is the yearly news from the National Tax Agency that the person some believe is the world's richest individual is listed nowhere near the top of Japan's greatest taxpayers.[17]

Journalists have long accentuated the complex business and personal relationship between the Tsutsumi brothers. Although he is the younger, Yoshiaki became Yasujirō's heir apparent about the time Seiji rebelled against their father as an undergraduate at Tokyo University. When Yasujirō died in 1964, Yoshiaki inherited nearly all the family property as well as control of the railway group; Seiji received only the right to operate the department stores—not even ownership of their land or buildings. Since then Yoshiaki has evolved as a conservative, cautious, and autocratic manager, whereas Seiji has become the most dynamic and innovative figure in Japanese retailing. The brothers are widely portrayed as distant, and sometimes acrimonious, toward each other. They have had less personal or business contact since Seiji resigned from the board of Yoshiaki's railroad in May 1986, an episode that generated great attention from the media amid predictions of an all-out commercial battle between the two in leisure services.

Still the characteristics shared by Seiji and Yoshiaki are many. Whether acknowledged or not, both show the mark of their father's philosophy and business methods. Like Yasujirō's early land company, Seibu and Saison each relies heavily on debt financing, minimizes current profits, and invests in the future by expanding its assets, operations, and influence in the industry. Just as Tsutsumi Yasujirō was a free-enterprise capitalist who defied the prewar *zaibatsu*, both Seiji and Yoshiaki have prospered outside the postwar *keiretsu* system of enterprise groups centered on a major bank. Seibu and Saison are the service-sector counterparts of Matsushita, Honda, and Sony—

exceptions to the *keiretsu* that dominated business after the mid-1950s. Neither brother is thick with the economic bureaucrats in the Ministry of International Trade and Industry, although each cultivates party politicians; neither plays a big role in the national business leadership (*zaikai*) or corporate associations like the Japan Chamber of Commerce and Industry. Both operate within the economic establishment but outside its system of reward and prestige, respected but not embraced by the manufacturing barons who reigned over the world of Japanese business in the 1970s and 1980s.

The Tsutsumis remain outsiders partly because their companies are only loosely tied to major banks, instead capitalizing on the great wealth in land accumulated by their father—assets unmatched by any other enterprise group in Japan. But the main reason they are not fully accepted is that, like low-ranking merchants in the premodern social order, they operate in the lightly regarded service sector of the economy, catering to middle-class customers in a country where national policy during most of this century has favored producers over consumers and exports over domestic demand. Government reports on comparative social indicators confirm that Japan rates high vis-à-vis other countries in health, economic stability, and family life but low in community activities, public libraries, learning and cultural opportunities, and leisure facilities[18]—services that are notoriously undernourished to this day.

In the widest sense, services represent all economic activities except the production of goods (mining, farming, fishing, forestry, and manufacturing). In this broad sense, services make up the tertiary or non-goods sector of the economy: transportation and communications, utilities, public services, wholesaling, retailing, and leasing, food and drink, real estate and construction, finance and insurance, education and culture, and leisure. By other reckonings, services are the residue after the tertiary sector is subdivided into financial, commercial, communications, and transport activity. Even in this narrower sense, services have accounted for a substantial majority of the Japanese tertiary sector since World War II. Although by international standards Japan employs a large number of people in wholesaling and distributing, Gary R. Saxonhouse has shown that services there have evolved more or less as in other industrialized countries. Productivity rose more slowly than for other sectors before World War II, then played catch-up in the 1960s even as the portion of the overall work force in service occupations rose from 26.0 percent in 1936 to 39.5 percent by 1969.[19]

Services for businesses boomed during the era of high-speed growth (1955–1973): shipping, warehousing, wholesaling, finance, insurance, real estate, and the like claimed about half of the tertiary sector. Services for individuals, such as retailing, life insurance, hotels, personal care, dining out, and recreation, represented 23.3 percent of tertiary activity in 1960 and 21.5 percent in 1970, then rose slightly during the next decade. Likewise services for society (government, railways, utilities, media, medicine, education) grew less fast than those for businesses during 1955–1973, then slowly expanded their share of total tertiary expenditures when Japan entered the phase of mature, lower-speed growth.[20] In short, the areas where Saison and Seibu focused most of their efforts—services for individuals and society—grew least rapidly during the 1960s and early 1970s, when the Tsutsumi brothers were scrambling to rebuild and expand their organizations following the death of their father in 1964.

Consumer prosperity, the information revolution, and steady conversion from a manufacturing-based economy to one grounded increasingly in services after 1980 led to what Japanese officials call softnomics—the adaptation of economic management to postindustrial society, in which investment and consumption are concentrated in the tertiary sector and manufactured goods have more and more nonmaterial (soft) content, such as design, packaging, and marketing.[21] Tertiary industries already represented 50.9 percent of gross domestic product in 1970; ten years later they claimed 58.1 percent. The Economic Planning Agency has estimated that this figure will rise to 64.2 percent by the year 2000,[22] about as high as it can go if Japan is to retain a substantial manufacturing base.

Services grew especially fast in the 1980s in areas where consumer demand shifted from material and quantitative to personal, qualitative fulfillment: matchmaking and wedding agencies, home-delivery firms, golf-club memberships, cultural activities, and travel. Services for businesses also expanded during the 1980s, driven by the belated but rapid spread of computing. Finance, insurance, advertising, leasing, information networking, and a variety of consulting firms performed extremely well. By the end of the decade, according to government statistics, tertiary industries represented 58.7 percent of employment and just under 60 percent of GDP.[23] Yet Japan remained a net importer of services; cultural facilities continued to be impoverished; and despite a preponderance of female workers and depressed wages, productivity grew relatively slowly in service industries. Nonetheless, as Miyata Mitsuru has observed, the demand for services continues unabated; they are consumed on the spot and cannot be stockpiled.[24]

These recent trends in services, together with sustained economic prosperity, have been both a godsend and a challenge to corporations like Seibu and Saison. The railway group reacted by spreading its network of resorts to twenty-five of Japan's forty-seven prefectures in the 1980s, doubling the capacity of its hotels, and marching boldly into urban development. Saison was the first department-store group to move successfully into supermarkets in the 1960s and insurance, credit, and finance in the 1970s. It has spent the last decade developing soft services like film distribution, publishing, videotex, and cable television as well as hotels, sports, catering, travel, theaters, advertising, and dining out—what Tsutsumi Seiji calls "a comprehensive lifestyle industry."[25] For the railway group, the key element in its recent growth remains the borrowing power it can muster because of its gigantic resources in land. The vital ingredient for Saison has been its ingenuity in response to a fast-changing market—one it has not always read accurately. Since each is deeply invested in recreation and tourism, presumably Seibu and Saison were cheered by the 1991 survey of 5,000 adults showing that only 13 percent thought work was more important than leisure, an astounding drop of 16 percent since 1989. Twenty-four percent rated leisure first, up from 11 percent in 1989, and nearly everyone else (59 percent) said leisure was as important as work—a judgment echoed by Prime Minister Miyazawa Kiichi when he decreed a five-day, forty-hour workweek for public servants starting in May 1992. A follow-up poll announced at the end of that year showed that among people in their twenties, barely three men in ten, and just two women in ten, thought work was the most important activity in life.[26]

This excursus into modern Japanese business history recounts the absorbing stories of Seibu and Saison largely in their own terms, for nowhere are there other enterprises quite like them; but comparisons with their competitors are offered when appropriate. Business history is a vigorous field of inquiry in Japan, sharply set off from economic history and usually lodged in a separate academic division of the university. Economic historians in Japan have been mostly concerned with theoretical questions and Marxist insights, whereas business historians are almost never Marxists and delve extensively into statistical data.[27] Few Japanese business historians study the period since 1945; apart from banking and securities, almost no writings by scholars of any nationality deal with the service sector of the Japanese economy. This book takes a step toward overcoming these temporal and topical lacunae.

There is no dearth of information about the Seibu and Saison enterprises, although the most salient data are sometimes elusive. Any major bookstore in Japan boasts a shelf of titles devoted to the Tsutsumis and their companies; the financial press and the sometimes gossipy weekly magazines write regularly about both groups. No American business leader—not even Lee Iacocca or Donald Trump—has been so extensively chronicled as the Tsutsumis or, for that matter, a number of other Japanese corporate managers. Neither the Seibu Railway Group nor the Saison Group makes its financial report or profit and loss statement public, but the essentials are often leaked to reporters, duly published, and then rarely disowned. The printed record is extensive for the period from 1920, when Tsutsumi Yasujirō started the Hakone Land Company, until the Seibu Railway and Saison groups separated in 1970. There are several company histories, one of them written with reasonable detachment, and a number of biographies of the founder and his sons. I have relied extensively on the writings and published interviews of Tsutsumi Yoshiaki and Tsutsumi Seiji for the period since 1970, as well as information made public by both groups. Several of the Saison businesses, as well as the Seibu Railway Company itself, are listed on the Tokyo Stock Exchange, which obliges them to make semiannual financial disclosures for public distribution. Like other researchers, I have received more cooperation from the Saison Group than from the railway group. The editors of the recent two-volume history of Saison, covering 1940–1990, have given me wide access to company archives and other documents used in compiling the series, including much information on the founder and on the railway group. I have supplemented these sources by interviewing knowledgeable persons both inside and outside the two groups. The result is a business portrait, although incomplete at points, that is as disinterested as the available sources and proper skepticism allow.

The pages that follow interweave business biography with corporate history, concentrating on the public lives of the Tsutsumis except when more personal issues affect the fortunes of their companies. However colorful Seiji and Yoshiaki may seem as private persons, their roles as entrepreneurs and service-industry leaders are the real sources of their impact on contemporary business and society in Japan.

The first two chapters examine the career of Tsutsumi Yasujirō from his student days at Waseda University through his involvements in real estate, railroads, and politics—mostly a record of failure until the 1950s, but not for any want of energy or imagination.

The next six chapters take up the parallel growth of the Seibu Railway and Saison groups from the 1960s to the 1980s as they diversified from railroads, land, and retailing into two of Japan's most far-flung consumer-services organizations. Both groups read the changing market with skill, although hardly omniscience, thanks mainly to the insights of their respective leaders, so that the railway moved beyond land development into recreation after 1970 just as the department-store company was carrying out a retailing revolution to accommodate shoppers' new-found preferences for quality and individuality. Then while Tsutsumi Yoshiaki turned Prince into Japan's largest hotel chain and the Lions into the country's best professional baseball club in the late 1970s and 1980s, Seiji diversified his companies beyond retailing into specialized consumer markets in finance, insurance, and food services—what he styled the "sale of information" in Japan's era of mature affluence.

Chapters Nine and Ten analyze the complementary approaches each group took to the sudden domestic demand for leisure in the later 1980s: skiing, golf, and mountain resorts for the railway, vacations, travel, and fine dining as well as hotels for Saison. These chapters, together with the eleventh and last, illustrate the contrasting styles and differing management philosophies of the two brothers by examining fields where their enterprises most nearly converge, now that Japan has entered an age of "creating lifestyles through leisure." Chapter Eleven recapitulates the elements of success for the two groups and stresses the enduring points in common—as well as those of sharp divergence—between Seiji and Yoshiaki.

My goal is to discover what the rise of these interconnected businesses reveals about the growth of services and consumerism in a partly planned economy that has favored producer goods and export-led manufacturing for most of the twentieth century. Often faced with official policies unfriendly to their activities, how did these private enterprises manage to develop outside the *zaibatsu* and *keiretsu* establishment and prosper under conditions where until recently consumption has been dampened, savings encouraged, and services retarded in favor of manufacturing? How has each group responded to changing social values, ideas of personhood, and consumer needs as information and leisure have become increasingly in demand? The answers to questions like these promise to tell a good deal about the interaction between entrepreneurship and social change that has characterized Japanese national life ever since Tsutsumi Yasujirō's "golden trains" carried human fertilizer to shore up food production and his own company's treasury in an economy savaged by war.

CHAPTER ONE

THE LURE OF LAND

Tsutsumi Yasujirō often exulted that "I'm twenty years ahead of other people."[1] This was true at several levels. He was a precocious, quick, and ambitious youth who mapped his future long before most classmates. In his twenties he knew two former prime ministers and an array of national leaders before most contemporaries had even thought to enter politics. He bought land for mountain resorts at Karuizawa and Hakone starting in 1917, well before other major developers; and in the 1920s he built college towns in the Tokyo suburbs on a scale unmatched for the next three decades. In private life Tsutsumi was a generation ahead of conventional social mores, in that he openly acknowledged children born to unions outside his marriages, registered them as his own, and allowed all his offspring to share in the family businesses.

But prescience often brings penury to investors who try to tap a market before it develops. Being twenty years ahead of his time was bittersweet for Tsutsumi: it showed his foresight, but it also delayed him from earning recognition and reward. As late as age fifty he was just one of thousands of energetic, moderately successful entrepreneurs in a country of small businesses where most of the labor force worked for firms with fewer than one hundred employees. Tsutsumi's early enterprises, like most small and medium concerns before World War II, existed outside the *zaibatsu* system; had he not turned his into giants after 1945, their beginnings would hold little interest today. The

FIGURE 1. Tsutsumi Yasujirō at home in Hiroo, 1960. (Saison Group)

lure of land development is what enabled him to excel others and eventually rival the postwar *keiretsu* in wealth.

LEARNING AND LABOR

Perhaps it is poetic justice that the person who built the richest private real-estate portfolio Japan has ever known should have been born on the soil to a small owner-cultivator household with two hectares—or that as soon as he inherited the family land he sold it for a profit.[2] Tsutsumi Yasujirō was born on March, 7, 1889, in Shimoyagi, a village of fifty households between Ōmi Hachiman and Hikone along the eastern shore of Lake Biwa in Shiga Prefecture. He died April 26, 1964, in Tokyo. The signal event of his childhood happened at age four when his father Naojirō died of typhus and his mother Mio was persuaded or forced to surrender Yasujirō and his two-year-old sister Fusa to the care of his paternal grandparents, Seizaemon and Kiri. Another brother, one-year-old Junjirō, was adopted by a family named Hirota. Mio returned to Hokkaido, never remarried, and apparently had no contact with her children thereafter.[3] Yasujirō later ritually acknowledged his grandparents' "many sacrifices" on his behalf, but at age fourteen he was once again separated from maternal care when Kiri died.[4] Yasujirō had finished eighth grade the previous year, but his grandfather barred him from going on to Hikone Middle School because, as Yasujirō later remembered it, "you'll associate with bad people"[5]—rich children from the city. Instead he became a farmer for the next four years.

Those who detect in Tsutsumi tinges of the Ōmi merchant point to his early attraction to stock speculation and risky ventures. Ōmi merchants trace to the fifteenth century in the area near Lake Biwa. Like Yankee peddlers, they sold their wares throughout Japan, often bilking customers and gradually undercutting village self-sufficiency. In the Tokugawa period (1600–1868) they opened pawnshops, offered loans, established a network of branch outlets, and devised an ingenious account-book system. The merchant-philosophers Nakae Tōju (1608–1648) and Ishida Baigan (1685–1744), both born in Ōmi, provided a rationale for commerce in an era when traders were ill regarded by the authorities.[6] Tsutsumi may have felt akin to this tradition when he began speculating in rice futures at age fourteen and sought exclusive rights to distribute a new chemical fertilizer in Shiga the following year. By age seventeen he had begun investing in the new South Manchurian Railway Company, about the time he gave up field labor to enroll in a concentrated year-long program at a naval preparatory school in Kyoto.[7] Tsutsumi graduated on schedule in 1907, worked for a short time in the municipal offices in his native county, and then lost the last adult relative at home when his grandfather died in April of that year. He decided to sell the family farm, earning himself ¥5,000 (roughly $2,500),[8] and headed off to Tokyo, where in 1909 he entered the faculty of politics and economics at Waseda University. On New Year's Day of that year his first child, a daughter named Shukuko, was born to Nishizawa Koto; Tsutsumi and Nishizawa married the following autumn.[9]

Judo and debating quickly distracted Tsutsumi from classwork at Waseda, which he had chosen for the entrée it would give to a career in politics. His personal finances also worried him. To avoid using up the ¥5,000 proceeds from the farm on educational expenses, he took a side job printing university lecture notes and selling them. Tsutsumi quickly became acquainted with Nagai Ryūtarō, a newly hired assistant professor of politics who eventually served in the Diet and as a cabinet minister. According to Nagai Michio, "My father apparently told him to go into business to earn money if he wanted to be able to afford to graduate."[10] Soon Tsutsumi invested ¥2,000 in the Gotō Woolen Goods Company and within six months earned a return of ¥60,000.[11] He immediately squandered most of his profit trying to operate a steel foundry in Shibuya. By now he had become one of Japan's first "arbeiters," undergraduates who put their jobs first and hardly ever attended classes.[12] In 1911 he paid ¥10,000 for a license to operate a third-class post office in Nihonbashi Kakigara-chō, one of whose employees, Iwasaki Sono, bore him his eldest son Kiyoshi two years later.[13] Nineteen thirteen is also when he divorced Koto and drew close to Kawasaki Fumi, a journalist and graduate of Japan Women's University whom Tsutsumi eventually admitted had written his graduation thesis for him. They were married in 1915, separated in 1923, and finally divorced in 1954 when he was speaker of the House of Representatives. Fumi reared Koto's daughter by Tsutsumi, Shukuko, but had no children of her own.[14]

Somehow Tsutsumi found time at Waseda for athletics (he eventually achieved the sixth degree in judo), studying Russian from an

Orthodox priest together with Nagai Ryūtarō, and making speeches in a booming voice that could fill a hall without amplification on behalf of the political candidate Nakahashi Tokugorō. On campus he was best known as a gold-medal debater in the university's mock Diet, where he first met former Prime Minister Ōkuma Shigenobu, the founder and president of Waseda. Tsutsumi also helped to start the Rikken Dōshikai political party in 1913 and met Katsura Tarō, its moving spirit and also a former premier, shortly before Katsura died in October of that year. Katsura introduced him to Gotō Shinpei, a top bureaucrat and cabinet minister whose patronage, together with Ōkuma's, helped to launch Tsutsumi on his career in land development. Many years later Tsutsumi reiterated his boundless respect for Ōkuma but gave him poor marks for his tips on the stock market.[15]

Ōkuma, however, offered Tsutsumi priceless access to the politics of the future when he installed the new graduate as president of an antigovernment magazine for young people called *Shin Nihon* (New Japan) in 1913. Ōkuma used this journal, originally published by Fūzanbō, as an organ to criticize the cabinets of the day and debate the essence of Taishō democracy. Nagai served as chief writer during most of its brief life, 1911–1918. Tsutsumi both managed its finances and churned out articles, as did critics from the left such as Yamakawa Hitoshi and Yamakawa Kikue before the magazine turned apologist during the second Ōkuma cabinet of 1914–1916. Although it suffered the fiscal fate of nearly all little journals, *Shin Nihon* put Tsutsumi into circulation with important party and intellectual figures when he was on the threshold of his own career in politics.[16]

Tsutsumi's original aim may have been to become governor of Shiga, but the contact with Ōkuma, Nagai, and Katsura redirected his ambition toward the lower house of the Diet. Business when he was in his twenties was a means to pay for college and start him off in politics. Later in life he recalled, "I didn't want to go into politics by taking money from others. I wanted to earn my own money."[17] Actually he made very little from his business ventures between graduation in 1913 and election to the Diet in 1924. Through Katsura Tarō and Gotō Shinpei he met Fujita Ken'ichi, a top officer of the Kobe-based Suzuki Shōten (predecessor to Nisshō Iwai) and later head of the Japan Chamber of Commerce and Industry. Fujita was the closest Tsutsumi came to a true connection with the business establishment; in 1916 he urged the recent graduate to buy into Chiyoda Rubber Company, a small manufacturer of tubing for medical instruments. Tsutsumi did so, became managing director, and the next year set up an affiliate known as Tokyo Rubber Company to produce bicycle tires. Tokyo Rubber is the direct ancestor of today's Seibu Polymer Chemical Industries, Ltd., and the first of all the Seibu companies to be controlled by the Tsutsumi family.[18]

Against this small accomplishment were soon set a score of business misadventures in the 1910s. Tsutsumi admitted to losing ¥100,000 in a botched coal-mining operation in Nagano Prefecture and to misreading the market for ocean freighters during World War I (both his wooden vessels were lost at sea in 1918). That same year he abandoned his investment in a pearl-culture firm in Mie Prefecture run by a charming but unproductive technician who had promised he could grow pearls in one-third the time required by Mikimoto. "These experiences," Tsutsumi wrote after World War II, "showed that my powers of judgment were like a five-year-old's."[19] A biographer quotes him, speaking retrospectively: "I have no particularly outstanding ability compared with others. It's just that when I was young I underwent all sorts of hardships, and that was a very valuable experience."[20] In short, as of the end of World War I Tsutsumi had learned much from his labor but was a failure in business and had no war chest for going into politics.

COTTAGES IN THE LARCHES

The resort town of Karuizawa sits 956 meters above sea level at the foot of Mount Asama, an active volcano about 140 kilometers northwest of Tokyo. Within its borders were two of the sixty-seven stations of the Nakasendō, the main inland route from Edo to Kusatsu during the Tokugawa period. The English missionary Alexander C. Shaw publicized Karuizawa's invigorating climate as a health resort among foreigners starting in 1886. Members of the Japanese imperial family built villas there in the 1920s; by the Meiji centennial in 1968 there were 200 hotels, inns, and lodges and about 3,500 vacation houses—3,000 of them built by Tsutsumi Yasujirō. Today the town draws several million visitors a year for skating, skiing, golf, and sightseeing in two national parks nearby.[21]

Possibly even more beautiful and certainly more popular with tourists is the mountainside resort of Hakone, 700 meters above sea level near Lake Ashi in the volcanic crater of the Fuji-Hakone-Izu National Park about 90 kilometers southwest of Tokyo. The Hakone toll station, constructed in 1618, was a famous checkpoint on the Tōkaidō highway connecting Edo and Kyoto under Tokugawa rule. Each year hot springs, temples, and more recently golf courses help to bring travelers by the millions to an area well stocked with hotels, sightseeing boats, sports facilities, and vacation cottages developed since 1920 by Tsutsumi Yasujirō and his son Yoshiaki. Hakone and Karuizawa are unrivaled as mountain resorts in eastern Japan. Tsutsumi Yasujirō was the first entrepreneur to open up Hakone to tourism and weekend housing; in Karuizawa he and his sons are almost the only developers the town has known in recreation and cottages. The two resorts remain keystones of the Seibu Railway Group because lands he bought up in the 1920s have appreciated so greatly in value.

"What led me to deal in real estate was trial and error,"[22] Tsutsumi reminisced in 1964, namely repeated business failures before he bought his first Karuizawa parcel in 1918. In an interview published in 1986, his heir Yoshiaki contended that "my father's idea about business was first to borrow money, then buy land. Once you've bought land, 99 percent of your work is finished. My job simply consists of applying some paint atop my father's 99 percent. But this leads to no growth. So maintaining the status quo means buying land for the future in order to carry on the Seibu company. It was a constitutional principle with my father not to touch manufacturing [after 1918], which is why I do the kind of work I do."[23] Actually in the early years buying property was just the beginning, the more so because land in Japan was not necessarily a profitable investment before World War II. With 1936 as 100, the index of urban land prices (which rose faster than other real estate) had barely doubled by 1955—well below the increase in the consumer price index. The true boom has been more recent: urban residential land in 1990 was worth 57 times its 1960 value, a period when consumer prices roughly quintupled,[24] and has diminished only slightly since. These figures show why the land he inherited gives Tsutsumi Yoshiaki an advantage over the competition—and why his father, unable to count on rising land values as a hedge against inflation, scurried to add value by putting in roads, water, electricity, hotels, cottages, and recreation facilities to attract customers.

Tsutsumi Yasujirō always credited Nagai Ryūtarō with suggesting he invest in Karuizawa, probably as early as 1915. Ōkuma Shigenobu added his endorsement in a 1917 letter to Tsuchiya Saburō, the village headman of Kutsukake who was in charge of approving the sale of 198 hectares: "Tsutsumi Yasujirō is one of the young persons I most trust."[25] After the purchase was completed in 1918, resurveying showed that the parcel contained 266 hectares, but the price remained the same—¥30,000, or about $15,000. By one estimate, in the early 1980s this land was worth ¥8 billion, or $33.5 million.[26] Strapped by losses in steel, mining, shipping, and pearls, Tsutsumi turned to his wife for cash. According to Tsutsumi's first cousin, Fumi not only borrowed money from her family toward the purchase but also pawned a graduation gift watch.[27] Ōkuma, Nagai, and Gotō Shinpei lent moral support but few funds; the only other important investor was Fujita Ken'ichi of Suzuki Shōten, whom Tsutsumi persuaded to serve as president of Sengataki Yūenchi, Ltd., when it was founded in 1918 to develop the site.[28]

The terms of sale stipulated that the new company subdivide the tract, located in what is now Sengataki in Naka Karuizawa, into fifty lots for vacation homes and begin selling them within two years. It was a tall order for an entrepreneur without funds, heavy equipment, or experience to turn forest and swampland filled with bears and wild boars into salable resort cottages in the midst of a postwar depression. By selling stock in the land company, Tsutsumi raised money to build roads, set up a power station for electricity, pipe in water from 10 kilometers away, and install telephones at a cost of ¥5,000 by running lines from Karuizawa Post Office.[29]

To publicize the development, he opened a hot-spring spa at Sengataki in August 1919; the guest of honor was Katō Takaaki, president of the Kenseikai political party and a future prime minister. Katō suggested that Tsutsumi buy several hundred nearby hectares in Onioshidashi, a lava plateau with remarkable scenery of volcanic rocks that became a tourist attraction after 1945. Tsutsumi was ready to sell lots with roads and utilities, thirty to a hectare, by November 1920. To market them, he mailed out picture postcards showing a modest but bright cottage surrounded by larches, advertised at ¥500 complete.

He was counting on a new clientele of urban consumers, now that Karuizawa was accessible by train, who could afford vacation homes a notch below the villas of the wealthy in Kyū Karuizawa.[30] There were few purchasers at first but many more after the Kantō earthquake and fire of September 1923.[31]

Sengataki Yūenchi became a branch of Hakone Land Company when the latter was founded in March 1920, with Fujita lending his prestige as president. Tsutsumi bought more parcels near Sengataki that year and in Minami Karuizawa the next, adding roads and a scheduled bus service in the summer. To attract prospective cottage buyers and visitors to his new horse racetrack, he opened the Karuizawa Green Hotel in December 1923. Two years later he constructed an airfield at Minami Karuizawa and soon offered regular air service to Tokyo using former army cargo planes. The day it opened, Tsutsumi later recalled, a crowd of thirty thousand gathered to watch landings and takeoffs, but few passengers used the facility, "so that although my idea was a good one, it was not successful."[32]

Kyū Karuizawa had long been favored as a summer refuge from Tokyo's humidity by members of the imperial family. The resort's prestige was fortified when Prince Shirakawa bought an existing villa in 1925 and Prince Takeda moved into a new one two years later. The cachet of Tsutsumi's development soared when Prince Asaka built a residence in the Sengataki tract, completed in June 1928. From this point on, Hakone Land Company added additional parcels, installed tennis courts and a swimming pool in 1929, opened bowling lanes in 1933, and constructed the Oshitateyama Hotel in 1937 to accompany the ski facilities it operated on Mount Oshitate. Surprisingly, even though Karuizawa had a golf course as early as 1920, Tsutsumi did not build links there until after World War II when the sport spread to the middle class. In 1947 he took over Prince Asaka's villa and renamed it the Sengataki Prince Hotel, for use by the imperial family; three years later he assumed management of the Seizan Hotel in Karuizawa and built an indoor ice skating rink. Tennis, golf, and more skating facilities were added in the 1950s, and Japan's first snowmaking machines appeared on the Tsutsumi ski slopes in Karuizawa in 1961.[33] Although the scale of his financing, expenditures, and revenues at Karuizawa is unclear, the many new hotels and sports installations in the 1950s—all of which helped sell cottages—suggest that Tsutsumi's land acquisitions in the 1920s and 1930s paid their real dividends starting a decade after World War II. Having sold three thousand vacation homes in Karuizawa, Tsutsumi was the king of middle-class leisure in Japan when he died in 1964, flouting official norms that valued manufacturing, exports, frugality, and devotion to work in order to promote the recreation that more and more people could afford after 1955.

Reflecting on his properties in Karuizawa and Hakone, Tsutsumi Yasujirō often boasted that his axiom was to "do only things that other people haven't done and can't do."[34] Actually what he did was to buy cheap land, improve it, and sell it for a profit like all other real-estate developers; what was different was the scale and location of his sites. When he bought 33 hectares in Gōra at Hakone in 1919, no one else had tried to build vacation houses that far up the mountainside. Next he added 232 hectares north of Lake Ashi at Sengokuhara and another 330 along its eastern shore in Motohakone and vicinity. These big land deals soon attracted other entrepreneurs, driving up the costs of acquisition, but Tsutsumi's early achievements at Karuizawa together with support from Ōkuma and Gotō made it somewhat easier to win local cooperation and backing from investors. Eight years after it was founded, Hakone Land Company had, in 1928, met its original target of ¥5 million of paid-in capital.[35] It continued developing Karuizawa, Hakone, and housing in the Tokyo suburbs to the end of World War II, changing its name to Kokudo Keikaku Kōgyō in 1944. The same company, which in 1965 became simply Kokudo Keikaku, was the axis of the Seibu Railway Group.

Like other land operators in the 1920s and 1930s, Tsutsumi typically paid only a small fraction (sometimes only 1 percent) of the purchase price for his Hakone properties as a deposit, the rest to be paid later but development to begin at once. Improvements drove land values up, letting him sell lots for a big profit before he had finished paying for them at the original low price. In some cases the terms of sale permitted him to stretch out repaying the original owners for many years.[36] Even under these generous conditions, and even with the respected Fujita as president, Hakone Land Company was saddled with big debts from the start. The company renewed its bonds to assure long-term financing, but it depended heavily on cash flow from property sales in suburban Tokyo and seldom showed much profit before World War II. Indeed, even in July 1963, according to the *Shinano mainichi* newspaper, Tsutsumi revealed that the company had borrowings of $140 million.[37] It is unsurprising that his sons Seiji and Yoshiaki have operated two of the most highly leveraged business groups in Japan ever since.

Tsutsumi Yasujirō built cottages on his Hakone lands and put up eight hotels, mainly hot-spring resorts, in the 1920s. At nearby Yunohanazawa Kōgen, which has a spectacular view of the sea, he bought 33 hectares in 1921 for ¥135,000, or roughly $67,500[38] — nearly 35 times the cost per hectare of his first parcel at Karuizawa three years earlier. Although there were few buyers for the fresh lots, he acquired two more tracts of 50 and 100 hectares, the latter purchase requiring thirty-five years until postwar taxes forced one holdout property owner to capitulate. After subtracting for lots it had sold, Hakone Land Company owned about 200 hectares of choice resort land in the early 1950s at Yunohanazawa Kōgen, to which it connected Lake Ashi and the Hakone Prince Hotel by a ropeway and cable car as well as adding luxurious golf courses. Tsutsumi also acquired the rights to operate sightseeing ferries on Lake Ashi, which began service in 1926, and even proposed landing seaplanes on the lake.[39]

The Izu Peninsula immediately south of Hakone is eastern Japan's other main resort because of its location on the Pacific Ocean. Although his competitors eventually surpassed him, Tsutsumi pioneered tourist facilities there through the Sunzu Railway (now Izu-Hakone Railway), which he took over through his own money and Fujita Ken'ichi's good offices in December 1923. This line from Mishima to Ōhito and Shūzenji hot springs gave Tsutsumi his first big opportunity in the transportation business. He eventually expanded the company into buses, limousines, trucking, hotels, and beachfront development. He earned the nickname "Pistol Tsutsumi" in 1924 when Iwata Fumio, a thug loyal to the railway's long-time president, pulled a gun and demanded that Tsutsumi sell his newly obtained shares. As a sympathetic biographer has it, when Tsutsumi refused, Iwata fired a shot that may have grazed his neck, then flung aside the weapon after Tsutsumi stared him down.[40] There is no reason to think Tsutsumi himself was armed, then or at any other time. This episode may or may not show that he was intrepid, but it has become a trivial, yet pungent, symbol of the antagonisms his acquisitions might arouse.

The world depression flung the Hakone Land Company into a deep trough, especially in 1930–1931. Land prices slumped, interest payments had to be met, and Tsutsumi later recalled that he was forced to raise cash by selling off some choice land to the Odakyū Railway for one-seventh of its value before the crash.[41] By 1932 things brightened a bit in the mountain resorts and soon after that in the Tokyo suburban developments. During 1932–1936 Tsutsumi pressed ahead with constructing a ten-kilometer toll road from Hakone to Atami for passenger cars only, a project the Home Ministry had held up for six years before approving in 1931. As Japan spent its way out of the depression through heavy military procurement in the mid-1930s, Hakone Land Company improved its income enough to afford more roadbuilding, hotels, and recreation sites in the region in anticipation of the 1940 Tokyo Olympics, which were never held.[42] Appropriately, one of Tsutsumi's final projects was to build the Tokyo Prince Hotel, opened several months after his death just in time for the Olympics of 1964.

Nonetheless Tsutsumi's ventures were still underfinanced on the threshold of the Pacific War. Hakone Land Company had paid-in capital of ¥7.55 million as of 1940, annual revenues of ¥3 million, and combined borrowings and promissory notes of ¥14 million. The book value of its landholdings was ¥11.2 million,[43] a sum its creditors presumably believed understated its actual or potential market worth. After 1940, as income from railway operations gradually improved, the company was able to retire some of its debt, only to have it swell greatly after the war when the scale of Hakone Land Company's operations expanded under its new name, Kokudo Keikaku Kōgyō. Like most of the leisure industry, the firm went into hibernation during the Pacific War for want of labor and construction materials, although it absorbed various small real-estate companies in Tokyo and Kanagawa Prefectures without adding much land.[44]

Hakone was the site of a famous standoff starting in 1950 between Tsutsumi and his long-time rival Gotō Keita, head of the Tōkyū Railway interests. In that year Odakyū, a Tōkyū affiliate, sought permission from the Ministry of Transportation to extend a bus line around Lake Ashi that would use a toll road owned by Tsutsumi, running from Hakone to Kowakien. Once friends, by the 1950s Gotō and Tsutsumi competed bitterly in both Hakone and Izu. Tsutsumi opposed the petition; the ministry delayed a decision for years; and then when a Tōkyū bus tried to enter the toll road on July 1, 1956, Tsutsumi's employees blocked the way and brawled with Tōkyū personnel. The two owners denounced each other in the media, and Tsutsumi bought 1.2 million shares of Odakyū stock to try to unsettle Gotō, whose personal holdings in his own enterprises were relatively small. Tōkyū eventually lost its court battle with the Seibu Railway Group over the roadway, but Gotō retaliated by assaulting the Tsutsumi fortress in Karuizawa. He bought 50 hectares for middle-class cottages, then added more properties, installed a bus line to compete with Seibu Bus, and vied with Tsutsumi for influence with the town assembly. The competition drove land prices up but did little damage to Seibu's grip on Karuizawa, where by the late 1950s it owned as many as 4,300 hectares.[45] The Tsutsumis have never dominated Hakone as they have Karuizawa, but their lands, luxury hotels, and premier golf courses at Hakone are unmatched by any rival.

CULTIVATED DWELLINGS

The earthquake and fires that destroyed much of Tokyo on September 1, 1923, speeded up the suburbanization of the capital, which had already outgrown the city limits established in 1868. The census of 1920 showed a population of 3.6 million in Tokyo Prefecture, about two-thirds of it in the fifteen Meiji-era wards that formed the city portion of the prefecture. By 1932, just before twenty new wards were added, the city contained a bit more than a third of the nearly 6 million persons who by then were estimated to live in Tokyo Prefecture.[46] Most of the growth was in the areas just outside the old city that were taken in as new wards in 1932. After the earthquake Tokyo's entertainment districts began to drift westward to Shinjuku, Shibuya, and other stations along a national rail line built in 1885 to link Shinagawa in the south to Akabane in the north. From 1923 on, new housing sprouted in tracts along various private railways established early in the century that ran from this national line into open areas west and southwest of the city. Many of the home buyers had fled central Tokyo after the earthquake; others migrated in from outlying prefectures, lured to Tokyo by new jobs. One of the many real-estate operators exploiting this lucrative market was Tsutsumi Yasujirō.

Even though he broke his leg during the earthquake, Tsutsumi summoned his workers as soon as the fires burned out and set up tents to sell land in a suburban parcel he had begun to develop the previous year in Shimoochiai. He also used his lands in Karuizawa and Hakone as collateral to borrow funds for small-scale housing projects in parts of the city like Gotanda, Azabu, Shibuya, Koishikawa, and Mejiro— mainly expensive dwellings for the elite to replace homes demolished by the earthquake. In 1923 he also opened an arcade (*hyakkenten*) on Dōgenzaka in Shibuya, a precursor of the fashion center called Parco through which Seibu Department Stores transformed Shibuya a half-century later.[47]

The Shimoochiai project, known as Mejiro Cultural Village, occupied ten choice hectares on high ground along the present Yamanote Dōri thoroughfare north of Nakai station, on the Seibu Shinjuku Line. Tsutsumi began buying this land in 1917 and gradually planted trees, ran utilities underground, built tennis courts, and then on request would put up "cultural dwellings" with a single Western-style room. These houses were intended for artists, intellectuals, and other cultivated persons on the model of Count Abe's Nishikatamachi or more recent suburbs like Seijō and Tamagawa. In fact the purchasers were mostly salaried corporate employees who paid about ¥6,700 (approximately $3,350) for lots of 375 square meters. The nearby Takada Agricultural Bank helped to finance Mejiro Cultural Village, but to what extent is unknown. Evidently Tsutsumi did quite well there: the prices he fetched rose five times per square meter within the first year of development.[48]

But he ran into problems with his next suburban property, an academic city (*gakuen toshi*) on 330 hectares of orchards and dry fields at Ōizumi Gakuen, to the northwest of Tokyo. Here the idea was to build moderately priced tract housing for commuters along perfectly regular streets laid out around a college or university. Tsutsumi constructed a new Western-style station for Ōizumi Gakuen and donated it to the nearby Musashino Railway, which connected with the national line at Ikebukuro on the fringes of the city. Although he could not persuade Tōkyō Shōka Daigaku (Tokyo Commercial University, now Hitotsubashi University) to relocate in Ōizumi, for a time the Toshima Normal School gave the community an academic tone. At its grand opening in 1925, Tsutsumi used cars to drive prospective customers to the site from Tokyo, entertained them with plays and dancing, and displayed a variety of model homes.[49]

Demand was strong at first, but then Hakone Land Company ran into cash-flow snarls and in the latter 1920s had an overall deficit of perhaps ¥10 million. Tsutsumi later told an interviewer, "At that time the success or failure of an enterprise was 90 percent determined by whether money could be borrowed from the bank."[50] The Kanda Bank helped by acting as trustee for a large bond issue to sustain the company, but Tsutsumi sold only a fraction of the lots at Ōizumi and converted about half for food production during World War II. Ōizumi Gakuen turned into an attractive suburb starting in the mid-1950s, finally earning Hakone Land Company a large payback thirty years after breaking ground for what the owner hoped would become a Cambridge on the Musashi Plain.[51]

Nonetheless, long after his death in 1964, Tsutsumi was still resented by some people in the area for buying the original parcel for a song and persuading at least certain landlords to let him pay with stock in his company, which in the 1920s was worth little. Sellers who needed cash disposed of the stock for almost no proceeds—in effect giving him the land almost free.[52]

Hakone Land Company did little better with an academic city at Kodaira, which it constructed beginning in 1924 between two commuter lines directly west of Tokyo. This property, which was comparable to Ōizumi Gakuen in scale and intended market, managed in 1933 to attract Tsuda Eigakujuku (now Tsuda College) and the preparatory unit of what is now Hitotsubashi University. But sales lagged, as at Ōizumi; and by 1939, land there could be bought for less than half its price a decade earlier. Much of it was turned to fields and gardens during the war. This project likewise was a commercial success only during the last years of the owner's life.[53]

Kunitachi alone turned into a busy academic city for Tsutsumi, if more so after the war than before. This site, now a half-hour train ride west of Shinjuku, consisted of 350 hectares of farmland and red pines assembled by Hakone Land Company between 1925 and 1930 at a cost of roughly ¥1 per square meter.[54] As elsewhere, the firm paid sellers only a fraction (up to 10 percent) of the purchase price in cash, the balance due when the land had been developed and resold. The area at the time contained a population of 3,000; Tsutsumi told the village head it would eventually reach 50,000, which it did in 1967.[55] The company built a stylish half-timber station and gave it to the national railway, which was then obliged to stop a few of its Chūō Line trains there each day beginning in 1929. Tsutsumi sold prime commercial land in front of the station for about ¥25 a square meter, after originally asking more than ¥40; there he built a plaza around a large fountain decorated with sculptures of cranes and pelicans, from which ran a perpendicular boulevard nearly 40 meters wide and two radial avenues, each 12 meters in width. Middle-class housing lots farthest from the station, similar to those in Ōizumi and Kodaira, were offered for ¥5 per square meter.[56] Sports facilities, a concert arena, and other amenities soon followed, as did the move by Hakone Land Company to its new national headquarters there in 1927. Perhaps most remarkable was that nearly 25 percent of the development was used for roads.[57]

What made Kunitachi especially inviting was the arrival of the forerunner to Hitotsubashi University in 1929, fulfilling a goal that had eluded Ōizumi a few years earlier. The university's president, Sano Zensaku, cooperated with Tsutsumi's plans for the town in return for the gift of new grounds after the 1923 earthquake had damaged its old site in Kanda. Two universities of music, Tōhō and Kunitachi, also occupied campuses there, although the latter relocated its high school and university some years later in Tachikawa. Seven other schools also moved to Kunitachi, giving something of the feeling of Göttingen as Tsutsumi evidently dreamed. But in 1927 he was outflanked by Gotō Keita and the Tōkyū Railway when he tried to bring another top university to Kunitachi: Keiō instead accepted 24 hectares in Hiyoshi, along the newly completed Tōyoko Line, for its lower-division campus. Hiyoshi, together with Ohara Kuniyoshi's hundred-hectare development at Seijō and the Minasawa project on 20 hectares at Jiyū Gakuen, formed a rival set of academic cities in the 1920s that were better located but usually less generously appointed with cultural and recreational facilities than Tsutsumi's.[58]

Yet even the presence of Hitotsubashi, one of Japan's most prestigious national universities, could not draw enough home buyers to distant Kunitachi for Hakone Land Company to begin to recover its ¥10 million in development costs there—when it was also overbuilt in

Ōizumi, Kodaira, and the mountain resorts. To raise cash, Tsutsumi had no choice but to sacrifice properties that he had planned to sell just a few years earlier for many times the ¥15 or so per square meter he received for them at the end of the 1920s. By one calculation, the same land in 1984 was worth nearly ¥3 million a square meter.[59] Of course, the real estate Tsutsumi managed to hang onto appreciated just as much, and there were vast amounts of it.

A financial journalist, Narushima Tadaaki, estimates that Tsutsumi sold 1,273 hectares of housing lots in the Tokyo region between 1922 and 1955, nearly all of it in the 1920s and 1930s (he sold much other land after 1955). Of this, about 9 percent by area was located in wealthy districts in the city: Hiroo, Kioi-chō, Hirakawa-chō, Koishikawa, Kawada-chō, Sendagaya, Tokugawayama (Nanpeidai), Shimazuyama (Shirokanedai), Ikedayama (Gotanda), and Gotenyama (Gotanda). These are prestigious and costly neighborhoods, and presumably they yielded considerably more than 9 percent of Tsutsumi's income from real estate in Tokyo and environs. Another 47 percent by area comprised properties in Mejiro Bunka Mura, Ōizumi, and Kunitachi,[60] the main places where he sold to new commuters. Kodaira, Fuchū, and many other small parcels in the suburbs account for the rest. Taken as a whole, housing properties sold through 1955 in the Tokyo region represented about 13 percent of the total area Tsutsumi developed nationwide during his four decades in the business[61]—most of them projects that fitted his forecast of growing consumer power in the urban middle class.

IN POLITICS

Tsutsumi Yasujirō entered electoral politics not when he had earned enough money to afford it but when the opportunity for office came in 1924. Even though his land company was encumbered with heavy borrowings, he decided to run for the lower house of the Diet from his home prefecture, Shiga, and managed to upset his opponent in the general election of May 10, 1924. Tsutsumi was reelected to twelve additional terms, capped by service as speaker of the house in 1953–1954; until his final illness, apparently he harbored the hope of one day being chosen prime minister.

Like many self-important officials, Tsutsumi liked to say that "politics is the highest calling of human life."[62] At least he was consistent: he entered Waseda to pursue politics, he met lots of party moguls through *Shin Nihon,* and he went into business to be able to support his chosen vocation. As his son Seiji noted in an interview published in 1991, "My father was very progressive at the beginning of his career and only later became conservative."[63] Tsutsumi grew up in the era dominated by Ōkuma, Katsura, and Gotō Shinpei; in mid-life he was associated with Premier Wakatsuki Reijirō and Nagai Ryūtarō; after 1945 he grew close to Ogata Taketora and three postwar prime ministers, Yoshida Shigeru, Ikeda Hayato, and Satō Eisaku. He belonged to the Kaishintō-Kenseikai-Minseitō-Nihon Minshutō lineage of political parties that in 1955 merged with its rivals in the Seiyūkai-Jiyūtō line to form the present Liberal Democratic Party.

Tsutsumi has been praised for his sincerity, good faith, and politician's memory for names but reviled for his self-interestedness, miserliness with contributions to other candidates, and lack of achievements in politics.[64] He gained campaign experience from helping Nagai win election to the lower house from Kanazawa in 1920. Four years later Nagai was a key source of funds when Tsutsumi toppled the favorite in Shiga, Horibe Kyūtarō, on a platform calling for land reform, something he denounced after World War II when the occupying American forces actually carried it out. Evidently it was a popular position to take in Shiga in 1924: "Progress for the farm villages," he later wrote, "would come from making sure every tenant was given land."[65] Attacking Horibe as a member of the old Shiga elite, Tsutsumi stressed his own origins as "a son of the soil"—and indulged in the novelty of campaigning from an automobile. He saw himself as a progressive and as an ordinary commoner, elements of the Taishō democracy to which he was much drawn.[66] Tsutsumi buried his rival in a landslide and never lost an election for his seat throughout his life.

Unlike many politicians, Tsutsumi was not notably tied up with geisha, but in almost every other way his domestic life was exceptionally complex in the 1920s. He grew distant from his second wife, Kawasaki Fumi, to whom he transmitted a venereal disease that crippled her in 1923, the year they effectively separated. According to Tsutsumi's first cousin, Kamibayashi Kunio, this is also when Tsutsumi became intimate with three of the four daughters of Aoyama Yoshizō, an aristocratic business acquaintance and former president of a failed local bank who later headed a small construction company. In this account, Aoyama's second daughter gave birth to a son by Tsutsumi named Seiji, whose birthday is registered as March 30, 1927; the youngest daughter gave birth to Tsutsumi's daughter Kuniko the following February 21.[67] Both were officially recorded as the children of Aoyama Misao, the third daughter, who became Tsutsumi's mistress about 1923, when she was sixteen, and his third and last wife in 1955. Apparently she bore no children. Seiji and Kuniko were reared by Aoyama Misao under her surname until they reached their teens. From 1941 on, Misao, Seiji, and Kuniko lived with Tsutsumi in a large new house near Hiroo, a compound where Seiji has built a Saison guest house and memorial to his father next door to his private home. Misao, who developed into an accomplished poet of the Araragi school under the penname Ōtomo Michiko, played a great part in the Seibu Railway Group in the 1950s and 1960s.[68]

In the late 1920s, Tsutsumi turned into an outspoken figure in the Diet in favor of capitalism free from state intervention. He enraged the Tanaka cabinet in April 1929 by opposing a bailout sought by the government: "Kokusai Kisen is a dying company. There is no need to save such a firm."[69] After winning reelection in 1930, he became chair of the Minseitō Party Affairs Committee and, in January 1932, director general of the party. After the assassination of Prime Minister Inukai Tsuyoshi by rightists on May 15, 1932, Saitō Makoto headed a new national-unity cabinet in which Nagai, representing the Minseitō, became minister of colonial development. Nagai named Tsutsumi his parliamentary vice minister for the next two years, then a position of much greater influence than it has become in the postwar system. This responsibility took Tsutsumi to Manchuria, recently proclaimed Manchukuo by Japan after it forcibly took control of the Chinese province in September 1931. There he conferred with Lieutenant General Koiso Kuniaki of the Kwantung Army about further railroad construction by the South Manchurian Railway Company, in which Tsutsumi had held stock as a teenager. In 1933, as Japan prepared to walk out of the League of Nations after being condemned for seizing Manchuria, Tsutsumi is credited with having joined Wakatsuki and other party heavyweights in protesting Japan's withdrawal as much as they could.[70]

The year 1933 is also when Tsutsumi drew close to Ishizuka Tsuneko, who bore him three sons and remained his mistress for the rest of his life. Born in 1913, she was six years younger than Aoyama Misao, whom she addressed as "elder sister." Ishizuka's father, Saburō, was a prominent dentist from Niigata who entered the Diet with Tsutsumi in 1924. Tsuneko graduated from Yamawaki Jogakuen in 1932 and came to know Tsutsumi after she was hired as a clerk in the Diet offices. She gave birth to Tsutsumi Yoshiaki, Yasujirō's heir, in 1934; to Tsutsumi Yasuhiro, who became president of the Toshimaen amusement facility, in 1938; and to Tsutsumi Yūji, who served as head of the Prince Hotels and later became president of Seiyō Continental Hotels, in 1942. Ishizuka was known as the "moonflower" mistress, staying mostly in her Takagi-chō (now Nishi Azabu) home, teaching tea ceremony to women in the neighborhood. Tsutsumi Yasujirō's house after 1941 was about 500 meters away in Hiroo (now Minami Azabu). Almost two years after his death the Tsutsumi family held a lavish reception at the Tokyo Prince to celebrate the wedding of Ishizuka's eldest son Yoshiaki. She was not included among the 1,500 invited guests because Misao was the widow of Yoshiaki's father.[71] This sad moment was a poignant outcome of the complex web of business, political, and personal connections Tsutsumi Yasujirō had constructed decades earlier while buying up land for development and resale long before almost anyone else.

CHAPTER TWO

THE FAST TRACK

The city came to the countryside surrounding Tokyo after World War II, and private railways like Seibu served as the go-betweens to bring them together. Today Seibu all but monopolizes commuter services in a forty-five-degree wedge of northwestern Tokyo, where in 1928 Tsutsumi Yasujirō opened his first line and took control of a major railroad four years later. Each morning an eight- or ten-car train trimmed in vivid yellow and stainless steel departs or arrives at Seibu's Ikebukuro terminal in the capital every seventy seconds at the peak of the morning rush, the inbound expresses jammed with more than twice their rated capacity of 1,568 passengers each. A parallel Seibu line to Shinjuku intersects Kanpachi boulevard at Iogi, where for years a notorious grade-level crossing was closed to cars and trucks for forty-three minutes of each rush hour until a train overpass was completed in 1991.[1] Since 1945, when the present Seibu Railway Company was established, its two trunk lines have helped to knit city and countryside as the population of the capital has spilled steadily outward. Seibu, which once meant the western Musashino Plain, came to signify the areas of Tokyo and southern Saitama Prefecture traversed by the city's most overcrowded private railway, where Tsutsumi had planted some of his biggest prewar housing developments and undertaken many more after 1945.

RAILROADS AND WARTIME

Unlike most rail barons, Tsutsumi Yasujirō started as a real-estate entrepreneur and only later was drawn into train lines. In 1923 he had taken a substantial position in the Sunzu Railway in order to build houses and tourist sites in the Izu Peninsula. His first Tokyo line, the ten-kilometer Tamako Railway, opened service in 1930 from Koku-bunji on the Japan National Railways' Chūō Line to Murayama, where he hoped one day to turn the shores of Lake Tama into a rec-reation area. Likewise his investments in the Musashino Railway (now the Seibu Ikebukuro Line) were prompted by the academic city he inaugurated at Ōizumi Gakuen in 1925.[2]

The Musashino Railway began in 1915 with about 1,200 passengers and 100 tons of freight a day on its forty-four-kilometer line between Ikebukuro and Hannō, Saitama Prefecture. Within a year of the 1923 earthquake, its daily passenger volume had risen above 9,000, but new construction costs and hard times at the end of the decade drove the company into debt. Tsutsumi increased his stake and took control in 1932, yet by the end of the next year its accumulated losses had reached $450,000.[3] He submitted a bankruptcy petition in 1934, clearing the track for compulsory administration by a foundation responsible to the Ministry of Railways. In this status the railroad could defer repay-ments on its loans while attempting to reorganize. But angry creditors chafed at the unpaid debts, and the power company retaliated by turn-ing down the voltage it supplied, forcing locomotive engineers to reduce speed. This drove passengers away, creating "ghost trains" and sending the company deeper into debt—$1.6 million by September 1936.[4]

Bedridden with typhus, Tsutsumi nonetheless staved off an attempt that year by Gotō Keita to add the enfeebled Musashino line to his Tōkyū network. Tsutsumi also managed to preserve its independence when the Ministry of Railways asked Gotō to consolidate suburban private lines under wartime controls.[5] The Tokyo District Court approved a reorganization plan in August 1937 under which creditors would excuse 75 percent of the debt in return for cash or preferred stock in the Musashino company. By 1939 the line was back on its feet and able to pay a dividend for the first time in ten years.[6] It absorbed the Tamako Railway, which by now reached to Lake Sayama, in 1940;

a year later the company had revived so dramatically that it recorded profits of $125,000 on revenues of $1.3 million.[7] The court-sanctioned restructuring scheme was indispensable to the turnaround, but so was economic prosperity driven by war preparations after 1935, which favored communities with military installations along the Musashino right-of-way.

Wartime is also when Tsutsumi began managing the Ōmi Railway in his native Shiga Prefecture, starting in 1942, the same year he purchased the old Seibu Railway in Tokyo. Because the Ōmi, founded in 1895, could no longer make a profit once wartime controls were in place, it turned to Tsutsumi, the Diet representative for the district who by now was experienced with reviving ailing railways.[8] His acquisition of the old Seibu Railway is a classic example of buying up a competitor you can't beat. This enterprise was formed in 1922 by merging several private suburban lines tracing their roots to 1895. It took its name from one of its components, the Seibu Tramway Company, which from 1921 until 1951 operated single-track streetcars from Shinjuku to Ogikubo on a route now served by the Marunouchi subway. Seibu inaugurated a new line in April 1927 from Higashi Murayama to Takadanobaba that directly threatened the weaker Musashino route a few kilometers to the north. The two became heated competitors at Tokorozawa Station in Saitama, where their lines intersected. Because the fare to Ikebukuro or Takadanobaba was the same, passengers often bought Seibu tickets and cheated by using them to ride the rival Musashino line to Tokyo. Each company built additional stations in Tokorozawa to corral more customers, so that this inconspicuous rural town soon had four terminals in operation.[9]

As Musashino sank into bankruptcy, its employees battled Seibu train crews in hand-to-hand combat during the 1930s. Eleven workers lost their lives and several dozen were injured in the violence, which had become chronic when Tsutsumi laid plans in 1940 to buy Seibu. "I had always thought about somehow putting the two together,"[10] he later recalled. The incessant labor friction evidently stirred him to act. Hara Kunizō, originally president of the extensive Tōbu Railway, was Seibu's major shareholder; for a time he tried to buy Tsutsumi's interest in the Musashino line. Instead Tsutsumi bought Hara's holdings in Seibu, which by 1942 was doing less well than its rival, and installed his son-in-law Kojima Shōjirō as managing director the following year.

Both Musashino and Seibu hauled sewage from the city after June 1944, always late at night; and each used some of its workers to grow food along the lines—which suffered remarkably little war damage.[11]

Tsutsumi tried to merge Seibu, Musashino, and a foodstuffs firm into a single company in 1944, but Horiki Kenzō, director of the railway-affairs bureau of the Ministry of Transportation and Communications, balked. His refusal may reflect the influence of Gotō Keita, the Tōkyū leader who served as transport minister under Prime Minister Tōjō Hideki in 1943–1944.[12] It is said that Horiki was furious with Tsutsumi for his tepid support of Japan's military policies, telling him: "Since you're against the war, we'll have to investigate you."[13] The merger was approved immediately after Japan's surrender in mid-August 1945, and the next month the new Seibu Agricultural Railway officially began operations. A year later it became, less rustically, the Seibu Railway Company of today.[14]

Horiki's claim that Tsutsumi opposed Japan's war policies touches on the crucial issue of how businesses, political parties, and individual citizens accommodated themselves to the conflict. Writing autobiographically near the end of his life, Tsutsumi said he had made "earnest efforts to prevent war"[15] between 1936 and 1941. He spoke against restoring the principle that only active-duty military officers should serve as the war and navy ministers, implemented by the cabinet of Hirota Kōki in March 1936. He wanted business leaders, not bureaucrats, to run essential industries under national mobilization for war.[16] When Nagai Ryūtarō joined the pro-military cabinet of Konoe Fumimaro in 1937 and then bolted the Minseitō to help support a restructuring of politics three years later, Tsutsumi broke with his mentor in order to defend the existing party system. His biographer contends that "Tsutsumi also hated Konoe. He was simply unable to like someone reared as a prince of the nobility. Tsutsumi hated Konoe's aristocratic effeteness to the point of foaming at the mouth."[17] Tsutsumi refused Nagai's suggestions that he meet the prime minister, and he chose to remain in the Minseitō, even when it was subsumed with all other parties under the Imperial Rule Assistance Association in October 1940.[18]

But the break between the two was far from total. Tsutsumi evidently believed that Nagai was working from the inside to keep the military from dominating Japanese policy right to his death in 1944, and both of them bitterly resented the choice of General Tōjō as prime minister in October 1941.[19] Tsutsumi later told Nagai's son Michio that during the war Tsutsumi had been obliged to watch what he said for business reasons, whereas Nagai had been freer to speak out. In this sense "Tsutsumi was more conservative than my father," Nagai Michio said in a 1986 interview. "He was more skeptical about the war than was my father. Tsutsumi thought Japan couldn't win. He concentrated on business during the war, not saying much about the conflict."[20]

Like many who harbored reservations about Japan's war policies, Tsutsumi chose to stay quiet: "If I criticized the Government in the Diet during the war, however, it would tend to disturb internal unity, [so] I was patient and remained silent."[21] This stance may seem timid for a person who stared down a would-be assassin in 1924 and police investigators two decades later. Perhaps Tsutsumi's outlook was more a matter of patriotism and politics than of conscience:

> I had no inclination to cooperate politically during the entire Konoe-Tojo period, and refused to accept any official position. Of course I was against the war. Once the declaration of war had been issued, however, the war should be won. Therefore, I made serious efforts from my position as a man in the economic world. . . . To compensate for being negative in the political field, I devoted myself to those enterprises which had to be done for the sake of the country, and which other people did not choose to take up because they were not profitable [food production and sewage disposal]. In this way, I withdrew from the political field and had nothing to do with the New System Movement or the two Imperial Rule Assistance organizations. I continued to hold to the proper line of parliamentary government.[22]

Tsutsumi was purged from politics by the occupying authorities after the surrender not because of any ambiguity, moral or otherwise, in his wartime conduct but because he had been a candidate recommended for reelection by the Imperial Rule Assistance Association in April 1942. It turns out the recommendation was only nominal, because, paradoxically, he was also listed by those who chose which candidates to support as someone with views unfriendly to the military. Tsutsumi mobilized former Prime Minister Wakatsuki Reijirō and retired General Ugaki Kazushige to support his petition for removal from the purge list in 1949–1950, and eventually he won reinstatement on August 6, 1951.[23]

Wartime and the American occupation were also a chaotic period for Tsutsumi personally. He lived with Aoyama Misao after 1941 in a grand villa at Hiroo, installing his estranged wife Fumi in a detached residence next door and visiting Ishizuka Tsuneko nearby in Takagichō. By degrees he grew disillusioned with his eldest son, Kiyoshi, a graduate of Tokyo Imperial University who was Yasujirō's heir apparent. Although Yasujirō made Kiyoshi a director of his companies soon after graduation from college, evidently the son proved to be headstrong and was demoted to a mid-level position at a manufacturing affiliate. When Yasujirō began suffering from prostatitis in March 1943, Kiyoshi's wife Yoshiko helped to nurse her father-in-law. Yasujirō's condition caused him great discomfort until it was corrected by newly available surgical techniques in June 1952.[24]

Despite his illness, Tsutsumi made a virtue of necessity as Japan stumbled toward defeat and occupation. He strung two telephone lines into the air-raid shelter at his Hiroo house and talked business even during bombing attacks. Ōya Sōichi, the influential journalist, labeled Tsutsumi an opportunist for buying up land cheaply from devastated owners who fled Tokyo after the fearsome incendiary raids in the spring of 1945.[25] Tsutsumi Yoshiaki later told an interviewer: "I remember my father's telling a story from the time of the air raids. People grabbed their money and tried to escape elsewhere. Those who didn't have faith in money exchanged it for goods, but nobody thought to buy land. My father, on the contrary, did not flee even as Japan was losing but tried to buy land in the city."[26] Yoshiaki also said his father was not concerned about a socialist coup after the surrender: "Win or lose in the war, he knew he'd grow rich buying land."[27] In fact it is not at all clear that in 1945 Yasujirō could count on riches from these properties, but there is no question that he snapped up lots that turned out to be lucrative.

Among them were several parcels he bought early the following year just east of the Ikebukuro terminal of the Seibu Railway. They added up to 6.6 hectares and cost him about ¥300 per square meter. He sold the larger portion to Tokyo Prefecture in 1949 for at least twice what he paid, although no known record of the transaction exists; inflation probably wiped out any profit on this segment. What proved a gold mine was the part he retained: two hectares on the street by the station, which became the site of the Seibu department store. By the time his son Seiji took over the store in 1955, the land was worth ¥2.4 billion ($6.7 million) expressed in devalued yen at 360 to the U.S. dollar—more than four times its 1946 value in constant dollars.[28] In this way Tsutsumi parlayed burned-out real estate in a neglected corner of the city into a pillar of the postwar Seibu edifice.

OPPORTUNITY COSTS AND BENEFITS

Like most Japanese survivors of World War II, Tsutsumi Yasujirō had a bittersweet experience with officialdom during the 1945–1952 American occupation of Japan. He headed a policy group on food production for the Higashikuni cabinet immediately after the surrender, agreed to a government request to take over a foundering fertilizer company in the fall of 1945, and was even approached early the next year by the Americans to head the Japan National Railways until he reminded them that the occupation had just purged him from political life, along with 20,000 others who had held office during the war. The postwar campaign against the giant *zaibatsu* also targeted smaller firms that could be considered oligopolistic, such as Tsutsumi's Kokudo Keikaku and Seibu Railway; but by November 1948 Tsutsumi had persuaded the authorities to exempt his companies, although by what means is unclear.[29] He also opposed redistributing rural property, according to Tsutsumi Seiji: "My father, who came from a farm village, always said the greatest mistake of American occupation policy was land reform and that modernization in Japan had opened the way to communism"[30]—a widely held view in Yasujirō's generation.

The survival of the Tsutsumi "Konzern," as some critics now called it, was almost without parallel once the occupation's program of economic deconcentration took hold. Nonetheless the family interests were barely profitable at war's end, and Seibu was little more than a low-rated suburban railroad with a rank image because of its night-time cargoes. Immobilized from politics and slowed by disease, Tsutsumi seized the moment to expand his businesses by taking advantage of the postwar boom that was bound to sweep across Tokyo as economic recovery gained force. Patronage of the railway picked up as fast as new cars could be built atop damaged chassis that Tsutsumi had bought from the national railways for next to nothing. Seibu sprang back to life faster than other private lines because it had plenty of lumber for rolling stock and train stations, much of which it culled from the Arakawa and Sumida Rivers right after American bombing raids near the end of the war. Then beginning in 1945 several big U.S. army and air-force bases along its routes gave Seibu's freight business a lagniappe as well.[31]

Seibu also avoided the epidemic of strikes and other labor disputes that afflicted nearly all the other railroads after the war. Part of the reason it was a "no-strike railway" was that its employees had little desire to repeat their bloody violence of the 1930s before the Musashino and old Seibu companies merged. Part, too, must have been the owner's paternalism: supplying seat cushions from his own house to train engineers; distributing flour, salt, and bread to workers during the food shortages of 1945–1946; and inviting employees in groups of one hundred to his Hiroo villa at New Year's, when he poured them sake and entertained them on his lute. His son Yoshiaki continues the custom each year on Yasujirō's birthday.[32]

Another element in the railroad's postwar recovery was diversification, which mostly meant following Hankyū's pattern by setting up subsidiaries in buses, taxis, motor freight, construction, and amusement parks. Seibu Motorcar Company (Seibu Jidōsha), formed in 1946, provided feeder transit to the main Seibu Railway lines as well as local routes in Gunma and Nagano Prefectures. It became Seibu Bus in 1969, adding charter service, and by 1972 carried 410,000 passengers a day.[33] A trucking affiliate of the railway was begun in 1950, taking its present name, Seibu Motor Freight Company (Seibu Un'yu), in 1959 when it merged with two other shipping firms. In 1962 it had nearly sixty offices in the Tokyo, Nagano, Izu, and Osaka areas; a decade later it operated a fleet of 3,000 vehicles.[34] Seibu Construction Company (Seibu Kensetsu) started in 1941 as a construction-materials business. By 1961, when it assumed its current name, it also built housing, railroad cars, and farm equipment. Tsutsumi realized a twenty-year-long dream in 1951 when he opened the popular Seibuen amusement park at Lake Tama. At the same time he began operating UNESCO Village at nearby Lake Sayama, a wooded hillside with typical houses from each of the sixty-four member nations when Japan joined the organization in 1951. Equally famous for high admission prices was the Toshimaen amusement park in Nerima, fifteen minutes from Ike-bukuro on the Seibu line. Tsutsumi took over this venerable but money-losing attraction, built on the site of a fifteenth-century castle, just before Pearl Harbor and turned it into such a hit that it became an independent company in 1956.[35]

Each of the subsidiaries became a building block of the eventual Seibu colossus, but even more important—especially for the retailing division—was the autumn 1945 takeover of Asahi Chemical Fertilizer Company (Asahi Kagaku Hiryō) in Amagasaki, west of Osaka. Asahi Chemical Fertilizer began making phosphates in 1935 but was destroyed in an air raid at the end of World War II. Matsumura Kenzō, the minister of agriculture and forestry, asked Tsutsumi to revive it because Japan's food situation was so desperate after the surrender. Tsutsumi agreed, scoured the country for phosphate ore, and soon had the company producing 6,500 metric tons of fertilizer per month; by 1950 the output was up to 10,000 tons a month.[36] New technology from Germany and a second plant in Saitama Prefecture brought a measure of prosperity by 1954. The firm added concrete pilings and steel construction materials to its products within a few years and in 1960 changed its name to Seibu Chemical Industries (Seibu Kagaku Kōgyō). At that point its annual sales were $12.7 million, but profits were very low.[37] Nonetheless the company owned valuable real estate that was a godsend to the Seibu Department Stores when Seibu Chemical joined the retailing group in 1970.

The subsidiaries gave the railroad and the land company wider market compass in consumer services during the first postwar decade. Seibu Railway Company recovered from wartime fast enough to stretch its line from Takadanobaba to Ōme Kaidō boulevard in Shinjuku by March 1952, although to its chagrin land-use restrictions caused the extension to stop a few hundred meters short of Shinjuku Station on the national rail lines, Japan's busiest terminal. As the northwest suburbs brimmed with new homeowners, the number of passengers on the railway grew by 48 percent between 1955 and 1960, versus 21 percent for private railroads in Japan as a whole. The company's revenues rose from $11.4 million in 1956 to $13.9 million in 1959, and profits doubled to $583,000 during the same period.[38] The affiliated Izu Hakone (formerly Sunzu) Railway, 50 percent of whose stock was owned by Kokudo Keikaku and the Seibu Railway, showed revenues of $3.1 million and profits of $103,000 in 1957.[39] Still Tsutsumi's enterprises suffered from a bad image as rustic, bothersome to motorists (in this era the Seibu lines had as many as 736 unstaffed grade crossings), and not doing their share at tax-payment time. Public relations are the main reason Tsutsumi Yoshiaki promoted sports—especially crisp, cool skiing and ice hockey—as soon as he joined the family business after graduating from Waseda in 1957.[40] Not coincidentally, sports proved to be highly profitable as well.

FROM VILLAS TO HOTELS

Tsutsumi's greatest postwar killing did nothing to burnish his tainted image as a profiteer: his quiet takeover of residences belonging to former imperial relatives who were forced to sell off their properties to pay taxes during the occupation. Under circumstances that remain murky, prime locations in Takanawa, Shinagawa, Azabu, Akasaka, and Karuizawa fell into his hands and became the nucleus of the Prince Hotel chain, Japan's largest and gaudiest. Using tax documents and other records available to the public, Japanese researchers have brought out enough details to verify that Tsutsumi bought these lands without competitive bidding, that they cost him surprisingly little, and that in at least some cases he paid for them with small deposits and drawn-out completion schedules, as had been true of his purchases in Hakone and Kunitachi in the 1920s. Tsutsumi Yoshiaki told a journalist many years later that déclassé nobles found it "quite difficult to sell your property safely" after the war[41]—as though Seibu provided a discreet service, like disposing of jewels at Cartier. Tokyo residents who knew of the modest taxes, assessed partly on the low book values of the Prince real estate, might be excused for thinking instead that Tsutsumi victimized the fallen nobility, and probably the public treasury as well.

Kokudo Keikaku and the Izu Hakone Railway had entered the hotel business before World War II as a part of Tsutsumi's strategy for developing resorts. Then in 1947 the Seibu Railway Company began taking over lands in Karuizawa and the Shirokanedai section of Tokyo belonging to the former Imperial Prince Asaka, who had given Tsutsumi's development at Sengataki in Karuizawa instant prestige when he moved into a secluded villa there in 1928. This building became the Karuizawa Prince Hotel in 1947, served as a resort for occupation officials until 1950, and then, renamed the Sengataki Prince, became a summer residence for the exclusive use of the present emperor, Akihito, when he was crown prince.[42] The Shirokanedai site comprised several choice parcels totaling 3.5 hectares, where Seibu hoped to construct a Prince Hotel until relentless protests from neighbors forced Tsutsumi Yoshiaki to back down. He arranged to sell the property to Tokyo Prefecture for $55.4 million in 1982, the income conveniently balanced for tax purposes by the costs of building the New Takanawa Prince Hotel that opened the same spring.[43]

The original Takanawa Prince opened in 1953 in a baroque Western-style house purchased without fanfare by Seibu two years earlier from the family of former Prince Takeda, not far from Tokyo's Shinagawa Station. In 1971 a blocky main hotel building in subdued tan brick was added, situated on a hillock surrounded by a fine Japanese-style garden.[44] Far more problematic was a larger adjoining tract of 5.3 hectares owned by former Prince Kitashirakawa where the New Takanawa Prince, faced in dazzling white tiles, now stands. The Kitashirakawas owed a ¥6.5 million tax bill on this land when they became private citizens in 1947; their lump-sum payment from the government to assist with the transition was only ¥5.4 million.[45] Between 1950 and 1952 they sold their former villa and 1.4 hectares to the state to serve as an official residence for the speaker of the House of Representatives until a more convenient site was found in 1961 in Nagata-chō. The remaining 3.9 hectares were sold to the Seibu Railway Company after a multi-year negotiation that was finally recorded on July 24, 1953. Of the ¥96 million purchase price agreed to in 1948, Tsutsumi evidently paid just ¥5 million in cash and another ¥10 million not long thereafter. He paid only annual interest of 10 percent on the remaining ¥81 million, in effect leasing an enormously valuable property that had officially appreciated eighty times its 1953 worth by the time the Seibu Railway finally paid for it in inflated yen in 1979. The rising value of this land more than offset the constant annual interest outlays; the low initial cash payment, although attractive enough to the impoverished Kitashirakawas, greatly reduced the taxes they might otherwise have owed.[46] As a part of the agreement, Seibu employed certain relatives and former retainers of Prince Kitashirakawa.[47]

The sale of 1.4 hectares to the government during 1950–1952 was widely publicized, but the transaction conveying the other 3.9 hectares to Seibu was hushed up, apparently by listing a former Kitashirakawa steward named Mitobe Makoto as the nominal owner. The reason was that Tsutsumi Yasujirō had become speaker of the house just two months before the sale was recorded; indeed, had he not held that post the recording might have been even further delayed. The subterfuge succeeded in preventing allegations of impropriety at the time, even though Tsutsumi may have attempted while serving as speaker to restore the 1.4 hectares owned by the government to private hands—in all likelihood his own.[48] Seibu installed Mitobe as head of a golf driving range it developed on the larger parcel, to extend the fiction that the Kitashirakawas still owned the property. Only in 1979 did the company disclose its ownership by completing the purchase, and only then because of Tsutsumi Yoshiaki's fervent determination to build an ultra-luxury hotel and gigantic banquet hall on the site.[49] The reason the Seibu Railway, not Kokudo Keikaku, bought these former imperial properties was probably that most of the payments were stretched out, as with those to the Kitashirakawas, so that it seemed less open to suspicion to have them controlled by a company whose stock was publicly traded.[50]

Seibu's array of new Princes in the Tokyo area was launched in October 1953 with the Azabu Prince Hotel on land once belonging to former Baron Fujita. Two decades later Tsutsumi Yoshiaki exchanged this site for one in Roppongi long occupied by the Finnish embassy; there he built the architecturally undistinguished Roppongi Prince, opened in 1984, whereas the Finns turned the Azabu property into a stunning new embassy complex. The Takanawa Prince made its debut in December 1953, by which time the hotel chain was using a variant of the imperial chrysanthemum as its logo—an impertinence, some thought. The Yokohama Prince followed in October 1954 on land that was once a secondary residence for former Prince Higashifushimi. Most valuable of all was a tract in central Tokyo once owned by the Kitashirakawas and, since 1914, by the family of the Korean Prince Yi, whose five-hundred-year-long dynasty ended with Japan's annexation of Korea in 1910. Tsutsumi Yasujirō bought this property, including its French Gothic residence (designed by Josiah Conder in 1884) with roomfuls of priceless antiques, for what is thought to have been a very low price in September 1954 and a year later opened it as the Akasaka Prince.[51] Today this hotel, twice augmented with modern additions, is the international flagship of the chain.

Among the Tokyo residences of the eleven families of former imperial collaterals who became commoners in 1947, the only major villa that escaped Tsutsumi was a prime location near Shinagawa Station once belonging to Prince Higashikuni. Although Seibu and the Keihin Kyūkō Railway both sought the property, which had recently come under state ownership, Tsutsumi's political rival Kōno Ichirō intervened to give Keihin Kyūkō control. Not to be outmaneuvered, Tsutsumi retaliated by buying a large block of shares in the rival line, which soon operated the Hotel Pacific Meridien on the site in direct competition with the Takanawa Prince nearby.[52]

These former imperial houses and the first-class hotels they spawned were the metropolitan counterparts to leisure facilities developed by Kokudo Keikaku elsewhere in the 1950s. The Ōiso Long Beach Hotel opened on Sagami Bay in August 1953 and added a hundred-meter-long pool four years later. A large outdoor skating rink began operating at Karuizawa in January 1957, enhancing the area's appeal as a winter resort. Summer visitors could now play golf at Minami Karuizawa, once Tsutsumi regained 660 hectares taken over with compensation by the army for an air field during World War II. Today the site includes the Karuizawa 72 Golf Course—actually seven eighteen-hole courses, all open to the public, as are nearby company-owned links at the Seizan and Karuizawa Prince Hotels. This flurry of investment helped Kokudo Keikaku's hidden assets soar in the 1950s, but at $35,000 its capitalization was so minuscule that it had to borrow extensively to install the new facilities.[53] Late in life Tsutsumi became enamored of trying to hold the winter Olympics at Karuizawa or nearby Manza—a dream that obsessed, but likewise eluded, his son Yoshiaki in 1990.

A COUNTRY STORE IN THE CITY

Tsutsumi Yasujirō's decision to operate a department store at Ikebukuro in 1940 stemmed partly from competition with other private railroad moguls and partly from a shrewd gamble that the region would turn into a major retail hub as Tokyo's suburbs burgeoned in the next decades. Ikebukuro became a stop on the national Takasaki Line in 1903 when a branch bending off to the east through mulberry and tea farms toward Tabata was constructed; the branch was eventually re-named the Yamanote Line when the loop was closed in 1925. The Musashino Railway began suburban service from Ikebukuro in 1915; three years later Rikkyō (St. Paul's) University helped to put the area on the map when it moved from Tsukiji to a new campus west of the station. In 1919 about 4,000 people a day used the national railways' Ikebukuro Station, but by 1932 the number had vaulted to nearly 57,000.[54] Streetcars and buses operated by the city began service there in 1935, the same year the Keihin Kyūkō Railway launched a depart-ment-store branch at Ikebukuro called Kikuya. The more powerful Shirokiya had opened a branch store in 1929 nearby in Ōtsuka, and other private railroads established retail outlets at their terminals along the Yamanote Line in the 1930s to sell food and daily-use items. By 1940, when Tsutsumi purchased the Ikebukuro Kikuya for roughly $45,000 and renamed it the Musashino Department Store, more than 100,000 passengers a day were entering or leaving the national rail sta-tion a few dozen meters away, and more than 50,000 were using Mu-sashino Ikebukuro Station. Both figures doubled by 1949 when the business assumed its current name of Seibu Department Stores, Ltd.[55]

Despite Ikebukuro's new look as a transit center and consumer mar-ket, 1940 was a terrible time to enter the retailing business because the state was relentlessly tightening wartime controls over commodities. The Musashino Department Store, a two-story wood-frame structure with 2,347 square meters of floor space, sold rationed clothing, sugar, matches, and other staples until inventories dwindled so drastically that it barely managed to stay in business at all after the Japanese attack on Pearl Harbor in December 1941. Despite the official restric-tions, Tsutsumi was able to operate a branch of the department store for summer residents of Karuizawa between 1940 and 1943. Deep in the war the main store moved to an idle building 300 meters from the Musashino Ikebukuro Station when the government began clearing wide swaths near railway terminals for fire breaks, but this new loca-tion soon burned in an air raid on April 13, 1945, leaving the Musa-shino Department Store with nothing at all.[56]

Right after the surrender Ikebukuro, like Shinjuku, Gotanda, Shin-bashi, and Ueno around the Yamanote loop, had a flourishing black market—portrayed by Hayashi Fumiko in her vivid novel *Ukigumo* (Floating clouds).[57] Potatoes, daikon, and other vegetables grown along the newly renamed Seibu Ikebukuro Line made their way to stalls set up near the east exit of the station. Next door Tsutsumi Yasujirō pitched a surplus army air-corps tent, in which he reopened the Musashino Department Store in November 1945. By the next summer the bucolic market was famous for fresh-water eels taken from rivers and snow cones from ice houses in the mountains along the Seibu lines. When a blizzard destroyed the tent in the winter of 1946–1947, it was replaced by a disused army barrack from Narashino, Chiba Prefecture, that burned down in a vagabond's bonfire on a cold February night just before the store was scheduled to reopen. Undaunted by three disasters within three years, Tsutsumi brought in another structure from Narashino to serve as a temporary location until a brand-new building for the renamed Seibu Department Store was opened next to the Seibu Ikebukuro rail terminal on November 1, 1949. This two-story frame-and-mortar venue, with just 2,742 square meters of floor space, was hardly imposing; neither it nor its gigantic successor of today was designed with a central atrium to define its character. Instead what made Seibu unique were the multiple arterial concourses on several levels that brought in customers from national and private rail lines, trolleys, buses, and soon subways as well.[58]

Tsutsumi's determination to revive the department store on a portion of the two hectares remaining from his early postwar land purchases in Ikebukuro may have resulted more from defensive caution than from the uncommon foresight with which his biographers usually credit him.[59] Had he really been interested in retailing right after the war, Tsutsumi could have bought a controlling stake in the well-established Matsuya Department Store or a major position in the even more venerable Shirokiya. But "I wasn't interested in making money in department stores. . . . I wasn't interested in overdoing it,"[60] he recalled in 1961. Instead, against the advice of most of the railway's directors, he erected the modest 1949 Seibu Department Store as a service to rail passengers who needed groceries and everyday items—and who would buy them from the competition if there were not at least a small Seibu outlet available. In the long run the Ikebukuro site paid off because the store had ample room to grow, provide parking, and put up auxiliary buildings, whereas the other major Tokyo department stores have been chronically pinched for space.

Seibu's choice of name in 1949—*hyakkaten,* no longer *depāto*—stated an ambition more than a reality. The new name implied that it carried a full range of goods, not just food and sundries, and it unmistakably emulated the industry leaders like Mitsukoshi and Daimaru, both of which called themselves *hyakkaten.* In fact it was only an ordinary terminal department store, catering to daily needs of passengers who routinely traveled on to giant stores elsewhere in Tokyo when they wanted the variety and selection of a full department store. But demographics were in Seibu's favor. By 1950 more than a quarter-million people a day entered or exited the national railway station at Ikebukuro, and daily patronage of the Seibu terminal had risen to 107,000, even before the suburban real-estate boom of the 1950s made Seibu the fastest-growing private railway in the region.[61] However uninterested in retailing Tsutsumi may have been, he recognized by 1949 that rail passengers were willing shoppers if the merchandise was conveniently close to the station.

A defensive response to his bitter rival Gotō Keita partly explains why Tsutsumi decided the very next year to construct a much grander, seven-story department store in concrete and steel right beside the new Seibu building. Gotō's Tōyoko Department Store had announced plans in 1948 to open a branch at the west exit of Ikebukuro Station, to be ready in December 1950 in a district widely predicted to thrive from postwar housing developments in nearby suburbs. At the opening reception the owner bragged, "Tōyoko is building Ikebukuro culture,"[62] by which he meant building market share. This company was a Gargantuan presence at Seibu's doorstep: its overall sales of $11.1 million in 1951 ranked sixth in the industry,[63] forcing Seibu to grow or resign itself to minor status. Shocked into building a real department store, Tsutsumi completed the nucleus of today's Seibu building in September 1952 and expanded it again in 1953 and 1954. Whether or not Gotō deserved his nickname of "usurping demon" (*nottori ma*), his foray into Ikebukuro failed miserably because his store was at the less-developed west exit, price wars in Ikebukuro were endemic, and Seibu replied with an estimable counterstrategy by the mid-1950s. Finally Tōyoko was forced to sell out to Tōbu Department Stores in 1964.[64]

Another reason why Tsutsumi borrowed heavily through the Seibu Railway to erect the seven-story concrete building was the decision in December 1949 to build a subway route, eventually called Marunouchi, from the east side of Ikebukuro Station to Ochanomizu (opened in 1954) and on to Tokyo Station (1956), Nishi Ginza (1957), and Shinjuku (1959). This line traveled quickly to the heart of the city's high-fashion zone and helped transform Ikebukuro's image from pastoral outpost to bustling in-town commercial district. Seibu soon built a concourse bringing subway passengers directly to its basement grocery section and to banks of elevators leading to the main store above.[65]

The new building meant that Seibu was a full-fledged department store by the autumn of 1952, but as an amateur in retailing Tsutsumi ran it cautiously, depending heavily on advice from wholesalers and turning its financial affairs over to accountants from the railroad. (He seems to have regarded the railway, department store, and Kokudo Keikaku as a single business from a fiscal point of view.)[66] The Nihon Kangyō Ginkō, a bank that was eager to install a branch at the east Ikebukuro exit, lent $1.7 million to complete a second expansion of the department-store building, finished in June 1953; further construction in 1955 brought the total floor space to about 43,000 square meters, suddenly one of the largest in Japan. By now the total cost of completing the 1952 store and additions exceeded $5.5 million.[67]

Modern as the building was, Seibu's reputation in the mid-1950s remained that of a merchant with floors muddied by the clogs and straw sandals of lower-class shoppers from the country. The main advertising theme in those days was still "reputable Seibu foodstuffs." Its cafeteria and grocery section were popular and its prices in all departments relatively cheap—partly because 700 of its 788 employees were women, most of them ill-paid. Tsutsumi's wife, Aoyama Misao, took an interest in how goods were displayed and how wrapping paper was designed in an effort to offset the store's deficiencies in facilities, stock, elevators, and stairwells.[68]

Still the investment in an ever-larger store paid off: sales roughly quadrupled between 1951 and 1954, to an annual rate of $8.8 million, and pretax profits more than quintupled—but total borrowings caused by the expansion shot up from $95,000 in 1951 to $790,000 in mid-1954.[69] Even though its land and buildings were owned by the Seibu

Railway, the department store had irrepressibly outgrown its subsidiary status: in 1956 it rang up sales of $14.8 million, versus $11.4 million in revenues for the railroad.[70] By the mid-1950s, in short, the chief engines of Tsutsumi's business legacy were all on track: the land company, the railway, and the department store. He devoted the final decade of his life mainly to satisfying his political aspirations.

THE POLITICS OF CONTROVERSY

Tsutsumi Yasujirō presided as speaker over two of the most rowdy sessions in the hundred-year-long history of the Japanese House of Representatives. These episodes won him praise for his tough-mindedness but probably cost him any chance at realizing his dream of becoming prime minister. While Premier Yoshida Shigeru's power ebbed, Tsutsumi won election as speaker on May 18, 1953, with the backing of the main parties opposed to Yoshida's Jiyūtō. Tsutsumi immediately quit his own party, Kaishintō, in an attempt to quell partisanship during the political confusion of the times, and he remained independent until his term as speaker ended on December 11, 1954. Under his leadership the lower house repealed or modified a number of laws enacted during the American occupation, but best remembered are the scuffles that surrounded its efforts to deal with a strike-control bill on July 31, 1953, and the revision of the Police Law on June 3, 1954.[71]

The violence on these occasions won the Diet the wry nickname of "Nagata-chō wrestling arena," but unlike sumo, no rules seemed to be in effect. In the July 1953 encounter the Japan Socialist Party fiercely opposed Yoshida over the pending budget; incited by this smoldering dispute, about 110 representatives from various parties pushed, beat, kicked, and threw ashtrays at one another in a melee that broke out over extending the Diet session to deal with the anti-strike bill. Tsutsumi held firm and eventually restored order. When he acted to extend another session the following June over the Police Law, opponents surrounded him, ripped his jacket and trousers, and choked him until his face turned purple before he was rescued. As Tsutsumi later wrote, he took "drastic but correct measures . . . without any hesitation" to deal with the violence; "I surmounted these two crises at the risk of my life."[72] From this point on he drew closer to

FIGURE 2. Former Prime Minister Yoshida Shigeru (center) chats with foreign guests in March 1960 as Tsutsumi Yasujirō (left of Yoshida) and future Prime Ministers Ikeda Hayato and Satō Eisaku (right of Yoshida) look on. (Saison Group)

Yoshida and his successors, centering on future Prime Ministers Ikeda Hayato, Ōhira Masayoshi, and Suzuki Zenkō.

Even though Tsutsumi belonged to the new Liberal Democratic Party, formed in November 1955, he broke with the cabinet of Hatoyama Ichirō over the Japan-Soviet Declaration signed on October 19, 1956, to end the state of war and resume relations between Tokyo and Moscow. Like most business leaders, Tsutsumi mistrusted the Soviets and believed that Japan should emphasize ties with the United States.[73] Nagai Michio, the son of Nagai Ryūtarō and a former minister of education, recalls that "Tsutsumi was more interested in private enterprise than my father, and he disliked the Soviet Union. When Prime Minister Hatoyama visited the USSR to discuss a peace treaty with Moscow, Tsutsumi told me he thought Hatoyama was 'a soft prime minister.'"[74] Tsutsumi was so disillusioned with the party leadership that he tried to resign his Diet seat in November 1956, but changed his mind two weeks later.[75]

Controversy also eddied around Tsutsumi's political influence over decisions affecting his companies. Some critics believe he used his position as speaker to expand his businesses as much as possible, especially by holding up applications to the national bureaucracy from wouldbe competitors seeking approval in areas dominated by Kokudo Keikaku or Seibu. Intimations of bribery persisted during the later years of his career.[76] By one account Tsutsumi used his political muscle in the late 1950s to prevent the Takashimaya Department Stores from installing a branch in a new Shinjuku Station building, which would have threatened the largest store in the area, Isetan. In return, Kosuge Tanji, president of Isetan, apparently abandoned plans to build a branch store on land he had recently bought in Ikebukuro.[77]

There can be no question of Tsutsumi's impact on his Shiga electoral district, where Ōmi Railway, Seibu Bus, and Kokudo Keikaku did a great deal of business by the 1950s. While serving as speaker, he pushed through approval of the Ōse highway linking the eastern shore of Lake Biwa with Ise Bay. He helped to arrange for dams, roads, and other public works that presumably benefited the prefecture, and certainly his companies. He joined the unsuccessful attempt by Shiga to merge with Kyoto Prefecture in 1959 and tried to have the proposed Kyoto International Conference Hall awarded to the city of Ōtsu in Shiga, just across the mountain from the ancient capital, even if the hall had to retain "Kyoto" in its name. When a site at Takaragaike in northern Kyoto was chosen instead, his son Yoshiaki built a sumptuous Prince Hotel next door. Shiga residents remember Tsutsumi's maneuverings to promote Seibu's tourism businesses when the Shinkansen rail line and Meishin expressway were under construction in their prefecture in 1963.[78] The Japan National Railways compensated Tsutsumi's Ōmi Railway $417,000 for improvements in safety and staffing made necessary by the Shinkansen, which paralleled Ōmi tracks for 7.5 kilometers. The national railways paid an additional $278,000 for damage to the scenery from Ōmi's passenger cars—an unprecedented award that was questioned by the transportation committee of the House of Representatives on March 8, 1963, leading to charges of graft.[79]

By this stage Tsutsumi's political power was waning: he had barely won reelection in 1960, and did so again in December 1963, despite failing health, only at the cost of charges that his staff had bought votes and committed other election-law violations. Eventually one hundred persons were found to have broken the law; a few cases from this tainted campaign were still tied up in the courts in 1990. When Tsutsumi died in April 1964, his mantle passed to Yamashita Ganri, a former finance-ministry official and protégé of future Prime Minister Tanaka Kakuei.[80] Perhaps it is fitting that Yamashita, too, was eventually snarled in controversy when the Tsutsumi family shifted its allegiance to another candidate as Yamashita stood for reelection.

COMPANY AND FAMILY

People who ten years earlier had scorned Tsutsumi Yasujirō as a scavenger of lumber and sewage were saying by the early 1960s, "you must have amassed the most property in Japan."[81] Yet his personal tax returns, as uncovered by the researcher Miki Yōnosuke, showed an income of just $18,667 in 1958, rising to $73,138 in 1962.[82] These were extraordinarily low figures for someone whose personal wealth at the time was thought to be anywhere from $3 to 30 million.[83] Tsutsumi brushed such estimates aside: "I have no assets of my own. This house belongs to the Seibu Railway. My income is my salary from the Seibu Railway, the Izu Hakone Railway, and one or two other companies plus my dividends from the Seibu Railway."[84] This mixing of personal and company interests—the so-called Tsutsumi Konzern—is why his businesses were sometimes called typical extended-family (*dōzoku*) enterprises. Not only were railroad workers treated paternalistically, but also some of the directors were related by marriage. Kojima Shōjirō, president of the railroad after 1955, was married to Tsutsumi's elder daughter Shukuko, and Morita Jūrō, head of Seibu Chemical, was the husband of her younger half-sister Tsutsumi Kuniko. Both Seiji and Yoshiaki served as directors after the mid-1950s.[85]

While Tsutsumi was alive, there was no president's office at any Seibu-related company, no directors' offices, nor any rooms for department or section chiefs. His power was so great that the directors had little authority (outsiders called him "chair," or *kaichō*, but insiders referred to him as "boss," or *ontai*). Each Tuesday he held a board meeting, known as Kayōkai, at his Hiroo residence where Seiji and Yoshiaki sat to either side, along with Yasujirō's wife Misao (then in charge of hotels), Kojima, Morita, and Miyauchi Iwao, vice president of the railroad.[86] Even though the Seibu Railway was a regulated utility with stock traded on the Tokyo exchange, it was the least publicly held of the seven private railways in Tokyo as of Tsutsumi's death in 1964. Financial institutions owned just 3.6 percent of its shares, compared with 25.1 percent for Tōbu and 49.8 percent for Keiō. At 799 shareholders, Seibu was far less widely owned than Tōbu (2,451) or Tōkyū (25,217). Even so, individuals represented nearly three-fourths of its shareholders, and the Tsutsumi family controlled a majority of the stock.[87] In fact it was, and in some ways still is, virtually a private company.

The founder began grooming Yoshiaki to succeed him when the boy was a teenager, warning him against close friendships because "friends will cause you harm and serve you no good purpose."[88] Instead Yoshiaki should run things himself, which he began to do at the Ōiso Long Beach Pool and Karuizawa Skate Center while still a Waseda undergraduate (Yasujirō is supposed to have been surprised and very pleased that he graduated).[89] Late in life Yasujirō spent more and more time vacationing at Hakone with his mistress Ishizuka Tsuneko, which gave Misao more influence over the weekly board meeting, although Yoshiaki remembered it differently in 1983: "My father . . . left business entirely to me. He could trust me most. This is when I was twenty-eight [in 1962]."[90] After Yasujirō died, the weekly Kayōkai reconstituted itself as the Brothers' Association (Kyōdaikai) and practiced a version of the management republicanism Seiji had evolved at the department store—a degree of autonomy for each Seibu company unthinkable while Yasujirō was alive.[91]

All told, Tsutsumi Yasujirō developed 9,700 hectares of real estate, of which about 13 percent represented housing ventures in Tokyo and its suburbs. In his lifetime he paved more than 500 kilometers of roadways to service his housing projects and resorts.[92] Tsutsumi was hurrying to catch a train to one of them in Atami, accompanied by Ishizuka, when a stroke toppled him in an underground passage at Tokyo Station on April 24, 1964. He was nursed at Shinjuku National Daiichi Hospital by his daughter Kuniko, visiting by chance from her home in Paris, and died two days later without regaining consciousness. As he had long wished, a punctilious funeral attended by 23,000 was held on April 30 at the Toshimaen amusement park. Many of those present, unaware that Yoshiaki had been picked as successor, were surprised to see his name listed as chief mourner rather than his elder half-brother Seiji's. Prime Minister Ikeda gave a eulogy and chaired the committee supervising the event, which approached a state ceremony under the aegis of the Liberal Democratic Party.[93] Perhaps only the Tokyo Olympics later that same year outdid the Tsutsumi funeral in elaborateness of ritual and number of dignitaries.

CHAPTER THREE

THE RETAILING REVOLUTION

Japanese turned into middle-class consumers in the late 1950s so quickly and enthusiastically that familiar prewar values such as frugality, restraint, and sales resistance were soon put to rout in the urban marketplace. Even though the Ministry of International Trade and Industry encouraged manufactures for export and dampened domestic consumption, families invested so heavily in durables and electronics that diffusion rates for refrigerators rose eighteen times and televisions twenty-two times between 1955 and 1959. Japan's per-capita income at the end of the decade ranked just twenty-seventh in the world (about two-thirds that of Italy); yet consumers both played catch-up, making purchases that had been delayed by war and occupation, and snapped up new goods resulting from technical innovation. Employees of large firms, who now earned significantly more than workers in small enterprises, formed the core of the new middle-class market. The 1960s consolidated and extended the transformation of household spending, as the national economy expanded at an average real rate of nearly 12 percent each year between 1960 and 1967.[1] By now millions of Japanese were purchasing status not through thriftiness, as before 1945, but by accumulating material goods.

Most of his competitors agree that the merchant who created postwar retailing in Japan was Tsutsumi Seiji almost from the moment he became head of the Seibu Department Store at Ikebukuro in 1955.[2] Tsutsumi took charge just as Japan's economy began its eighteen-year run of sustained, high-speed growth that gave consumers a spending power unimaginable before the war. He quickly became a leader in the era's two main institutional forms of merchandising, department stores and superstore chains. Department stores were the stars of the Japanese retailing revolution in the 1950s: their share of retail sales soared from under 1 percent before 1945 to nearly 10 percent in 1960 because of feverish expansion and aggressive marketing to a customer base willing and able to pay for the cachet they purveyed. The next decade belonged to superstores, or *ryōhanten* (lit., "volume-sales stores"), combining supermarkets and general-merchandise stores under one roof. Superstores recorded almost negligible sales before 1960 but by 1973 had surpassed department stores in percentage of total retail sales throughout the country.[3]

But Tsutsumi did much more than crest with the retailing wave of the times. He gave it force and direction by advertising heavily, creating markets rather than just selling goods, developing his own products so as to pare down dependence on wholesalers, and introducing foreign foods and fashions of the highest renown. Tsutsumi converted Seibu from a terminal outlet to a full department store in merchandise as well as facilities; by the end of the 1960s it was a front-rank company in both volume of sales and quality of goods. He also became the only department-store chieftain successfully to diversify into superstores when he turned his newly established chain of Seiyū markets into an overnight giant in the field. Tsutsumi revolutionized the industry via unheard-of borrowing to construct a highly leveraged network of superstores, department-store branches, and tie-ups with regional stores that since the early 1970s has constituted Japan's largest retailing organization.

ADAPTING TO THE JAPANESE CONSUMER

Retailing, like other services, is highly culture-specific in advertising and other marketing techniques, but its organizational metier in twentieth-century Japan combined native evolution with volume-sales mechanisms modified from Western business practice. In 1885 Japan already had more than a million retail establishments, or roughly one for every forty residents.[4] Many of these shops and restaurants derived from Edo-era forebears, and a number of them survive to this day. The department store as an institution piggybacked onto this elaborate retailing web in the first decade of the twentieth century; yet as late as the start of World War II, there were fewer than one hundred department stores or branches, and their impact on total national sales volume was small.

Just as Bon Marché (1852) in Paris and the American department stores of the 1860s reflected the rise of big cities, huge markets, swift rail transportation, and the proliferation of goods caused by the industrial revolution, their counterparts in Japan arose shortly after 1900 in response to urbanization, industrial growth during the Russo-Japanese War, and the spread of a nationwide railway network. Yet from the start these stores, although modeled on Western emporiums, were indigenized in expecting patrons to remove footwear, sit on cushions, and be served by clerks retrieving goods from enormous storerooms.[5] Only after the 1923 earthquake did Tokyo stores begin to emulate Bon Marché as places of entertainment where anyone was free to walk about, touch the merchandise, and choose any style that suited his or her taste—thus becoming one of Japan's great leveling experiences.

Department stores in Japan feature an abundance of goods, fixed prices, and quality guarantees, much as their Western counterparts usually have. They have also conventionally engaged in cash buying and selling, stocked many items from abroad, and offered full staffing at sales counters once these became common in the 1920s. Most department-store companies have used models called "mannequin clerks" sent by manufacturers for 40 percent or more of their floor sales force, and all of them emphasize superior service. The Japanese department store depends on its basement food section to set a tone of high quality, freshness, and good taste for the floors above. Its clothing division clamors to be a fashion trend setter in competition with domestic and foreign haute-couture houses, avant-garde designer boutiques, and specialty clothing chains—all of which are represented in miniature display areas at the major department stores. In a country where relatively few shoppers arrive by automobile, the department stores continue to provide home delivery of purchases or gifts at no additional charge.[6] Their main buildings are large, averaging 35,000 square meters of sales space and running more than twice this size at their largest, as with the 1992 Tōbu expansion at Ikebukuro. On a peak Sunday more than three hundred thousand customers enter a top department store like Isetan in Shinjuku or Seibu in Ikebukuro and spend well over $15 million in each.[7]

Two crucial elements conditioned how Japanese entrepreneurs adapted the department store to their customers' needs. First, all the major department stores established during 1904–1920 were founded by dry-goods companies, some of which had been in business since the seventeenth century. Mitsukoshi, which began as Echigoya in 1673, became Japan's first department store in December 1904, modeled on Harrod's in London; Matsuzakaya (1910) stems from a business that started in 1611. These department stores derived from dry-goods firms have been the industry leaders in sales and prestige for most of the twentieth century. But a second important factor is that private train companies in the suburbs began setting up department stores at their in-town terminals in the 1920s to sell food and sundries to their passengers in competition with the better-established department stores in the centers of major cities. Keiō founded a five-story department store at Shinjuku in 1927 that soon failed; the Hankyū market in Osaka's Umeda Station, dating to 1921, paved the way for an eight-story building opened nearby in 1929 that is the longest continuously operating terminal department store in Japan.[8] Only after World War II, spearheaded by Seibu, did the railway-company stores seriously challenge the older firms founded by dry-goods dealers; by the 1980s there was little difference between them.

Businesses like Mitsukoshi and Takashimaya responded to the upstart terminal stores by establishing branches in smaller cities in the late 1920s and early 1930s, but then eleven of the biggest department-store companies voluntarily agreed in 1932 to curb further expansion so as to reduce pressure from neighborhood retailers for legal restrictions on the big stores. Nonetheless the Diet passed a Department Store Law in 1937 of dubious value to small businesses; the occupation repealed the measure in 1947, but the Diet later reenacted it almost verbatim as the Second Department Store Law of 1956.[9] As soon as the occupation lifted commodity controls in 1950, the department stores got back on their feet and energetically remodeled, expanded, branched out, and founded new stores until the 1956 law imposed a cumbersome approval process for future department stores and branches over 3,000 square meters in sales space (1,500 square meters outside the six largest cities).

The restrictions had the predictable effect of preserving oligopoly for the existing stores, including Seibu, whose 1955 additions made it the largest terminal-store building in Japan. An unintended result was that self-service superstores, which were not covered by the law, moved quickly into markets where the spread of department stores was now encumbered.[10] Seibu alone of the big department stores successfully diversified by founding Seiyū Stores in 1963 to develop this unrestricted retail segment. Still, despite the impediments to expansion, department stores benefited mightily from urbanization as the proportion of Japanese living in cities swelled from just over 50 percent in 1955 to 75 percent two decades later. The surge of newcomers helped drive up department-store sales to their all-time peak of 11 percent of total retail sales in 1973 while also supporting both small businesses and the new superstores, so that all merchants may have come away winners under the 1956 legislation—an outcome infinitely easier to achieve thanks to sustained high-speed economic performance in the overall national economy.[11]

THE MERCHANT AS ARTIST

Like Edo-era business leaders who aspired to paint and write in the manner of the Chinese literatus, Tsutsumi Seiji has been a serious novelist and poet throughout his corporate career as well as one of Japan's most influential art patrons. Tsutsumi wanted to be a diplomat or scientist when he was young and might have majored in theoretical physics at Tokyo University had the department not been closed down by the occupation authorities. Perhaps more surprising, he immersed himself in Marxist-Leninist principles of action as an undergraduate and showed a deep interest in nihilism in his twenties.[12] These complex artistic and intellectual currents have inescapably affected his management of the Seibu Department Stores and helped to shape his goals for the Saison Group.

Tsutsumi was born in Tokyo on March 30, 1927, and grew up with his half-sister Kuniko in the home of Aoyama Misao, who was legally recorded as their mother. Her skill as a traditional Japanese poet exposed Seiji to writing as a child, but he did not turn out work of his own until "late"—age twenty-seven or twenty-eight.[13] He was ill following surgery as a third-grader and stricken with tuberculosis after college, taking nearly two years to recover. Tsutsumi first encountered Marxism as a student at Seijō High School in late 1945 and joined the leftist student movement after entering Tokyo University three years later.[14] His ten-person cell of the Youth Communist League once slept over at Tsutsumi's Hiroo house, under the lion's very nose, when his fiercely anticommunist father was home (it was a big house, and the young people were routed by Aoyama the next morning).[15] Although Tsutsumi worked as a labor organizer at Tōshiba and other firms, he was expelled from the Youth Communist League in 1950 after sectarian fighting between his Internationalist faction and the larger Impressionists, who were loyal to the Japan Communist Party headquarters at Yoyogi. Looking back at his youthful rebellion against both his father and the party leadership, Tsutsumi said in 1985 that his "antiestablishmentarianism was fairly unprincipled, so I was antiestablishment toward the Communist Party, too, and that's why I was purged."[16]

Whatever the resentments between father and son, Yasujirō seems to have wanted Seiji to join the Seibu department store as soon as he finished college in 1951; but Seiji chose to become an assistant to Nakano Shigeharu, the famous poet and intellectual who edited *Shin Nihon bungaku* (New Japanese literature). Soon he fell ill, recuperated at Karuizawa, and began writing poetry tinged with nihilistic views. After his father became speaker of the House of Representatives in May 1953, Seiji joined his staff as a secretary and served until the autumn of 1954, when he moved to the department store at Ikebukuro and began as a sales clerk in the book section. He married Yamaguchi Motoko, a fellow aide in the speaker's office, in 1955. They became parents of Kōji, now an official of Ciné Saison, but divorced about the time Yasujirō died. Tsutsumi then married Mizuno Asako, a former Yanagibashi geisha whom Mizuno Shigeo adopted shortly before the secret wedding in Paris in 1968. Mizuno, a former communist, was president of Kokusaku Pulp Company and the *Sankei shinbun*, a leading financial daily newspaper; his son Seiichi became president of the Seibu Department Stores in early 1990.[17] Tsutsumi is the father of a son, Takao, with his second wife.

He abandoned *waka* poetry after his teens "because it was definitely pre-modern, feudal in its delineation."[18] He turned to Chinese-style poems during his long convalescence from tuberculosis and published his first volume in 1955 under the penname Tsujii Takashi. He has won prizes for poetry and for his autobiographical novel *Itsumo to onaji haru* (1983; tr. *A Spring Like Any Other*, 1992).[19] Thus far the businessperson whom *Forbes* rates as one of the wealthiest in Japan, with personal assets estimated at $1.9 billion, has found time while heading the $35.21 billion Saison Group to publish more than twenty volumes of prose and poetry, including a selection of his poems translated into English.[20] A born outsider who was taunted as a "mistress's child" by schoolmates, excluded from his father's affections, and rejected by the alternative political party that claimed his allegiances, Tsutsumi has used his detached vantage to be a business leader who dares to be different because he is an artist, while also being an insider of the elite Japan P.E.N. Club who is an outsider because he is a corporate tycoon. As Tsutsumi himself put it in 1991, without evident false modesty, "I find that I can get rid of the business stress by writing. And I can avoid getting consumed by writing problems by being preoccupied with business."[21] This is an apt summary of the amateur ideal cherished by many Edo-period merchants—few of whom achieved it so fully as Tsutsumi.

FROM TERMINAL TO MAIN LINE

Japan's retailing revolution after 1955 coincided with a phase of high mass consumption when everyone with the wherewithal sought the same material goods: cars, color televisions, air conditioners, stereos. The older department stores, already challenged by terminal stores founded before World War II like Hankyū (1929) and Tōyoko (1933), were confronted by even more railway-affiliated rivals after the war: Hankyū in Tokyo (1947), Seibu (1949), Hanshin (1957), Tōbu (1960), Odakyū (1961), and Keiō (1964). Then in the late 1960s, as unceasing economic expansion drove disposable incomes upward, superstore chains began to pull even with department stores in market share, prompting major companies like Seibu to counterattack by setting up out-of-town branches and establishing ties with regional department stores. Nonetheless in 1972 Daiei, the giant among superstores, surpassed the venerable Mitsukoshi department stores as the largest single retailer in net sales and has remained number one since.[22]

Shoppers began to seek higher quality in the mid-1970s and started to abandon their fear of being different from everyone else, instead seeking goods that expressed their own sense of style. This shift toward quality and individuality forced superstores, which heretofore featured high-volume, low-profit sales of a limited range of products, to adapt more rapidly than department stores, which had long carried a huge selection of high-quality items. Some department stores remained complacent, until a downturn in the business cycle in 1982 jolted them into recognizing that superstores were innovating fast and riding out the mini-recession in good shape. Other department stores, like Seibu, transformed their buildings after 1975 into serried clusters of specialty shops to cater to consumers' quest for more selfhood in the products they bought. The early postwar department store was a city within the city, with park benches, small art galleries, restaurants, and rooftop playgrounds. By the 1980s, as middle-class families grew sated with possessions and sought experiences that were personally satisfying, both superstores and department stores began to construct entire shopping complexes, taking the city to the suburbs through what Seibu calls "creating towns" (*machizukuri*). The aim of the contemporary department store, the company confidently proclaimed in 1990, was now "marketing goods and services for particular lifestyles."[23]

When Tsutsumi Seiji joined the Seibu store at Ikebukuro as a trainee in 1954, he called it a "colony" of the railway to enhance the latter's value, not an enterprise in its own right.[24] At that point Seibu ranked number thirty-six in sales among department-store companies in the country as a whole.[25] Tsutsumi found it humiliating to visit wholesalers, be told that his store was considered second- or third-rate, and hear its name mispronounced "Nishitake" (an alternative reading of the characters of Seibu). More troublesome was his discovery that Seibu was losing money and that its financial reports were being adorned to cloak how much.[26] His father later admitted that he had only modest hopes when Tsutsumi first joined Seibu: "I didn't think he'd become head of the department store."[27] By November 1955 Yasujirō had changed his mind and made Seiji store manager, signifying renewed confidence in his once-recalcitrant son. Seiji at this point reconciled himself to being part of the family business and working under his father's tutelage.

Even before taking charge, Tsutsumi persuaded his father to rationalize labor relations at the store by setting up a union, formed in

December 1954 with seven hundred members. The next year he said he wanted the group to be a genuine critic, not "some sort of company union," and he hoped it would participate in a confederal leadership style he called "management republicanism" (*keiei kyōwashugi*).[28] Actually it remained a company union, but one with some impact in pressing for employee benefits that are still admired in the industry.[29] Unions in service industries tend to be weak, and retailing seldom sees organized conflict between labor and management, but Tsutsumi's companies surpass even the industry norm for labor peace and have been regarded as quite free of strife. A notable exception came to light in November 1968 when a Diet committee was told of allegations that Seiyū Stores had withheld $400,000 in overtime wages due its employees, partly because a store official had annulled the paycards and thus removed all evidence on which overtime claims could be based. An investigation by the Labor Standards Bureau the next month led to no resolution of the problem. Seiyū responded by forming a company union, yet by 1974 the cumulative amount employees said was owed for uncompensated overtime had soared to $2.8 million. Tsutsumi's rejoinder was that arriving up to thirty minutes early or staying up to thirty minutes late was not considered working overtime.[30]

A second major step Tsutsumi took was to recruit new employees for the department store more systematically. He sought to bring more men into a largely female work force and to hire university graduates for supervisory positions. As soon as he became manager in late 1955, he began inviting applications from college seniors and recent graduates. Six hundred responded, of whom twenty-one were hired the next spring. On April 4, 1956, he told the first class of initiates that he wanted to make Seibu "the best in Japan,"[31] even though at that point it was just number nine in Tokyo and carried few top-quality brands. Yet clearly he was stating an ambition, not just buoying workers' morale. The company also began to bring in senior executives from other firms because Tsutsumi was not content to make do only with officials on long-term loan from the Seibu Railway. As sales climbed and branches sprouted, the store mobilized new workers at all levels and ran them through orientation sessions replete with training manuals, product stories, and Tsutsumi's priorities. He told employees again and again that "when our company has a profit, we first of all use it to improve facilities for customers. Then we give it to employees in wages. . . . Only then do we give it to shareholders."[32] Within five years the work force reached 2,522, more than double its 1956 level, and males now represented 26.4 percent of the total.[33] (Tsutsumi says student activists are treated equally in hiring. "But the major companies reject them, so they expect that they can join Saison. This is not always possible" if they are not well qualified.)[34]

In addition to modernizing personnel practices and labor relations, the company discarded its old-fashioned ledgers and installed cost-accounting management, aided by $140,000 in brand-new office equipment. In 1957 Tsutsumi instituted daily sales reporting based on tags removed from each article sold and a Remington machine for punch-card control of inventory. More prosaic but no less important, Seibu mechanized its storerooms and warehouses and began using the most advanced floor-scrubbing machines available. Within two years the store became the most highly automated of its generation in the country.[35] The building itself kept on growing, in spite of directives from the Ministry of International Trade and Industry under the Second Department Store Law of 1956 to trim the scale of successive expansions. By January 1961 the Ikebukuro store contained 69,638 square meters of floor area, nearly seven times its original size in 1952, although only 42,549 square meters were devoted to sales space—second to Mitsukoshi at Nihonbashi with 48,103. Seibu, however, boasted the only rooftop heliport in the industry, at home or abroad.[36]

No era in the Cinderella story of the Seibu Department Stores is more striking than the 1950s, when the Ikebukuro store raced from last place to sixth in sales among the seventeen department stores or branches in Tokyo. Then by the end of fiscal year 1961, it had leaped three more notches and trailed just Mitsukoshi's Nihonbashi headquarters and Isetan's main store in Shinjuku—and during three separate months that year led all stores in Japan.[37] Net sales roughly quadrupled from a tiny base in 1951 to $8.8 million in 1954, then swelled to nearly $14.4 million in 1956, Tsutsumi's first full year as manager. From that year on, the company developed branch stores that soon began generating about a fourth of its revenues. Taking 1956 as 100, the index of sales for Seibu Department Stores jumped to 475 by 1961—an average annual increase of 35 percent, unprecedented in the industry. During the same period the index for all Tokyo department stores rose to 225.[38] What was a $2.2 million salesroom in 1951 had suddenly become a $66.7 million market cynosure ten years later.

Seibu in the late 1950s was blessed by the times and by its location. High-speed economic growth became a reality just when the firm expanded its building and completed the conversion from a terminal to a mainline department store, further reducing its dependence on the sale of foodstuffs from 26.3 to 21.2 percent between 1956 and 1961.[39] As Seibu began featuring high-fashion clothing and accessories, its market reach widened dramatically compared with its earliest days as a terminal store serving grocery shoppers in a territory limited by how far they could lug home perishables. With the new subway taking passengers to Nishi Ginza in nineteen minutes, Ikebukuro after 1957 seemed a major hub to consumers who began to discover haute couture from French designers at Seibu by the end of the decade. At the same time, rampant suburbanization catapulted the index of persons using all train lines to Ikebukuro from 100 in 1957 to 136 in 1960.[40] The volume of passengers on the Seibu Ikebukuro Line jumped 111 percent during 1955–1962, with more distant residential areas in Kitatamagun and Saitama making up a quarter of the market for Ikebukuro merchants by 1960.[41] Then during 1960–1964 these same suburbs claimed a further 4.9 percent of the Ikebukuro market, while the number of households living in the five wards closest to the station (Bunkyō, Itabashi, Kita, Nerima, and Toshima) increased by 30.9 percent at the same time.[42] Shinjuku's share of the total Tokyo retail market grew 4.1 percent and Ikebukuro's 5.9 percent between 1958 and 1963,[43] reflecting the astonishing population growth of western and northwestern Tokyo precisely when Seibu was leapfrogging to the top echelons of the industry.

BEYOND GROWTH TOWARD INNOVATION

The company might have expanded even faster had Tsutsumi Yasujirō not resisted Seiji's plans for branch stores, unless they were on Kokudo Keikaku or Seibu Railway lands. "As my father saw it," Tsutsumi Seiji said in 1984, "there was no need to build so many department stores all over Japan. . . . I'm afraid at the time I was not being very filial toward Yasujirō."[44] Bereft of financing from his father or the banks in the late 1950s, Tsutsumi built branches and affiliates mostly on company-controlled land. The first department-store branch to open was a summer outlet in Karuizawa (1956), evoking the Musashino shop there during World War II. Other small branches appeared in Numazu (1957), Kamakura (1959), and Ichikawa (1963). Separately the company also opened grocery outlets known as Seibu Stores in a dozen locations after 1956. Nearly all these branches and groceries were later abandoned, although Seibu Department Stores folded a few of them into its new subsidiary, Seiyū Stores, founded in 1963 as a self-service superstore chain offering general merchandise as well as groceries.[45] As of 1960 the department-store company was paying the railway $1.6 million annually to lease land and buildings—in effect, most of its profit on sales that year of just under $60 million.[46] Then in 1961 Tsutsumi became one of two representative directors of Seibu Department Stores and gradually broke its dependence on the railroad by borrowing increasingly from banks, which by now were dazzled by the company's growth and more willing to lend funds.[47]

Part of the glitter came from the store's new advertising campaigns and even more from its chic fashion lines from Paris. *Seibu of Your Dreams* was a popular radio jingle in the late 1950s (the store "full of dreams and plans" for young customers), but before 1960 most of its ads were simple newspaper announcements with detailed texts. Then the firm began a huge and very memorable campaign, including its first television commercials, "to create consumer recognition of Seibu as a first-class department store,"[48] as Tsutsumi put it. The main theme shifted from mood and atmosphere to new ideas for improving people's livelihoods. One proved to be a huge hit: wearing clothing by foreign designers. Celebrities like Christian Dior and Pierre Cardin had already visited Japan at the invitation of other department stores by the time Seibu brought the little-known Louis Féraud to show his women's collection in April 1959. Féraud's works were an instant success, propelling the store into imported women's fashions with unexpected éclat. Ted Lapidus arrived from Paris the following January with a men's line that set the fashion edge for "the Seibu man" in a distinctly European look—a real coup that projected the company into the men's clothing market at top speed. In 1961 Tsutsumi's half-sister Kuniko opened an atelier in Paris to create designs for the Japanese market, the first of eight overseas offices of the department store for acquiring merchandise to sell in Japan. From this fast start Seibu developed the reputation of carrying more high-fashion items by foreign designers than anyone else, many of which it also resold to competitors or manufactured under license for the Japanese market.[49]

But even when Seibu moved into the luxury market with exclusive imports of clothing, crystal, and jewelry, it was careful to nourish its mass customer base. The spirit of service (*hōshi*), Tsutsumi said in 1962, meant "the customer is boss" and "the consumer is king."[50] This did not mean shoppers were immune to being educated: Seibu successfully created a market by opening the first leisure-goods center in a Tokyo department store in June 1959, selling boating, bowling, golf, and mountaineering gear. Soon it operated a marina on the Miura Peninsula and offered ski lessons at Kokudo Keikaku resorts such as Naeba and Manza. This early foray into the recreation business did not pay off,[51] but it proved to be a lead-in to what Tsutsumi in March 1961 called the "department industry" (*hyakkagyō*)—which he explained as "new trading activity by the Seibu Department Stores to capture the mass market."[52] In effect this meant nonstore sales never undertaken by Japanese department stores before: automobiles, gasoline and oil, LP gas, vending machines, coin laundries, and marinas—mainly recreational products and services that showed little return at the time but set a pattern for profitable leisure activities two decades later.

The department industry also included a five-year misadventure in real-estate promotion, beginning in February 1961, that consisted mostly of selling suburban housing and mountain dwellings on Kokudo Keikaku land to customers of the department store. Tsutsumi made a splash in 1963 by unveiling Koala Homes, which were prefabricated bungalows with major appliances and a Mazda coupe included, for ¥1 million ($2,780)—reminiscent of the cottages in the larches his father sold by picture postcard forty years earlier. Surprisingly, the store's real-estate division also took over planning for the Tokyo Prince in late 1962, including funding and furnishing this 510-room hotel in Shiba Park. Included was Pisa (Prince International Shopping Arcade) in the basement, which eventually turned into a lucrative antiques and fine-arts affiliate of the Saison Group. The department store borrowed more than half the $83.3 million it cost to erect and furnish the building; but by the time it opened in September 1964, the store was saddled with $27.8 million in long-term debt, accumulated through store expansion and a disastrous branch venture in Los Angeles. To lighten this burden, its assets and liabilities in the hotel (except Pisa) were unloaded on the Seibu Railway in 1965, along with its real-estate operations in the mountains the following year. Perhaps it is understandable that Tsutsumi quietly dropped the idea of the department industry after 1965,[53] but this early experience with diversification taught him some useful shortcuts for expanding Seibu's retailing group in the 1970s.

More immediately rewarding was another Seibu innovation: slashing its dependence on what manufacturers and jobbers made available by developing its own products. Traditionally Japanese department stores carried whatever suppliers produced and exercised control only over patterns. Leftover merchandise could be returned. Then in the 1960s three parallel ways to stock goods came into use: 1) outright purchasing, which gave the company complete choice of the product mix and forced it to assume all the risks because items could not be returned; 2) consignment sales, in which the supplier bore all the risks, decided what was to be offered for sale, and conceded a high profit to the store; and 3) a variant on consignment, known as sales stocking (*uriage shiire* or *shōka shiire*), in which the store could choose a much wider variety of goods than under straight consignment, paying only for items actually sold, returning the overstock, and earning a reduced margin on retail prices set by manufacturers. Since the 1960s most stores have used some combination of the three. The latter method, long used in the industry, reduces risks but also greatly hampers a store's capacity to innovate.[54]

By 1962 Tsutsumi, who greatly admired Macy's for keeping prices down, paying cash to vendors, and protecting honest values in its wares, began to fulminate against Japanese suppliers who blocked him from emulating the famous New York firm: "The bad thing about Japan's department stores is their overreliance on wholesalers."[55] Every retailer knows the frustrations of dealing with distributors, yet without them it is impossible to stay in business; consequently Seibu attempted to prune the less desirable ones from its list of sources and work out better terms with the rest. Tsutsumi rather quixotically tried to forbid the store's buyers from fraternizing with outside salespeople; wholesalers, for their part, complained that Seibu did not promote their products aggressively enough and returned far too high a percentage of orders taken under sales stocking.[56]

Instead of depending on wholesalers Tsutsumi established a merchandise division in 1962 to begin developing Seibu's own lines, which meant hiring design specialists and doing careful market research before contracting with a manufacturer to produce the item. If it sold well, profits were great; if it flopped, so were losses. Tsutsumi was willing to accept the risk as a cost of overcoming the caution and blandness of wholesalers. Without its own brands Seibu could never introduce fresh ideas fast enough to pull ahead of other stores, who used the same distributors. Another factor was that the traditional method of sales stocking yielded too little profit for Seibu ever to climb out of its cycle of debt. As mass production and consumption boomed in the 1960s and superstores began pressing the department-store industry for customers, Seibu centralized its purchasing operations after August 1966 in order to cut personnel costs, design more of its own products, control their quality, and maximize buying in large lots at lower unit costs. Having its own brands also gave the store more leverage over its remaining wholesalers. In effect, by promoting house labels like Royal Weston in high-fashion clothing, as well as brokering foreign-designed goods manufactured in Japan under license, Seibu was trying to add maximum value through its own efforts, transforming the company from being a mere agent for manufacturers and distributors into a value-added enterprise.[57] By the late 1960s this venture in product development was well launched, and Seibu has carried private brands in great quantities ever since.

BAD MOMENTS IN IKEBUKURO AND LOS ANGELES

Tsutsumi Seiji's schemes to expand, diversify, and provide original merchandise helped send net sales at the Seibu Department Stores beyond $112.4 million in 1964, but pretax profits slipped from $1.0 million in 1961 to $694,000 the next year and then sank to just $15,000 in 1964, barely higher than the $11,400 in profits recorded back in 1955.[58] Company historians attribute the skid not to the heavy costs of financing new branches or the stuttering start of the store's leisure businesses but to a disastrous fire in the Ikebukuro building on August 22, 1963, and, even worse, the abject collapse of Seibu's branch in Los Angeles the following year. The fire started with a careless match that ignited insecticide being spread by exterminators on the eighth floor. Fortunately the store was closed to shoppers that day, but seven persons lost their lives in the day-long blaze. Tsutsumi announced a storewide fire sale two days later, which was cut short after an hour when fire officials ordered the doors closed because of the throngs. The sale was much criticized as profiteering in the face of others' misfortune, but still the fire was costly to Seibu: two floors were gutted, the rest of the building was damaged, and the outlays for reconstruction weighed down a balance sheet already burdened with heavy debts from the Tokyo Prince and Los Angeles projects. To make matters worse, Oda-kyū, Keiō, Isetan, and Mitsukoshi were all remodeling in nearby Shinjuku for the 1964 Olympics, a threat to Seibu in the best of circumstances.[59]

The undertaking on Wilshire Boulevard came about because of Tsutsumi Yasujirō's deep interest in cementing ties with the United States after he traveled to Washington, D.C., in January 1959. He instructed Seiji to set up a branch in Los Angeles, for which Seibu Department Stores took out loans from the Bank of America to finance $7.9 million in land, construction, and start-up expenses.[60] At 10,000 square meters on four floors, the building was too large to be merely a specialty shop selling antiques and souvenirs, like Takashimaya in Manhattan. Instead Seibu tried to operate as a regular department store carrying 60,000 items, roughly half of them made in Japan. The store was very Japanese in design and displays, yet Americans could buy pearls, cameras, and electronics more cheaply at discount houses and showed little interest in traditional art, textiles, or exotic foodstuffs.[61]

Soon after the branch opened in March 1962, Tsutsumi Seiji commented that marketing in Los Angeles "is very difficult. The competition is incomparably more severe than in Japan." He contended that because American management was more rationalized and offices more mechanized than in Japanese stores, "when they go abroad, they fail."[62] Seibu proved to be maladroit in dealing with its American employees and unable to cut costs to compete successfully with other department stores like the nearby May Company, let alone with self-service discounters. By the time the company pulled down the shutters for good in March 1964, the Los Angeles outlet had cumulative losses of nearly $13 million; shortly before his death that spring, Tsutsumi's father is thought to have apologized to him for causing such a huge headache in opening the ill-starred branch in California.[63]

With the benefit of hindsight, Tsutsumi liked to note that "we calculated it would take twenty years to make up the deficit" from Los Angeles, although actually it required only five. He attributed this successful egress to corporate boldness in the face of adversity: "There was no alternative policy but to expand our business, plan for diversification, and thereby absorb the losses."[64] The crisis was compounded by his father's illness and the consequent drift in leadership of the family companies during 1962–1964. Tsutsumi pressed forward with plans for more branches of his new superstore chain, Seiyū, and expanded the department store's operations dramatically in the late 1960s.[65] These moves helped to rescue the company from its nadir of unprofitability in 1964, but probably the leading reason why Seibu quickly erased its debt was that Japan was awash with economic prosperity and times were flush for everyone in the retail business for the rest of the decade.

THE SEIYŪ PHENOMENON

The Seibu Department Stores' most successful extramural enterprise in the 1960s involved mass marketing in a conventional but popular vein: the Seiyū Stores selling groceries and everyday items that heretofore had mostly been available in neighborhood shops. Building on the scattered Seibu Stores founded in the late 1950s and an experimental self-service outlet at Takadanobaba in 1962, the department store established the Seiyū Stores chain of superstores in April 1963 to capitalize on the discount revolution taking place in the Japanese market. Within three years Seiyū Stores rocketed to second place in sales among Japanese superstore chains; by 1972 it had become the fifth-largest retail company of any kind. Together with Seibu Department Stores, which was the number-six retailer, Seiyū Stores now formed part of the biggest retailing group in the country with yearly sales of just over $1 billion.[66] Seiyū, as it became known officially in 1983, has always been a top priority for Tsutsumi Seiji and from the start was one of the two main components of the Seibu retailing group that informally coalesced around the department store after 1966.

Japan's first self-service supermarket was Kinokuniya, which opened in Tokyo in 1953. The oldest superstore chain is Daiei, founded in Osaka by Nakauchi Isao in 1957 and the sale leader among individual retailing companies beginning in 1972, when it surpassed Mitsukoshi to symbolize the domination of superstores ever since. Spurred by the limits on department-store expansion enacted by the Diet in 1956, superstores borrowed directly from the American supermarket experience of the 1930s: chain-style operations with self-service, checkout lanes with cash registers, heavy advertising, high sales volumes, and low profit margins. Until the late 1960s Japanese superstores self-consciously distinguished themselves from department stores on the basis of lower prices (both types of stores carried groceries as well as daily-use items). Then they began to emphasize high-volume sales, as their name in Japanese (*ryōhanten*) implied. Starting in the late 1970s superstores shifted rapidly to stressing quality and diversity, with speciality shops, entertainment facilities, and attached shopping centers, as consumers sought more individuality and grew more discriminating about what they purchased wherever they shopped.[67]

Japan already had 1,465 self-service stores by 1960, prompting most of the department-store companies to establish superstore chains of their own. The railway-based department stores were at an advantage because they owned land for development along their passenger lines, but only Seiyū of the entire lot made a real go of it. Many department stores like Seibu also formed networks with regional department-store firms during the 1960s for collective buying and marketing in an effort to blunt the rise of superstore chains, but the out-of-town companies naturally resented the arrangements when they turned into mechanisms for the big-city stores to get rid of slow-moving merchandise. The largest and most prestigious department-store business at the time—Daimaru, Mitsukoshi, Takashimaya, Matsuzakaya—took the superstore threat the least seriously.[68] In this sense it may be an accident of timing that Seibu was still a newcomer which could not afford to dismiss the superstore phenomenon but instead became a part of it. Being affiliated with the most land-rich private railway in the country made it infinitely easier to put up Seiyū branches once Tsutsumi decided to develop the chain.

He set up Seiyū in 1963 as an independent company to underscore how different superstores are from department stores, but the change

75

of name from Seibu Stores to Seiyū Stores came about when government officials told him it was inappropriate for a department-store business and a superstore chain to bear the same name.[69] Mishima Akira, Ueno Kōhei, and Satō Hajime were the chief planners for the new firm, which was closely patterned after such American discount stores as E. J. Korvette, which had opened on Fifth Avenue in New York the year before. Each of these three executives was a graduate of Tokyo University, each was a specialist in principles of marketing, and none had direct experience as a line officer in sales.[70] Between 1964 and 1966 Tsutsumi moved an additional fifty managers from the department store to help Ueno deal with the spectacular growth of Seiyū. No personnel were brought in from Seibu Railway or Kokudo Keikaku.[71]

The new chain started off with ten locations inherited from Seibu Stores that had combined sales of $7.2 million in 1962. Tsutsumi told Seiyū employees in August 1963 that "Seiyū Stores aim at being an entirely new form of retailing. We intend to create a chain of supermarkets and superstores based on self-service and discounting."[72] He set a sales target of $55.6 million for 1965 and forecast that Seiyū would be comparable to Seibu Department Stores as a major firm by 1969. In fact Seiyū barely attained sales of $27.7 million in 1965, but in 1970 it had already surpassed the department store by recording $333 million in sales.[73] Seiyū's strategy for expansion began with building large supermarkets containing some sundries, averaging 3,300 square meters in sales areas, in contiguous districts roughly three stations apart to achieve market saturation along the Seibu, Chūō, Keiō, and other railway lines in the Tokyo suburbs—thus abandoning Tsutsumi Yasujirō's ban on stores along rival routes. Starting in 1966 the company decided to meet Daiei and Itō Yōkadō, its main rivals, head on by building even larger general-merchandise stores with groceries in the basement at a dozen major locations such as Tsuchiura, Ogikubo, and Akabane. Only Tokorozawa of these new superstores was on the Seibu line. Akabane became the site of a famous price war between Seiyū and Daiei in 1969 that plunged the cost of eggs as low as two and one-half cents each.[74] This was the first of many marketing skirmishes between the two that continue to this day. Nonetheless the trend by the late 1960s was unmistakably toward building large stores emphasizing high-quantity sales, no longer the deep price cutting characteristic of Seiyū's earliest years.

The company remodeled or closed its inherited buildings and began branching out further in 1965. Between 1966 and 1970 it added a dozen or more new stores each year, bringing the total to eighty-seven and prompting Tsutsumi to declare that Seiyū was moving beyond a big-store to a big-business strategy.[75] As part of this plan the firm decided to move outside the Kantō region near Tokyo and go national, establishing affiliates around Osaka in Kansai in 1970 and the Nagano region of central Honshu the following year. Seiyū also took control in 1969 of a twelve-store grocery chain, My Mart, that began six years earlier in the Tokyo suburbs as a joint venture among the Seibu Department Stores, Seiyū Stores, and the trading company C. Itoh. To cope with this breathless expansion, the firm introduced a centralized buying system, like the department store's, in September 1970 in order to standardize inventories, cut costs, and streamline the introduction of more clothing brands to each store large enough to handle them. It is not surprising that a rapidly growing business had troubled labor relations, such as the overtime dispute in 1968. But pay rose and hours grew shorter starting in 1970, and company historians assert that by 1973 wages "almost matched the competition."[76] Management, too, underwent vicissitudes at this time: Ueno Kōhei, who had been manager of Seiyū since 1963, was promoted to vice president in 1970 and then abruptly forced out by Tsutsumi the next year when business slowed somewhat.[77]

FROM DEPARTMENT STORE TO RETAILING GROUP

Tsutsumi Seiji inherited little personal wealth when his father died because Yasujirō's property was almost entirely corporate assets.[78] Even the Seibu Department Stores remained a part of the railroad; Seiji stayed on as manager but was subject to dismissal by the railway's directors. In practice all the Tsutsumi companies were such tightly held family concerns that the key decisions were made by the Brothers' Association (Kyōdaikai), which replaced the Kayōkai after Yasujirō's death as the de facto board of directors. Because Seiji's theory of management republicanism prevailed after 1964, the Kyōdaikai left the various companies alone, and Seiji's authority at the department store and Seiyū was not questioned.

Tsutsumi Seiji became a media favorite in the late 1960s when both enterprises shot to the top of their industries. His younger brother Yoshiaki, who inherited control of the railroad and Kokudo Keikaku, remained shrouded from public attention until he purchased the Lions baseball club and moved it to Tokorozawa in 1978. Once Seiji's risky ventures in the 1960s had succeeded, they were widely applauded as products of boldness, imagination, and insight into the future; but at the time he continually scrambled for financing to underwrite his enterprises. Already by 1964, thanks to the Ikebukuro fire and the Los Angeles fiasco, the department store's long- and short-term debt had jumped to $46.4 million (sales that year were $112.5 million), and profits were almost nil. These were poor conditions for obtaining further loans, and they were all the worse because banks historically took a dim view of service-sector businesses. Nonetheless borrowings increased another 350 percent between 1964 and 1970: in the latter year the department-store group, consisting mainly of Seibu Department Stores and Seiyū Stores, had loans of $202.5 million (the railway group's were $443.9 million, with impeccable assets to back them).[79] Many writers have recounted the lore about Tsutsumi's repeated trips, hat in hand, to city banks, local banks, mutual banks, and farmers' credit associations looking for funds that, by 1972, made him king of the largest retailing empire in Japan. Another source of capital was Mitsubishi Shōji, the giant trading company, which undertook $55.5 million in joint projects with Seibu Department Stores and Seiyū starting in the late 1960s.[80] Even judged by the heavy debt-to-equity ratios that prevailed in the era of high-speed growth down to 1974, Seibu Department Stores and Seiyū were very highly leveraged businesses. Company records clearly show what funds the banks did lend were tacitly guaranteed by the railway and Kokudo Keikaku for several years after the two brothers divided their businesses in 1970.[81]

As Seiyū raced to the front ranks of superstores in 1965–1966, Tsutsumi reorganized it and all the other companies associated with the department store so that each assumed more responsibility for developing and executing its own marketing strategies, in accordance with management republicanism. As a part of this readjustment of relations among the units, Tsutsumi was finally named president of the Seibu Department Stores in February 1966, and he remained the most powerful figure in the informal Seibu retailing group that began to emerge that year. Seiyū was entrusted largely to Ueno Kōhei's direction for the rest of the decade, so that Tsutsumi could focus on new department-store branches, more extensive advertising, new cultural promotions, and further diversification to stay ahead of Daiei as Japan's leading retailing group.

Advertising and cultural events became complementary dimensions of the department store's publicity campaigns after the mid-1960s. Seibu spent 3.5 to 4 percent of sales on advertising during 1966–1971, versus the industry ceiling of 3 percent; sales rose almost step by step with advertising outlays, as mass-marketing experience everywhere might predict.[82] One of its themes in 1967 spoke of the seasons, the first known use of the term *saison* that became part of the corporate name in the 1980s.[83] Image was the key to the store's arts promotions in the later 1960s, as was true for its competitors, but Seibu sponsored exhibitions that may have been better and certainly were bigger: Dali and German expressionists in 1964, Henri Rousseau two years later, Léger in 1972. The opening show at its new Shibuya branch in 1968, carefully chosen to strike a contemporary yet familiar note, featured works by Modigliani and drew 290,000 spectators. A Gaughin exhibit at Ikebukuro attracted 400,000 in 1969, and Renoir two years later claimed 550,000. Entrance fees and catalogue sales for a Millet show in 1970 seen by 400,000 earned $277,000 in net profit, split with Yomiuri Shinbun as cosponsor.[84] The store also held exhibitions of works by Japanese artists and a variety of events in other arts media. These activities served as highbrow advertising and brought potential shoppers to the store, but the main purpose was to set a cultured tone and create a reputation for Seibu as a patron of the best in both traditional and modern forms of art.[85] In time this image added luster to the new retailing group of which the department store was both mainstay and pilot.

CHAPTER FOUR

FROM LAND TO LEISURE: THE
SEIBU RAILWAY GROUP, 1964–1974

New Year's Eve for many Tokyo people means fireworks by the bay, revels in Roppongi, or temple visits for ritual bell ringing to expiate the evils of the year just ended. For six hundred management employees of the Seibu Railway Group it also means a predawn bivouac at Ikebukuro Station for a pilgrimage to the hilltop grave of Tsutsumi Yasujirō at Kamakura Cemetery, overlooking the sea at Asahina Pass south of Tokyo. Yasujirō's heir Yoshiaki arrives separately by helicopter to lead the chilled visitors, gathered under a large tent, in sunrise obsequies to the company founder. Day and night since April 26, 1965, the first anniversary of Yasujirō's death, male employees of Seibu have taken turns standing watch over the tomb in groups of two or three, sweeping the site, ringing a bell at six each morning and evening, and praying for the spirit of the departed.

The railway group says the graveside vigil began spontaneously among long-time Seibu workers who imagined that "the old man must be lonely, all alone,"[1] but as more and more new employees who never knew the founder joined the Tsutsumi enterprises, it became obligatory for managers to take a shift now and then at the cemetery. One who has done so three times in the span of ten years said, "It cleanses my heart" (kokoro)[2] to perform service (hōshi) to the deceased. These daily and annual memorial rites symbolize the unity of the railway group, helping to make Yasujirō's pet phrase "thanks and service" the ideological centerpiece of companies that are on the frontiers of Japan's service sector.

Yoshiaki's lifelong respect for his father is evident from everything he has said about him, in unmistakable contrast with his half-brother Seiji. Yoshiaki's praise for Yasujirō has seemed so limitless that scholars like Oda Susumu, a professor of psychiatry, have concluded that he probably suffers from "a father complex."[3] Others have contended that Yoshiaki cloaks himself in his father's mantle to excuse dubious business methods and that he lionizes an idealized version of the founder in order to improve his own image.[4] "My father's judgment and mine are 99 percent the same,"[5] he told a writer in 1978. "If my father were alive," he said to another in 1990, "I think he'd be developing the same enterprises as we are now, but on a scale ten times as big."[6] Whatever his deference to Yasujirō, Yoshiaki was not content merely to inherit the business in 1964 and maintain it intact; indeed, he recalls that Matsushita Kōnosuke of Panasonic told him in 1984, "I don't have any sense at all that you are second generation. Rather you are like a founder."[7] Even allowing for hindsight, Matsushita's assessment seems a much more useful way of grasping Yoshiaki's activities after 1964 than to take seriously Yoshiaki's claim that he honored his father's deathbed wish: "After I die, don't change anything for ten years."[8] The decade between Yasujirō's death and the first oil shock in 1973–1974 was a critical time of further diversification for the Seibu Railway and transition from real-estate development to leisure investments for Kokudo Keikaku.

GROOMED TO LEAD

Tsutsumi Yasujirō set out to prepare his third-born son for business and politics when Yoshiaki was a junior-high-school student at Azabu Gakuen in Tokyo. Born on May 29, 1934, to Ishizuka Tsuneko, Yoshiaki fled to Karuizawa at the end of World War II to escape American bombing raids but soon returned to Takagi-chō to resume elementary school. Within a few years his father took to giving him lessons in business ethics and practice during sunset walks around the pond in nearby Arisugawa Park. He also taught the youngster judo, telling him how to size up an opponent and stay calm in a crisis (Seiji was likewise adept at the sport, achieving the third level).[9] Yoshiaki recalls that his father often struck him to inculcate manners and respect. Evidently he learned the lesson: many years later Nakamura Toshio, chair of the Mitsubishi Bank, said of Yoshiaki, "What is splendid is that he is properly polite toward those older than he and scrupulously preserves the distinction between young and old."[10]

Tsutsumi made a number of friends when he entered Waseda University, some of whom joined his companies after he graduated from the evening session of the Faculty of Commerce in 1959. His father's aim in sending Tsutsumi to Waseda was to school him for a career in politics, which also meant running the family businesses in order to pay for it; evidently he readily accepted this role.[11] Tsutsumi wrote in 1984 that he learned management from his father, not at Waseda, where like many students he attended only a third of his classes as a freshman and none at all by senior year.[12] Through his father Tsutsumi became acquainted with Prime Minister Ikeda Hayato, who alerted him in 1963 to the dangers of land speculation and, as Tsutsumi recalled it two decades later, told him to "beware of politicians. A number will come around, but stop seeing politicians. They'll call themselves friends of your father and come around in an amiable manner, but they're dangerous."[13] Cautious as he may have learned to be, Tsutsumi soon started cultivating the leaders of various parties because "to know what Japan will become, I keep in touch with the politicians."[14] But he resisted the blandishments of such top Liberal Democrats as Tanaka Kakuei, Fukuda Takeo, and Ōhira Masayoshi to run for the upper house in 1974 and 1977. Apparently Yoshiaki proposed to Ikeda's daughter Noriko, but her family preferred a politician as a son-in-law; in 1966, instead, he married Ishibashi Yuri, the daughter of a Mitsui Bussan official. The couple had three sons.[15]

The management philosophy Tsutsumi learned from his father emphasized following out existing lines of business and minimizing risk. He has frequently declined opportunities to invest in new ventures on the ground that one money-losing company can wipe out profits from ten sound ones, putting all Seibu group employees and their families at risk. The senior Tsutsumi warned strictly against speculation as nothing more than gambling, which may account for his son's insistence on conserving the family's corporate assets.[16] But just as the father took chances with many of his earlier companies, so

Yoshiaki has not literally hewed to the injunctions against new investments, particularly in the 1980s. Still it is true that he acted deliberately rather than boldly once he inherited the businesses in 1964. Although he became representative director of Kokudo Keikaku while still a Waseda undergraduate in 1957, he assumed the presidency only in May 1965 and did not become vice president of the railroad until the next November. He once claimed that it took him five years to master both firms' finances after he became the principal owner.[17] Gradually he developed operating principles that owed much to his father, such as "don't undertake any new enterprises unless others are not doing them" and "don't undertake challenges outside your specialty."[18] To these he added the importance of winning local cooperation for new projects, letting employees do work they like, and hiring only at the entry level[19] — much more cautious guidelines than those at the department store.

BEYOND THE TRANSPORTATION BUSINESS

The mushrooming suburbs in northwestern Tokyo after the mid-1950s enriched not only the Seibu department store at Ikebukuro but also Kokudo Keikaku, which sold off what lots remained from prewar tracts and developed a battery of new housing ventures along the Ikebukuro and Shinjuku train lines. Coping with so many new passengers forced the Seibu Railway to strengthen its carrying power in 1961 by adding more frequent departures, extending the length of platforms, and converting certain expresses from six to eight cars. Two years later it became the first private rail company in Japan to operate ten-car expresses, and new spur lines in western Tama were incorporated into its system in 1968–1969. By then automatic train-stop (ATS, or dead-man's hand) equipment was installed on all its trains, and personnel, finances, and inventories were computerized. The company added air conditioning to its commuter expresses in 1972 and by the late 1980s had the highest rate of air-conditioned cars of any railroad in the country.[20]

Two of Seibu Railway's projects along its right-of-way in southern Saitama aroused both hopes and suspicions among local residents and illustrate its operating methods in the 1960s. Tsutsumi Yasujirō had long ago begun buying up mountains surrounding the 60,000-person city of Hannō, originally the western terminus of the Seibu Ike-bukuro Line. Throughout the 1960s the company spoke vaguely of turning Hannō into a second Takarazuka, the vibrant entertainment and cultural magnet developed by the Hankyū Railway in suburban Osaka before World War II. Then Seibu acquired more land outside the city in 1977 and finally admitted it had abandoned the entertainment center in favor of a great housing project and golf course on 450 hectares centering on Lake Miyazawa. Despite an outcry at the impending destruction of forests, the local authorities imposed only minor alterations on the scheme, and a gigantic bedroom town with few civic amenities soon took shape in the hills around the lake.[21]

The Seibu Railway also persuaded the mountain city of Chichibu, 40 kilometers northwest of Hannō, to sell it 300 hectares in 1963–1964 for $2 million, triggering both charges of a giveaway and hopes that the company would install a sports and leisure center in the old silk capital of Kantō that might stem the population loss in the area since the war. The railroad dug a 4,811-meter tunnel through the mountains and extended its line 19 kilometers from Agano to Chichibu, opening in 1969. It soon added the Red Arrow Express to Tokorozawa and Ike-bukuro, using plush coaches that provided frequent service to the metropolis in eighty minutes. The Chichibu Line earned Seibu a comfortable profit thanks to weekend sightseers and well-heeled commuters, but the firm was slow to develop recreation facilities on its property in the city itself. Local and prefectural authorities pressed Tsutsumi Yoshiaki to extend the line northward to the Seibu bastion in Karuizawa, a proposal now shelved because of a new and more direct JR superexpress that takes passengers from Tokyo to the famous mountain resort in just over an hour. Like towns everywhere that stood still while giant cities grew swollen during industrialization, Chichibu expected more return from its relationship with Seibu than has thus far materialized.[22] Yet local people have welcomed the additional train service and the tourists it has brought.

Incorporating the Chichibu Line and other short segments in the 1960s increased Seibu's total track length to 178.2 kilometers, to which 1.2 kilometers were added in 1983 when a snippet of the much-delayed Seibu Yūrakuchō subway went into service. Since 1969 the company has ranked fifth among private railroads in Japan in length of routes. Nonrailway operations such as tourism, recreation, and real estate have always accounted for a greater share of its revenues than is true of its competitors, among whom it has usually been surpassed only by Kintetsu in pretax profits.[23] Reports filed with the Ministry of Finance show that between 1960 and 1970 the Seibu Railway's visible assets expanded from $51.4 million to $158.8 million, but these figures mask the hidden wealth of properties acquired before the war or during the occupation that were carried at book value despite rapid appreciation during the 1960s.[24] The average daily passenger count had climbed by 1972 to 1.3 million and freight to 3,263 tons per day,[25] levels that showed only incremental growth during the next two decades because the northwestern suburbs had largely filled up by the end of the 1960s.

By then it was clear that future profitability for the railroad lay in building on the diversification begun by Tsutsumi Yasujirō right after World War II. Yoshiaki was fortunate that his father had established affiliates because the precedent made it much easier for the conservative managers he inherited to accept the need for further ventures to increase revenues and assets while maintaining current profits. Neither Yoshiaki's considerably older brother-in-law Kojima Shōjirō, who served as president of the railway from 1955 until the late 1960s, nor Miyauchi Iwao, its vice president and main financial officer, showed much initiative. Yoshiaki came to rely increasingly on Okano Sekiji, the last of his father's intimates, as well as Nagai Hiroshi (now president of Seibu Motor Freight) and Usami Fumio, a managing director of the railroad. To these he added Nisugi Iwao, a career bureaucrat with the national railways, as senior managing director of the Seibu Railway in November 1971.[26] Two years later Yoshiaki himself became president of the railroad and Nisugi vice president; at this point Tsutsumi Seiji resigned as a vice president and became a part-time director until he quit the board altogether in May 1986.

Nisugi, who quickly became the chief of rail operations for the line, tapped years of experience in labor relations with Japan National Railways to put down unrest among younger Seibu workers not long after the nationwide demonstrations of 1970 against the Vietnam War and the extension of the U.S.-Japan Mutual Security Treaty.[27] He was also helpful in the later stages of the drawn-out approval process for the Seibu Yūrakuchō subway, which is now expected to begin full service in 1997, fourteen years behind schedule. Taxpayer suits and land-acquisition difficulties slowed this and many other transit projects in Tokyo in the 1980s and early 1990s, so long as property values skyrocketed and landlords held out for ever higher settlements. More remarkable in the Seibu case were the generous financial terms whereby the Railway Construction Public Corporation agreed to build the underground section and add overhead express tracks to the existing Ikebukuro line for what in July 1974 was estimated at $252 million. It would turn the new facilities over to the Seibu Railway, which would then have twenty-five years to repay the construction costs, with any interest charges above 5 percent to be shouldered by national and local governments. The railroad had only to build the rolling stock.[28] Nisugi's role in these financial arrangements is unclear; he did not leave Seibu to become head of the Railway Construction Public Corporation until five years after the deal was struck. The terms themselves are strikingly reminiscent of Tsutsumi Yasujirō's method of acquiring land in the 1920s in Hakone and Kunitachi and from former imperial relatives in Tokyo after the war.

Still the firm has prospered since the 1960s mainly because of its auxiliary enterprises, especially in real estate, shopping plazas, the Prince Hotels in Tokyo and a few other inns elsewhere, and certain bowling alleys and other recreation facilities not controlled by Kokudo Keikaku, long its principal shareholder. After 1965 all the private railroads found their bus subsidiaries unprofitable because of restrictions on raising fares and competition from private automobiles. Like Seibu, they quickly diversified into tourism and land development: with 1965 as 100, the index of revenues for private railway companies from rail traffic in 1982 was 578, from buses 455, and from all other operations 940.[29] In effect, they were forced to become conglomerates because the mass-transportation business itself almost stopped growing after the 1960s in the areas they served, while costs kept creeping upward.

Seibu actually owned less land for development than most of the other private railroads, because a great deal of the Tsutsumi holdings were in the hands of Kokudo Keikaku, but the property it had was well located and evidently quite profitable before the real-estate market skidded in the mid-1970s. The company focused during the 1960s on high-quality developments in Yokosuka, Kamakura, and Yokohama as well as smaller projects in the Shōnan area to the south.

Finally in 1970 it began a new subsidiary, the Seibu Real Estate Company, Ltd. (Seibu Fudōsan), to construct housing, shopping, and recreation facilities on lands owned by the railway along its tracks. Once the real-estate business regained its equipoise in the early 1980s, the new firm plunged vigorously into apartment projects, hotels, and vacation houses in southern Saitama near Seibu's main lines. By this point private railways as a group found their real-estate divisions five times as profitable as their rail operations;[30] Seibu Real Estate would have been even more lucrative to the railroad but for transfers to take account of financing within the Seibu Railway Group itself[31]—a custom that dated to the Tsutsumi Konzern shortly after World War II.

ZONES OF LEISURE

In tones that might have been Tsutsumi Seiji's referring to the Seibu Department Stores, Tsutsumi Yoshiaki told an industry analyst in the late 1970s that "my father thought of leisure itself as a way of increasing the value of land. But I sensed that leisure itself would become a business."[32] Yoshiaki was most often portrayed before the 1980s as a cautious conservator of the family's wealth; but as his companies began to steamroller ever more resorts through to completion, a counterpoint of Yoshiaki the prescient began to be heard. Awed by the scale and lavish facilities of his ski, golf, and hotel complexes, parts of the financial press discovered the origins of the Yoshiaki myth in recreation centers he developed as an undergraduate in the 1950s. In this view, for example, he had the foresight to build a hundred-meter pool in Ōiso next to a stretch of ocean unsuitable for swimming. The Long Beach Pool was a success as soon as it opened in 1957; a Prince Hotel and golf course were added in 1964, and on a good day the pool still draws 20,000–30,000 swimmers.[33]

Even more storied is Tsutsumi's Karuizawa Skate Center, inaugurated in January 1957 in answer to his father's challenge to attract more winter visitors to the area. "At first it had ancillary value," Tsutsumi recalled in the early 1980s. "We built the skating rink to increase the value of the Karuizawa resort development. But we knew that the skating rink itself would be good business."[34] For a time it was, but then it lost its special appeal as other wintertime diversions multiplied in Karuizawa. Still it was an early tonic to the region's allure as a year-round playground, and far more profitable rinks soon followed on company-owned sites in Ikebukuro, Shinagawa, Agano, and elsewhere in the Tokyo area. Perhaps more innovative than either the pool or the skate center was an artificial, above-ground ski slope, supposedly the world's first when it opened in 1959, as a part of Seibu's skiing facilities in Sayama, Saitama Prefecture.[35] Whether or not any of these sports venues was Tsutsumi's own idea, he implemented them so successfully as a young man that many years later they were rediscovered as precursors of the vast resorts his companies have developed since.

Whatever his penchant for citing his father's deathbed injunction to do nothing for ten years, Tsutsumi began to convert Kokudo Keikaku from a real-estate company to a sports and leisure business in the 1960s and withdrew from land acquisition almost entirely by 1972, before many property investments turned sour in the first oil crisis of 1973–1974. The firm helped to create the bowling craze of the 1960s by opening mammoth hundred-lane facilities at Shiba, Shinagawa, and Ikebukuro. Kokudo Keikaku had to be cautious during the post-Olympics recession of 1964–1965, when the Tokyo Prince and other hotels were struggling and investments in both tourism and land had to be hedged. Although the railway had increased its paid-in capital to $5.8 million in 1962, the group as a whole remained undercapitalized, forcing Kokudo Keikaku to use a half-dozen major banks as sources for funds because it existed outside the *keiretsu* system and lacked a main bank.[36] Nonetheless it kept on adding smaller bowling centers at places like Saginomiya and eventually even Karuizawa, the latter in 1969. By 1972 it was first in the industry with 1,260 lanes at thirty-five locations—and then began selling out, citing overcapacity and the fact that anyone could now enter the business, just before the sport suddenly became passé and other operators took a beating.[37] Then it revived again in the early 1990s.

Tsutsumi also became a major entrepreneur of golf courses after 1964 because he controlled abundant land and a construction company, greatly reducing the investment required to build new ones from scratch. The first Seibu-related links date to 1952, at Hakone Yunohanazawa, soon matched by a companion course at Dai Hakone Country Club and others in Karuizawa, Saitama, and elsewhere. Tsutsumi said in 1984 that when he first opened a golf site, "I wasn't thinking of it as an enterprise to increase profits"[38] but rather to embellish the value of the nearby resort area. As with bowling, he correctly anticipated the arrival of golf as a mass sport, which its historians in Japan pinpoint to 1970 (the number of courses increased from 583 that year to 1,093 in 1975 and has roughly doubled since).[39] Most Japanese courses are private because huge membership fees are required to buy land and construct facilities; since the 1960s all but three of Tsutsumi's have been open to the public for a daily fee, allowing him to retain control over their design and operation. Most other courses accessible to the general public are seen as lacking in amenities, but his make superior fairways, greens, restaurants, and equipment available to anyone who can afford the stiff price of admission.[40]

Ice hockey, too, added sparkle in the mid-1960s to the group's new image of freshness and youthfulness through sports, but an equally useful function served by the Seibu Railway hockey team was to build corporate loyalty. "In an organization of thirty thousand-plus employees," Tsutsumi has said, "you have to have something to unite everybody. That was the motive for starting up ice hockey."[41] Left unsaid was that employees were regularly mobilized to fill the stands to cheer for the club, which began in 1965 and within five years became the national champion—whereupon the owner started a second team, Kokudo Keikaku, to challenge Seibu Railway to become even better. Prince Hotels sponsored an industrial-league baseball team for company unity and public relations as well,[42] although it doubled as a farm team for the Seibu Lions professional club.

"Skiing I began as a hobby and turned into a business, golf I began as a business and turned into a hobby"[43] is how Tsutsumi has explained his preoccupation with establishing ski resorts since the mid-1960s. The operative principle is "zone development," taking a 300–330 hectare site in rough mountain terrain and grouping hotels, restaurants, cottages, and condominiums around a ski facility that also has tennis courts, mountain trails, and ideally a golf course to render it a year-round leisure center. The oldest and most famous is Naeba, first developed in 1961 in a region of Niigata Prefecture boasting the best snow in central Japan. Until then Naeba had been a cedar forest, which Kokudo Keikaku gradually felled, reshaping the mountain with heavy earth-moving equipment and planting grass to form Japan's first engineered ski slopes. Tsutsumi, a superior skier, personally designed the championship courses, used since 1973 for World

Cup competition. Starting off with five lifts and a 28-room lodge in 1961, Naeba has gradually but relentlessly evolved in typical Tsutsumi fashion through high cash flows, low profits to minimize taxes, and piecemeal additions into a colossal mecca with thirty-six lifts, a 1,713-room Prince Hotel, more than 2,500 condominiums, and 2.7 million skiers each winter.[44] In 1976 Kokudo Keikaku built a golf course, pool, and tennis courts to help sell summer cottages in the remaining wooded areas nearby.

The zone-development principle holds that a loss-leader facility such as a golf course nonetheless adds value by drawing customers to hotels, restaurants, and bars—all owned by one of the Tsutsumi-controlled enterprises. Altogether Kokudo Keikaku invested $40 million in facilities at Naeba during the 1960s and 1970s,[45] and perhaps an equal sum in yen terms since. Although fewer than half the skiers stay overnight in a Seibu hotel, those who do spend $140 a day including room charges; and everyone uses the lifts, which generate more than $500,000 in daily revenues during the hundred-day season.[46] There is a big spinoff for local restaurants, shops, and inns, but Naeba is as close to a Seibu monopoly as exists in the Japanese recreation industry.

Naeba is both prototype and exemplar of the railway group's approach to building resorts. It emerged almost simultaneously with a smaller project begun in 1962 at Ōnuma, Hokkaido. Starting with a golf course for the Hokkaido Country Club, Kokudo Keikaku gradually added the Hakodate Ōnuma Prince Golf Course, log cabins for rent, and a hotel. Twenty minutes away is the Nanae ski area, opened in 1984, with a remarkable four-kilometer downhill course. Ōnuma was the first of a half-dozen zones that the Seibu Railway Group developed in Hokkaido, once it somewhat belatedly decided to challenge Tōkyū's dominant postion in tourism in the prefecture.[47] The leisure-zone idea was even modified for urban areas when the Seibu Railway began to construct a sports complex in Shinagawa, including a skate center (1962), bowling lanes (1963), and a swimming pool (1964) that were rounded out in 1978 by a no-frills Shinagawa Prince Hotel intended for single young people drawn by the athletic facilities.[48] In its latest version, the urban resort has become a health club and Prince Hotel built around an above-ground swimming pool with clear plexiglas sides in Tokyo's Roppongi district, the triumph of Tsutsumi's 1984 dictum that "leisure becomes business."[49]

OUT OF LAND BUYING

Because large land purchases and sales were evidently profitable for the railway group after 1955, nearly everyone inside and outside Seibu was shocked when Tsutsumi decided in 1972 to abstain from further big land deals. It is often said that Tanaka Kakuei, before becoming prime minister that year, warned Tsutsumi that the government must act to prevent a run-up in real-estate prices.[50] Against the advice of his managers, Tsutsumi stopped most real-estate transactions just before the wild speculation of 1972 that was sparked by Tanaka's blueprint for remodeling the archipelago. Then the oil shock of 1973–1974 ended the land fever and drove many real-estate operators out of business. The market recovered only in the early 1980s, when it charged ahead into another round of speculation, led by corporations. Both his employees and the business world praised Tsutsumi's acumen once the overheated land balloon collapsed, now realizing that his pullout from bowling centers had been prompted by the same fears of a serious real-estate slump. Tsutsumi's own explanation was that his father's warnings against gambling with the company's fate naturally led him to step to the sidelines,[51] with Japan's largest fortune in land safely intact. On the other hand, Tsutsumi Seiji, who had also used the period of high-speed growth in the 1960s to transform his businesses, made the mistake of plunging forward into land purchases and was severely hurt by the real-estate bust after 1973. For Yoshiaki the goal was to protect the company's strength, even at the cost of potential profits, out of the same concern for enterprise loyalty and unity that prompted graveside vigils and hockey championships. This insistence on building the group's asset base, rather than myths about prescience, almost certainly accounts for Yoshiaki's striking shift from real-estate operations to leisure development during the nominally do-nothing decade after Yasujirō's death in 1964.

"WHEN I SPEAK, A HUNDRED POLITICIANS JUMP"

Diffident though Tsutsumi Yoshiaki may have been about entering electoral politics after his father died, he did not hesitate to cultivate leaders of all the major Liberal Democratic factions as well as the opposition parties for information that might help his businesses.

Within a few years he grew to be so well connected that he could mobilize former and current prime ministers, imperial relatives, and foreign ambassadors to lavish receptions at his hotels. One former premier, Kishi Nobusuke, inherited an office in the old building of Tsutsumi's Akasaka Prince Hotel from another, Fukuda Takeo. Forty of sixty-six fundraising parties held by national politicians in Tokyo during 1984 took place at Princes. Even though he repeatedly denies any intention of running for office, political journalists never tire of speculating about when Tsutsumi will declare his candidacy for election to the lower house of the Diet from Saitama or Shiga.[52]

The Tsutsumi family's impact on Shiga politics since Tsutsumi Yasujirō's death has been as substantial as it is hard to pin down, according to the political scientist Takabatake Michitoshi. A long-time bureaucrat in the National Tax Agency, Yamashita Ganri, is believed to have worked out an inheritance-tax settlement favorable to Yasujirō's heirs,[53] presumably the reason why this favored lieutenant of future Prime Minister Tanaka Kakuei took over Yasujirō's local support association in 1964 despite weak ties to the prefecture. The Tsutsumis backed Yamashita's successful campaign for election to the lower house in 1967, but evidently they also contributed funds to Aoyama Shun, the candidate endorsed by then-current Prime Minister Satō Eisaku. It is surely not coincidental that Aoyama later joined the Seibu retailing group and became president of Seibu Urban Development Company.[54]

After Tanaka fell from power in 1974, Tsutsumi Yoshiaki diverted most of his support in Shiga to Takemura Masayoshi of the Fukuda faction and helped elect him to three terms as governor of the prefecture, 1974–1986. The railway group needed official favor because of its growing real-estate activities in the area, especially a 330-hectare parcel in the Seta district of Ōtsu that Tsutsumi Yasujirō had quietly obtained in 1958 for the price of a reported $83,000 loan to Seta so that Seibu could put in a golf course and other recreation facilities. In 1967 it became known that the company had used most of the site for tract housing and paid only 20 percent of the taxes appropriate for such a use. By supporting Takemura, Tsutsumi Yoshiaki evidently hoped that he could help resolve the many suits that were lodged after this disclosure.[55]

Seibu and Ōtsu clashed over financing a toll road and a new prison to be built there in the late 1960s and over a grandiose $1.7 million scheme to develop Lake Biwa for tourism initiated by Tanaka and advanced by Takemura in association with the railway group. Even more sparks flew in the mid-1970s when $40 million in public funds were committed to provide roads, utilities, schools, and parks for a $293 million Seibu housing project that critics said would pollute the lake and benefit only commuters to Kyoto and Osaka, not Shiga itself—the New Jersey syndrome replicated. Takemura is also thought to have helped smooth Shiga's purchase of an $8.4 million green strip next to a Seibu apartment complex and golf course near Ōtsu in 1984 for use as a nature conservancy, even though local environmentalists did not favor the plan.[56] Yet even Tsutsumi's staunchest detractors conceded that his influence on Takemura was indirect and hard to verify.[57]

Tsutsumi's ability to sway national politics became widely known during the forty-day struggle in 1979 between former Prime Minister Fukuda and then-current Premier Ōhira Masayoshi for control of the Liberal Democratic Party, when he drew attention for providing help to both sides. After Ōhira died suddenly in June 1980, Tsutsumi forcefully promoted Suzuki Zenkō as the next prime minister, angering another powerful contender, Nakasone Yasuhiro, who succeeded Suzuki in 1982. To Nakasone's chagrin, Tsutsumi three years later held a famous golf outing for three prospective prime ministers at the Dai Hakone Country Club while Nakasone was still in office. What was so inexcusable was Tsutsumi's brashness in inviting a hundred reporters and camerapeople to watch him in a foursome with Abe Shintarō, Miyazawa Kiichi, and Takeshita Noboru, the latter of whom succeeded Nakasone in October 1987 after an enervating intraparty impasse during which Tsutsumi angered all contenders by erroneously leaking a "top secret report" that "it'll be Miyazawa."[58] In fact it was Takeshita, a fellow Waseda alumnus to whom Tsutsumi provided a good deal of aid during his scandal-tarred administration. Many who follow politics think that, if elected, Tsutsumi would immediately head a large faction within the Liberal Democratic Party, but as it is, his backroom influence as a coordinator and occasional kingmaker seems very substantial. Apparently Tsutsumi agrees, since he boasted in 1988 that "when I speak, about a hundred politicians jump"[59]—more than listened to his father for most of his career.

CHAPTER FIVE

MERCHANTS TO NEW MARKETS: THE SEIBU RETAILING GROUP IN THE 1970S

Shopping arcades called Parco filled with high-fashion specialty shops for the young were the hottest retailing concept of the 1970s and the focus of the most influential marketing campaign ever conducted in Japan. In 1973 Seibu Department Stores unveiled a shiny steel and glass Parco building in the Shibuya district of Tokyo, the same year a worldwide oil crisis stunned the country. Parco defied the economic storm caused by the Arab oil embargo: "Ginza's neon was turned off because of the energy-conservation campaign, but Parco boldly left its neon lights burning. After the oil shock the economy entered a period of long-term stagnancy, but in the midst of this Parco increased the vigor of its [advertising] campaigns."[1]

This recollection by Masuda Tsūji, the firm's guiding figure, symbolizes how the newcomer challenged consumers to return to the marketplace through store promotions, events in its top-floor theater, wall paintings, and street fairs, parodying the prevailing mood of recession and sketching new fashion directions for well-heeled young people in the cities who were tired of both prêt-à-porter designer copies and the anti-styles of the Vietnam War era. Parco's neon in the Shi-

FIGURE 3a. Tsutsumi Seiji in 1991. (Saison Group)

FIGURE 3b. Tsutsumi Yoshiaki in 1989. (Kyōdō Tsūshinsha)

buya darkness aptly captures the Seibu spirit of the 1970s: flouting the prevailing wisdom and mapping out new markets unexplored by earlier Japanese retailers. Tsutsumi Seiji's daring in the face of ill economic winds nearly sank the company in the mid-1970s, but it also positioned the group at the front of the industry in both diversification and specialization by the end of the decade.

THE TWO BROTHERS' COMPACT

The critical event that freed Tsutsumi Seiji to develop the Seibu retailing group was an extraordinary business-splitting agreement with Tsutsumi Yoshiaki in 1970 that marked out spheres of activity for the railway and the department-store enterprises. When their father died in 1964, Seibu Railway Company owned most of the department store's shares. Under the 1970 noninterference pact Yoshiaki pledged to sell his stock in the department store to the retailing group, hand over its land and buildings, and move a subsidiary that produced fertilizer and steel to Seiji's group. Henceforth Seiji would concentrate on manufacturing and distribution while Yoshiaki would emphasize transportation, real estate, and tourism. Both agreed to show respect to their father's memory as their various businesses evolved in the future.[2]

This informal compact gave Seiji recognition as owner and representative of his group but also total responsibility for its financial health. Having decided to expand in order to earn his way out of the debts piled up in the 1963 fire at Ikebukuro and the 1964 flop in Los Angeles, Seiji needed bank loans and thus collateral. Rather than backing his brother each time he sought capital, Yoshiaki gave Seiji control over Seibu Chemical Industries and 1,655 hectares of land it owned at Yatsugatake and Osaka as a kind of dowry, worth an estimated $138.8 million at the time,[3] so that he could be independent financially—and psychologically. Yoshiaki reportedly said that "I try to decide difficult things the way my father would if he were alive. On this point, Seiji thinks our father is dead, so he has come to do things his own way."[4] In fact Yoshiaki kept on helping out his brother for years after the gentlemen's agreement: monthly meetings of the Brothers' Association continued throughout the 1970s, and the transfer of land, buildings, and stock occurred in several stages from 1972 to 1985.[5] Evidently some or all of Yoshiaki's shares were transferred to Seiwa Sangyō, nominally a manufacturing, trading, and leasing company that is still listed as the largest shareholder of Seibu Department Stores. Although some of Seiwa Sangyō's officers have had strong ties to the railway group, a top Saison executive states flatly, "Seiwa represents Tsutsumi Seiji's family interests, not those of Tsutsumi Yoshiaki. The railway now has no say in the management of the Saison Group."[6]

As is often true in the histories of diversified corporations, the little-known subsidiary Seibu Chemical Industries was the hinge on which the two brothers' agreement turned. Founded in 1935 as a producer of chemical fertilizers, this firm was taken over by Tsutsumi Yasujirō right after World War II. By the late 1960s it began investing in a dozen bowling centers, only to see the market for them suddenly collapse in 1972. That same year Tsutsumi Seiji divided the company into a manufacturing concern under the same name of Seibu Chemical Industries and a real-estate business called Seibu Toshi Kaihatsu (Seibu Urban Development Company, Ltd.). Seibu Chemical, Asahi Foods, and a seaweed business acquired in 1983 merged two years later to form Asahi Industries, Ltd. (Asahi Kōgyō), a subsidiary of the department store that had sales estimated at $400 million in the year ending March 1990 and anchored a cluster of affiliates with aggregate sales of roughly the same amount. In April 1992, when annual sales reached $432.7 million, Asahi Kōgyō was divided into Asahi Food Processing Company, Ltd. and Asahi Industries Company, Ltd. Asahi Food Processing was made a member of the Seiyo Food Systems Group; Asahi Industries was conspicuously profitable in construction materials and agricultural technology.[7]

Much more problematic was Seibu Urban Development because it was saddled from the start with failing bowling alleys, which prompted its president (and Tsutsumi Seiji's brother-in-law), Morita Jūrō, to resign in February 1973 to assume responsibility.[8] Despite its name, Seibu Urban Development first turned to making over its 993 hectares of hillside at Yatsugatake, Nagano Prefecture, and a site on Nishiomotejima as a marine resort. The company also began work on a members-only hotel in Osaka that opened in 1976. At this stage Tsutsumi Yoshiaki evidently was not ruffled by his brother's foray into real-estate projects because they appeared to be directed toward the department store's more affluent patrons.[9] But Seiji himself became very disturbed when he found that Seibu Urban Development, swept along by Prime Minister Tanaka's illusion of remodeling the archipelago, had bought lands it could not sell once the effects of the oil shock in 1973–1974 were felt, leaving the company with loans of $233 million secured by land worth $167 million.[10] This crisis, in tandem with stagnation at Seiyū in the mid-1970s, provoked a new atmosphere of peril in the retailing group just a few years after Tsutsumi's daunting expansion of department-store branches and superstores had erased the accumulated debt from the mid-1960s.

Still the advent of Seibu Chemical in 1970 allowed Tsutsumi Seiji to constitute his enterprises around four core companies: the department store, Seiyū, the scaled-down Seibu Chemical, and Seibu Urban Development. When the group held its first formal meeting on September 22, 1971, at the Tokyo Prince, Tsutsumi reiterated his principle of management republicanism: a federation of firms with central direction that freely engaged in self-criticism.[11] At the same time he began to sound a theme that grew more audible at the end of the decade: the gradual conversion of the Seibu Retailing Group into a "consumer industry" (*shimin sangyō*) responding to the needs and aspirations of "autonomous urban consumers."[12] The corporate focus on the urban consumer industry coincided with a broader shift, both at Seibu and elsewhere, from quantity to quality as consumption evolved to a new phase of maturity in the late 1970s.

THE SIEGE OF SHIBUYA

The greater Shibuya marketing sphere (including Aoyama and Harajuku) is now such a cynosure of fashion and excitement to Japanese below age thirty that it is hard to remember a time twenty-five years ago when the area was a dowdy backwater of tired movie halls, grimy concrete apartment houses, and rundown civic auditoriums. Once a fiefdom of Gotō Keita's Tōkyū interests, Shibuya was transformed by the Seibu Retailing Group after the late 1960s into the centerpiece of its highly leveraged strategy of building new department-store branches as a response to complex pressures: the turmoil of high-speed economic growth, increasing competition from superstores, growing demands from small shopkeepers to limit all large retailers, and chronic financial difficulties within the group itself. The Seibu assault on Shibuya is a

remarkable chapter in Japanese commercial history and an indispensable ingredient of the postwar retailing revolution in that country.

Tsutsumi Seiji's entry into Shibuya was the keystone of an expansion plan that included new department-store branches in Funabashi
(1967), Shibuya (1968), Ōmiya (1969), and Hachiōji (1970), as well as
tie-ups with out-of-town stores in Shizuoka, Hamamatsu, Utsunomiya, Kansai, and Hokkaido between 1970 and 1973. In the 1960s it
was enough to stock a rich abundance of goods, but in the 1970s these
new stores paid much more attention to the installation and presenta-
tion of displays as new levels of fashionable marketing were attained.
(By the 1980s the emphasis shifted again to the essence of the product,
not sentiment or environment as in the 1970s, and a wide variety of
sizes and colors was de rigueur.)[13] While branching and regional networks swept the industry during the late 1960s and early 1970s, the
Big Six department stores (Mitsukoshi, Takashimaya, Seibu, Isetan,
Daimaru, and Matsuzakaya) distanced themselves from the rest, especially by developing more private brands and asserting overwhelming
sales power in the largest urban centers. Tokyo, with 11 percent of the
nation's population in 1972, accounted for 31.8 percent of wholesale
and retail trade; during 1975–1983 it and the other five biggest cities
rang up 62 percent of all department-store sales.[14] Seibu's designs on
Shibuya, Tokyo's only remaining underdeveloped market among the
affluent, were perfectly timed to ride these industry-wide trends.

Yet in other ways all department stores were at risk in the 1970s.
Although the index of department-store and superstore sales jumped
from 100 in 1972 to 178.8 in 1976, most of the growth occurred in superstore chains. Likewise, even though the same index fell from 100 in
1979 to 88.5 in 1982 after the second oil shock, the contraction was
entirely attributable to the department stores.[15] Superstore chains
increased their outlets from about 2,000 in 1972 to more than 3,100 in
1977 and promoted standardized clothing and household items, not
unlike a European hypermarket, to balance their strong food sales
(food accounted for 42.5 percent of revenues in 1977).[16] By then their
largest out-of-town branches were damaging those regional department stores that lacked affiliations with big-city counterparts. The lag-
gard rationalization of wholesale trade (the number of distributors
actually rose by 60,000 during 1979–1982)[17] hurt profitability at the
department stores, to the extent that the latter still relied on jobbers

for their merchandise. Chain specialty stores, led by such mass-market clothing arbiters as Suzuya and Ropé, surged so fast that by 1977 they accounted for 34 of Japan's top 200 retailing companies.[18] This was also the decade when small department stores based on installment credit took root, especially in the youth market, with 70 percent of their sales in clothing.[19]

Potentially even more damaging was the Large-scale Retail Store Law of 1974—modeled after legislation in France—together with amendments in 1979 and administrative rules three years later. Now all new retail stores with more than 500 square meters of sales space were subject to a tedious local-approval mechanism that meant the average period for opening a new store stretched to six years.[20] In effect the only chains that could freely expand were convenience stores. This legislation sliced the number of applications for new large-scale stores from 1,605 in 1978 to just 402 in 1981, after which there was a steady rise to 655 in 1988 and 791 in 1989, as pressures from chain operators and the United States trade representative led retailers to expect speedier approvals.[21] Finally in February 1990 Prime Minister Kaifu Toshiki announced that the law would be applied more flexibly; by then the number of planned large stores, more than 1,500, exceeded the total already in operation (1,429). The Diet formally abolished the local-consultation requirement in May 1991, greatly accelerating the clearance process.[22] The administrative rationale for the law was that it protected neighborhood businesses during a transitional phase, before labor shortages and the lack of successors began forcing them to close permanently, while at the same time giving the superstores and discount houses a foothold from which they could expand in the future.[23] Under these restrictions, department stores were the most vulnerable to being whipsawed by superstores on one side and small retailers on the other, but the most imaginative of them managed to thrive and expand nonetheless.

Faced with these developments in the overall retailing industry, Seibu's approach to Shibuya was daring, even defiant. It occurred in two phases: a medium-sized branch of the department store in 1968 and a Parco shopping arcade five years later, both northwest of Shibuya Station. Between them these outlets rewrote the face of the district and inspired a youthful style in fashion and the arts variously known as Seibu or Parco culture. Although Tsutsumi Yasujirō had briefly operated a shopping center there as early as 1923, Shibuya became a Tōkyū monopoly in the late 1920s and remained so for the next forty years. The Nihon Kangyō Ginkō, Tsutsumi Seiji's main bank, evidently suggested in 1962 that the department store advance into the area; the idea was formalized in November 1963 in an internal memorandum, *Seibu Hyakkaten no atarashii shinro* (New course for Seibu Department Stores).[24] Within a year Seibu arranged with Tomizuka Kōkichi, the owner of some disused Tōei movie theaters on a main street near the station, to build and lease the two connected structures that in 1968 became the A and B wings of the Shibuya branch store.

Although critics at the time thought the debt-burdened Seibu company was foolhardy for challenging Tōkyū on its own sidewalks, documents recently published by Saison show that Seibu reached an extraordinary and highly secret coexistence agreement with Tōkyū in February 1964, whereby the latter acquiesced in the construction (Tōei was part of the Tōkyū Group) if Seibu would lease it some badly needed office space until Tōkyū's own department-store headquarters was ready in 1967 at Dōgenzaka. Seibu Department Stores, which turned operation of the Haneda Prince Hotel over to Seibu Railway later in 1964, likewise agreed to sell the hotel to Tōkyū in 1967–1968,[25] and Tsutsumi Seiji also exerted influence to give Shizuoka Prefecture the family's private roadway at Hakone, where Seibu and Tōkyū had battled in the 1950s.[26] It is not surprising that when the 28,000 square meter Shibuya branch opened in 1968, Gotō Noboru posted huge banners on the main Tōkyū Department Store: "congratulations! Seibu opens!"[27]

In a formal sense Gotō, who had succeeded his father Keita as Tōkyū's chieftain when the latter died in 1959, was powerless to prevent Tsutsumi's Shibuya venture. Someone who might have was Tsutsumi Yoshiaki, especially when the traditionalist managers of the railway group closed ranks against the project after the founder died in April 1964. Many years later Yoshiaki told an interviewer that "the Seibu Railway asked what sort of thing this was; because we didn't understand it, we were forced to oppose it."[28] These words, although technically accurate, befog the fact that Yoshiaki stood up for his brother, helping persuade the railroad's directors to let Seiji try the strategy and later convincing Taisei Construction Company to sell the Shibuya

Parco site to Seibu. As Seiji freely acknowledged in 1983, "When I asked headquarters for help in expanding into Shibuya, only Tsutsumi Yoshiaki supported me."[29] The web of interconnections between the two was far too durable to be severed by a single gentlemen's agreement to divide their businesses in 1970, and there is reason to believe the brothers still assist each other covertly in the 1990s.

Against the advice of the railway's directors and many department-store managers in Ikebukuro, Tsutsumi Seiji pressed forward in Shibuya, relying on his high-school friend Masuda Tsūji to help plan the branch's operations. The first-year results seemed half empty to the company itself, with sales just a third the volume of the main store's, but half full to the rest of the industry, which thought the outlet had done well to chalk up revenues of $40.8 million in Tōkyū's home territory.[30] Still the new store did not hit full stride until after its $3.7 million renovation in the mid-1970s, when it abandoned the amorphous theme of "young prestige international" in favor of more selective high-fashion marketing in a downsized format the company called a "70 percent store" (nanajūkaten), rather than a full-range department store. The remodeled building capitalized on Ralph Lauren's new Polo line, introduced in 1976 as a marriage of tradition and innovation, and since then has been as popular among style-conscious clothes shoppers under age forty as any store in the industry. Not surprisingly, it is now also one of the most profitable, the more so because of its ideal location near four train lines that bring customers from Tokyo's wealthiest suburbs.[31]

By some estimates as many as two million people pack into the Shibuya district each day, thronging the "scramble" intersections that are among its hallmarks. Two others are the studios of NHK, the national broadcasting corporation that began moving there from Atagoyama in 1964, and Park Avenue (Kōen Dōri), a strollers' paradise connecting NHK and the station, with Parco as its pillar. Shoppers tend to linger in Shibuya, somewhat offsetting its lower population compared with Shinjuku or Ikebukuro. The target for merchants is young people, who consistently rate the Aoyama-Shibuya-Harajuku triangle more exciting than establishmentarian Ginza, touristy Asakusa, middle-class Shinjuku, or commuter-dominated Ikebukuro. Youths congregate in Shibuya to express themselves, as in Westwood or Winnetka, by showing off their cars and sauntering at streetside to see people and

FIGURE 4. The original Parco building in Shibuya (built in 1973) as it appeared in 1990. (Saison Group)

be seen.[32] Virtually everyone agrees that the single most important stimulus to the youth culture of Shibuya has been Parco, which opened the first of its current four buildings on Park Avenue in 1973 and has never turned off its neon since.

Parco is the transfigured descendant of the ill-fated Tokyo Marubutsu, which operated a 10,000-square-meter department store next door to the main Seibu store in Ikebukuro from 1957 until it was bought eleven years later by Seibu Department Stores. Seibu then re-modeled it as Japan's first rental arcade of women's specialty stores to offer multiple shops in each merchandise line (e.g., accessories, shoes). Both Tsutsumi Seiji and Yoshiaki have claimed credit for the con-cept,[33] but Masuda Tsūji was the marketing genius who made it work. Its first building opened at Ikebukuro in 1969 and assumed the name Parco the following spring; a second began operating at Shinsaibashi in Osaka in 1971. Shibuya became the third in 1973, and a dozen others have followed since, almost always in high-traffic urban areas on lots too small for use as a superstore or department-store branch.[34]

Parco is a textbook case of a value-added company: Parco itself sells no goods; besides renting space to stores that do, it is in the business of producing images. "I realized Ikebukuro was an area with few places to have fun and one with no specialty shops,"[35] Masuda recalled in 1977. He took deposits from tenants in advance, collected 10 percent of their sales in lieu of ordinary fixed rents, and in return proffered expert marketing advice and produced clever advertisements, promo-tions, and cultural events for the arcade as a whole. He persuaded tenants that the lack of down escalators would keep shoppers in the Ikebukuro building longer and lift sales. Despite some early resistance to the notion of including competitor stores selling the same product lines, the Ikebukuro Parco opened in November 1969 with a full com-plement of 169 merchants, mainly in women's fashions, accessories, sundries, and restaurants.[36] What made it different from previous ar-cades and station buildings was 1) its unified focus on evening shop-ping for big-city working "women on their own," ages eighteen to twenty-nine; 2) its segmentation of interior space into nests of shops without a large anchor store; and 3) its elaborate decor to create a shop-ping environment that would draw the beautiful people who in turn attract other well-to-do customers—quite a task for that time and loca-tion.[37] But the idea worked: tenants found their sales increasing 15–25 percent a year, and within five years the new company had wiped out Marubutsu's accumulated debt of $5 million, making it the most profitable member of the retailing group after the parent department store itself.[38]

Parco brightened the sheen of the Seibu retailing group still more after moving into Shibuya in 1973. The choice of site—far from the glitter of Dōgenzaka, reminiscent of Tsutsumi Yasujirō's turning hardscrabble into housing—challenged the company to landscape the street, put utilities underground, widen the sidewalks, and install British phone booths, redirecting the flow of traffic from other parts of the district to "Park Avenue in Shibuya, where the person you pass is beautiful."[39] Borrowing a venerable Bloomingdale's come-on, Masuda promoted "the shopping street as a theater," both through plays and concerts in the 478-seat Seibu (now Parco) Theater on the top floor and through street festivals, outdoor art shows, and gentle parodies like the faux Trevi fountain or the bicentennial replica of the Statue of Liberty on the sidewalk in 1976.[40] Yet Masuda was frank to admit that the Seibu Theater "was not necessarily intended to elevate theatrical culture. Essentially it was a device to create a show space, a fashion environment"[41] where people could look beautiful and see fashion all around them—a trademark of Japanese audiences since at least the Genroku galas at the end of the seventeenth century.

The building itself was a gamble because, unlike Ikebukuro or Shinsaibashi, it carried only women's fashions—no other boutiques or restaurants. But it and the nearby Seibu department-store branch did well in good part because they were located in Japan's richest residential zone. Management insisted that each tenant show sales growth compared with the previous year, and it helped shaky stores with buying, inventory control, and displays based on the Seibu Department Stores' expertise. Still, faltering tenants were soon replaced, so that the building had a 10–15 percent turnover per year. After 1973 Parco devoted most of its efforts to promoting its shopping centers to "power" customers who elsewhere were called yuppies: young, urban, wealthy. The firm based its advertising on market segmentation, targeting this carefully defined niche through electronic, print, poster, and direct-mail announcements so as to avoid the inefficiency of mass marketing. Avant-garde art work, African American models, catch phrases printed horizontally (often in English, such as "young," "chic," "international"), and daring copy like the 1973–1976 challenge "don't look at a nude, go nude" sought to tap the freshness and energy of the baby-boom generation (an all-time high of 2.4 million Japanese turned twenty in 1969; as of 1975 half the population had been born since the war).[42] For a time this cohort was labeled the New Families. Then after 1975 the modal consumer was called the New Young, someone used to electronic information and highly conscious of fashion who responded to humor and lighthearted advertising. Even more crucial than shifting values was demographics: the number of persons turning twenty dipped to 1.6 million in 1978 and again in 1981, a new low since the war.[43] There is no question that the effort paid off. By the end of the decade, above all in Shibuya, Parco meant youthful fashion and not just a building.

Parco prided itself in the 1970s on being "more Seibu-like than Seibu itself."[44] As soon as it earned logo recognition with meaningless TV ads showing foreign models and the tag line "it's very Parco," the company focused its attention on well-to-do young women in their twenties through frank appeals to individuality and even narcissism. Female commercial artists like Yamaguchi Harumi and Ishioka Eiko created ads with unsmiling, noncomplaisant models who seemed to show themselves deliberately, without waiting to be noticed—women who seemed to live for no one but themselves. "I love me," a 1973 poster said in English—a self-absorbed theme still found in the late-1980s ad, "I'm the cutest."[45] Parco also emphasized role models such as Faye Dunaway and the idea of fashion as something natural, not contrived, in commercials that stressed ecology and textiles like cotton at their place of origin in India. Even the ads for men's clothing were unprecedented: a 1976 poster read, "fellows, let's try to be more good-looking for the women."[46] Still the company kept its marketing budget within the industry rule-of-thumb (3 percent of sales);[47] it was the quality and pinpoint targeting of advertising, not its quantity, that mattered.

Parco expanded fast during the 1970s in cities like Sapporo, Gifu, Chiba, Ōita, and Kobe, often by taking over failed Seiyū or Midoriya outlets. Parco Part 2 opened an art-nouveau building at Shibuya in 1977, showcasing some of Japan's trendiest contemporary designers, and four years later Part 3 followed in cool art deco with sports, sound, and interiors. The number of tenants in all its buildings passed 1,000 in 1977 and stood at 1,352 in 1983, by which time Studio Parco and SRG, both of them showrooms, had been added at Shibuya. Net sales rose from an initial $25 million in the first year at Ikebukuro to $186.7 million in 1975 (up 6.2 times in yen terms) and $470.2 million in 1980 (nearly double again in yen terms).[48] By now Parco meant Shibuya to most residents of Tokyo, and Shibuya more and more meant

Parco, for its creativity and social impact, even though Seibu's main competitor in the young people's market, Marui, was busy installing buildings of its own on Park Avenue. By now, too, the so-called East-West War in the district between Tōkyū and Seibu was effectively settled in favor of Seibu and Parco, which in 1987 were thought to draw three customers for every one of Tōkyū's.[49] After opening its headquarters department store in 1967, Tōkyū failed to take Seibu seriously and did not add a major retail building until 1978 with Tōkyū Hands, a highly successful hardware and do-it-yourself emporium that has recently been eclipsed by Seibu's more artistic counterpart, LoFt. The following year Tōkyū unveiled its 109 building, a close copy of Parco in a superb location—but with little of the ambience of youth culture so crucial to Parco's allure.[50] The successful struggle for Shibuya was the brightest aspect of a stormy decade for the retailing group, which found itself diversifying into financial services for consumers in order to reduce its reliance on the department store at a time when the industry faced a shrinking market share and legal restrictions on growth.

BEYOND RETAILING

Shoppers were surprised and merchants disconcerted when the Seibu Retailing Group and Sears, Roebuck and Company, then the world's largest department-store chain, signed a contract in December 1972 for catalogue sales of Sears products in Japan. At the time it was Japan's policy to exclude imports for the mass market and restrict foreign investment, yet suddenly a major Japanese firm was bringing in this overseas giant that might destabilize the domestic industry at a time when superstores were already setting other retailers back on their heels. It turned out Seibu was less interested in Sears's goods than its technical knowhow: market research, private-brand development, employee-management systems, inventory control, and especially its nonretailing operations like the Allstate insurance companies.[51] Particularly fruitful to the retailing group was that Sears invested in Seiyū, helping to streamline its personnel system and inventory controls; the Chicago-based firm still holds a 2.2 percent position in the chain.[52]

Hardly anyone was taken aback when "catalogue sales of Sears products through the department store proved difficult,"[53] as Mizuno

Seiichi, president of Seibu Department Stores since 1990, puts it. But Sears's immensely profitable experience with Allstate, one of the largest life and casualty insurers in the United States, quickly persuaded Tsutsumi Seiji to make Seibu the first department store in Japan to branch into consumer financial services when it inaugurated a joint venture with the American megaretailer in 1975, the Seibu Allstate Life Insurance Company, Ltd. (now Saison Life). Sears later surmounted a severe marketing slump in the United States by diversifying at the end of the 1970s into real estate, securities, precious metals, and consumer finance, which led Tsutsumi to concede in 1983 that what he had learned most of all from the American corporation was that 70 percent of its profits came from nonretailing operations.[54] This was a clear signal to Seibu to move beyond goods into an even wider array of services.

Life insurance was likely to be lucrative to Seibu because Japanese families put nearly half their savings into policies, so that the country had by far the highest per-capita amount of life insurance in force in the world. Despite much greater consumption in the late 1980s, thrift continued to grow: the average household in 1990 had savings of $94,615, making life insurance a reliable source of cash flow ever since Tsutsumi entered the field in 1975.[55] Yet Seibu was considered both radical and foolhardy for going into the business because at first it sold policies, like Sears, at walk-in counters in its department stores, not via an army of saleswomen selling to their friends as all twenty other life insurers did. Moreover Seibu Allstate initially emphasized term policies without cash value or dividends, not endowment plans as was customary for other providers.

"Seibu Allstate is a sign of the internationalization of Japan," Ikuno Shigeo, president of the company, pointed out in a 1986 interview. "For forty years no new life-insurance company had been started in Japan, and before Seibu Allstate was founded there was very little foreign participation in the Japanese life-insurance industry."[56] It took the Ministry of Finance nearly two years to approve the new company because no firms had been founded since 1934 and there was no precedent for a foreign joint venture. Spurred by Sears's successful diversification, Tsutsumi and Ikuno established another venture with the American conglomerate beginning in 1984, Allstate Automobile and Fire Insurance Company. That same year the retailing group also set up Seibu Mortgage Securities Company (Seibu Teitō Shōken) and in 1986 acquired a small brokerage, Saiō Shōken, to sell stocks and bonds in split lots to the group's retail customers.[57] By now Tsutsumi had converted his businesses into what he called a "generalized corporation"[58] providing services within the urban consumer industry as a whole, no longer confined to retailing.

Another lesson Sears taught Seibu was to develop consumer credit, a concept slow to blossom in a country where savings and cash payments have long been favored. The Singer Sewing Machine Company introduced installment-plan sales to Japan early in the twentieth century, but Marui became the real credit pioneer among department stores after it was founded in 1937. Later Marui was surpassed for a time by Midoriya, established in 1946, thanks to a network of seventy-eight small monthly payment stores in the Tokyo suburbs. Then Marui repositioned itself in the young people's market, built large outlets near major train stations, and regained the lead over its more conventional rivals in the late 1960s. Still the idea caught on very slowly: installment plans represented only 1 percent of total retail sales in Japan as of 1970, and credit sales of any kind were in their infancy among the major department stores like Seibu, which first experimented with credit cards in 1962, only to face consumer resistance and stiff government regulation.[59]

Seibu Department Stores first invested in Midoriya in 1976 after the monthly payment chain stumbled badly during the 1973–1974 oil crisis. "I wanted it," Tsutsumi recalled in 1988, for its customer base of 5 million and its credit potential.[60] He put Sakakura Yoshiaki, a top lieutenant recently arrived from Mitsukoshi, in charge of gradually converting the dowdy retailer into a "consumer bank" offering financial services on behalf of the entire group. Many of its twenty-nine remaining branches were closed; other profitable ones like the Midoriya in Fuchū were handed over to Seiyū; and some of its best locations were transformed into a Seibu sports building (Kichijōji), Habitat furniture center (Ikebukuro), or gallery of restaurants (Prime in Shibuya). Still the company struggled. Midoriya changed its name to Seibu Credit in September 1980 and two years later began issuing general-purpose Saison credit cards, usable almost everywhere, to the group's 800,000 existing store-card holders and millions of new customers mobilized during the mid-1980s. It also set up loan counters and cashing services in more than 140 Seibu branches, Seiyūs, and Parcos. By 1985 Seibu Credit was realizing 38 percent of its revenues and 85 percent of its profits from financial services.[61] Having long since conceded leadership of the installment-plan to Marui, the firm set its sights on becoming the top retail-credit company in Japan.

The Seibu Retailing Group's third big excursus beyond merchandising in the 1970s owed much less to the example of Sears than to the sudden rage for family dining out that swept the country during the decade. Few countries boast a longer or livelier history of restaurants, teahouses, drinking establishments, and meals served at inns, but traditionally families dining out together in Japan almost always did so on trips rather than near their homes. The period of high-speed economic growth during 1955–1973 led to a privatized focus on "my-homeism" (including family activities), higher incomes, and more housewives drawn back to work by inflation and a shorthanded labor market. By the 1970s a growing slice of household income was devoted to eating in the country's 537,000 restaurants, coffee shops, dining halls, and sushi bars.[62] Young people also drove up restaurant sales, especially in the fast-food industry, as new urban lifestyles among unmarried students and workers began to replace living at home or in a company dormitory.

The Seibu Retailing Group responded belatedly by widening the compass of its cafeteria division, which began in 1947 and was reorganized in 1963 as Seibu Dining (Seibu Shokudō) to operate food services in Seibu department-store branches and Seiyūs. Soon Seibu Dining expanded into wedding halls, banquet facilities, company cafeterias, and country clubs, changing its name to Restaurant Seibu in 1969. An internal memo two years later stated the firm's new aim: to "develop specialty chains with à la carte items or limited menus."[63] Restaurant Seibu took a big step toward profitability in 1973 when it founded a chain of restaurants called Los Arcos and even more so when it launched the suburban chain Casa in 1978—its main brand name in family dining today. The company soon followed these ventures in Mediterranean-style food with chains serving Chinese, Japanese, and French cuisine as well as coffee shops, Lenôtre bakeries, and franchises of the Dunkin Donuts Company from the United States. Although it trailed giants like Daiei and New Tokyo,[64] Restaurant Seibu was strong enough to absorb the perennially red-ink Kinkei

Foods Company when Tsutsumi took it over in 1976. He split off the manufacturing division of this well-known producer of curry and sauces, eventually assigning it to Asahi Industries, and transferred most of its other assets to Restaurant Seibu.[65] This merger was followed by a much larger rescue in 1980, the beef-and-rice chain Yoshinoya. By the end of the 1970s, in short, the Seibu Retailing Group was spreading far beyond conventional store-based merchandising and rapidly becoming the generalized consumer corporation projected by its leadership. But en route it faced great turbulence that shook the whole conglomerate.

FALLING BEHIND, PLUNGING AHEAD

Like the rest of the national economy, consumer-service industries were forced to adapt fast to the oil embargo of 1973–1974 that brought an end to the era of high-speed growth, leading to 24 percent inflation and negative GNP expansion in 1974 and a long-term reduction of the annual real rise in economic output from nearly 11 percent to just over 5 percent. Although the Seibu Retailing Group diversified fast enough to ride out the shift to a moderate-growth economy, two of its companies were badly jolted. Seiyū's sales dropped from second to third among superstore chains because the firm failed to adjust fast enough to market changes. At the same time Seibu Urban Development, the real-estate company established in 1972, pressed forward too quickly with ambitious projects just as the land market was turning flat.

Even before the petroleum crisis of 1973–1974 Seiyū was in trouble. The company managed a profit in the early 1970s, but its glamour of the previous decade had given way to stodginess, and the Tokyo-based Itō Yōkadō chain replaced it in second place behind Daiei—a ranking unchanged for the next twenty years. By the 1970s Seiyū's stores seemed small and often shabby; customer surveys showed that the company appeared to be quiet, conservative, and expensive, especially compared with Daiei.[66] Although it had become a national network through subsidiaries in Kansai (1970) and Nagano (1971) as well as tie-ups with regional superstores, Seiyū was far less active outside its home territory than Daiei. Even though sales tripled between 1969 and 1973, to $762.7 million, nonoperating losses of $13.3 million in 1973 cut deeply into the company's slender operating profits of $20.6

million that year.[67] But the real problem was strategic, according to Tsutsumi Seiji: "The greatest obstacle to market development is using conventional concepts."[68] In 1970 he attacked the superstore industry, especially his own chain, for neglecting quality in the pell-mell rush for high-volume sales, expanding too fast, and growing bloated without internal controls.[69] He expressed his concern for product quality by pressing Seiyū to develop its own source of tofu (Asahi Foods) in 1972, against the advice of both bankers and store managers who regarded it as a declining diet item. The project ran in the black from the start and soon uncovered a demand for other fresh, high-quality traditional foodstuffs like seaweed and buckwheat noodles.[70] This episode shows Tsutsumi's well-known penchant for latching onto new consumer trends (which sometimes prove to be only fads, and thus costly to Seibu) and also his preoccupation with vertical integration, an idea he learned from American management specialists in the 1960s, by designing and contracting for Seiyū's own products rather than remaining at the mercy of suppliers.

The entire superstore industry suffered from inflation, high interest rates, and a huge jump in procurement costs after the oil embargo of 1973–1974 and the government's subsequent overstimulation of the economy. Just at this time Seiyū had the bad luck to open large new branch stores in regional cities like Ōita, Maebashi, and Kōfu; most failed or were converted to Parcos and department-store branches. Ironically Seiyū achieved a listing on the lower-ranked second section of the Tokyo Stock Exchange in September 1974, before the extent of its difficulties was known. The combined pretax losses of Seiyū operations in Kyushu, Hokkaido, and Nagano were $8 million in 1974, driving the company as a whole into the red for the first time ever.[71] Saison's official historians put the matter bluntly: "During the two or three years after the first oil emergency, the Seibu Retailing Group confronted a life-or-death crisis."[72] Tsutsumi's response was to take personal command of Seiyū by reassuming its presidency in March 1975.

He soon found that there was little agreement among different Seiyū stores about marketing, that the management structure at company headquarters had grown rigid in its determination to press volume sales, and that the firm was drifting without a distinctive strategy. He told his managers in March 1975 that "we must return to the basics of retailing."[73] Later that year he called for a "cultural revolution" at

Seiyū that amounted to reeducating management to shed the pre-1975 approach: "The idea of the volume-sales store is fading away. . . . The essence of retailing is to serve the customer. The logic of humanity must come before the logic of industrialism."[74] He said Seiyū should become a "quality-sales store" (*shitsuhanten*) by responding to people's needs rather than those of mass-production manufacturers. These themes resounded in the group's marketing for the next decade. The irony is that Tsutsumi was leading Seiyū away from a high-volume approach that was rapidly carrying Daiei further ahead of its rivals toward becoming Japan's first trillion-yen superstore in annual sales ($4.4 billion, achieved in 1980).[75]

More concretely, Tsutsumi held endless staff meetings, directed store managers to select their own product mix depending on local market conditions, and exhorted stores to remodel with more fashion touches. The company reclassified its branches into small supermarkets under 2,000 square meters, general-merchandise stores with groceries in the range of 3,000 to 7,000 square meters, and Seiyū department stores about 10,000 square meters in size. New outlets were to be in large buildings with substantial market areas; about one per year was planned to anchor a shopping center. Tsutsumi also set ceilings for borrowing, tried to put cash flow to better use, and slowed the rise in labor costs by systematically monitoring productivity. Seiyū now pledged to increase its capital through retained earnings, convertible bonds, stock splits, and new offerings.[76]

Despite its slowdown in the first half of the 1970s, Seiyū was strong enough to be promoted to the prestigious first section of the Tokyo exchange in 1976. This allowed the firm to reduce its long-term indebtedness, sell bonds at more favorable rates, and (by 1980) finance its short-term loans at the prime rate. The fiscal upturn was possible because sales roughly tripled again, this time between 1972 and 1978 (to $2.25 billion),[77] driven in good part by the opening of new branches. Even so, this growth lagged the industry as a whole by an embarrassing margin.[78] Seiyū surprised the business community in 1980 by appointing the first woman store manager in any superstore chain. The company also benefited from a two-year technical and product exchange in 1979–1981 with Jewel, the innovative Illinois supermarket operator.

Japanese superstores remained low-profit enterprises in the 1970s, and it is understandable that Tsutsumi's 1975–1980 program to modernize Seiyū while repositioning it toward consumer needs which were only beginning to emerge did not whip the rather plodding company into a gallop overnight. At the very least his plan redirected Seiyū away from gentle decline and toward the solid growth that characterized its results in the 1980s.

Seibu Urban Development faced the opposite problem in the mid-1970s, namely too little caution. This company overcommitted itself and ran up debts of $233 million in its first two years of operation, 1972–1973. "The $13 million or so we invested in bowling echoed the loudest,"[79] Tsutsumi Seiji admitted after closing nine bowling centers in 1973. The retailing group, with no experience in real-estate development, bought forests in Gunma, hillsides in Kyoto, and farmland near Sendai without the resources to improve them, precisely when Tsutsumi Yoshiaki was shying away from further land deals. Seibu Urban Development's sales in 1972 were said to be $26 million, little more than a third those of Seibu Real Estate in the railway group and barely more than the $23 million a year it soon faced in debt-service costs alone.[80] Although Tsutsumi Seiji hoped to sell suburban residences and vacation cottages to department-store customers, much as his father had done fifty years before, this time the inflation and economic stasis produced by the Arab oil embargo sent the housing market into a tumble, and Daiichi Kangyō Bank grew worried about the company's ability to repay its loans.

Hariki Yasuo, a former editor of the financial magazine *Zaikai*, has written that in May 1976 Seiji went to Yoshiaki for help in rescuing Seibu Urban Development.[81] The retailing group has always denied this claim, and its recent fiftieth-anniversary history does not mention any role by Yoshiaki.[82] But no one disputes that Ishida Masatame, managing director of Kokudo Keikaku, stepped in to help restructure the imperiled company's debts and reorganize its management. (The department store's version is that Ishida happened to be available, so came aboard.) The retailing group dealt with Seibu Urban Development's borrowings out of its own resources without turning to Yoshiaki for cash or, so far as is known, guarantees.[83] At the very least, however, the presence of one of his senior aides must have reassured the new firm's bankers that it was a worthy investment.

Eguchi Rentarō, a confidant of Tsutsumi Seiji's who became vice president of Seibu Urban Development in October 1975, helped to raise $65 million from banks and other companies in the retailing group during the next two years.[84] Seibu Urban Development reportedly disposed of more than $37 million in assets to reduce long-term debt; it cut back on new purchases and, with the help of lower interest rates after 1978, staged a recovery in its housing operations that put the company in the black by 1982.[85]

The troubles at Seiyū and Seibu Urban Development in the mid-1970s were the gravest symptoms of the retailing group's danger after the first oil shock. Company sources say the group rode out the storm thanks to renovations in the Seibu Ikebukuro store at the end of the decade, refinancing Seiyū through the equity markets, and the cash generated by the Ikebukuro and Shibuya Parcos.[86] Ikuno Shigeo, president of Seibu Allstate and a key financial planner for the retailing group, said in 1979 that in the previous year or two "the department store's profitability rose dramatically, and our financial situation improved suddenly. Now the department store is creditworthy, so we're able to expand Seiyū Stores on this base."[87] Even so, the retailing group had overall borrowings of $1.3 billion as of March 1979, whereas Isetan had just $55.6 million and Mitsukoshi and Hankyū none at all.[88] The revival of Seibu Urban Development was no doubt speeded by the group's strong performance in the late 1970s; but it remained a relatively small actor in a highly leveraged retailing empire until January 1986, when it merged with two other companies to form today's mid-sized Seiyō Environmental Development (Seiyō Kankyō Kaihatsu)—a name so oxymoronic that Tsutsumi prefers to call it simply Seiyō Corporation.

NEW MARKETS FOR THE DEPARTMENT STORE

> The decade of the 1970s was one in which the social value of consumption gained greater recognition. At the same time, consumer behavior itself began to change. First, individuals were able to choose from a wide range of products according to personal tastes. Second, they began to place as much or more emphasis on human interaction and personalized service as on the products themselves.[89]

This capsule of the Japanese service sector, written by the playwright Yamazaki Masakazu and others in a 1985 report to the Ministry of

Finance, points to the maturing of the retail market as shoppers began looking for more than material satisfaction in the 1970s. The previous decade had been the age of prêt-à-porter in Japan, a time when Seibu began offering off-the-rack fashions by the Paris designer Ted Lapidus, manufactured under license by Seibu in Japan—the first of many ready-made lines by arbiters of foreign fashions for both men and women.[90] Prêt-à-porter appealed especially to the frugal, cautious generation born before Pearl Harbor, whose hard work had made national prosperity come true in the postwar era. Then in the 1970s the department store quickly adjusted to a very different market by developing strategies that were new to Seibu in both place and time.

Spatially the company expanded beyond the Tokyo suburbs to various regional locations. During the same decade Seiyū added eight compact department stores under the name Seibu in even smaller cities. Unlike most competitors, Seibu avoided franchising its out-of-town locations. Instead it borrowed heavily for what amounted to a large venture-capital operation, sometimes refurbishing properties already owned by the group but more often investing in local retailers or conducting joint operations with them. Seibu also became the driving force behind the Japan Management Association, a loose federation of twenty-three regional department-store companies for joint purchasing, market research, and employee training.[91] Apart from standardized wrapping paper, the out-of-town Seibus at first had less in common with their Tokyo siblings than might be expected in a highly concentrated, media-soaked economy like Japan's. The parent company in Ikebukuro was careful to refer to its affiliates as regional (*chiiki*) rather than provincial (*chihō*).[92] Its first ads catered to local sensibilities, such as the poster of a woman's face surrounded by the Kai mountains when the Kōfu Seibu was announced (see Figure 5). Echoing Tsutsumi Yasujirō, the firm's publicists avowed that Japan's regions were the building blocks of a democratic society—but gradually Seibu's commercials began to sound themes such as "this is young Tokyo" at all its locations, now that a more unified distribution system was turning the whole country into a single market at the end of the 1970s.[93]

Predictably enough, the retailing group found the fiercely competitive Kansai district in western Japan hardest to penetrate, the more so after the energy crisis of 1973–1974. Seiyū entered Kansai in 1970, fol-

FIGURE 5. Seibu poster for the opening of its new department store in Kōfu, March 8, 1979. (Saison Group)

FIGURE 6. "The New Family": Seibu poster for the opening of its refurbished Ikebukuro department store, September 19, 1975. (Saison Group)

lowed the next year by Parco and the department store—the latter with heavy capital participation by local partners.[94] The first Seibu department store in the region, at Takatsuki, got off to a tragic start when fire killed six persons at the new building shortly before its scheduled opening in September 1973, delaying the ribbon cutting more than a year. Sales at the Shinsaibashi Parco, opened in 1971, proved to be slower than expected, and by 1976 it was clear that Seiyū was in trouble in the region, too.[95] Eventually the Takatsuki department store, and another at Ōtsu that opened in 1976, drew ample numbers of customers, but they produced pretax profits of only 1 percent as of 1980.[96] A more ambitious shopping center anchored by both a Seibu and a Seiyū began business at Yao in 1981; but this venture did not achieve its annual sales target of $125 million until 1985, three years behind projections, and operated in the black for the first time in 1991.[97] By then the Saison Group counted 4 department stores, a Parco, a LoFt home-improvement center, 38 Seiyūs, 68 restaurants, and 252 convenience stores in Kansai, with several billion dollars in sales[98] but very small profits.[99] As Tsutsumi Seiji said of his regional strategy in an interview published in 1991, "The age of mergers, capital participation, and other hard [i.e., direct] cooperation has ended."[100]

The Seibu Retailing Group also chose the early 1970s to move out of the era of uniform mass consumption toward cultivating a more relaxed generation, the baby boomers born immediately after World War II. Often called the New Families, these shoppers were conspicuously interested in quality, not quantity, and sought a more fashionable lifestyle than their prêt-à-porter predecessors. Then in the late 1970s Seibu refocused on an even younger cohort, the New Young, for whom Parco held such particular fascination. Born during 1955–1960, these people took quality for granted and were much more interested in artistic and cultural fulfillment than previous generations of consumers. In 1974 Tsutsumi Seiji branded the New Young "highly selective" and summarized their preferences as individuality and diversity, a reaction against the depressing sameness favored by their parents in trying to keep up with the neighbors and by employers in coloring their lives with bureaucratic gray.[101]

The main Seibu building at Ikebukuro was still a local department store, the Dentsū advertising agency concluded in 1972, and it was losing market share to its neighbor Tōbu as new suburbs sprang up along the Tōbu Tōjō rail line.[102] In the following three years Seibu completed a $67.3 million overhaul and expansion at Ikebukuro, making it one of the largest retail buildings in the country and giving it something of the steely, flattop look of the U.S. aircraft carrier *Enterprise*, henceforth its double-edged nickname. The 1975 remodeling pumped up sales by 25 percent in the twelve months after the project was finished; it indisputably transformed Seibu from an Ikebukuro to a Tokyo department store.[103] Now the marketing tactic was to "turn the department store into a shopping street," with parks, plazas, specialty shops, restaurants, and leisure services like books, hobbies, music, and sports—upscaling the fashion level of food, clothing, and shelter in a comprehensive shopping environment under one roof.[104] In this sense the 1975 refurbishing was Seibu's last stab at preserving the traditional omnibus department store; all further changes since then have redefined its institutional character in the direction of more selective functions.

The company summed up its underlying marketing principles for the newly expanded store in an August 1975 memorandum called *Kihonteki kangaekata* (Basic thinking):

1. Presenting products in response to the values associated with changing lifestyles;
2. Presenting a wide range of goods in response to the individualization and diversification of consumers;
3. Tending toward responding to changing values, especially among the growing numbers of people born since the war.[105]

The key words were *lifestyles, individualization*, and *diversification*— very much in tune with Tsutsumi's observation that the oil shock was a turning point for Japanese capitalism (from goods to services) and for Japanese civil society (from mass to segmentation).[106] A Seibu pamphlet issued in 1975 pointed out that "the basic structure of the economy and the composition of society are undergoing qualitative changes." With material abundance finally available to nearly everyone, "what consumers now want" is for "each individual to protect his or her own livelihood through material and spiritual satisfaction."[107] As if to flaunt the point, Seibu painted giant Mona Lisas on the shutters of the Ikebukuro store to advertise its new twelfth-floor art museum, while the company's commercial artists announced the remodeling with posters of a New Family: casual father with collar-length hair and wire-rims, sporty mother with a pageboy and bangs, and nude three-year-old boy with a Prince Charles haircut (see Figure 6).[108]

The museum was supposed to set a tony image for the revamped store by attracting both publicity and customers but not to earn the company money from inflated art prices. The Seibu Museum of Art (the first in a Japanese department store) was concertmaster of a well-orchestrated campaign in the mid-1970s to burnish the retail group's corporate identity at a time when both the economy and consumer habits were being rapidly restructured. "A department store amid abundance" was the slogan, but most customers noticed only the visuals, like Tanaka Ikkō's new all-caps logo, blue-and-green bull's eye wrapping paper and shopping bags, and cobalt-blue uniforms — packaging, not substance. Kinokuni Ken'ichi, Seibu's marketing chief at the time, drew on his earlier experience with corporate identities at the Dentsū and McCann Erickson Hakuhōdō advertising agencies to start using the Ikebukuro and Shibuya stores for productions and turn the art museum into a lodestar of prestige for the retailing group.[109]

The rise of the New Families and then the New Young meant a declining demand for mass-produced goods and thus a conversion from maker-based to consumer-based merchandising. By the late 1970s manufacturers dispatched fewer "mannequin girls" to staff sales counters and no longer controlled how goods were displayed in department stores. Demand gradually diversified because of new consumer generations, higher educational levels, more double-income families, an aging society, and mature levels of national prosperity; retailers like Seibu consequently found it essential to do more buying (and less ordering) and to design, develop, and procure specialized products from sources of their own. This reorientation from upstream to downstream merchandising, always with an eye on consumers' increasingly disparate lifestyles, meant that stores now determined their own mix of imports and Japanese-made items, national and private brands, house labels and foreign designer lines manufactured under license[110] (often slimmed to fit Japanese physiques).

The changing market, not management theory, is what allowed Seibu to reorganize its product flow according to the principle of vertical integration—developing more and more of its own items from initial design to sourcing to final point of sale. As the largest retailing group in the country by now, with $4.25 billion in revenues in 1976,[111] Seibu commanded such great selling power that it could create house brands to challenge the national manufacturers or else jawbone the big makers into offering volume discounts for large orders—a foretaste of the Wal-Mart phenomenon of the 1990s. Ikuno Shigeo of Seibu Allstate isolated Seibu's advantages: "The things we value most highly are the ability to develop products and the ability to do planning."[112] Vertical integration proved especially availing in clothing lines and at Seiyū, where Tsutsumi set up Asahi Foods to make tofu in 1972, Seiyū Farm for hogs the following year, and Kaika Bakery in 1977. The group also integrated its foreign sourcing in the 1970s and 1980s, opening more than a dozen offices to order or adapt foreign goods according to the turnabout principle of "Western spirit, Japanese technique" (*Yōkon, Wasai*).[113] An authoritative study in 1984 concluded that, despite heavy borrowings, the Seibu Retailing Group prospered because of its skill in planning, its knack for developing new products, the great buying clout of Seiyū and the department store, and the drawing power of the Ikebukuro and Shibuya stores. The study quoted Tsutsumi: "These two account for 60 percent of the operating profits of the department stores."[114]

No sooner had Seibu crowned its expanded Ikebukuro flagship with the glittering art museum than it began yet another remodeling, completed in 1980, that made the store Tokyo's largest, at 65,647 square meters. This renovation catered to the New Young's pursuit of culture in the sense of leisure, knowledge, and beauty. The company's goal was to wean this generation reared in affluence away from the brand names their parents preferred and to teach them that Seibu was synonymous with self-realization. Giant posters showing two blondes swabbing the decks of a ship proclaimed "the age of the woman" in 1979,[115] a nod to the narcissism Parco had begun to tap among its clientele of beautiful people several years earlier. By now Tsutsumi regularly reminded employees that theirs was a "consumer industry" for city dwellers who were reasonably well-off, conscious of quality, and eager "to lead peaceful, humane lives."[116] Retailers had to be ready for shoppers' diverse quests for meaningful lifestyles, which went beyond the material goods people could now take for granted to cultural activities at many levels of taste. In a speech inaugurating the Seibu department store at Ōtsu in 1976, he recalled that his father often spoke in the 1920s of "thanks and service," a management philosophy that "to someone like me born in the Shōwa period means 'the consumer industry'—the idea is the same."[117] This refocus on the consumer, as well as the firm's vertical integration, was mainly ideology for internal use. It helped Tsutsumi sell the inevitable to his workers: the traditional department store was passé; to prosper Seibu must sell services as well as goods.

Tsutsumi's notion of serving changing consumer needs was scarcely unique. In the 1970s Itō Masatoshi of the Itō Yōkadō superstores regularly declared that "the consumer comes first"; Nakauchi Isao of Daiei insisted that his employees honor "customer rights."[118] But as early as 1973 in *Seibu Ryūtsū Gurūpu no keiei kihon rinen* (Basic management theory of the Seibu Retailing Group), Tsutsumi had begun to redefine the corporate mission as "supplying not only merchandise but also information for daily life"[119]—Seibu's major theme of the following decade. In 1980 he told an interviewer that modernization in Japan was based on "the logic of capitalism,"which had come to overshadow "the logic of humanity. . . . Because retailing is on the boundary between these two kinds of logic,"[120] Seibu's goal was to bring them into balance by denouncing the excesses of capitalism ("opposing pollution, war, and dictatorship")[121] and taking account of the needs of consumers as well as manufacturers. It is probably incidental that Tsutsumi was a former Marxist: he made no effort to disguise that this was a retailer's self-interested view of postindustrial society, in which Seibu would benefit immediately from the demand for services as well as goods, now that middle-class Japanese could expect to lead the good life. His outlook was openly profit-oriented—and also an accurate reading of social values in the era of mature economic growth and industrial restructuring after 1973.

SPECIALIZATION: SHOPPERS AND WORKERS

The remodeling at Ikebukuro in the late 1970s was meant to be a spatial representation of the consumer industry, on the premise that customers increasingly sought self-actualization rather than conformity. Abandoning the 1975 slogan of "fashionable food, clothing, and shelter," Seibu now aimed at "responding to humans one by one who are seeking a diverse, individualistic lifestyle."[122] Although these ideas had been voiced before, the real point was that no longer could the department store be comprehensive and still make money. Its president, Sakakura Yoshiaki, said that now it must be "a large store bringing together many specialties."[123] Sakakura swept away whole merchandise departments and replaced them with specialty shops like the Wise Fool clothing section (1979), which sold theater fashions to surprisingly large numbers of shoppers interested in expressing themselves without going on stage. Nearby the company opened specialty buildings (rather ponderously styled "halls," or *kan*) for food, interiors, and sports—the latter featuring a "community college," with noncredit lessons in studio and domestic arts, that never managed to turn a profit.[124] The sports building itself, which cost the company $20.5 million to construct, trumpeted "do sports!" and featured thirty-five specialty shops carrying 800,000 items—Japan's largest athletic-goods mart, and instantly its most lucrative.[125] The food building opened in 1981, two years after the sports one, and managed to pay off its $18.6 million construction cost quickly, even though its main value was not in adding sales revenue but drawing more customers to the main department store (Tsutsumi called this effect "synergy").[126] The interior building, operated with the British firm Habitat, opened in 1982 across the street from the sports building but soon flopped. "This situation is difficult," said Egashira Keisuke of Seibu International in 1986. "Furniture is the last boom area," but a lack of space in homes and a traditional preference for simplicity may have worked against the project,[127] which was converted to a music store at the end of the decade.

Specialization was also a motif of Seibu's employment system in the second half of the 1970s, mainly because of diminished worker loyalties and a pinched labor market. Even before Japan adjusted to more moderate economic growth after 1973–1974, it was clear that the values of New Families and the New Young permeated the work force as well as the clientele. No longer were clerks willing to walk eight kilometers a day, as Seibu once estimated of its female sales staff.[128] Isetan shocked the industry by giving its personnel five-day weeks as early as 1965; Seibu managed to provide them only after 1970. Seibu and its company union, which Tsutsumi Seiji had helped to start in 1954, agreed on a five-year plan to improve wages during 1970–1975 if productivity increased (in 1966 productivity had been 32 percent higher at both Isetan and Tōkyū than at Seibu). By year three of the plan it was clear that advances in pay were trailing Mitsukoshi, the industry leader; and then the oil crisis the next winter set the plan back even further before it was finally declared a success in October 1975.[129]

A second labor plan, emphasizing working conditions and welfare benefits, was implemented in 1976–1980. Quasi-managerial titles went into effect, to offset fewer promotions, and more married women were recruited as nonregular workers. A Seibu Welfare Promotion Center began operating in March 1977 to administer employee insurance, housing, health, and pension benefits more systematically than in the past.[130] Nonregular employees were excluded in principle from these fringe benefits. To overcome monotony and give veteran salespeople a morale boost, the company introduced a shopmaster system in 1975 so that departments or specialty subdepartments could be managed almost autonomously by experienced salaried employees. The shopmasters, of whom a third were women, were responsible for ordering, sales strategies, displays, and accounts. Some also helped with buying. No longer were departments to be managed by untutored college graduates; any employee with experience and qualifications could apply. The shopmaster system was soon copied by other department stores, although the anthropologist Millie R. Creighton has pointed out that many women avoided managerial positions, including shopmaster, because of the long hours and possible impact on their personal lives.[131] Still the program proved to be very popular, and today there are nearly 250 shopmasters throughout the department store's two dozen branches.

The job title "specialist" was adopted in November 1978 for non-managerial workers who were tired of general duties and wished to concentrate on one of eighty-six job categories in eight classifications, including shopmaster.[132] Tsutsumi tried to put a good face on the worker alienation that made the new job specifications necessary: "This system is a response to the diversification of the marketplace and also a response to the diversification of workers' consciousness about their own lives."[133] The idea became so popular that 97 percent of Seibu employees surveyed in June 1980 expressed the hope of being promoted to specialist once they had served their four-year probations.[134] Seiyū adopted the specialist system in March 1983. As Tsutsumi recognized, such was the denouement of company loyalty in an age of individuality and self-expression.

So, too, was the company's new pragmatism about female employees, who before 1970 were not hired above the level of salesclerk on the self-fulfilling premise that they would merely use their jobs as stepping-stones to the altar and then quit. Seibu appointed seventeen women university graduates in 1970 as regular, permanent employees, a move that was considered pathbreaking at the time. Women made up 75 percent of the department store's work force (and customers) in the 1970s, and they benefited from the shopmaster and specialist systems as well as from a Ladies' Board established in 1979 to express female employees' ideas to management. Wholesaling and retailing employ perhaps half of all women who work for wages in Japan, and department stores are more liberal than most other employers in utilizing them as managers.[135] Greater opportunity for women workers in the 1970s stemmed mainly from the tight labor market that resulted from continuing economic growth and a smaller population of young employees; but at Seibu it also paralleled the firm's efforts to sell to working women and twin-income families after 1977 in the marketing climate of greater individuality, diversity and appeals to women's self-worth.[136] Still it would be wise not to overestimate the changes. As Tsutsumi told an interviewer in 1991, "I'm always trying to better the position of women in my companies, but it is very difficult. Men are very jealous, even under the guise of being protective. I have to use fifty to sixty times more energy to make a woman an executive then to make a man one. Still, women are gradually increasing their power and position in all my companies."[137] He added that men and women were paid equally.

In upper-management echelons Tsutsumi strengthened the Seibu Retailing Group in the 1970s by recruiting senior officials from government, banking, and business, including a few women. Neither Tsutsumi Seiji nor Yoshiaki has been an insider in Japanese corporate circles, but Seiji drew on his youthful connections at Tokyo University and his father's political offices to attract top outside managers when the retailing group expanded after 1963. The goal was to bring in experienced talent with strong ties to the banking industry, given Seibu's thirst for capital; most turned out to be capable leaders, although Miyoshi Motoyuki stumbled as president of Seiyū in 1973–1975 and had to be replaced by Tsutsumi himself.[138] Aoyama Shun and Tanabe Noboru rode golden parachutes (*amakudari*) from the Ministry of Finance, soon earning their keep by helping the retailing group arrange critical land transactions.[139]

Of the several dozen executives appointed from outside, the best known was Sakakura Yoshiaki. Passed over for the presidency of Mitsukoshi in 1972, Sakakura brought a brilliant reputation to the Seibu Retailing Group when he joined the department store as vice president in April 1974. He held one other position within the group—president of Midoriya, the predecessor of Seibu Credit—before succeeding Tsutsumi as head of the department store in 1977, the year Tsutsumi turned fifty. Sakakura is universally credited with restoring prosperity to Seibu at the end of the 1970s, but he was eased out in May 1984 after a policy battle and rejoined Mitsukoshi as second in command the following year, rising to president in March 1986—the sole person ever to head rival department-store companies in Japan.[140] Sakakura was far from the only manager to be recruited by Tsutsumi, then later cashiered; Hiraoka Shigeki came from Mitsubishi Shōji to head Seiyū's operations in 1979 but within four years was exiled to the group's helicopter company. These executive transfers signaled the end of Seibu's heavy raids on other companies and agencies; by the 1980s the organization had plenty of homegrown leaders ready for senior positions. Still, as Kizu Haruhiko of the Saison Group noted in 1986, "There is relatively great equality among Seibu managers because many were brought in from outside and traded around within the group. As a result there is relatively little hierarchy or patron-client relations."[141]

The department store's balance sheet for the 1970s reflects the company's rapid expansion and diversification, but it also shows ever greater nonoperating losses because of continual borrowing. Sales rose 278 percent in yen terms between 1970 and 1980, to $1.68 billion. Operating profits improved even more, rising 825 percent during the same period to $62.6 million. But nonoperating losses also grew by 789 percent, to $49.9 million in 1980, leaving the company with pretax profits of just $12.7 million that year, less then eight-tenths of 1 percent of sales.[142] The low point for operating profits came in 1975, after the Arab oil embargo and subsequent inflation shook the entire retailing world. The department store's interest payments on loans that year were double their 1973 level.[143] After that sales grew substantially, which allowed operating profits to surpass the industry average during 1979–1983.[144] But pretax profits lagged because of the great cost of building regional branches in the mid-1970s and then refurbishing each of the older department stores at the end of the decade. The company also invested heavily in other members of the retailing group. By one estimate, the department store's borrowings rose from $333.3 million in 1974 to $758.3 million just four years later (up 60 percent in yen terms.) The group as a whole is thought to have had debts of $1.23 billion that year. By this point Seibu Department Stores probably had a debt:equity ratio exceeding 70:30, whereas Daimaru was perhaps 25 percent dependent on borrowings and Mitsukoshi had no debt at all.[145] On the other hand, the department store's fixed assets—already substantial compared with the competition—rose 337 percent in value between 1972 and 1983, nearly twice as fast as the industry overall.[146] Like the Japanese economy as a whole, Seibu exemplified the bicycle phenomenon: furiously pedaling to keep its balance and press ahead, with little margin for spills.

The Seibu Retailing Group finished the decade where it had begun: Japan's largest in revenues, estimated at $8.14 billion (including nonretailing operations).[147] A business of this scale that opened more than 160 retail outlets during the decade ran the risk of ill coordination or even balkanization because of its utter complexity. With ninety-seven companies to supervise, Tsutsumi Seiji was forced to delegate more functions than was true of Nakauchi Isao at Daiei or Itō Masatoshi at Itō Yōkadō. Since the 1960s the Seibu Retailing Group has operated in federal or republican fashion to a greater degree than most of its rivals, although the department store and Seiyū have been its cash cows. Tsutsumi set up a liaison unit in 1971 to link the four core companies (the department store, Seiyū, Seibu Chemical Industries, and Seibu Urban Development). This unit provided planning services and general staff functions for member firms that were growing more and more unlike one another as the group diversified. In 1982 four more firms were designated core companies—Seibu Allstate Life, Restaurant Seibu, Seibu Credit (Midoriya until 1980), and Asahi Helicopter. What is distinctive about the Seibu Retailing Group is that it was clustered not around a bank, as with the postwar conglomerates called *keiretsu*, but around the personality of Tsutsumi Seiji. Well aware that banks survive much longer than individuals, Tsutsumi told an interviewer in 1985 that "I'm here now, so it's okay, but after I'm gone, it's already been decided that the presidents of the core companies will run things democratically."[148] Inasmuch as democracy has a rather impoverished history in most corporate boardrooms, this may prove to be one of Tsutsumi's least durable forecasts, but it indicates a realistic judgment that the group has long since become too disparate to be ruled by one person.

CHAPTER SIX

PRINCES AND LIONS

If you take a look at hotels in Tokyo, the Imperial, Ōkura, New Ōtani, and Palace have all owned their land for many years. These are the strong ones, together with Prince. Next come ones like the Keiō Plaza or Pacific that bought their property a bit before the land boom. They are the next strongest. Then come the people who have built more recently. There is absolutely no way they can compete with these older hotels.[1]

This terra-deterministic explanation by Tsutsumi Yoshiaki in 1984 only slightly overstates how important the silver spoon was to the Prince Hotels, Inc., when the company was born in August 1971 to operate Princes for the Seibu Railway Group. Owning so much land in such prime locations, especially in Tokyo, gave Prince a priceless head start and made it almost impossible for any competitor to catch up, even if it were willing to match the funds Tsutsumi lavished on architects' fees and superior facilities during the next two decades. The same rich endowment in land has helped the Seibu Lions overcome all giants on their way to the top of the Japanese professional baseball world, playing in a handsome stadium in a huge suburban meadow that has guaranteed the owner a profit ever since it opened in 1979. Princes and Lions are the chief reasons why Tsutsumi became a celebrity the equal of his brother Seiji in the 1980s and the best signifiers of how his businesses evolved during the second decade after he inherited them in 1964.

HOTELS FOR EVERY SEASON

"The Tokyo Prince was built at the request of the government" for the 1964 Olympics, Tsutsumi Yoshiaki recalled in 1987. At the time "we had absolutely no interest in city hotels,"[2] only in the small Princes that opened during the 1950s in rambling villas once owned by titled aristocrats. Seibu so completely lacked managers with any experience in the hotel business that Tsutsumi's stepmother, Aoyama Misao, was called on to manage the Tokyo Prince. The Haneda Prince, another monument to the Olympics, was sold to Tōkyū a few years later. Indeed, the next in the chain did not open until 1970 at the Naeba ski resort. Business was very slow for all the major Tokyo hotels after 1964, recovering a bit at the end of the decade and then dipping again in 1971. Nonetheless, on the principle that "you have to plan enterprises in ten-year units or they'll not succeed,"[3] Tsutsumi devoted the rest of the 1960s to winning the confidence of Seibu's bankers and mapping out a group of new urban and resort hotels that suddenly started springing up one after another in 1971, the year he split off the tourism division of the Seibu Railway and established it as Prince Hotels, Inc.[4]

Today Prince is Japan's largest hotel chain in number of rooms and the unquestioned leader among first-class hotels catering mainly to Japanese businesspeople and resort-goers. From 8 hotels with fewer than 1,000 rooms when it became an independent company, Prince expanded during the next twenty years to forty-one locations in Japan and six more abroad, with a total of 17,447 rooms. Another eighteen inns, hotels, and lodges in Japan and one in Alaska, with 1,168 rooms, bear other names but are closely affiliated with Prince.[5] These modest figures are dwarfed by Holiday Inn and similar chains in other countries; even in Japan Princes represent only a tiny fraction of the nearly 5,000 hotels and 80,000 inns, with a combined 1.3 million rooms, that compete for business.[6] Instead what distinguishes the Prince Hotels is their domination of the top end of two markets: resorts serving skiers and golfers and the first-class hotel segment in Tokyo—where eight well-located Princes offer 5,833 rooms, almost four times the number at Tōkyū's top-quality hotels and nearly triple the scale of Tokyo's largest hotel, the New Ōtani, which has 2,057 rooms.[7] Prince is also unusual in operating so many hotels directly owned by itself, its parent

Kokudo Keikaku, or the Seibu Real Estate Company; only three of its hotels in Japan and one in Singapore are leased from or managed on behalf of other owners.[8] As a result, it is virtually a family enterprise that closely guards its financial condition from outside scrutiny.

New Prince resort hotels appeared at a dozen spots between 1970 and 1984, including the longtime Tsutsumi strongholds in Karuizawa and Hakone. Both of these resorts had Kokudo Keikaku hotels dating to the 1930s, but in each case Tsutsumi wanted to provide ultramodern facilities and excellent service to make customers feel like royalty, justifying the high room charges and helping to sell land for vacation cottages on part of the 2,230 hectares he controlled in Karuizawa and on smaller parcels in Hakone. The Karuizawa Prince opened in 1973 with 782 rooms surrounded by tennis courts, the skate center, a ski area that eventually expanded to fourteen lifts, and the Karuizawa 72 golf facility, which waived its $80 greens fee for guests of the new hotel (on a summer weekend by 1992 the fee had risen to $300). Today the Karuizawa Prince has grown to 895 rooms, including 527 cottages, the most extensive resort hotel in the chain after nearby Naeba, which has 1,713 rooms.[9] The Hakone Prince, unveiled in 1978, is one of the company's few luxury hotels by world standards and the centerpiece of Seibu's eleven lodgings in one of Japan's most picturesque settings, along the shore of Lake Ashi looking toward Mount Fuji. Not surprisingly, it is also the most expensive of Prince's resort hotels; even so, Tsutsumi has estimated, its annual operating loss of $3.4 million must be recovered through profits from his golf courses and other recreation facilities in Hakone.[10] Most of the other Prince Hotels he built in the 1970s and early 1980s in ski areas or at the waterside ranged from 50 to 250 rooms.

These new buildings established Tsutsumi as a resort hotelier second to none, but his greatest impact on the industry occurred in Tokyo, where between 1971 and 1984 he radically transformed older Princes at Takanawa (1971) and Akasaka (1983) by adding huge wings and constructed brand-new ones at Shinjuku (1977), Shinagawa (1978), Sunshine City in Ikebukuro (1980), New Takanawa (1982), and Roppongi (1984)—adding a remarkable 5,153 rooms to hotel space in the capital. Neither before nor since has a Japanese entrepreneur erected so many top-quality hotels so close to one another in so brief a time. Only because he already owned the land in every case except Ikebukuro could Tsutsumi indulge in such a frenetic undertaking. The bills for design, construction, and furnishings ranged from $18.5 million at Shinjuku to a hefty $104.4 million for the New Takanawa[11] — at that price, "it's truly a work of art more than a hotel,"[12] Tsutsumi told a financial journalist when it was completed. More than half the expenditures for this showpiece were presumably covered by the sale of the former Asaka property in Shirokanedai to Tokyo Prefecture in 1982 for $55.4 million.[13] A safe assumption is that the other five new wings or entire buildings cost an average of $35 million apiece, exclusive of land, bringing the total for all seven to almost $300 million—whereas the Prince chain's overall sales in 1984, the year the flurry of construction ended, were an estimated $247.9 million.[14] His bankers evidently believed Tsutsumi's hidden wealth in land was now very great, inasmuch as he had little trouble borrowing to meet these expenses; and of course no other hotel operator in Japan could have put up seven high-quality buildings in the same period for $300 million because only Tsutsumi had both prime land and his own construction company.[15]

Seibu's one extravagance was using big-name architects, even though some of them were inexperienced at designing hotels. Tsutsumi hired Murano Tōgo and Tange Kenzō, both recipients of the government's medal of culture, to create resort hotels as well as several of the new Tokyo buildings. By one reckoning, their combined fees for all Seibu projects may have approached $75 million.[16] Murano, the architect of the Nissei Theater in Hibiya and of the refurbishing of the Akasaka State Guest House, designed the Hakone Prince (1978), New Takanawa Prince (1982), Takaragaike Prince in Kyoto (1986), and the reconstruction of the Yokohama Prince (1990)—all of them luxury hotels showing his fondness for rounded forms and white surfaces (see Figure 7). Before he died in 1984, he also did the preliminary plan for a twenty-one-suite addition to San'yōsō, the pure *sukiya*-style villa in Izu Nagaoka acquired in 1947 by the Izu Hakone Railway from Iwasaki Hisaya of the Mitsubishi interests.[17] The architect's fees alone ran about $780,000 per suite for this sumptuous 1988 expansion of Seibu's premier hot-spring resort, where the daily charge per person in 1992 started at $595.[18] Tange is Japan's best-known architect abroad but had never done a hotel until 1972, when he designed the accordion-like white wing of the Akasaka Prince that was not opened until 1983

FIGURE 7. The Yokohama Prince Hotel reopened in 1990 after a facelift by Murano Tōgo. (Prince Hotels)

because of the oil crises of the 1970s. Long interested in trying a mirrored look, Tange first attempted it with the hemispherical Ōtsu Prince (completed in 1988) and modified it for the triangular Marine Tower of the Makuhari Prince Hotel (1992). Yet another costly architect employed by Tsutsumi was Kurokawa Kishō, creator of the tweezer-shaped Roppongi Prince, opened in 1984.[19]

The leading Tokyo hotels in 1970 were the Imperial, the Palace, and the group constructed for the 1964 Olympics: the New Ōtani, Ōkura, New Japan, Hilton at Nagata-chō, and the Tokyo Prince in Shiba Park. Then the Keiō Plaza opened in 1970 at Shinjuku, and the next year the Pacific (now Pacific Meridien) followed at Shinagawa together with the expanded Takanawa Prince almost next door to the Pacific. At 418 rooms, the Takanawa Prince was not far from the Tokyo Prince in scale, but the Pacific was a gigantic thirty-story, 954-room investment by the Keihin Kyūkō Railway for a quiet area already dotted with hotels. Even though Japanese hotel companies find weddings, banquets, and receptions far more lucrative than room rentals, it is not surprising that the competition in Shinagawa and elsewhere led Tsutsumi to ask rhetorically, "Isn't the hotel business the least profitable of all?"[20] To keep ahead of the Pacific, Tsutsumi supervised the Takanawa construction closely: the day before it opened he ordered his brother Yūji, the president of Prince Hotels, to take up the new carpet and replace it. Somehow it was accomplished overnight, and the ribbon cutting occurred on schedule.[21]

The company began to encircle its rival in 1978 when it launched the 1,016-room Shinagawa Prince next door to the Pacific on property once belonging to the Mōri family, members of the prewar nobility. Seibu intended the new building for customers at its 104-lane bowling center, year-round ice arena, swimming pool, and tennis courts that today draw almost 5 million visitors a year to the railway group's largest sports facility. The owner designed the hotel as part of a recreation package for unmarried young people and planned most of its rooms as singles. Other guests soon discovered its convenience as a business hotel, but still Tsutsumi had difficulty raising the occupancy rate from its initial 70 percent to 90 percent by the time of the hotel's tenth anniversary.[22]

Yet Seibu's pièce de résistance in Shinagawa, and perhaps all of Japan, was the 946-room New Takanawa Prince by Murano, opened with gaudy fanfare on April 23, 1982, when the owner held three parties for a total of twenty thousand guests, headed by Prime Minister Suzuki Zenkō and former Prime Ministers Tanaka Kakuei and Fukuda Takeo. Construction of the plush sixteen-story building took five years, including elaborate decor for the Hiten banquet hall accommodating five thousand persons. A copper-roofed convention center of seemingly Himalayan proportions, named Pamir to mark the historical flow of culture across the Silk Road, was soon added next door. By now the Pacific was surrounded by Princes on three flanks, yet after one year's operation the new Takanawa was filling barely half its rooms. "Yes, certainly the occupancy rate is low," Tsutsumi told the *Nihon keizai shinbun*, "but if we can just support a rate of 50 percent, there'll be no loss" because no land costs remained to be repaid.[23] To the extent to which Seibu sees its leisure facilities as sets or zones, the lack of profit at a hotel is more than offset by the prosperity of adjacent sports venues. Still, as a hedge Tsutsumi had the New Takanawa built with inner entrances, connecting rooms, and balconies so that it could be turned into condominiums if the hotel business soured. Converting the building might bring in $345 million in condominium sales, according to a 1987 estimate[24]—a very resilient safety net for the cautious owner.

What turned Tsutsumi into a true Tokyo hotelier, according to the financial press, was not the Shinagawa cluster surrounding Seibu's sports attractions but the far more modest Shinjuku Prince, dating to March 1977. This slender twenty-five story building, faced in russet tiles, offered few extras to the guests in its 571 rooms; yet it was an instant success and, with the Tokyo Prince, became what is thought to be the most profitable of the company's locations in the capital. Perched atop the Shinjuku terminus of the Seibu Railway, the hotel stood immediately beside the city's largest and most vibrant entertainment district and closer to the national railways' Shinjuku Station than any other high-quality hotel. These attributes dictated a more middle-class clientele than was true of other Princes on lands once belonging to nobles. Even though there were dozens of love hotels in the neighborhood, the Shinjuku Prince retained a reputable image, partly through relatively high prices, despite considerable dependence on last-minute walk-in guests. Although it had no banquet halls, the occupancy rate was immediately so high (above 95 percent) that this hotel broke even within a year, whereas the nearby Keiō Plaza required nine.[25] Tsutsumi admitted in 1984 that he had grown tired of hotels after adding the new wing to the Takanawa Prince in 1971, only to see it struggle for the rest of the decade: "I had no strength left to build hotels. I began to have confidence that I could operate only after opening the Shinjuku Prince."[26]

The owner's self-assurance was apparently not shaken by the recurring deficits at the Sunshine City Prince in Ikebukuro from the moment it made its debut in 1980, for he never expected to earn money there. Although he was reluctant at first to build in such a remote part of town on leased land, Tsutsumi agreed to put up the 1,166-room hotel as something of a civic contribution to reconstructing the former Sugamo Prison site, a project initiated by his father a quarter century earlier. Originally the corporate leaders in charge of rebuilding the district asked Tsutsumi Seiji to build a hotel, but when he backed off, Imazato Hiroki of the Nikkeiren business federation prevailed on Yoshiaki to step in. Yoshiaki did so unstintingly: he installed German featherbeds and many other amenities, but the rooms were small and the location distant even from Ikebukuro Station, Tokyo's least inviting major hub. Because he did not own the land, Tsutsumi needed 70 percent occupancy to stay in the black at Sunshine City; it is not surprising that the cumulative losses there had reached $35 million by 1990.[27] Stretching his idea of zones only a little, he saw the profits at the Shinjuku Prince as canceling out the losses in Ikebukuro, much as the prosperous Tokyo Prince balanced the anemic performance of the Akasaka Prince after its stark new wing went into service in 1983.[28]

Whether or not Japanese critics were correct that the forty-story Tange addition in Akasaka was notably American in style, the owner was determined to build a city hotel there that would attract foreign guests as none of the other Princes in town had quite managed to do. He instructed the architect to make it hospitable to foreign businesspeople; at the very least Tange made it big, with 761 rooms averaging 43 square meters, the size of a standard condominium in Tokyo and nearly 25 percent larger than rooms in the other top hotels. Kajima Shōichi, president of the building firm that was the lead contractor, acknowledged that Tsutsumi micro-managed the construction at the 3.1-hectare site, which consultants valued at $100 million in the mid-

1970s.[29] No one was surprised when the Akasaka Prince topped out at 138.9 meters high, 8.9 taller than its next-door competitor, the New Ōtani, whose new building was the work of Tange's pupil Kurokawa. Neither the new Akasaka Prince wing nor Kurokawa's Roppongi Prince proved to be financial successes after opening in 1983 and 1984, respectively. The former, like the New Takanawa Prince, was designed for potential conversion to offices in case it failed in the hotel business; if sold as office space, the wing might bring in $700 million in such a premium location.[30]

When Tsutsumi cut the ribbon for the Roppongi Prince in February 1984, he declared that "with this, our construction plans for Prince Hotels in Tokyo are completed."[31] From then on, he said, the railway group would concentrate on hotels in Hawaii and ski facilities, golf courses, and resort hotels throughout Japan. The group preferred word-of-mouth publicity to media campaigns because Tsutsumi believed that "the special nature of the tourism industry means that advertising isn't too effective."[32] He readily admitted to a journalist in 1986 that "we can operate the Prince Hotels inexpensively because of the land left by the previous generation [his father]."[33] The same held true for golf: he wrote two years earlier that "if I have ¥1 billion [$4.2 million], I can do the whole thing from land to clubhouse,"[34] whereas it cost other operators three to five times this much to open a new course because of land prices.

The year 1984 also marked the end of an era in a more personal sense for both Tsutsumi Yoshiaki and Tsutsumi Seiji when, by strange coincidence, their mothers died within eight days of each other in November. Although Tsutsumi Misao, Seiji's adoptive mother, was the more outgoing of the two women and had appeared at the opening ceremony for the new Seibu Department Store in Yūrakuchō at the end of October, she preferred a quiet funeral (eight hundred persons nonetheless attended the rites). Ishizuka Tsuneko's death was solemnized before a crowd ten times this size at Zōjōji near the Tokyo Prince, ceremonially bestowing full recognition as a Tsutsumi on Yoshiaki's mother in death as never in life. Employees at Kokudo Keikaku later said with full sympathy that when his mother died, Yoshiaki was so grief-stricken that he took five days off from work, unheard of for him.[35]

PROFITING FROM TEAM SPORTS

"I was the first to approach sports as a 'business,'"[36] Tsutsumi Yoshiaki reminded writers after his Seibu Lions won the Japan professional baseball championship in 1982 and made their owner a tabloid celebrity the equal of any team magnate in other countries. By the time he bought the Crown Lighter Lions for about $3.3 million, renamed them the Seibu Lions, and moved them from Kyushu to Tokorozawa in 1978, Tsutsumi's skiing, skating, swimming, bowling, and golf enterprises already ranked him as the leading marketer of individual sports in Japan. "The reason I built a ballpark was likewise to expand my tourism business,"[37] not merely for public-relations benefits for the parent firm or simple indulgence in an expensive plaything, as was true of most other Japanese teams. Like many of the Prince Hotels, Lions Stadium was part of a larger amusement and recreation zone that included UNESCO Village and the 330-hectare Seibuen park, where patronage tripled after the ballpark opened in 1979.[38] What surprised the sports industry was how quickly Seibu turned a money-losing franchise into an efficient business, even though no other team in the Pacific League was either profitable or well-run.

Pro baseball in Japan dates to 1936, when a seven-club league modeled after the American major leagues began play. Four of the original franchises survive: Yomiuri, Hanshin, Chūnichi, and Orix (formerly Hankyū). Another remains in spectral form, the Senators, one of whose owners was Tsutsumi Yasujirō—yet another example of his dream of profiting from middle-class consumerism. Because the club did poorly, it was sold to the Nishi Nihon Railway in 1943 and disbanded the next year, then revived in 1950 as the Nishitetsu Lions. Yasujirō had plans drawn up for a baseball stadium near the Takanawa Prince before the 1964 Olympics but abandoned the idea when Keihin Kyūkō wrested control of the former Higashikuni property, on which the Hotel Pacific opened in 1971.[39] Since the family's interest in pro baseball goes back to the start, there is a certain serendipity in Yoshiaki's purchase of a franchise in whose antecedent his father was an investor.

Tsutsumi Yoshiaki broke into pro baseball in 1976 when Nakabe Kenkichi, owner of the floundering Taiyō Whales, asked for help in stanching the club's $1.1 million yearly deficit. The Whales were then renting the decrepit Kawasaki Stadium for home games and drawing poorly. Even the mighty Yomiuri Giants, one of two well-run franchises in Japan along with the Hanshin Tigers, paid rent to Kōrakuen Stadium as a home field, but Tsutsumi startled Nakabe by suggesting that he build his own modern facilities in an attractive setting as a way to put the club in the black. The two leaders secured land from the city of Yokohama, sold forty-five-year season tickets to 800 businesses for $9,260 each, and raised another $7.4 million in the stock market thanks partly to the power of Tsutsumi's name.[40] In this way Tsutsumi helped Taiyō expand its assets, offer fans a comfortable ballpark, and reestablish itself as a quality franchise—all without spending any of his own money. Still, as with some of his hotels, he ended up building a multipurpose stadium capable of accommodating other sports, including American football, in case baseball did not do well in Yokohama.

The Lions' franchise was operated by the Nishitetsu Railway until the early 1970s, then briefly by the Taiheiyō Corporation, a leading construction firm, until the Crown Lighter Company took it over in 1976. Two years later the new owners threw in the towel, having run an annual deficit of $1.1 million and attracted just 780,000 spectators in Heiwadai Stadium in Fukuoka in 1978.[41] Tsutsumi, who was already building a $14.8 million American-style ballpark in Tokorozawa for use as a rental facility when it was ready in March 1979, decided to buy the Lions and move them to the Kantō area. Even though this shift meant that six of the twelve professional clubs were now in the Tokyo region, none of the other owners objected, presumably because Tokorozawa seemed rural. The players spent two months in spring training at Bradenton, Florida, working out with the Atlanta Braves, then returned for their first season as the Seibu Lions and promptly lost their first twenty-one games. Still management reported that the team drew 1.3 million customers in 1979 despite a losing record on the field (Japanese baseball attendance figures are notoriously padded).[42]

This outcome illustrated Tsutsumi's dictum that a club didn't have to win in order to turn out crowds: "If you build a good ballpark and treat the fans well, no matter how often you lose, you can draw a million fans or more each year. It doesn't matter whether the team is strong or weak."[43] This doctrine was both heretical and in the end untrue, because attendance rose when the Lions were winners and dipped when they were not. But by providing comfortable seats, excellent restaurants and beer halls, handy transportation on the Seibu Railway, and an array of rides and amusements next door at Seibuen, Tsutsumi made facilities rather than the club itself the key variable for profitability: everyone could have a good time even if the Lions lost. The result, he said in 1988, was that Seibuen and UNESCO Village used to handle 3 million customers a year in the mid-1970s but now drew 10 million, comparable to the resorts at Hakone or Hankyū's Takarazuka amusement center. Games at Seibu Stadium also earned the railway an estimated extra $6.5 million in revenues each year.[44] Nonetheless Tsutsumi showed his customary caution by building the ballpark at a low level, dug into a hillside, so that if it failed he could convert it into an outdoor theater or a housing development[45] — now a remote likelihood, based on the Lions' popularity in western Tokyo and Saitama, where the club calculates 10 million people live within a thirty-minute train ride of home plate.

Seibu now means the Lions to more people than the railroad or the department store, partly because of the marketing power of electronic media in spectator sports and partly, *pace* Tsutsumi's dictum, because the team won nine Pacific League pennants and eight Japan Series during 1980–1992. The owner's stated goal from the outset was to promote baseball as family entertainment by bringing people to the ballpark as the focal point of a daylong visit to other Seibu enterprises in the zone. Tsutsumi claimed he rarely discounted his attractions or let people in free because he operated leisure facilities as a business, not a public service. In line with his arch-conservative views about the primacy of physical education, he insisted that athletes live up to their roles as idols for the young through clean living: "I will not renew the contracts of players who use alcohol or tobacco or who moonlight."[46] The owner even prohibited them from appearing in television commercials or endorsing products, ostensibly because doing so distracted them from the game but actually because he wanted to project a clean and pure image for his companies.[47] He also banned gambling, beards, mustaches, and long hair and demanded that players wear white suits and ties on road trips. In return team members enjoyed very high salaries, second only to those of the Yomiuri Giants.[48]

Ice hockey and skiing were Tsutsumi's main athletic interests as a young man, but he turned to baseball because of its "popularity" and "mass appeal" to assure that Seibu teams and events were in the news and on the air all year round, helping to promote business at company-owned sports centers.[49] The Lions set up a much larger publicity department than the Giants and relentlessly marketed hats, shirts, and other souvenirs branded with the club's logo, a pet Leo by the cartoon artist Tezuka Osamu—$11.5 million worth in the first year alone.[50] Tsutsumi selected both the Leo mark and the team color, a pale Columbia blue, because "kids love blue skies" and he wanted the Lions to be heroes for children.[51] Like other franchises, Seibu formed fan clubs (250,000 members by 1988) and posted photographs of recent games in all its trains and stations throughout the season. No team has outdone the Lions in cultivating its local consumer base, showing the effect of efficient business methods in a sport still treated as a diversion by many club owners. "The real judgment of me will be if customers stop coming,"[52] Tsutsumi said in 1984; but in fact the club's massive public-relations campaigns and game broadcasts kept Seibu at the top of its league in attendance from 1979 until the Tokyo Dome opened in 1988, allowing the Nippon Ham Fighters to edge ahead.[53]

When Seibu defeated the Chūnichi Dragons in Nagoya for its first Japan Series title in October 1982, the owner was in Tokyo watching a hockey game. But he scarcely took a hands-off approach to the Lions' success: he awarded Japan's first $1 million contract in 1980 to Steve Ontiveros, a former San Francisco Giant and Chicago Cub, and each year sent young Seibu players to the United States for training. He provided the club with an indoor synthetic-turf field as well as an outdoor grass field for practice. His investments paid off most notably in 1983 when the Lions defeated Yomiuri, Japan's most popular team, with a come-from-behind rally in the seventh game of the Japan Series—whereupon Tsutsumi Seiji ran a national victory sale in Seibu Department Stores and Seiyūs, drawing scorn for his opportunism but envy in the industry for the 350,000 customers who jammed the Ikebukuro store for day one of the four-day event.[54]

Even though Seibu won five championships in the 1980s compared with only one for Yomiuri, the Lions continued to draw just half as many fans. One reason was the Giants' long history and Yankee-like record of domination (they won nine series in a row during 1965–1973); another was the much greater strength of the Central League, where both the Giants (preferred by 60 percent of Japanese fans in the mid-

1980s) and the Hanshin Tigers (favorites of 25 percent) performed. Seibu, which tore up the weaker Pacific League during the 1980s, claimed the allegiances of just 10 percent of those who followed baseball.[55] The Giants benefited from greater television exposure and media backing from their owner, *Yomiuri*, Japan's most widely circulated newspaper. Starting in 1988 the Giants, like the Fighters, had the advantage of playing home games in the Tokyo Dome ("Big Egg") at Kōrakuen, which seated 46,314 and sold out for nearly all Giant contests until the novelty of watching a game in Japan's first domed ballpark began to wear off in 1991. Seibu stadium had just 37,008 seats; even with standees it could hardly approach Yomiuri's total attendance figures across a 65-game home season. These factors help to explain why the Giants were able to claim 3.4 million admissions to their home games in 1988, versus 1.9 million for the Lions.[56]

Tsutsumi is a skilled athlete in golf, swimming, tennis, and especially skiing, personally supervising construction sites with a user's sense of function and detail. Baseball was another matter. Because he did not know the game intimately, he elected to endow the Lions with a strong management structure and leave baseball decisions to his field manager, a standard piety for owners everywhere but one he upheld more faithfully than most. Within the organization of the railway group, he made the Lions coordinate with Prince Hotels and Seibu Golf, directly under the control of the Kokudo Keikaku president's office. The club's president has always been a top officer of the Seibu Railway; since 1988 it has been Nisugi Iwao, president of the railroad and perhaps the most influential executive in the group after the owner. The Lions' financial and marketing officials were similarly well-qualified professionals from the start, in keeping with the goal of making a business of sports.

On the field Seibu was regarded as one of the strictest, most disciplined organizations in Japanese pro baseball. Tsutsumi was tempted to hire the former Giant legend Nagashima Shigeo as the team's manager but decided not to because Japan's best-loved baseball star was a media favorite for his many commercials and endorsements—anathema to the Lions' philosophy. The owner was happier with Hirooka Tatsurō, a fellow Waseda alumnus and an unceasing disciplinarian in training and game tactics. Hirooka whipped the club into line and won its first championships in Tokorozawa during 1982–1985, then left

Seibu after a dispute with Tsutsumi that reportedly involved front-office authority (Hirooka was believed to wish more of it for himself). Tsutsumi then hired Mori Masaaki, another stiff regimentarian who nonetheless overlooked some of his players' high jinks, like cartwheels at home plate after home runs, in the interest of placating some of the younger stars. By the late 1980s the Lions had players as talented as any in Japan; it was natural that Ishige Hiromichi, known as Mr. Lions, and Kiyohara Kazuhiro, who hit thirty-one homers as an eighteen-year-old rookie in 1986, should have become immensely popular with young fans for their individuality rather than their membership on a disciplined team.[57] To some degree Mori's small concessions to his younger players may be the key to pro baseball's survival in Japan, since few fans under age thirty admire the work ethic and spartan training that Japanese ball clubs epitomized into the late 1980s, well after these values had lost ground in the workplace.

Tsutsumi twice found reason to criticize team members in the late 1980s and ended up with reams of bad press as a result. A star pitcher, Higashio Osami, was questioned by police in 1987 for gambling with gangsters and suspended by the owner for half a season, with a sizable loss of pay. When the *Hōchi shinbun*, owned by Yomiuri, reported the details soon after the Lions defeated the Giants in the Japan Series, Tsutsumi banned the *Hōchi* from newsstands controlled by Seibu along its rail lines. Like most attempts to blame the messenger, this fit of pique boomeranged and earned Tsutsumi more negative publicity than the pitcher he punished. Two years later the owner reportedly castigated Manager Mori after the Lions failed to win the Pacific League pennant for the first time in five years: "If you were a man, you'd bite the bullet and resign."[58] The episode drew Tsutsumi many barbs and Mori much sympathy. The Lions ran away with the league title the next season with Mori still at the helm and swept the listless Giants to win the 1990 Japan Series. This time the unsmiling owner was present for his team's championship, shown for an instant on national television just before the final out as he looked down imperiously from his austere presidential box with no one else except his wife Yuri anywhere nearby.

TSUTSUMI YOSHIAKI AND THE BUSINESS ESTABLISHMENT

Even though Gotō Noboru, the Tōkyū leader, capped his career by heading the Japan Chamber of Commerce and Industry, bankers and manufacturers dominated the four main business associations so completely from the 1950s to the 1980s that very few executives from service-sector enterprises had much standing in the top echelon of corporate Japan or voice in its influential policy pronouncements. Even if Tsutsumi Yoshiaki collected art, attended concerts, and enjoyed socializing with associates instead of sitting by himself in presidential boxes, there is no assurance that his achievements with the Seibu Railway, Kokudo Keikaku, the Prince Hotels, or the Lions would win him acceptance among the industrialists who controlled Japan's *zaikai*, or business establishment. His lack of clout among the inner corporate elite was all the more striking in the light of his undoubted influence over party politics.

Tsutsumi shunned fellow hoteliers, even though he ran the leading chain, and rarely attended gatherings of golf entrepreneurs or railway owners. His public service was confined mainly to sports organizations in the 1980s, especially the Japan Ice Hockey Federation, the Japan Athletic Association, and the Japan Olympic Committee, until his humiliating resignation as chair of the latter in April 1990 amid suspicions of a conflict of interest. Part of his reticence presumably derived from the exceptional secretiveness of the railway group and from its lack of connections with the securities market.[59] Tsutsumi needed bankers but not underwriters throughout the 1970s and 1980s as his companies built new hotels, resorts, and sports facilities; the banks were generally quick to lend because of the prestige of doing business with Japan's richest landlord. Otherwise, he told a reporter in 1986, "I'd like to see the business community dissolved. . . . The political world is necessary, but there's no need for the business community."[60] As someone who grew up outside the establishment with little need to beg for its services, he contended that industrial federations and the *zaikai* as a whole inhibited competition and stood in the way of free entrepreneurship. It was hard for most ordinary Japanese to feel much sympathy for one tycoon's quarrel with others in a country where privilege was greatly stacked against consumers in favor of corporations, yet Tsutsumi's plaintive summary had an unmistakable antiestablishmentarian ring: "It would be better if there were no business elite. This is because Japan is a capitalist country."[61] Here was a chord that presumably resonated with the general public, American trade negotiators, and even his brother Seiji.

CHAPTER SEVEN

FROM ABUNDANCE
TO AFFLUENCE

Retailers everywhere know that nothing is staler than last year's marketing plan. In an industry where change is the only certainty, the past evaporates like yesterday's shower as company soothsayers struggle to determine what will capture the shopper's fancy a season or two ahead. If merchandisers have a weak sense of history, they also have great trouble looking beyond the next advertising campaign toward genuine long-term planning. Scrambling to anticipate the next consumer fad leaves little time to ponder the underlying changes in society that retailers must discern if their enterprises are to remain healthy.

The early 1980s were a vital moment for Seibu and other Japanese merchants because the country was moving beyond an abundance of material goods toward lifestyles of real affluence, reflected in personal choices about culture, entertainment, fitness, and fashion as well as a growing indulgence in travel and leisure. Gone was the view that all citizens were equally middle-class, entitled to the same civil minimum of amenities without regional variations. In its place was an ever louder clamor for satisfying individual preferences, so that the decade as a whole, as in other wealthy countries, became one of self-aggrandizement, symbolized by rocketing land prices and a "bubble economy" that finally started to sag at the end of 1991.

The advertising executive Fujioka Wakao wrote in *Sayōnara, taishū*

(Farewell to the masses), published in 1984, that the compact camera and the Sony Walkman were the last universal products everyone had to have; henceforth niche markets (*shōshū*), segmented according to style and sensibility, would replace mass markets (*taishū*).[1] That same year the playwright Yamazaki Masakazu said in *Yawarakai kojinshugi no tanjō* (Birth of mellow individualism) that consumers were sated with goods and now sought self-discovery in the products they acquired.[2] The model shopper was no longer the New Young but the first entirely urban generation in Japan, known as the New Breed (*shinjinrui*), born in the 1960s and reared to take material abundance for granted. Like the New Young, these people were highly selective consumers with a penchant for culture and the arts, but they were also a media-schooled electronics generation who knew life and nature mainly through television and often understood marketing messages about new products better than the salespeople in the stores.[3] Many were single and most were concerned with self-expression—and with showing off their distinctiveness to others in the clothes they wore, the cars they drove, the skiing and scuba diving they did, and especially the music they played and the comic books they read, or at least carried. Some thought the New Breed desultory, irresolute, inconstant, directionless—but the Seibu Retailing Group recognized that this was the most powerful marketing phenomenon since the prêt-à-porter generation of the 1960s. The company went to great lengths to cultivate new customers in the early 1980s by further diversifying and reorganizing itself into what Tsutsumi Seiji called "a comprehensive lifestyle industry."

SYNERGY THROUGH DIVERSITY

Once Japanese retailers found their bearings after the second world petroleum crisis of 1979, superstores managed to rebound nicely during the next four years but department stores experienced their slowest growth since World War II. The stagnancy stemmed partly from a disbelief that shoppers were surfeited with artifacts (consequently stores kept piling up inventories) and partly from a long-term restructuring of how goods were sold in Japan. During 1964–1973 consumer spending and department-store sales grew in tandem; then during the next ten years department-store sales rose only 63 percent as fast as consumer spending,[4] because of competition from superstores, discounters, specialty outlets, and mushrooming convenience stores—the latter leavened by the curbs on building new large retail stores after 1974. Another reason department stores fell behind was that household outlays for the things they sold—semidurables and nondurables—dropped more than 5 percent while consumption of services rose nearly 6 percent between 1975 and 1983. On the whole the department stores bore up better than small shopkeepers, who accounted for nearly all of the 92,000 decline in the number of retail establishments between 1982 and 1985,[5] although regional department stores were wounded by new shopping centers anchored by national superstores or branches of big-city retailers.[6] The previous twenty years had been an age of suburban sprawl for the top department stores; now in the 1980s they rediscovered urban development as a way of overcoming the torpor that immured them at the beginning of the decade.

What did patrons expect from merchants in the 1980s? Tsutsumi detected a shift in the psychology of consumption from possession to function, from mere ownership to actual benefit for individuals' lives. This inevitably meant more variety, he wrote in 1981, in the same way that art and music were more diverse than before: "If superstores stagnate in this regard, they're bound to drive customers away. This same problem is bound to extend to department stores, too."[7] He asserted that "people are searching for genuine things that will satisfy them spiritually as well as materially. Now is the era for creating genuine articles."[8] Tsutsumi surprised his employees the following year by declaring that "the era of the department store is over"—a perplexing claim at a time when the Ikebukuro building had just surpassed Mitsukoshi at Nihonbashi to become the national leader in sales. He explained, "Japan's postindustrial movement is proceeding at a fast tempo. Because of this fundamental trend, retailing, too, is probably facing a big turning point"[9] in its social function: appealing to customers' search for lifestyles they could call their own. For example, Wada Shigeaki, a key Seibu executive, worried in 1982 that the group had underestimated the purchasing impact of working women, a force that "has produced drastic changes in eating habits in the past few years."[10] Postindustrialism also meant a rising senior-citizen market, new information systems, a mania for fitness, and a big increase in hobbies—all of which drove consumers to specialty stores to find value for their lives.[11]

FIGURE 8. Front façade of the Ikebukuro Parco (right) and attached Seibu department store as they appeared in the 1980s. (Saison Group)

One of the main ways Seibu reacted to the unsettled market was to reorganize the group in 1982 to allow for more "strategic diversification."[12] As Japan's leading retailer with $8.14 billion in sales as of 1980, the Seibu group was already quite diversified before this restructuring began, with department and superstores, specialty shops, and restaurants; more manufacturing and food-processing subsidiaries than its competitors; financial and leisure services; and real-estate and transportation businesses. The department store alone had fifty-five affiliated companies and Seiyū another fifteen.[13] When Seibu Credit, Restaurant Seibu, Seibu Allstate Life, and Asahi Helicopter joined the four original core companies in 1982, the revised inner circle signaled the group's expansion beyond retailing into more service areas than any other department-store or superstore operator in Japan. Each core company was now expected both to specialize on carefully defined customer segments and to diversify into new activities,[14] cutting its reliance on business as usual and instead devising new services that would help convert Japan's economic affluence into social satisfaction—and profit for Seibu.

Retailing analysts often credited Tsutsumi Seiji with greater skill at forecasting consumer trends than at managing his extensive empire. The 1982 reorganization added incentives to create further spinoffs and subsidiaries, making the group even more complex and potentially unruly. Like large organizations elsewhere, Seibu countered this centrifugality with fresh doses of company ideology to serve as corporate glue—or at least façade. To preempt bureaucratic rivalries and offset intragroup competition, Tsutsumi trotted out the American business shibboleth "synergy," urging his constituent enterprises to interact, share information, and rely on one another for services like credit and insurance. He told his executives that "managing is an eternal revolution" and that the purpose of the group "is to activate the various companies and undertakings to produce the effect of synergy."[15] Tsutsumi defined the collective goal as "moving from the consumer industry [shimin sangyō] to the comprehensive lifestyle industry [seikatsu sōgō sangyō],"[16] with greater attention to "soft" services, information, and internationalization. He also began running full-page ads in the newspapers, starting in 1980, to cut a sharper corporate identity for the group.

Internally the retailing group continued to be dominated in capital terms by the department store and Seiyū, but with renewed effort to nurture management republicanism as a leadership style after the 1982 shake-up. Biweekly headquarters staff meetings were convened at Beisōkaku, a company guest house on Tsutsumi Seiji's property in Minami Azabu, starting in September 1983; bimonthly meetings of representatives from the core enterprises were instituted the next spring. The headquarters staff group, originally consisting of Tsutsumi and six senior executives but expanded by three more in 1989, exercised initiative in policy questions. The core-company representatives met to find out what the headquarters staff had decided, coordinate how each firm would implement group policies, and discuss broader issues not directly related to business like technological developments, new media, the financial markets, and social changes. Each core company now underwent regular review, usually every summer, conducted by Tsutsumi or other top officials from the group, with the inevitable mounds of documents to be assembled beforehand. Seibu also began holding regional conferences for local managers of each core business operating in the district to discuss their particular markets and strategies with senior leaders from Tokyo.[17]

Little about this management system distinguishes it from other Japanese conglomerates structurally; Seibu officials are tight-lipped about it as a leadership style in practice. How effectively it promoted republicanism doubtless depended on the particular issue at hand, how strongly Tsutsumi was committed to it, and how widely it affected the group as a whole. Company historians point out that, for all the talk of synergy, the group was difficult to administer in the uncertain retailing climate of the early 1980s and that Tsutsumi was hard put to assemble the capital required for further diversification.[18] Nonetheless it is notable that the retailing group created, spun off, strengthened, or reorganized forty-two of its member firms between 1981 and 1985 and that aggregate sales for the latter year were $10.98 billion, an increase of 42 percent in yen terms since 1980.[19] (Sales at the Seibu Railway Group, by contrast, were $3.36 billion in 1983.)[20] About four-fifths of the revenues still came from Seiyū and the department store; altogether the group now had more than eight hundred places of business and 67,500 employees.[21] But pretax profits barely grew at all between 1982 and 1984 and then increased somewhat the following year to $84.5 million, still less than 1 percent of sales.[22] It is understandable that the quest for fatter profits became an urgent concern for the reorganized group in the second half of the decade. Since they took in most of the cash, the department store and Seiyū were expected to show the way.

THE NEW SELF

The Me Generation found its expression in Japan as the New Breed of the 1980s, to whom Seibu Department Stores pitched its marketing under the slogan "responding to each individual's lifestyle." A poster for the remodeled Ikebukuro store in 1980 showed a nude three-year-old swimming underwater in a pool, with the tag line "Myself. A new revelation."[23] The message was obviously not "new goods" or "the new Seibu" but "the New Self"—no longer competing with other people but discovering your own style. Some other showy examples of the company's mood advertising in the early 1980s were "street of humanity," "mystery: I love it," "Genroku renaissance," and "delicious living" (the last on a poster showing Woody Allen). Such abstract and apparently meaningless ads created an atmosphere that shoppers could easily sense, if not understand, subsuming Seibu's earlier image-setting campaigns in the 1960s so that mood now became the predominant public image of the store. This approach to a more splintered and elusive market, not bargain sales or a "loss-leader strategy,"[24] helped the company enhance its reputation for quality among those who now wanted it for themselves more than to impress others. These campaigns were so efficient that Seibu could afford to underspend Mitsukoshi, Takashimaya, and Daimaru on advertising as a percentage of sales (2.5 percent in 1983).[25]

Appealing to the New Self took a great deal of consumer research and some basic rethinking of merchandising tactics. For Tsutsumi it meant shrewdness in identifying market niches when more conventional retailers hunkered down during the "wintertime of the department store."[26] He reminded his managers that "creativity is produced by a sharp clash of values—the clash of warm and cold currents, the clash of Asian and Western styles."[27] For Wada Shigeaki, a managing director of the department store in 1982, selling to the New Self meant shifting from quantity to quality, from material to psychological, from fast flow to varied stock, from sets to parts, from possession to function.[28] Both of them knew that the New Breed was the hardest sell of all, especially in department stores. Tsutsumi wrote in 1982 that "young people in their early twenties clearly show a tendency to search in earnest for psychological values. You can see this in books, records, and the increasing admissions to art museums. Even travel is not just for leisure, it's to increase their horizons of experience"[29]—a point lost on their work-oriented parents, who criticized the travel not realizing the personal values young people were seeking.

Private brands were a key point of entry to this youthful cohort. Seibu already dealt with more than six hundred makers, at home and abroad, and was unsurpassed in the variety of foreign designers it carried (both directly imported and manufactured under license in Japan). But in the torpid sales climate of the early 1980s, national brands on consignment often sold poorly, returns were heavy, and prices crept higher in response. Seibu and Isetan were particularly quick to design and order more private labels of their own, assuming the risks but cashing in on the self-image of lines available only from a single high-quality store. As one financial journalist put it in 1985, the growth of "designer and character" brands "is a reflection of the development of the individualistic, more diversified lifestyles that characterize modern Japan."[30] Seibu therefore began offering more such labels of its own for maximum distinctiveness. Private brands were one among many ways the department store labored to shed the industrywide doldrums by reaching this fickle young market through precise specialization and a much broader variety of offerings than before.

Another tactic to shake off sluggishness was to blitz the competition with a fresh round of store renovations, new branches, and tie-ups with regional retailers. Like the other big department stores, Seibu was abashed that the superstores kept on growing after the 1979 oil crisis; Tsutsumi once again chose to expand rather than play safe. In the early and mid-1980s Seibu refurbished many of its locations, began joint operations with Darumaya in Fukui (1980) and Gobankan in Sapporo (1982), and unveiled new stores at Yūrakuchō (1984), Tsukuba (1985), Tsukaguchi (1985), and Tokorozawa (1986).[31] These investments naturally produced a jump in sales for the department-store company (up 40.5 percent in yen terms between 1980 and 1985, to $2.24 billion),[32] but operating profits were almost entirely consumed by the growing costs of debt service in order to finance the expansion. As of 1983 Seibu Department Stores carried five times as much long-term indebtedness as the average of fourteen major companies in the industry; even more ominous was that its capital was just 3.7 percent of debt plus equity, in contrast to the industry average of 32.1 percent that year.[33] Still the entire group celebrated buoyantly in 1982 when the once-muddy Ikebukuro store finally overtook Mitsukoshi at Nihonbashi to become the number-one building in the country in sales at $971.9 million, nearly five times the volume at Seibu's second-busiest store in Shibuya.[34]

Since the labor pool available to the retailing group was both shallower and more self-absorbed than in the 1970s, Tsutsumi Seiji took further steps to attract and retain the best workers he could find, abandoning the stale vinegar of company loyalty for the fresh honey of job specialization. In 1980 the group began offering special licenses to capable women employees who had six years' service and whose family duties forced them to stop working. These licenses allowed the women to return to their positions at the company up to ten years later without losing seniority or benefits. Within a year 161 licenses had been issued, and thirty-one recipients had already returned to work.[35] Tsutsumi told the *Nikkei* in December 1981 that "hitherto, only those women 'who have stopped to be female' could continue to work in the company where the work is organized by and for male employees. We started the License System so that female employees could remain being female at work"[36]—and because the company could no longer function unless it enticed them and their expertise to return.

In 1982 the group began sending certain newly hired university graduates for on-the-job experience in design, architecture, and other specialties before starting their regular employment at Seibu. In the first seven years of this program sixty-one men and six women received advanced training in Japan or abroad.[37] Nineteen eighty-two is also when the retailing group hired the first of many dozens of foreigners as regular employees. Borrowing from the theater, Tsutsumi instituted a cast system in 1984 whereby specialists like management consultants, sports coaches, architects, and others who performed staff rather than line functions could work full or part time on a fee-for-service basis at Seibu Department Stores. More important, the whole group adopted a new "multiple" personnel scheme that same year which allowed ambitious employees to take on added duties, moonlight elsewhere within the group, or shift entirely to another Seibu company. The multiple system provided far more openings for specialization than the shopmaster category established in 1975.[38] This principle of job or company selection was soon extended to the group's new hires as a recruiting ploy, starting in 1986, through the Order Entry System.

This highly popular program helped turn the Seibu group into one of the most desirable of all employers among college seniors because they could choose either to apply to a specific member company, as in the past, or to one of thirteen training courses in specialties such as marketing, finance, tourism, and international operations. (High-school graduates were not eligible for the courses.) About a quarter of new employees each year elected these training tracks, with the promise of a job in the chosen specialty somewhere in the group. The motive, according to Seibu, lay in "workers' improving their job skills and in respecting individuals' preferences"[39] about the kind of work they wanted to do. The plan was broadened in 1990 to include college graduates already working for the group who wished to transfer to other member companies by preparing for specific positions.[40]

Few experts on the subject doubted that the Seibu Retailing Group was an innovative employer. It had to be agile in a scarce labor market; but the company generally acted faster than the competition to provide in-store day-care, flextime for both male and female workers to care for children under two at home, and (since 1988) the right for women workers to refuse transfers to other locations without penalty.[41] Although no female leader at Seibu has yet risen so high as Ishihara Ichiko, the executive director of Takashimaya whose slogan is "think like a man, act like a lady, work like a dog," both the department store and Seiyū have a number of women managers, whose presence is thought by the male executives to improve morale among female employees.[42] What is less clear is whether innovation since the early 1980s materially or psychologically improved working conditions. The Ladies' Board created in 1979 to give women employees more voice may have had more form than content; a similar Junior Board for workers in their twenties probably told the front office more about how to market to that age group than about how to improve job conditions. A study conducted by Alice C. L. Lam in 1988 found that Seibu Department Stores had made efforts to comply with the Equal Employment Opportunity Law of 1985 but also that the company stopped well short of providing full opportunities for its women employees.[43] Wages for both males and females remained close to the industry average; hours were long and competition among employees was steep, as in most retailing organizations, although the department store managed to introduce more generous vacations and four-day workweeks in 1990. Tsutsumi had a reputation for leaving employees to their own devices but also for removing them fast if they were outperformed by others in similar or overlapping jobs.[44] Morale was difficult to assess in such a fast-paced line of business or in so far-flung a corporation, but the impression was strong that Seibu's progressive structure of benefits outran most workers' appreciation of it.

Nonetheless, there is little question that the New Breed of the

1980s found the Seibu group a more congenial corporate setting in which to seek self-fulfillment than was true of most other employers. Tsutsumi for many years recruited people with initiative and a street sense, rather than those with long academic résumés, so that the retailing group was seen as a good place to prove oneself and get ahead. Nowadays "sincerity, earnestness, and hard work are big demerits," he said in 1985, because they mask dullness and an absence of creativity.[45] Three years later the managing director of the department store, Ido Kazuo, pointed out that "someone who only cares about the company cannot really be creative. . . . We want people who have their own goals, can think for themselves and make their own decisions."[46] This sort of employee, according to the company's siren song, would find Seibu attractive because it sought "peaceful and humanistic livelihoods" and was an internationally minded firm "that has direct contact with people's lives."[47] Job seekers were lured both by Tsutsumi's image as an artist-businessperson who understood their generation and by the company's orientation toward the future, where self-discovery was possible. Two thousand of them applied in 1987 for seventeen openings in the group's training program in culture and media.[48] Even though the Seiyū in Yokosuka denied credit to an otherwise eligible candidate in 1981 because he was a Korean Japanese, Tsutsumi contended ten years later that "my companies progressively employ more Koreans and Chinese and Burakumin. But discrimination in Japan is very deep and people use delicate words to camouflage wrong attitudes."[49] Mizuno Seiichi, president of the department store, described its hiring policy as "liberal" in a 1991 interview: "Our philosophy is not to discriminate in employment. We emphasize that we are open to all."[50] At the same time the group does not go out of its way to solicit applications from minorities; no affirmative-action plans are known to exist.

Total employment at the Saison Group as of 1990 was 110,575, including 12,383 at Inter-Continental Hotels (nearly all of them overseas). The group hired 3,855 new full-time workers that spring, about double the number a decade earlier. Women represented 55 percent of the new employees, although a slight majority of the college graduates appointed to managerial positions were men. By 1992 the group claimed more than 145,000 workers.[51] Noting that "the company as a community has begun to crumble . . . the Japanese have the least sense of belonging"[52] among young people in any of the wealthy countries, Tsutsumi stopped holding formal initiation ceremonies for new employees in 1988—abandoning ritual recitations of corporate ideology because by now the worker as well as the customer sought to become the New Self.

SEIYŪ: QUALITY AND CONVENIENCE

Japan's superstores rode out the second petroleum crisis of 1979 in better condition than the department stores, but most of their growth in the early 1980s stemmed from opening new stores, and profits were dangerously thin by 1983. Grocery purchases slumped because more and more twin-income families preferred to dine at restaurants and fast-food chains. A sudden boom in all-night convenience stores triggered partly by the restrictions on large-scale retailing challenged superstores for the first time on their home territory, self-service. The broad consumer trend toward items to suit particular lifestyles further menaced those superstores whose operations were still geared toward the mass market. The largest of them, Daiei, actually ran in the red for a time; its response was to transform itself into a giant volume-sales conglomerate. Itō Yōkadō chose to streamline technically by reducing inventories, pruning slow sellers, adding new lines, and speeding up both ordering and delivery. Both chains were far stronger financially by 1985 as a result.[53]

Seiyū's strategy in the early 1980s was to emanate a new image as a quality rather than quantity store, particularly in its new branch outlets and private-brand lines, and also to diversify by promoting a lucrative chain of convenience stores in the Tokyo area called FamilyMart. Tsutsumi Seiji had been beating the drums for quality at Seiyū ever since he reassumed its presidency in 1975. In their earliest years superstores had used price and volume as their chief ploys, but their wares had a Marcusean sameness that no longer attracted shoppers who were thoroughly accustomed to abundance by the 1980s. By quality Seiyū meant selling no products below a certain standard, offering good merchandise that met people's everyday needs without matching the top items in luxury stores, and shedding the self-service warehouse ambience by providing attractive displays and helpful service[54]—from Kmart to Macy's, if not quite Bloomingdale's. By dropping "stores" from its name to mark its twentieth anniversary in June 1983, Seiyū meant to escape its image as a storehouse of artifacts and to highlight its new attention to quality of life by supplying convenience, services, and cultural diversions to "prosumers" who actively sought to devise personal lifestyles,[55] a stiff task for a slightly dowdy chain widely seen as a reliable supermarket with inexpensive clothing and housewares on the floors above.

A key route to reaching the New Breed and other self-oriented shoppers was to build small department stores, operated by Seiyū but labeled either Seiyū or Seibu, where the company could offer higher quality, spiffy decor, and greatly improved services compared with its older superstores. Gambling on the fact that affluence (*yutori no aru*) had now spread beyond the most comfortable suburbs, Seiyū in the early 1980s targeted shoppers with big mortgages living in hew housing developments in the hope that their fashion sense would find satisfaction in its freshly built department stores. Seiyū opened a 12,000-square-meter branch at Kotesashi in June 1981 and another at Ōizumi in April 1983, both in the northwestern outreaches of Tokyo, that became models in scale, appearance, and market radius for its new stores for the rest of the decade. More striking was the Ōmori Seiyū, launched in March 1984 with 12,500 square meters of sales space and heralded as "the consumer's information station." The building contained groceries, general merchandise, restaurants, and three movie theaters as well as travel, insurance, and real-estate counters—a forerunner of Seibu Department Stores' splashy Ginza showcase that opened six months later. Seiyū unveiled even larger department stores with a wider range of services at Kinshichō (November 1986, 30,700 square meters) and Hikarigaoka the following spring, the latter of which abutted a mammoth housing project on the site of a former army base known to a generation of Americans as Grant Heights.[56]

Seiyū's workers should feel confident competing with major department stores, Tsutsumi told them in 1983: "A store's size does not determine whether it is weak or strong. What does are the strength of management and quality of goods."[57] No one who shopped at them doubted that Seiyū was going to great lengths to achieve "freshness and style" at its new department stores—except at Kiyota in Sapporo, where 7,879 customers suffered food poisoning during the opening week in October 1982 because of fouled well water that critics blamed on construction shortcuts caused by Seiyū's haste to debut on schedule. The retailing group paid $8.3 million to the victims as compensation,[58] but the public-relations disaster took many years to overcome. The financial sting was very great because each of the small department stores Seiyū opened between 1979 and 1983 cost the firm $40–45 million to build and decorate,[59] at a time when it was also introducing new outlets on a more modest scale in seven out-of-town locations.

Another entrée to a more personalized market was to develop high-quality private brands that catered to a growing interest in natural materials and foodstuffs without additives or preservatives. Seiyū was already so vertically integrated that by the late 1970s it purchased 20 percent of its merchandise and nearly half its foodstuffs from its own subsidiaries.[60] This structure made it easy for the company to develop, test, and market products to its own specifications and test standards, which unlike house brands in the United States usually exceeded those of national manufacturers. One of Seiyū's most extraordinary coups was Mujirushi Ryōhin ("Nonbrand good items"), introduced with little fuss in December 1980 but soon the envy of every one of Seiyū's rivals.

The Mujirushi Ryōhin label was a pet project of Tsutsumi's. As with Parco, the names Seibu and Seiyū were not mentioned, yet everyone knew these generics were theirs. Appealing to the themes of environment, simplicity, and authenticity, these unadorned foodstuffs and housewares came in see-through packages, natural tans and browns, and plain labels emphasizing function and contents. So extreme was their romantic appeal to the green counterculture that no English terms were used. Mujirushi Ryōhin were priced 25–30 percent below national brands and 10–15 percent under Seiyū's own lines.[61] An apt symbol was the basic white bicycle for $50: you could personalize it by spending up to $30 more for a basket, mud flaps, and other accessories, and you could paint it whatever color you wanted (pink and purple were favorites). Mujirushi Ryōhin opened a 103-square-meter toehold shop on posh Aoyama Dōri in June 1983, with plain woods and floor tiles, recycled shelving, and the slogan "love is unadorned!"[62] Carrying just 450 items, this public-relations outpost in Japan's richest shopping triangle was an instant hit with the New Breed, taking in revenues nearly four times the company's projections during its first year.[63]

From an original 31 items in 1980, Mujirushi Ryōhin soon added clothing to its repertoire and swelled to 1,111 products in 1985, about

1,550 in 1990, and an estimated 5,000 by 1993. Sales were a remarkable $45.5 million in year one and then tripled in yen terms by 1986; at the end of the decade they reached $282.8 million,[64] marketed throughout the group's retail outlets as well as in twenty-six separate Mujirushi Ryōhin stores. So successful was this venture that Seiyū and the British firm Liberty PLC opened a Mujirushi Ryōhin shop in London in July 1991. By then Mujirushi Ryōhin had long since become a part of the established consumer culture and a brand name of its own, known to just about everyone in Japan.

Seiyū also appealed to ecology, resource conservation, and the handicraft tradition among city-born shoppers when it introduced a private label called Furusato Meihin ("Country-home gems") in 1981. These foodstuffs and handmade items brought touches of nature and distinctiveness to superstore shelves that otherwise bulged with monotonously similar products, often with artificial ingredients, which bore no traces of local flavor. Two years later the company began marketing a private brand of housewares known as Shufu no Me ("Housewife's eye") and, in October 1984, a fifty-eight-item line of single-portion frozen foods called Gourmet Express—both intended for working couples and singles too busy, or too maladroit, to cook and keep house the way their mothers did. Store brands of all sorts earned Seiyū $250 million in 1985 and rose more than one-third in yen terms by the end of the decade to $625.8 million, the proceeds from sales of roughly 5,700 private-label items.[65]

Another way Seiyū tried to distance itself from its stolid past as a supermarket chain was to set up a Strategic Operations Division in 1983 to deal with shopping-center management, cultural enterprises, restaurants, financing, travel, direct marketing, and convenience stores— the latter of which was its most conspicuous success. Convenience stores began in Japan when the Southland Corporation of Texas and Itō Yōkadō opened their first 7-Eleven in Toyosu, Tokyo, in the early 1970s. Their growth paralleled the rise of a night-owl population of single persons in the biggest cities, as well as a spreading fondness for going shopping by car. By the end of 1980, 7-Eleven had more than a thousand locations throughout Japan, well ahead of Daiei's Lawson and Sun chains (which merged in 1988). Seiyū traces its FamilyMart convenience stores to a shop in Sayamagaoka that opened in 1973, but as of 1980 there were just fifty FamilyMarts in existence. The following year Seiyū spun off the chain to form a subsidiary, FamilyMart Ltd., that by 1990 had shot ahead of both 7-Eleven and Lawson to claim top rank in sales and number of stores in the Tokyo region, even though it was just number three nationwide in an industry with hundreds of competitors.[66]

The Seibu Retailing Group made much of the homegrown character of its convenience stores, although it freely acknowledged the technical assistance it received from Jewel's White Hen Pantry chain during 1979–1981.[67] Like 7-Eleven and Lawson, FamilyMart franchised its outlets to local investors, often small shopkeepers who already owned their properties; unlike its main rivals, FamilyMart gave out area franchises only in distant parts of the country where direct single-store franchises were hard to arrange, and it also owned 6–8 percent of its locations outright, operating them through licensees. The company redecorated each store, trained the franchisee and other employees, installed and serviced equipment, and provided advertising as well as advice on merchandising. Franchisees agreed to operate the stores 365 days a year, carry about 3,300 items including some selected to meet their local customers' needs, stay open 24 hours (in all but 10 percent of cases today), and pay a franchise fee averaging 11.5 percent of net sales.[68]

Since convenience stores are indistinguishable in size (about 100 square meters), prices (expensive), and services (quite varied), what brought the 775 customers on an average day to FamilyMart? Location was uppermost: the company went to great lengths to pick sites along the outbound lanes of major thoroughfares to catch the evening homebound traffic, the more so because 60 percent of its patrons were males. Much late-night business also came by car. Although 70 percent of sales were food items, a magazine shelf well stocked with comics and men's magazines was crucial for luring browsers late in the day, and photocopiers, packaged sandwiches and salads, personal products, and the ubiquitous panty-hose rack all had much appeal. Open refrigerator cases were widely used at FamilyMart because as early as 1980 the company discovered women didn't like opening doors. To keep store inventories low, the firm provided point-of-sale accounting and overnight delivery to all its franchises. Crowded traffic and a lack of drivers did not prevent FamilyMart from bringing freshly made lunch items each day, just in time for the noon rush. It was the first Japanese convenience-store chain to combine with gasoline stations, in the universal American fashion; the first to sell Japan Railway tickets; and the first to deliver fresh flowers via catalog order, starting with Mother's Day 1990. All its outlets carried Seiyū's private brands, including Mujirushi Ryōhin.[69] Still the company staked its future on good location more than any other factor and deliberately chose to cultivate Japan's car-owning young people, of whom the New Breed were the archetype.

From the 50 stores it counted in 1980, FamilyMart expanded to approximately 500 in 1985 and added roughly three times this number during 1986–1990. Fifty of them were joint ventures with C. Itoh in Taiwan, known as Ch'uan Chia convenience stores under the FamilyMart logo.[70] This strong record allowed the firm to gain a listing on the Tokyo Stock Exchange in July 1987 and a promotion to its first section two years later. Total sales at FamilyMart's 2,000 locations leaped more than 35 percent annually during 1986–1990, to $1.9 billion in the latter year, and pretax profits were $78.8 million, a 600 percent increase since 1986. By March 1992 sales had risen to $2.52 billion per annum, and the number of locations stood at 2,652.[71] Nonetheless 7-Eleven and Daiei's pair of Lawson and Sun each has about twice as many stores as FamilyMart and more than twice the sales, so that even with 6,000 outlets by the end of the century, FamilyMart could not expect to capture more than 10 percent of the very fragmented national market[72]—a good reason to expect the company to focus on Tokyo, where it and its erstwhile parent Seiyū are strongest.

Seiyū managed a remarkable shift in its image from volume sales to quality and convenience in the early 1980s, but its profits were shriveled by heavy borrowing to finance so many new stores and by still operating many antiquated grocery stores: as of 1985, nearly 40 percent of Seiyū's 164 stores were smaller than 3,000 square meters.[73] Seiyū and its subsidiaries (exclusive of Kansai and Nagano) generated sales of $3.93 billion in 1980, or 48.3 percent of the entire retailing group's revenues. The superstores alone took in $2.41 billion that year, a figure that rose to $3.2 billion by 1985 (up 40 percent in yen terms) thanks in good part to Seiyū's newly opened branches. But pretax profits as a percentage of sales fell from 1.31 to 1.05 percent during the same period,[74] so that the company ranked third in its field in sales but only fourteenth in profitability. Seiyū's short- and long-term borrowings as reported to the Ministry of Finance increased 187.9 percent in yen terms between 1974 and 1984, to $816.7 million (the company's liabilities for 1984 also included $172.5 million in corporate bonds).[75] Daiichi Kangyō and Mitsubishi banks headed a long list of creditors; no shareholder except Seibu Department Stores and the Tsutsumi family held more than 2.7 percent of Seiyū stock. As was common in the chain-store industry, most of the firm's land and buildings were leased, including eleven locations owned by the Seibu Railway Company as of 1990[76]—yet another link between Seiji and Yoshiaki that endures.

LOW-BUDGET BAILOUTS

To press the Seibu Retailing Group forward in the early 1980s also meant exploring new pathways, despite the fact that the conglomerate was highly leveraged and chronically starved for investment capital. If he were not already notable as a retailing innovator, Tsutsumi Seiji would probably have been honored as the sultan of corporate rescues after overcoming fire in Ikebukuro, failure in Los Angeles, and demoralization at Marubutsu (now Parco) in the 1960s and reviving Kinkei Foods, Restaurant Seibu, and Midoriya (later Seibu Credit) in the 1970s. Even more critical was the recovery of the whole group from peril in the mid-1970s, thanks mainly to turnabouts at Seiyū and Seibu Urban Development.

Still it was remarkable that the retailing group undertook further rescues after the second oil crisis in 1979. The effort was reminiscent of Tsutsumi Yasujirō's philosophy of doing "only things that other people haven't done and can't do."[77] Each instance proved to be strategic in his son's vision of a comprehensive lifestyle industry for the affluent. In one case he expanded a familiar member of the group, Asahi Helicopter (now Aero Asahi); in another he turned around a faltering fast-food chain, Yoshinoya, and added it to an existing member firm; in a third he acquired J. Osawa & Co., Ltd. (Ōsawa Shōkai), a respected trading company that was awash in debt, and added it to the group as a new core enterprise.

Asahi Helicopter was the most problematic of the three, both financially and in terms of anticipating a market that has yet to blossom. Founded in 1955 and added to the Seibu group in 1959, this company primarily hauled freight and sprayed pesticides until Tsutsumi merged it with Tōyō Airways (Tōyō Kōkū), a red-ink aerial surveyor, and renamed it Aero Asahi (Asahi Kōyō) in 1982. The firm absorbed Osaka Airways in 1985 and as a result ranked first among Japanese helicopter services with ninety-four aircraft and annual operating revenues of $68.4 million.[78] These acquisitions permitted Asahi to offer passenger as well as freight service and to undertake airborne investigations. Then a merger with Japan Industrial Airways (Nihon Sangyō Kōkū) later in 1985 increased its fixed-wing fleet to nine and took Asahi into scheduled airplane service among Hiroshima, Matsuyama, and Ōita beginning in April 1987, sixty years after Tsutsumi's father had tried regular flights between Tokyo and Karuizawa. Like the earlier venture, this one ran up huge losses ($15.6 million in the first year) and as of 1990 managed only a 37.8 percent load factor.[79]

The company also started up scheduled helicopter service among Yokohama, Haneda, and Narita in 1988, with Japan Air Lines as a partner to supply passengers; but in its first two years City Air Link averaged only thirty fares a day and a load factor of just 23.5 percent.[80] Nonetheless Asahi's overall sales reached $139.6 million and pretax profits $4.4 million in 1989 as its more established areas of business thrived along with the national economy. Then the company suffered a series of crashes in 1989–1990, including three with fatalities; a cutback in public-agency contracts for aerial surveying because of the business slowdown in late 1991 set Asahi back still further, yet its overall sales, including affiliates, stood at $203.3 million for the year ending March 1992.[81]

Far more successful than the reorientation of the helicopter firm toward passenger travel was the bailout of Yoshinoya, the beef-in-a-bowl chain, after 1980. Yoshinoya began franchising itself in 1958, then ballooned from 11 stores in 1972 to 260 in 1980, the most extensive in the fast-food business—despite its single product, marinated beef on a bed of rice, and its virtually all-male clientele. This overheated expansion led to annual sales of $96.9 million but debts of $50.7 million, so that the company filed for protection under the Corporation Reorganization Law in July 1980—the largest collapse ever in the Japanese restaurant industry.[82] Spurning an approach from Daiei, Yoshinoya's stockholders turned to Seibu for help, even though Restaurant Seibu in 1980 ranked just sixteenth in the business, with sales of $97.8 million (barely larger than Yoshinoya's).[83]

Why the retailing group decided to rescue a failing chain purveying a conventional product of little interest to women or youths is less puzzling than it may seem. "Everybody opposed me" when he first suggested taking over Yoshinoya, Tsutsumi crowed in 1987, "but now they all look as though they've forgotten their opposition."[84] He decided many of the franchises were sound and could soon prosper with better management at the center; adding nearly two hundred strong locations would greatly boost Restaurant Seibu, which lacked a high cash-flow chain like Skylark or Denny's that could help carry its smaller businesses. Executives from Restaurant Seibu cut prices, added a breakfast menu, and closed the weakest franchises. They restored flavor by getting rid of dried beef and powdered sauces. The company began operating more than 40 percent of the stores directly, adding curry and noodle outlets as well as an upscale beef-and-rice Yoshinoya in fashionable Akasaka. From their low point of $68.6 million in 1981, sales climbed to $94.5 million in 1984 (up 49 percent in yen terms), and pretax profits more than doubled, to $13.9 million.[85] By February 1987 Restaurant Seibu had fully paid off claims against Yoshinoya and taken it into the Seibu Saison Group, and the following month Yoshinoya was declared fully reorganized by the Tokyo District Court.[86]

So remarkable was the turnabout that Yoshinoya was sent to the rescue of Nihon Dunkin Donuts, an affiliate of Restaurant Seibu with 130 shops but weak sales of just $48.3 million in 1987, far behind Mr. Donut.[87] Yoshinoya merged with Dunkin Donuts—an improbable conjunction of tastes—in March 1988 to form Yoshinoya D & C, a member of the Restaurant Seibu Group. Yoshinoya's economies of scale and franchising experience helped sell sweet doughnuts as well as salty beef, and the new company's yearly sales reached $375.8 million by March 1992.[88] One of its first steps was to add pizza at Dunkin Donuts counters; another was to appeal to young women with more inviting decor and menus at Yoshinoya as well as at Tweener's Harajuku,[89] a glittering and highly successful restaurant launched in November 1989 in Tokyo's mecca for the young.

Seibu's biggest rescue of the decade involved the venerable Osawa trading house, which sank in a sea of debt in February 1984—the third-largest business failure in postwar Japan.[90] Tsutsumi's interest in Osawa was obvious: adding its prestigious international brands would make Seibu the leading importer of foreign retail merchandise, with more than a hundred lines, and taking over its strong domestic network of a thousand retailers would widen the group's wholesaling and trading capacity. The previous summer Tsutsumi had assumed control of the huge World Import Mart at Sunshine City in Ikebukuro, an enfant terrible established by Mitsukoshi and others in 1977 to promote imports through trade fairs and consulting services.[91] Adding Osawa to the Import Mart now cleared the track for Seibu "to establish a trading division based on Osawa without all the functions of a trading company"[92] and reduce the group's dependence on retailing still further.

Privately held by the Ōsawa family for most of its existence, this medium-sized trading company began in Kyoto in 1890 and quickly became a major importer of watches, jewelry, sporting goods, and other luxuries for the Japanese leisure market as well as an exporter of high-quality cameras and photographic equipment. Although it had an excellent reputation and an eminent board of directors, Osawa was not allied with a city bank and tumbled precipitately into collapse in February 1984 when it could find no lender to back its ambitious marketing plans for Mamiya cameras abroad. At this point its annual sales of roughly $325 million were overwhelmed by its accumulated debt of $431.1 million.[93] Under the court-approved plan for reorganization, Seibu assumed $324.8 million of this burden; the amount was reduced to $140.8 million in the final plan, just 22 percent of the original debt in yen terms.[94] Tsutsumi put Egashira Keisuke, a managing director of the department store and a close confidant, in charge of Osawa; an unexpected irony was that Egashira and the outgoing head of the firm, Ōsawa Zenrō, had studied together at Princeton in 1954–1955.

"Imports represent about 40 percent of our domestic sales, very high for a Japanese trading company," Egashira pointed out in 1990. Another 40 percent were foreign products manufactured under license, such as Lacoste or Trico wiper blades. "Only 15 to 20 percent of our sales are purely Japanese goods."[95] Aided by huge demand during the economic bubble of the late 1980s, Osawa's sales soared from $99.6 million in 1985 (only a third of their level before the firm failed) to $426.4 million in the year ending March 1990, a 147 percent rise in yen terms, and then climbed further to $723.0 million by March 1992. A $4 million loss in 1985 was replaced by pretax profits of $4.6 million just three years later. When subsidiaries and affiliates are included, the sales were even more remarkable: $662.1 million for the year ending March 1990 and $848.3 million a year later.[96] The revived Osawa phoenix was the most robust symbol of Tsutsumi's strategy of rescuing companies in order to capitalize on Japan's new age of personal affluence. Perhaps it is fitting that a few months before Osawa's hundredth anniversary in 1990, Tsutsumi promoted it to full status as a core member of the Seibu Saison Group.

CHAPTER EIGHT

INFORMATION FOR SALE

Nowadays "it's not enough to sell just goods," Tsutsumi Seiji said in April 1987. "This is the age of selling information and aesthetics. Goods themselves are still selling, but the way we sell them is changing completely."[1] Design, packaging, and "the creation of value" constituted "the act of product development in the broad sense."[2] By adding value through information, Tsutsumi believed, retailers now offered not just tangible artifacts (*mono*) turned out by industrial capitalism but also intangible experiences (*koto*) generated by postindustrial "information capitalism."[3] Arguing that the department store "must change its nature into a place to present values and information," he concluded that "information sells. Because information moves, goods move. The sale of goods is the result, not the objective . . . The concept of consumption is changing. The relationship of goods and information has changed. Originally after goods sold, services and information were tacked on. Now . . . goods sell, gold sells, tickets sell, hotel rooms and services sell"[4] all at the same time—what the former Ministry of International Trade and Industry leader Sakaiya Taichi called "the economics of conceptual values" rather than material wealth.[5]

Information became both gnomon and grail for the Seibu Saison Group in the mid-1980s, and even today it is the main way the group distinguishes itself from other retailing conglomerates. By information Tsutsumi meant both the addition of value to products and information for individual consumption: financial data, real-estate listings, travel advice, insurance, tickets for events, the production of film and the live arts, the distribution of electronic media, and many other forms of information as a market commodity. As Tessa Morris-Suzuki has pointed out, the production of innovation has employed more workers in Japan than manufacturing ever since 1978.[6] Although Tsutsumi tried to develop this as a retail market faster and more assiduously than the competition, there is no known link between him and the Japanese government's program of nurturing an "information society" after the 1973 oil shock. Instead he recognized its significance early on and took steps to benefit from it commercially. By the late 1980s somewhere between 10 and 20 percent of sales at the Seibu citadel in Ikebukuro derived from information and services,[7] even though nationally they comprised just 1 percent of department-store sales in the year ending March 1990.[8]

RETAILING IN THE LATER 1980S

Meeting secretly at New York's Plaza Hotel in September 1985, high financial bureaucrats from five rich nations—including both Germany and Japan—undertook to correct imbalances in world trade by strengthening the mark and the yen. This plan succeeded but also failed: within three years the Japanese currency rose from ¥245 to the dollar to ¥123, yet Japan started the 1990s with a current-account balance slightly greater than the level that helped trigger the Plaza accord.[9] The stronger yen made Japanese exports more costly, stimulating further efficiencies in production; it also sliced the cost of imported energy, raw materials, and manufactured goods almost in half. The Japanese government, pressed by the United States to increase domestic demand, committed large amounts to public works and procurement; and private investors poured funds into housing, equipment, and urban development. This restructuring blurred the traditional boundaries between industries, bringing about multi-industrial clusters and a greater focus on domestically led growth. As a result, after a slight slowdown in 1986 attributable to yen revaluation, the Japanese economy went on a spectacular roll for the next five years. Greatly hastening this restructuring and prosperity were advances in electronics and information, such as point-of-sale and value-added networks, on-line systems, intelligent buildings, and more sophisticated medical equipment[10] – information capitalism in both producer and consumer goods.

Inviting as it may be to criticize this bubble economy for its soaring land prices, inflated stock values, and greedy financial scandals, the period through late 1991 was undeniably one of great consolidation and reorientation of domestically focused industries, leading to sound, sustained expansion. The Japanese GNP grew in real terms at an average annual rate of 4.7 percent during the five years ending March 1991, faster than that of any other mature industrial country; for 1990 the figure was a remarkable 5.2 percent; and even for the year ending March 1992 it was 4.4 percent.[11] Much of the new wealth ended up in workers' pockets: the ratio of living expenses to net income for Japanese households fell as fast during the five years starting with 1985 as it had during the previous fifteen;[12] and the average increase in net household income, after inflation, was more than 2.2 percent a year during the latter half of the 1980s.[13] While retail prices were rising only 2 percent a year, families increased their real consumer spending by an average of 3.8 percent annually during the last half of the decade.[14] Then household spending kept right on rising through the year ending March 1992, fueled particularly by greater earnings by women.[15]

Retailers of all sorts smiled amid this vigorous prosperity, especially department stores and large superstore chains. By the early 1980s the latter reported about twice the sales volume of the former; together they commanded about a quarter of the total retail market in Japan, a proportion unchanged for the next decade. Retailing as a whole was sluggish during 1983–1985 but then improved to an average yearly increase of 4.6 percent during the rest of the decade.[16] By March 1990 retail trade in Japan was estimated to generate between $623 and $906 billion in annual business, depending on which transactions were counted.[17] Whereas superstores had outstripped department stores in the early 1980s, the Ministry of International Trade and Industry calculated that department-store sales grew faster at the end of the decade (a nominal 7.2 percent, versus 5.0 percent for superstores during April 1986–March 1990)[18] because customers preferred the service, selection, and prestige of department stores in an age of great affluence. Gross revenues at seventy-seven leading department-store companies grew even faster: 7.8 percent in 1988 and 9.8 percent in fiscal 1989, ending March 1990.[19] The twenty-six department-store buildings in Tokyo registered a further jump of 7.9 percent in sales during calendar 1990, by which time they accounted for nearly 30 percent of department-store sales countrywide (the Tokyo metropolitan area as a whole represented 47.3 percent of the national total). Only with the economic slump of 1992 did revenues ease: sales at the nation's largest department stores fell 5.7 percent that year, the first annual decline since 1965,[20] while no-frills discount stores were mushrooming throughout the country.

Bankers believe the greatest momentum behind the consumption boom of 1986–1991 came from yen appreciation because of the flood of inexpensive imports it set loose, especially from newly industrializing economies in East and Southeast Asia. The stronger yen also invited Japanese manufacturers to refocus on domestic markets. Department stores outpaced the superstore chains in bringing many of these products to market: whereas the ratio of food, clothing, and all other items sold in superstores hardly varied during 1987–1990, the share of food and clothing sales at major department stores fell more than 4 percent during the same period. The fastest growth, according to the Japan Department Store Association, occurred in furniture, household items, and miscellany.[21] Upsizing (*ōgataka*) was especially common: big-screen televisions, large refrigerators, automatic washers, better plumbing, more substantial furniture, and videocassette recorders all sold very well at department stores, which also profited when their best clients visited to buy luxury foreign cars, jewelry, and information services relating to art objects, fitness, real estate, overseas vacations, and even matchmaking agencies. To gild their edifices still further, several cash-rich retailers invested in American partners at the end of the decade: Jusco in Talbot's, Mitsukoshi in Tiffany and Company, Tōbu in Gump's, and Tōkyū in a joint venture with Bloomingdale's and other partners to open a branch of the New York company in 1995 at Makuhari,[22] the Hoboken or Secacus of Tokyo.

Why the high-image department stores outperformed the superstores in the late 1980s may be a matter of psyche as much as statistics. Nakauchi Isao, the Daiei superstore magnate who was Japan's closest analogue to Sam Walton, readily conceded in 1986 that "real affluence is not simply an imitation of other people's lifestyles, but instead is the freedom to develop one's individuality and find the lifestyle appropriate to oneself. People have begun to realize that real affluence lies in buying only what is necessary and rejecting purchases that are inconsistent with personal values."[23] To find a good match with those values, consumers now sought items of high quality and style that incorporated greater information costs in planning and design, according to the dean of Japan's information society, Hayashi Yūjirō of Tokyo Institute of Technology.[24] Quality and creativity gave department stores the edge, in Tsutsumi Seiji's view: "Today's consumers are much more quality minded,"[25] he told a reporter in 1988; two years later he wrote that "one of our aims has been to inspire consumers and give them the means to be creative on their own. Until now the Japanese market has merely expanded; now the creative route is one which must be further developed"[26]—a frank recognition that without creativity, Seibu would soon be just another department store.

Tsutsumi redefined the Seibu Saison Group's mission in 1984 in terms of lifestyle, culture, and information. He posited that people were looking beyond food, clothing, and housing to the rhyming pairs *yū, kyū, chi, bi:* recreation, leisure, knowledge, and beauty.[27] His fascination with information services perplexed the same Seibu oldtimers he had shocked with his earlier dictum that "the era of the department store is over," but his employees usually admitted that he had clairvoyant powers about consumer tastes. Having correctly anticipated the boom in kimono sales that began in 1986 and accurately predicted the fad for hot-spring bathing that swept the New Breed at the end of the decade, Tsutsumi stocked the store accordingly—even though his senior managers muttered in disbelief that "the chairman has begun to have the tastes of an old man."[28]

By 1990 the entire Saison Group was committed to selling both goods and information to consumers who sought "new amenities" that pampered the self.[29] Mizuno Seiichi, who became president of the Seibu Department Stores that year, noted "the gradual shift in our values from the efficiency orientation typified by business to desires for personal enrichment and comfort." Seibu's aim, he said, was to achieve "lifestyle marketing": "We are dedicated to creating greater value in our products and information services"[30]—the group's quest from the moment it opened its "information lifestyle building" near Ginza in October 1984, the newest branch of the Seibu department store.

HIGH-INFORMATION DEPARTMENT STORES

The central avenue of Tokyo's Ginza district has been the most chic shopping promenade in Japan for a century. The name Ginza carries such cachet that nearly five hundred streets lined with shops and restaurants from Hokkaido to Okinawa have renamed themselves after the Tokyo original. Every retailer in the land dreams of opening a branch in Ginza for prestige, if not necessarily profit, inasmuch as the area ranks only third in sales revenues behind Shinjuku and Ikebukuro. When Seibu Department Stores opened its Yūrakuchō branch next to the Ginza subway station in 1984 (see Figure 9), the arrival of this upstart jolted the $2.57 billion Ginza retail market, about $840 million of which belonged to five well-entrenched department stores that alternately scorned and feared the newcomer from humdrum Ikebukuro.[31]

The Yūrakuchō Seibu store occupied eight floors and the basement in the north half of the striking fourteen-story Mullion Building, newly built in emerald glass and ivory trim on the site of the former Nichigeki Theater and Asahi newspaper offices at the Sukiyabashi intersection. Although Seibu shared the structure with a conventional department store, a bank, a gallery and event hall, and five movie theaters, many people called the graceful 78,631-square-meter building "Seibu at Ginza," heedless of the successful campaign by worried local merchants that forced the company to identify the new branch by its postal address (Yūrakuchō) rather than as Ginza. The advent of a gleaming, innovative Seibu store on an east-west thoroughfare three hundred meters from the main intersection of Ginza redirected the pedestrian flow from the north-south central street without harm to preexisting shops[32]—as though a new emporium at 42nd Street and Lexington Avenue rerouted Manhattan shoppers without hurting Fifth Avenue because of the great rush of newcomers flooding the whole area.

The Yūrakuchō Seibu, Tsutsumi announced, was to be "a theater of the mind" that offered the future now: information and new media as well as merchandise that was fresh in design, materials, and display. At 12,900 square meters, the branch was the smallest of the three department stores that opened at Sukiyabashi that year, and the second smallest of the eight in the entire Ginza area; consequently it had to

FIGURE 9. Mullion Building shortly after the Seibu department store opened at Yūrakuchō in 1984. (Saison Group)

make an impact through quality rather scale. Uchimura Shun'ichirō, the general manager, jumbled the usual floor plan and saw to it that 70 percent of the items for sale were original to Seibu. He introduced computers, holography, 177 closed-circuit television monitors for shoppers, and point-of-sale accounting and schemed to make the narrow interior an interesting place to browse, with mini-displays and unexpected visual effects to relieve the tedium of shopping. The upper floors had counters offering insurance, real estate, concert tickets, precious metals, and soon enough securities, in the hope that information and services might eventually claim half the store's sales[33]—a turnabout from the era when service at a Japanese department store was always free.

"We want the Yūrakuchō store to be used as the show window and keystone of the group," Tsutsumi declared the day the Mullion Building opened. "I think of it as techno-minded, contemporary-minded, post–department-store theater of the mind."[34] Such rhetoric baffled his less adventuresome employees and brought scorn from his critics, who dismissed the venture as the "7-Eleven of Ginza," selling convenience.[35] His goal was to make Seibu exciting and attract more young people to Ginza (just 27 percent of customers in the area were under age twenty-five in 1984, versus 64 percent in Aoyama and Harajuku) for shopping as well as for movies in nearby Hibiya. By 1986 200,000 customers a day were visiting Japan's largest retail edifice, prompting Edward Seidensticker to conclude that Mullion "more than any other force has brought a rejuvenation of Ginza"[36] by luring back the young.

What they discovered at Seibu were private labels like U 251 (for Yūrakuchō 2-5-1, the store's address), P & P, or The Market, each of them with a fashion sense to match the most stunning designer and character brands sold elsewhere. The Yūrakuchō branch's relatively small size intensified its exclusiveness and drove demand higher, the more so because 90 percent of its merchandise could be found at no other Seibu outlet. Yūrakuchō carried no national clothing lines at all; the big apparel makers like Renown, Wacoal, Kashiyama, and San'yō Shōkai were behind the times and held little appeal to the New Breed. "Famous brands are still popular in regional stores," Tsutsumi told *Asahi* in July 1988, "but in the cities, the 'brand myth' is over. Above all, the product must suit the individual's taste and style."[37] The company emulated small but profitable designer lines like Comme des Garçons and Nicole; it found that fashion shows plus ads in magazines such as *Nonno* and *An'an* assured publicity among the niche it sought. The private labels sold mainly at Yūrakuchō accounted for 2.2 percent of Seibu Department Stores' sales in 1987; house brands of all kinds developed by Seibu, including foreign lines, represented 14 percent of the company's gross that year.[38]

The first year's results at Yūrakuchō disappointed Tsutsumi not because of their volume ($95.8 million, 4 percent above target) but because information and services accounted for only 12 percent of the total.[39] The financial press estimated that the break-even point for the store in 1985 was $15–30 million higher than sales.[40] Both costs and revenues rose sharply after that,[41] but evidently the company was willing to operate this branch at a loss because of the discussion it generated and the information beachhead it was gradually solidifying. In 1987 the store shifted direction somewhat when it added a 2,747-square-meter annex featuring interiors, fine jewelry, elegant Japanese crafts, and a basement stocked with a 2,100-bottle wine cellar and a fine selection of gourmet fish—all of it intended for the middle-aged New Rich who sprouted in the economic boom of the later 1980s.

General Manager Uchimura noted that "from now on the department store has to fulfill dreams. It's a space where customers can purchase dreams when they want to create new lifestyles."[42] Those new-found parvenu lifestyles included luxury vacations at Club Med sites and the costly accoutrements of the arriviste homestead for which Seibu had a particular marketing flair. Evidently the investment paid off, since the company refurbished the entire Yūrakuchō store in 1990 to emphasize still more furnishings as well as imported lines.[43] Even so, the branch still has not reached Tsutsumi's goal of earning 50 percent of its revenues from information and services. Seibu's appearance in Ginza stimulated waves of redecoration by its rivals and reams of reportage about Tsutsumi as "the savior of Ginza"[44] with "the capacity to do wild things."[45] Yet no department-store building in the district ranked higher than twenty-ninth nationally in sales (Matsuya) as of March 1990,[46] whereas numbers two and three (Mitsukoshi and Takashimaya) were less than two kilometers to the north, and number one (Seibu at Ikebukuro) was a nineteen-minute subway ride away.

With the panache typical of his trade, the new president of Seibu Department Stores, Yamazaki Mitsuo, declared 1984 to be "year one of our metamorphosis from a traditional department store"[47] via a new round of expansion, mainly high-information stores in the Yūrakuchō pattern. One was a 17,000-square-meter branch unveiled at Tsukuba in March 1985 to coincide with an international science and technology exposition. Tsutsumi branded this latest outlet a "lifestyle-information building harmonizing people and science"[48] through a storewide data network for shoppers to direct them to goods and services, videotex, 120 television monitors for advertisements, environmental-management controls, and an automated flow-of-goods system as well as service counters for insurance, travel, real estate, and personal finance. By one estimate about $8 million of the $37.7 million the company spent on this ultra-smart building went to information and mechatronic systems,[49] which the retailing groups developed jointly with Fujitsū, Mitsubishi Electric, Nissan, Japan IBM, and a number of other firms.

The Tsukuba Seibu was transparently a media ploy, with miniature remote-control forklifts, small carts to retrieve merchandise, and robots to carry the customer's purchases to the exit—and win attention from the press. Certain homes in the Tsukuba area were linked to the new store by cable television, forming a small shopping channel that was Japan's first. Even though the building's automation cut personnel costs, the huge start-up expenditures ruled out any hope of breaking even for the rest of the 1980s. Nonetheless sales grew by nearly 20 percent per annum from their first-year level of $46 million,[50] and yet Tsutsumi was far from pleased because Yasumori Ken, the general manager, had used mechatronics (e.g., computer-operated retrieval from storerooms) to keep costs down but otherwise not explored its possibilities for merchandising.[51] As at Yūrakuchō, the impression was strong that Tsutsumi failed to make his goals clear to his subalterns for the high-information, high-technology outlets they were asked to staff.

An even costlier investment opened in 1985 when the newly renamed Seibu Saison Group inaugurated its first major shopping center, on a 60,000-square-meter site at Tsukaguchi in the western suburbs of Osaka. This $81.6 million project, known as Tsukashin, contained a medium-sized Seibu, 263 specialty shops, and such come-ons as a wedding chapel, multipurpose hall for performances, riverside park with ducks and playgrounds, and more than 20,000 trees and shrubs to landscape the site (formerly a Gunze underwear factory). Perhaps the greatest amenity was that no bicycles were allowed inside the complex, only in underground storage lots.

Tsutsumi labeled the project an experiment in "building a shopping district for spending time,"[52] in frank emulation of suburban malls across the Pacific. Travel advice, insurance information, financial consulting, and other services were well represented in the anchor store, so that Tsukashin attempted to marry the Seibu Saison Group's campaign to sell information with a new focus on creating "a lifestyle amusement park."[53] Arai Minoru, president of Seibu Urban Development and head of the construction phase, noted in 1986 that "it is not a fortress shopping center. We want to make it a 'lifestyle playground' where anyone can enter at any time."[54] Evidently the strategy worked: Seibu found that three-quarters of the visitors to Tsukashin stayed two hours or longer.[55] Dining out there was especially popular.

The new center drew crowds at first—11.4 million persons in the first year, 8.6 million in the second[56]—from its market area of 2 million, about 40 percent of whom came by car. The company said sales in the first year totaled $174 million, of which the department store inside the complex took in $116 million, 7.9 percent above projections.[57] In the second year sales rose 8.8 percent, including a jump of 14.8 percent at Seibu; but Takatsu Yutaka, general manager of the center, told reporters in 1987 that he was frustrated by Tsukashin's location far from mass transit and admitted it was "probably unreasonable" to expect to attain the initial goal of breaking even by 1990 and paying off the project's debt by 1992.[58] In fact sales at the Seibu branch barely increased at all between 1986 and 1989,[59] yet the company higher-ups were naturally optimistic amid the great publicity Tsukashin generated. Yamazaki Mitsuo, president of the Seibu Department Stores, brushed aside queries with "Tsukashin is no problem—it is very satisfactory."[60]

Yūrakuchō, Tsukuba, and Tsukashin were the most expensive of the Seibu Department Store's projects in the mid-1980s, the three main gemstones of a showy expansion program that plunged the company into an estimated $418.4 million of additional debt[61] but carried great public-relations value. Tsukashin was a tonic to the group's struggle to broaden its operations in the Kansai suburbs and emboldened Tsutsumi to develop the Plenty Mall in western Kobe, opened in late 1989, and the Kobe Harborland Center in 1992. In the Tokyo area the department store added medium-sized branches in suburban Tokorozawa (1986) and industrial Kawasaki (1988), the latter a part of the city's effort to revive its commercial district even though Tokyo's large department stores were only twenty minutes distant and Yokohama's only ten. Perhaps the 22,500-square-meter Kawasaki Seibu was Tsutsumi's David-like tweaking of Sogō, which had opened a Goliath of a store in Yokohama three years before. At 68,413 square meters, it nosed out the Ikebukuro Seibu to become the largest department-store building in sales area in the country, until the revamped Tōbu in Ikebukuro surpassed both in 1992 at 83,000 square meters.[62]

CORRALLING THE NEW BREED

Few governments anywhere track the habits of their young people more breathlessly than the Tokyo metropolitan authorities, who plot a good deal of the city's future based on the latest developments among its youths. A clear indicator that big changes were afoot was the 44 percent rise between 1976 and 1988 in the number of Tokyo residents ages fifteen to twenty-nine whom city poll takers classified as either easygoing or else discontented yet politically inert—two of the most common traits of the New Breed. By 1988 just a fourth of the young women and men in the sample accepted the conventional values of the Japanese social system; the rest seemed inclined to follow their own.[63] Tsutsumi Seiji apparently agreed with this appraisal when he told a reporter in 1990 that "youth would like to rebel against their fathers, or any other figure. They want to say, 'I'm different,' but not fight or overcome or pull their fathers down."[64] Many of the New Breed chose to do so through fashion rather than the factiousness of their predecessors.

In 1988 the Dentsū advertising firm branded high-school-age youths in the Tokyo area as Ranchōzoku, after Luanniao, a mythical Chinese bird symbolizing narcissism. More than 60 percent of the males and 83 percent of the females surveyed by Dentsū agreed that "fashion is an important factor in leading an enjoyable life." The average amount of spending money at their disposal was $125 per month.[65] This wherewithal, and the propensity to part with it, gave rise to the so-called Marui phenomenon of the 1980s. Aoi Tadao, who succeeded his father Chūji as president of Marui monthly payment chain in 1975, transformed it during the next decade into Tokyo's most powerful magnet for stylish young people, especially those in their teens and twenties on middle-class budgets.

Aoi rebuilt the company's Shinjuku redoubt into a series of functional buildings such as "fashion," "men's," and "sports," diverting customers over age thirty to the firm's suburban branches. By the mid-1980s nearly 80 percent of youths in Tokyo carried Marui's Red Card, which shoppers used for almost two-thirds of their purchases there.[66] A gift from Marui enjoyed special favor among the young unmatched by any other department store. Much of the allure came from Aoi's relentless marketing of designer and character brands at prices young people could manage. Top lines such as Kenzo, Hanae Mori, or Kansai Yamamoto were rarely within reach, but character labels—in which several designers cooperated to establish an identifiable style, like Nicole or the Bigi Group—found their exact marketing niches among the hundreds of thousands of young suburban shoppers who flocked into the city's main commercial districts on weekends. At the height of the designer and character boom in the mid-1980s, Marui may have claimed as much as half the market for these brands, and they still accounted for a respectable part of the company's $3.94 billion sales for the year ending January 1990.[67]

Seibu Department Stores dealt with Marui's succès fou by moving beyond specialty products and services to concept stores that it called "lifestyle houses": "information outlets that help people choose their lifestyles."[68] The company focused on upscale Shibuya, where well-to-do young clients with a high fashion sense headed for Seibu's sleek new Seed building, opened in March 1986 on Park Avenue, for designer and character brands with more flair and steeper prices than most at Marui. Mizuno Seiichi, then general manager of the Seibu branch at Shibuya, spearheaded the idea of a polished yet hip environment where the firm could showcase young designers and offer character brands of its own. This windowless building, faced in striking black and gray, employed nearly two dozen house designers and also offered clothing and accessory lines created by outsiders.

The 3,600-square-meter structure became a proving ground for fashions developed by the Seibu Department Stores that could be marketed in all its outlets. Kikuchi Takeo, Yokomori Minako, Hosokawa Noboru, and more recently Shiozawa Naoki were some of Seed's most outstanding designers for an audience that averaged 23.9 years old for women and 25.7 for men.[69] The new building was an inventive competitor to nearby Parco, which by now drew such crowds that its fashion edge was somewhat dulled. As an antenna shop, Seed did not have to be an instant commercial success, but it provided great publicity for new Seibu products by showcasing them for the hundreds of thousands of young shoppers who passed its front door each day en route to Marui and Parco. Thus Seed's location allowed for ideal niche marketing at virtually zero cost.[70]

Even more successful, if less trendsetting, was Mizuno's coup de main against Tōkyū Hands, the do-it-yourself center near Parco that first touched off the explosion of Sunday carpentry in Japan in 1978. Mizuno and the department store launched another lifestyle house next door to Seed in October 1987 under the faintly stealthy name of LoFt,[71] inspired by SoHo garrets, that was intended for the artist in each of us as well as the handyperson we sometimes have to be. The deliberately cluttered multilevel interior created the ambience of a friendly studio by reducing materials to a human (and carryable) scale while offering a wider array of lumber, hardware, colored drawing paper, brushes and pigments, and decorative household gadgetry than any other in-city store in Japan. Tōkyū Hands had been to youthful creativity in the late 1970s what Marui became to young fashions in the mid-1980s; but whereas Seed took up the high end of the clothing market after 1986 and in no way challenged Marui's broad-based appeal, LoFt instantly outflanked Tōkyū Hands to become young people's favorite locale for things they could touch, manipulate, and use to express themselves.

Another LoFt followed in April 1990 at Umeda in Osaka; a third opened in November of that year on the uppermost floors of the Ikebukuro department store. Mizuno pointed out in 1991 that "compared with our youth-oriented LoFt in Shibuya, the LoFt in Ikebukuro reaches a more general market."[72] The company predicted that sales at this newest LoFt would reach a very health $268 million in its first year, 9 percent of the Ikebukuro building's overall intake of $2.98 billion in the year ending March 1990.[73]

Saison's third concept house for the young was a record, tape, and video building called Wave, opened in November 1983 in the Roppongi entertainment district of Tokyo. Tsutsumi advertised Wave as a "sound-and-image information-transmission base," implying electronic pulses but also trends or waves of fashion.[74] The 6,200-square-meter store included Ciné Vivant, which was a mini-theater for art films, and a half-dozen floors of recordings, videos, listening rooms, and studios for composing and performing. Wave patronized avant-garde music at various levels of taste but mainly targeted those among the New Breed who knew contemporary music ranging from jazz and soul to the more enduring semipopular vocalists. Generally only mass-market pops (*kayōkyoku*) by Japanese singers sell really well; Wave carried little such music and stocked mainly slow-moving foreign recordings. Nonetheless the group installed new Waves in other sections of the city during the late 1980s. Like Yūrakuchō, Tsukuba, and Seed, Wave in its first years ran in the red but provided the retailing group much attention and set a high profile among knowledgeable music lovers unsurpassed by any other outlet in Japan. Marui's answer came in September 1990 when it opened a large music and video shop called Megastore in the basement of its Shinjuku fashion building, in partnership with the Virgin Group of England, with plenty of popular recordings for its huge middle-income clientele.[75]

Saison's leaders profess their satisfaction with Seed, Wave, and especially the very profitable LoFt; yet despite Tsutsumi's long record of automation and his relentless effort to market information, the group has been surprisingly cautious about investing in new media. The Seibu Information Center Company, Ltd. (Seibu Jōhō Sentā) was formed in 1981 by combining units within the retailing group to promote a value-added network for the core companies and operate data services for Seibu Credit and other Seibu retail outlets.[76] In 1986 Saison merged two advertising agencies to create I & S, now Japan's sixth largest, to promote the group's five thousand retail locations.[77] Tsutsumi's companies have experimented with videotex and invested in FM Japan, a radio station also known as J-Wave that is aimed at well-heeled listeners ages eighteen to thirty in the Tokyo area. But apart from FM, a small stake in ESPN-Japan, and a temporary joint venture with Time Books, the group has very limited ties with the media. "Cable television is not profitable in Japan because we already have pay TV–NHK," a top Saison executive said in 1986;[78] and the situation has begun to change only since deregulation of commercial broadcasting has taken effect in the mid-1990s. Mizuno disclosed in

1991 that Tsutsumi would form a marketing and communications group within Saison to coordinate broadcasting, publications, and information services;[79] but clearly Tsutsumi has been more interested in turning information into a commodity accessible to everyone, by circulating it as widely as possible to consumers for a fee, than in sinking money into new media themselves.[80]

IS SEIBU NUMBER ONE?

"The term Seibu Retailing Group no longer expresses the real substance of our group,"[81] Tsutsumi Seiji said in 1985 when he announced its new name, Seibu Saison Group. Now that the enterprise had diversified beyond selling goods into "creating lifestyles," it also began renaming many of its member companies and adding new core firms to the group. Seibu Chemical Industries moved further into foodstuffs and became Asahi Industries in 1985; Seibu Urban Development turned into the Seiyō Corporation the following year; Seibu Credit was renamed Credit Saison in 1989, the same year Restaurant Seibu became Seiyō Food Systems; and Seibu Allstate Life changed to Saison Life in 1990.

FamilyMart and Parco gained the status of core companies when they were first listed on the Tokyo Stock Exchange in 1987. They were joined by Osawa and the newly acquired Inter-Continental Hotels two years later, bringing the number of core enterprises to twelve.[82] Then in 1990 the much-transformed conglomerate shed "Seibu" to become simply the Saison Group. Most experts think Tsutsumi restyled his companies to dissociate himself further from his brother Yoshiaki; but the kingpin among Seiji's companies, the department store, would suffer from dropping "Seibu" and retains the name to this day.

"Yūrakuchō for information, Shibuya for fashion, Ikebukuro for profit"[83] was how the industry regarded Seibu Department Stores in the late 1980s, even as the company thrashed through several reorganizations to position itself for better earnings in the 1990s. Tsutsumi had Issey Miyake come up with new uniforms for female employees, taught clerks to engage customers in conversation side by side (not confronting them across a counter), and declared a campaign in 1986 to improve profits for the company and the group through further diversification. A sign of the convolution in running this vast company is that it took three years to establish a Profit Management Committee and begin to unsnarl the tangles in clothing inventories.[84] In the spring of 1989 the department store and its subsidiaries restructured themselves into seven operating divisions, only to be "deconstructed" and then recast in March 1990 when Mizuno succeeded Yamazaki as president.[85]

One outcome from the makeovers was a strong and evidently very profitable[86] trading division that sold both company-developed products and imported designs manufactured under license by Seibu to other retailers around the country. Separately the firm promoted non-store sales of precious metals, medical equipment, care for the elderly, and a range of environmental services related to recycling. Direct marketing by catalogue, telemarketing, and cable television (in Tsukuba) started up, including the distribution of Amnesty International brands to raise funds, starting in 1991.[87] Thanks to strong sales by the trading division, by LoFt and Seibu's book and art shops, and by its car dealerships, the Seibu Department Stores Group began the new decade earning nearly one-third of its revenues from divisions and subsidiaries other than the department-store division itself.[88] In March 1990 the highly successful entertainment, trading, and automotive divisions were transferred to the Seiyū superstores, but even so, Seibu now constituted much more than just its best-known stores in Yūrakuchō, Shibuya, and Ikebukuro.

All its branches gradually added counters in the late 1980s with insurance, credit, travel, real-estate, and investment counseling in a cluster known as Saison Square. Seibu also sought the patronage of the New Rich through Osawa's luxury imports, the interiors annex at Yūrakuchō, and its subsidiary Pisa, which since 1964 has purveyed antiques, art objects, and expensive fashion items to the recently gentrified. The New Rich of the late 1980s were families with more than ¥100 million (about $775,000) in assets, a surprising 1.8 million households in a country long known for its flat income pyramid.[89] Many of them consumed even more readily than the younger and less flush New Breed, but both flouted middle-class frugality as well as aristocratic restraint.

After years of catering to a small market segment from a single shop in Shiba, Pisa began cultivating the new wealth at branch stores in Yūrakuchō, Osaka, Fukuoka, and Sapporo, bringing in annual revenues of nearly $150 million.[90] A sign of how closely these clienteles converged was the 1990 merger of Pisa, Wave, and Reborn Sports Systems, so that those with time and money could work out at Reborn fitness centers, play golf at U-raku resorts, and find quality music and videos at Wave to enjoy in their Pisa-decorated homes. Even with the economic slowdown of the early 1990s, Saison expects a strong market for the combined amenities this subsidiary offers, inasmuch as sales leaped to $615.6 million for the year ending March 1992.[91]

The department store also exploited the graying of Japanese society by promoting new values and enriched lifestyles for those seniors who could afford travel, leisure, or simply more comfortable homes. Another cohort in the procession of "new" generations, Mizuno noted in 1991, was the New Middle Age: "Heretofore the department store's sales have been 30–40 percent to the young market and 60–70 percent to the adult market. But our image has been the reverse: mainly the younger market. Nowadays, as the baby boomers get older, we are targeting them as the New Middle Age. The difference is that, unlike middle-aged people in the past, the New Middle Age group is very conscious of fashion. This is how we are developing the mature market."[92]

Seibu closed the generational circle by also redoubling its appeal in the well-to-do children's market when it cut the ribbon in September 1990 on Kids' Farm, a 4,125-square-meter bedlam of euphoric youngsters and beaming adults on the seventh floor of its Ikebukuro store. This juvenile utopia was far more than an upscale toy store: it carried designer fashions for tots, character clothing for juveniles, and cassette players and televisions intended for children, including a line called My First Sony. Mizuno said in 1991 that Kids' Farm was really for parents,[93] but one presumes he meant grandparents, too. The young mothers who came to the store belonged to the so-called An-Non-zoku generation of fashionable youths from the 1970s (named for two fashion magazines) and now wanted stylish clothing for their offspring—but Seibu also welcomed grandparents with fat wallets who by custom provided the thousand-dollar gold-brocade kimonos that small children wore for holiday shrine visits. As Japan's birth rate dipped to just 1.5 per woman in the early 1990s, the combination of fewer children, a wealthy economy, and grandparents who lived longer than ever before led to great indulgence of the young—a $21 billion annual market in which Kids' Farm was the single most lucrative outpost. Spending on children continued to rise in 1993, even though department-store sales as a whole fell 6.6 percent in August of that year compared with August 1992.[94]

These tactics to reach across the generations were captured in Saison's new corporate identity for the 1990s, "I want to gaze softly." The department store pursued the theme with an ad showing a mother dalmatian and four nursing pups, with the legend "warm to the touch." Warm perhaps, but not soft: Mizuno announced plans to expand the number of department-store branches from thirty to forty by 1995 (including tie-ups with regional retailers), and Seibu pressed ceaselessly forward, in spite of great local opposition, with a large shopping center on a 113,000-square-meter parcel at Shin Yurigaoka in Kawasaki, ready in 1993.[95] Mizuno predicted in 1990 that the key marketing angles of the decade would be individuality, popular fads, and the environment, and he expected that sales of fashions would grow more slowly than other items.[96] If he proved to be correct, Seibu Department Stores could expect to remain number one in the business—at least by certain criteria.

The most conventional criterion is sales, in which the Ikebukuro store became the single most lucrative retail building in the country in 1982. By March 1990 it led second-place Mitsukoshi at Nihonbashi, $2.98 billion to $2.51 billion.[97] Seibu publicists report that the Ikebukuro headquarters averages 300,000 customers each day and more on Sundays.[98] The department-store company as a whole overtook Mitsukoshi in the spring of 1988 to become the national sales leader, at $4.47 billion for the year ending in March. The firm absorbed its Kansai affiliate in 1989, adding another $1 billion to its gross, and by March 1990 it had achieved annual sales of $7.21 billion—a remarkable growth of 103.6 percent in yen terms since March 1985. Sales climbed still further, to more than $8.2 billion, in the year ending March 1992.[99]

Seibu by 1990 led all its rivals except Marui in the number of stores it owned (eighteen, compared with Marui's thirty-three). By comparison, at this point Bloomingdale's had seventeen stores in the United States and yearly sales of $1.26 billion; the figure for the Saks Fifth Avenue Company was $1.24 billion.[100] The entire Seibu department-store group, including the entertainment, trading, and automotive divisions that were later transferred to Seiyū, took in $11.27 billion during the year ending March 1990[101]—so that Seibu ranked first in sales among single buildings, department-store companies, and department-store enterprise groups.

Because assets are less useful for measuring a company's standing in retailing than in manufacturing or finance, the other chief index for evaluating Seibu, in addition to sales, is profitability. As a privately held business, Seibu does not publish a complete financial statement, but it is estimated that construction of new branches and shopping centers drove up the department-store company's borrowings from $1.26 billion in 1986 to $2.29 billion in 1990, a rise of 56.2 percent in yen terms.[102] The great nonoperating losses from debt service kept pretax profits very low (just $22.8 million for the year ending March 1989),[103] far behind first-place Daimaru and the other Big Six firms.[104] Retailers also evaluate the health of their industry by gross sales area (Seibu was first among department-store companies in 1990, at 459,794 square meters), number of employees (Seibu also led, with 20,625),[105] sales per employee (very low, trailing all the top competitors), and sales per square meter (behind all except Marui, although the crowded Ikebukuro store ranked second among individual department-store buildings, after Takashimaya at Nihonbashi).[106]

Sales alone do no make a department-store company best in its field—or else Sears, with retail revenues of just under $32 billion in 1990, would enjoy top prestige in the United States.[107] This fact led Seibu's historians to admit, even after overtaking Mitsukoshi in 1988, that "in profitability and corporate image . . . it cannot be said that the company was number one in the industry."[108] If Seibu Department Stores outdid its rivals in the late 1980s qualitatively, it did so through inventiveness, sensitivity to young people, speedy adjustment to plush times, and the company's knack for identifying new market segments from spoiled children to self-indulgent seniors. Tsutsumi generated an aura of dynamism and a sense of excitement across the generations in his drive to convert Seibu into a business that helped customers create lifestyles—a theme Prime Minister Miyazawa picked up in his 1992 campaign to turn Japan into a "lifestyle superpower."[109]

SEIYŪ AND PARCO BRANCH OUT

Both Seiyū and Parco in the early 1980s were successful companies with positive images and strong cash flows, but each faced powerful competition and could no longer afford to serve up more of the same if it was to retain its vitality and establish momentum for the 1990s. Having earned a solid reputation for quality and convenience, the superstore company diversified into entertainment, media, finance, and direct marketing as well as shopping-center management during the latter half of the 1980s; at the same time Parco expanded into hotels, restaurants, health and beauty salons, and suburban commercial development. Saison's goal for Parco might equally have been said of Seiyū by 1990: "to plan a highly fashionable urban lifestyle by creating an attractive environment and the dissemination of a high level of ultramodern information."[110] What did this actually mean?

Seiyū decided in 1985 to emphasize higher profits and an image as the store that is "now." Inventories were chopped back, branches were told to update their product mixes by learning from one another which items sold well, and point-of-sale accounting was hastened. Tsutsumi brought in Ueda Hiroshi from Yamato Transport Company to become Seiyū's president; Ueda promoted far more house brands than any other superstore and imposed company-wide automation using an American system, Tandem, that cost the firm at least $93 million.[111] For its thirtieth anniversary in 1993, Seiyū announced a follow-up program touting the Saison Group's ritualized aim of creating a "comprehensive lifestyle industry."[112]

Tsutsumi and Ueda recognized that much more than computers and inventory adjustments was needed to make Seiyū truly competitive. The firm bought into Nikō Mail Order Company (Nikō Tsūhan) in 1987 and turned this sizable but faltering catalogue-sales concern into the nucleus of a direct-marketing operation for the Saison Group, with projected sales of $384.6 million in 1993.[113] Although direct marketing was underdeveloped in Japan compared with other countries, the growing number of working women who might prefer home shopping and the sudden popularity of L. L. Bean products—which Seiyū agreed to help distribute starting in the fall of 1992—are reasons why Saison wanted a bigger slice of the $10 billion market.[114] At the same time Seiyū concentrated its in-store merchandising on high-volume branches selling $72.5 million or more per year, of which it had twenty in 1990, and on the eleven outlets in its department-store division, the latter of which had yearly sales of $913 million in February 1990.[115] Because the department stores were so thriving, the company decided in 1990 to transform two of its largest Seiyūs, in Kōfu and Akabane, into "fashion buildings" for shoppers who were not quite the New Rich but wanted to emulate them.

The tide of urban development also washed across Seiyū in the late 1980s. The Large-scale Retail Store Law forced Seiyū to cooperate with local merchants (who put up much of the capital) when it developed its first shopping center, opened in March 1988 in Nagahama, a castle town in Shiga Prefecture established by Toyotomi Hideyoshi in 1573. The 6,300-square-meter Seiyū building at Nagahama (see Figure 10) offered Saison's financial and other information services, and the project included restaurants, high-tech amusements, and a drive-in movie theater. No chain-store operator had ever made a go of it with local businesses in a project like Nagahama before. Its early success emboldened the superstore to plan at least ten more centers, beginning in 1992, from Hokkaido to Kyushu.[116] Seiyū also put in a "leisure complex" with a pool and health club at Urayasu in 1989 and shopping arcades a bit more middlebrow than Parcos in Osaka and Nagasaki Prefectures the same year.

Although it was not nearly so far-flung or adept at operating satellite companies as the Seibu department-store group, Seiyū and its subsidiaries entered the 1990s with sales of $7.97 billion, almost $1.22 billion of which derived from development, finance, media, and other non-store activities that hardly existed on the company's menu ten years before.[117] In 1990 Seiyū and subsidiaries employed 11,307 full-time workers and enough part-timers to equal another 10,171 positions in 264 locations.[118] Sales more than doubled during the 1980s in yen terms, and pretax profits for the superstores rose 58.5 percent in yen terms between February 1984 and February 1990, to $90.8 million, well behind Daiei and Itō Yōkadō in both receipts and profitability.[119] Pretax profits for the Seiyū Group as a whole were $209.1 million at the same time.[120] As in the past, operating profits for the superstore company were ravaged by nonoperating losses brought about by so much construction and investment in expansion; as a result Seiyū's outstanding interest-bearing debt rose 42.8 percent dur-

FIGURE 10. Seiyū shopping complex in Nagahama, Shiga Prefecture, opened in March 1988. (Saison Group)

ing the year ending February 1990, to $6.87 billion, which the company calculated as 75.6 percent of its total assets at the time[121] —a pattern of high leverage, steep debt, and investment in future assets that was little changed from Tsutsumi Yasujirō's time.

Parco from the start pursued "a highly fashionable urban lifestyle," but like Seiyū it sought new customers in the later 1980s through enterprises unknown to the company a decade earlier. Parco was the golden child of the Seibu group in the 1970s but its prodigal by the 1980s. Imitation may have been flattering, but the rise of competitors like Mori's La Forêt, Tōkyū's One Oh Nine, and Keiō's Lumine proved very damaging. Even though it remained Saison's third-ranking core enterprise in operating revenues, Parco's business virtually leveled off in the mid-1980s (and actually fell at both Ikebukuro and Shibuya), with a predictable squeeze on profits.[122] At length the firm invested heavily in remodeling, raised its credit limit for customers, and shuffled the tenants in its arcades to offer more international fashions—

yet its president, Masuda Tsūji, conceded in May 1988 that "we were a step behind in responding"[123] to changing tastes among the well-to-do.

Parco began to diversify fast in the late 1980s under Yamada Masatoshi, who succeeded Masuda in June 1988 and soon had to dampen an uproar over violations of the Commercial Code by two former company officials who paid $12,000 to thugs connected with the underworld in 1986–1987.[124] Yamada capitalized on Parco's image as "trendy" but otherwise "pretty vague" ("a vague image is vital to Parco—it's our main sales point")[125] to branch into producing and distributing films, operating movie theaters, managing chic restaurants and luxury beauty parlors, and developing suburban shopping centers anchored by Parcos and often including Creston Hotels. The goal of the firm's efforts to create a "new Yamanote" commercial loop from the Tama Hills to Yokohama was to reach those in their forties who had once shopped in Shibuya and their internationally minded teenage children. Parco's shopping centers tried to create an urban lifestyle without going into town[126]—bringing the city to the suburbs, as Tsutsumi's father had done in the 1920s.

The 1989 Parco "urban resort" at Chōfu, a western residential zone of Tokyo, contained 20,096 square meters for 229 specialty shops, a Creston Hotel, shape-up salon, cinema, and hall for live entertainment, designed to siphon customers from Chōfu, Fuchū, and Hachiōji along the Keiō Line who would otherwise stay aboard another twenty minutes to reach sprawling Shinjuku. A month after inaugurating Chōfu, the company opened its largest arcade and shopping center in Nagoya, where it arrayed 329 tenants in a 30,801-square-meter building and offered the same companion amenities, including information counters for the Saison enterprises. The two complexes raised the total number of shops in Parco's thirteen locations to 2,400. Operating revenues at Chōfu and Nagoya during their first year of operation displayed an annual rate of $385 million between them, of which the company skimmed off a flat basic fee and 8–10 percent of gross from each merchant as rent.[127] Both new plazas reported a higher proportion of men customers than at other Parcos, drawn partly by sports as well as conference facilities in the hotels but also by some of the 150 restaurants the company offered in its arcades, half of them directly owned and managed by Parco.[128]

To spread operations still more widely, Yamada and Tsutsumi added a fourth building at Shibuya in 1988, called Quattro by Parco and designed like a country house, with 35 shops under the theme "international and unisex" with casual Italian, French, and American imports. The main draw was Club Quattro on the fourth floor, a 310-seat live-music house that helped the building break even almost at once and continued to attract the young to Shibuya while Ginza merchants suffered poor sales in mid-1993. Another money maker was Across, a subsidiary chain of speciality shops with imported fashions, sporting goods, books, and interiors that filled in marketing niches in each arcade and also operated independent stores around the country. Its sales for the year ending in February 1990 were $200.6 million, about 11 percent of Parco's total operating revenues.[129] The parent company targeted another select audience in September 1990 when it unveiled the four-story Nos Vos arcade at Ōizumi Gakuen in the northwest suburbs of Tokyo. Its shops, arranged in the manner of a Parisian shopping street, were the first in any Parco aimed specifically at married women[130] – of whom there were now more than ever before, while the young population the company once cultivated exclusively continued to shrink.

To raise capital for this flurry of expansion, Parco gained a listing in the second section of the Tokyo Stock Exchange in 1987 and in the premier section the following year. As new buildings opened in Chōfu, Nagoya, and Ōizumi and ground was broken for others in Ikebukuro (1992) and Atsugi (1992), operating revenues shot upward and so did pretax profits. Gross income as of February 1990 stood at $1.79 billion, a rise of 53.3 percent in yen terms from five years earlier, and pretax profits during the same period increased 189.7 percent, to $25.6 million. Gross income by February 1992 had increased to $2.13 billion per year.[131] Better credit management and an improved point-of-sale accounting system also helped to lift profits. The company's bank borrowings in August 1990 stood at $118.2 million, down slightly from the year before, and the equity ratio rose from 16.3 to 23.8 during the same period. Parco and all other core companies also had access to cash from Seiyū and the department store. Stockholders who knew of the rift between the Tsutsumi brothers may have been surprised to read in their annual reports for 1990 that Seibu Railway still held the second-largest bloc of shares in Parco, 10.9 percent (to Seibu Department Stores' 26.1).[132] New leadership, quick diversification, fresh capital, and expansive marketing to matronly suburbanites and their children revived the company from its gloom of the mid-1980s. But the price was corporate commercialization, middle-age spread, and the dulling of Parco's formerly sword-sharp fashion image on the only Park Avenue that young Japanese once wanted to stroll.

MONEY WHEN YOU NEED IT

Financial deregulation in the early 1980s and the robust economy after 1986 finally allowed the Seibu Saison Group to win a respectable return on its commitment to life insurance and other financial services a decade earlier. Seibu Credit and its Saison Card quietly became the propellers of a groupwide campaign to offer credit, money dispensing, loans, investments, and insurance to those whose desire to create a personalized lifestyle outran their capacity to pay for it in cash. Seibu Credit turned into a diversified financial-services company for individual consumers after 1986, even though the group had no bank and little experience in the field. As Ikuno Shigeo, president of Seibu Allstate Life, pointed out, "the concept of sales is fundamentally different in the financial-services area compared with retailing";[133] even so, by the late 1980s Seibu Credit was well on its way to becoming a nonbank bank.

Consumer credit, excluding housing loans, expanded from 6.5 to 11.2 percent of family disposable income in Japan between 1975 and 1985, comparable to major European countries but less than the United States (20 percent) in 1985.[134] Seibu Credit's share of this market lagged until Takeuchi Toshio replaced Sakakura Yoshiaki as president in April 1983 and immediately invested $210 million in computerization, soon cutting the company's unusually high rate of delinquent loans to 0.3 percent.[135] "When I moved from Restaurant Seibu to the presidency of Seibu Credit," Takeuchi said in 1987, "it was about $84 million in debt. At that point I had to press forward with building a credit system" through automation, but still "I thought any number of times that the company was doomed."[136] He eliminated unprofitable Midoriya stores, slashed employment, and persuaded the banks to share the burden of stabilizing the firm's financial base. He touted the Saison Card, which traced to 1982, as an instrument linking the

entire Seibu Saison Group through a database on millions of customers' buying habits and credit histories; and he introduced new financial products via affiliated companies that offered consumer loans,
corporate financing, mortgage securities, and investment counseling—
all of this eased by liberalization of Japanese financial markets after
1983. Seibu Credit's pretax losses that year were $6.2 million; by Jan-
uary 1987 the firm was able to report a pretax profit of $12.4 million,
more than double the year before, and to resume dividends after skip-
ping the nine previous periods.[137] The company renamed itself Credit
Saison in October 1989, "to strengthen cardholders' identification of
the Company with the Saison Card,"[138] and faced an even rosier
future for its lucrative revolving-credit business with the complete
deregulation of this part of the credit-card industry in 1992.

When Seibu Credit began signing up merchants outside the Saison
Group to accept the Saison Card in 1984, it took the first crucial step
toward becoming a full financial-services company with a national,
not just a house, card. Since then the number of credit cards in use in
Japan tripled to 166 million in 1991, according to the industry association; the majority of credit purchases occurred with cards issued by
banking institutions rather than credit companies or retailers like Saison.[139] Credit Saison calculated that more than 3 million blue-and-
green Saison Cards were in circulation by 1985 and that the number
rose to 7.3 million in 1990, aided by tie-ups with Visa and MasterCard
starting in August 1988[140] for use overseas by the young women who
were Saison's most numerous cardholders.

Credit cards accounted for about 80 percent of Credit Saison's
annual operating revenues of $360 million derived from a handling vol-
ume of $7.24 billion during the year ending March 1990. Two years
later operating revenues rose to $457.9 million.[141] Shoppers used the
Saison Card for approximately 30 percent of their purchases at Seibu
Department Stores and avoided the 15 percent annual percentage-rate
finance charge if they paid the monthly bill promptly. Much more
profitable were cash advances from automatic teller machines, for
which cardholders paid 28.2 APR in fees without a grace period.[142]
The card also provided instant entrée at 156 Saison Counters in Seibu
department stores, Seiyūs, and Parcos where personal loans and
expanded shopping credit could be arranged or life and casualty insurance purchased. Among the few places the Saison Card was not wel-

come after March 1985 were Tsutsumi Yoshiaki's Prince Hotels and golf courses, evidently because of animus toward credit cards in general, not toward his brother.[143]

Takeuchi also strengthened Seibu Credit's ties with several affiliates in the finance and securities business. Seibu (today Saison) Barclays Finance offered leasing, discounted commercial paper, project finance, and factoring to companies outside the group. Established in 1979 as a joint venture with Barclays Bank, the firm achieved operating revenues of $42 million in the year ending March 1990[144] and gave Saison a toehold in the world of commercial finance. Ace Finance provided wholesale financing for enterprises within the Seibu Saison umbrella, in cooperation with Japan Long-Term Credit Bank. Ace, which began in 1983, reported annual operating revenues of $58.1 million in March 1990.[145] Much larger than either Seibu Barclays or Ace was another affiliate, Seibu Mortgage Acceptance Corporation (Seibu Teitō Shōken), founded in 1984 to lend mortgage funds, sell mortgage securities to small investors, and finance stock purchases during the bull market of the late 1980s. The bulk of its business was making real-estate loans with funds supplied by its partners in banking and the securities industry. This company (now Saison Fundex) took in $166.2 million in revenues in the year ending March 1990,[146] a double-digit improvement in percentage terms over the previous year, as was also true of Saison Barclays and Ace Finance.

Of all Seibu Credit's moves in the 1980s, what especially caused anxiety among competitors in the stock-and-bond business was Tsutsumi Seiji's joint capital venture with a little-known securities dealership in the suburbs, Saiō Shōken, starting in 1986. Opening up the financial markets made it much easier for Japan's 244 securities houses to sell small lots. Barred by government regulations from starting a new investment firm, Seibu Credit cooperated with Saiō (today Shin Seiyō) to establish sales counters in Seibu department stores, Seiyūs, and other Seibu Saison locations.[147]

What surprised the retail industry was that Tsutsumi would plunge his cash-starved company headlong into the volatile brokerage business, inviting shoppers to become first-time gamblers in a stock market which had little more respectability than the racetrack. Life insurance, by contrast, was a staid and stable industry familiar to the families who patronized Seibu, and it had been in a relatively tranquil condition when Tsutsumi entered it a decade earlier. He relished the publicity for his venture with Saiō but avowed that it was "just filling a niche":[148] "We have absolutely no intention of becoming a big securities house . . . we're filling a gap where people have found it difficult to deal with the existing securities market."[149] In fact Shin Seiyō became a full-service dealer in 1990 when it received permission from the Ministry of Finance to engage in underwriting, but those who feared its potential as a Gargantua may have been surprised to learn that its annual operating revenues at that point were just $24.9 million.[150]

Credit Saison and its affiliates turned into profitable enterprises for the Seibu Saison Group very quickly in the late 1980s, unlike many of the new diversified projects Seiyū, Parco, and the department store undertook at the same time. Credit Saison's pretax profits in the year ending March 1990 swelled to about $56 million, up 163 percent in yen terms compared with the 1987 figure. Affiliates added another 30 percent or more to pretax profits for the same period.[151] The entire Credit Saison Group thrived because of deregulation, smart leadership by Takeuchi, and the relatively undernourished state of consumer finance in Japan—but also because of the happy accident that the firm's new initiatives coincided with the most sustained prosperity its customers had ever known. To enjoy it they needed a convenient way to spend and borrow, and Saison was happy to supply the necessary plastic.

Japanese families needed money for security as well as consumption, leading to exceptional growth in life insurance, casualty insurance, and personal annuities as the population aged and grew richer in the late 1980s. The demand was so great that by 1991 about 85 percent of men and 72 percent of women were covered by life-insurance contracts in Japan, with a total face value of $12.7 trillion, by far the highest on a per-capita basis in the world.[152] Many of the policies provided pension income and payments for medical expenses as well as death benefits. Seibu Allstate Life Insurance Company (founded in 1975) and the much smaller Allstate Automobile and Fire Insurance Company (established by Allstate in 1983, converted to a joint venture with Seibu Saison in 1984) both benefited from the flood of consumer assets that poured into insurance and annuities at the end of the decade. Thanks in good part to the great sales power of the Saison Group, each was well established in its field by the end of Japan's five-year economic boom in late 1991.

Seibu Allstate Life stumbled badly in 1976–1978 and then turned its first profit in 1981, when its operating revenues reached $33.9 million.[153] The firm finally erased its accumulated deficit in 1986, three years behind schedule, and at the same time appointed Matsubara Mikio from the Ministry of Finance to develop new products. Before he signed on, Matsubara told an interviewer in 1990, "I had the impression that Seibu Allstate Life relied too much on the Seibu Saison Group, so I thought it might be well for it to move boldly into the general marketplace."[154] As a result, the company joined forces with its banks to begin offering medical insurance and individual annuities through a network of representative offices with legions of saleswomen, as was customary in the industry, to supplement its counters in Seibu department stores and Seiyūs.

Matsubara was proudest of a combined term and whole-life policy with favorable savings features called U-Flex, introduced in 1987, but medical plans (56.1 percent), whole-life (18.7), and annuities (11.4) accounted for most of the company's sales to individuals as of March 1989.[155] At that point there were 3.5 million group life-insurance certificates and 305,000 individual life policies in force, although the face value of the latter was roughly 20 times larger.[156] Even though interest rates rose in 1989, making other investments more attractive, Seibu Allstate Life heavily promoted the medical-payment provisions of its life-insurance policies, so that the amount of individual life policies in force rose 16.3 percent and group life policies 18.4 percent during the year ending March 1990, to a combined total of $21.79 billion.[157] Premium income doubled in yen terms between 1980 and 1983, then rose another 72.9 percent during the next three years, to $114.2 million. Mainly because of strong sales of annuities and single-payment endowment policies, premium income rocketed to $879.2 million in the year ending March 1989, then fell off to $644.2 million a year later (down 21 percent in yen terms).[158] The company blamed the decline on high interest rates and the consequent slower growth in demand for annuities, but these still showed a healthy rise over the previous year. Operating profits in the year ending March 1990 were $11.7 million, a rise of 7.8 percent from the year before, but plunged two years later because net premium income sank to $508.1 million in a saturated market.[159]

Most important in the long run was that Seibu Allstate Life managed to double its assets during the year ending March 1990, to $1.64

billion, allowing it to rise two notches to number nineteen in the field.[160] Even though the market for life insurance may now be sated (the industry's premium income dipped in 1991 for the first time since World War II), the sale of personal annuities in Japan rose 40 percent that same year because of high demand from women, who outlive men in that country by an average of six years.[161] Saison can expect to carve out a profitable share of this retirement market because of the group's strong standing among female customers.

As with so many Tsutsumi projects since the 1920s, Allstate Auto and Fire, the newest and smallest of Japan's twenty-three casualty insurers, seemed a step or more ahead of its time when it became a joint venture of Allstate and Saison in 1984. The market for casualty insurance in Japan was immature: income from premiums in proportion to GNP was less than half that in the United States.[162] After a long struggle to find its feet, the company established itself well enough to achieve a 24 percent rise in earned annual premium during the year ending March 1989 (net premium income at that point was $61.2 million per annum, rising to $90.6 million three years later).[163] Predictably, more than half its sales derived from auto insurance, but 20.2 percent came from savings schemes, versus only 11.7 percent from fire insurance.[164] Even though this company accounted for only 6.5 percent of Seibu Saison's total insurance business at the end of the decade (Seibu Allstate Life had the other 93.5 percent), it tripled its assets between 1986 and 1989, to $179.9 million, and expected to triple them again by 1993.[165]

Seibu Allstate, which had likewise stumbled at the start, entered a new phase in April 1990 when the firm changed its name to Saison Life Insurance Company, Ltd., without altering its 50:50 capitalization between Allstate and Saison. The company somberly gave as reasons for the new name "to create a new corporate image appropriate for the era we are entering" and "to indicate that you will receive from us the quality service that you expect from Saison."[166] Most people in the industry took the change as the latest in a series of steps by Tsutsumi to distance his corporate identity from both Sears and his brother's Seibu Railway Group. The chief public vestige of the latter was the hardest of all to give up—yet the financial pundits have not stopped speculating that Tsutsumi would soon cap the age of information for sale by renaming his retailing enterprise the Saison Department Stores.

CHAPTER NINE

JAPAN AT PLAY: THE SEIBU
RAILWAY GROUP IN THE 1980s

"The service industry sells luxury," Tsutsumi Yoshiaki said in 1983. "We get down on bended knee for our customers." Whereas the Saison Group professed to offer self-realization through the various forms of information it sold in the 1980s, Kokudo Keikaku focused on only one specific form of it, leisure-time activities. Tsutsumi echoed his brother Seiji's high-minded rhetoric about lifestyles when he claimed that "our customers don't seek services in the sense of leisure [i.e., idleness]. . . . They buy our services as recreation—re-creation."[1] By the end of the decade Kokudo Keikaku earned 95 percent of its revenues from tourism, sports, and the overall leisure industry and just a small amount from real-estate operations. Luxury and recreation were the twin dreams the railway group tried to satisfy among customers with growing amounts of cash and free time to afford them. The 1980s completed the group's reorientation from a land and transportation business to a diverse leisure-services enterprise. Yet as the decade ended Tsutsumi started to redirect his attention to fresh ventures like shopping centers and suburban development—some of the newest expressions of middle-class consumerism in Japan.

STRENGTHENING THE RAILWAY

The basic demographic fact facing Seibu and all other railways was that between the 1960s and the 1980s automobiles replaced trains as the most widely used form of transportation in Japan. During 1965–1988 railroads and motor vehicles (overwhelmingly automobiles, since bus ridership fell dramatically) traded places as the most popular means of travel: in 1965 trains claimed 66.7 percent of all passenger-kilometers, versus 31.6 percent for motor vehicles; by 1988 trains accounted for just 30.4 percent and motor vehicles 65.6. Total domestic travel tripled during this period, but rail passenger-kilometers grew just 41.9 percent, with private lines performing somewhat better than the overextended Japan National Railways.[2] Even in urban areas where roadways were clogged and private commuter lines legion, motor vehicles carried more commuters than trains by the 1980s in Nagoya and accounted for more than 40 percent of passengers in Tokyo,[3] a city with a rail system second to none among world capitals. Ridership on the nation's private lines increased about 2.5 percent per year during 1985–1988[4]—a low-growth condition that prompted the biggest among them to redouble their efforts to diversify into non-rail operations.

Seibu already depended less than its competitors on passenger and freight revenues by 1980, when real estate (22 percent) and tourism (29 percent) represented a slight majority of its $418.1 million sales. Ten years later real estate was about the same (21 percent), but rail revenues had fallen in importance to 38 percent, and tourism now accounted for 41 percent of sales, which were at an annual rate of $1.4 billion (up 117 percent in nominal yen terms over 1980).[5] During the same decade Kokudo Keikaku increased its stake in the railway from 29.4 percent of shares to 48.7 percent, and paid-in capital grew from $63.6 million to $151.5 million, up 50 percent in yen terms. Another sign of the railroad's activity was that total borrowings almost tripled in yen terms during 1980–1990, to $2.7 billion as of September 1990.[6]

Because of greatly increased cross-holding of shares by various Seibu enterprises in the 1980s, the Seibu Railway Company is now one of four core companies constituting the Seibu Railway Group. At the apex is Kokudo Keikaku, descended from Tsutsumi Yasujirō's original Hakone Land Company and now capitalized at a nominal $733,000.

Kokudo Keikaku directly controls the Seibu Railway and the Prince Hotels (since 1986 a wholly owned subsidiary). The fourth core company, Seibu Golf, is wholly owned by the railway but has its offices in the Kokudo Keikaku building at Harajuku. Except for the Lions and Seibu Travel, which are also directly beneath Kokudo Keikaku, all the other companies in the group are owned by the railway or its subsidiaries. The most important include Seibu Construction (Seibu Kensetsu), a 50:50 venture with Kokudo Keikaku, and four wholly owned subsidiaries: Seibu Real Estate, Seibu Trading (Seibu Shōji), Roppongi Prince Hotel (which in turn owns Seibu Motor Freight and Seibu Bus), and Seibu Polymer Chemical Industries (Seibu Porima Kasei). Together with its own subsidiaries the railroad also owns Seibu Garden Construction (Seibu Zōen), the Izu Hakone Railway, and the Ōmi Railway.[7]

Collectively the seventy-six companies in the group are believed to do about $7.2 billion in business each year and employ nearly 45,000 persons, although precise data are scarce because only the Seibu Railway and the Izu Hakone Railway are listed on any stock exchange. Even though it controls most of the other companies in the group, the Seibu Railway generates only 22 percent of the sales;[8] its subsidiaries, Kokudo Keikaku, and the Prince Hotels take in nearly all the rest. Because he is by far Kokudo Keikaku's largest shareholder at 40 percent, Tsutsumi Yoshiaki is the de facto owner of the group. As of 1990 he was president of Kokudo Keikaku and board chair of the other three core companies, as well as board chair of the Izu Hakone Railway and the Seibu Construction, Real Estate, Trading, and Motor Freight Companies.[9]

A symbol of the steadily more diversified railroad company was its new $23.7 million headquarters building in Tokorozawa, unveiled in August 1986 with offices for the railway, Seibu Real Estate, Seibu Trading, and Seibu Limousine in a city Tsutsumi expected would grow from 270,000 residents into a regional metropolis of a million. He had long planned the move to this crossover point of the main rail lines because it was part of a zone of development that included Lions Stadium, Seibuen amusement park, two golf courses, a branch campus of Waseda University on a site partly donated by Tsutsumi, and extensive housing investments, as well as the potential for suburban shopping-plaza growth centered on hotels. Residents of the region might be excused for sometimes seeing the forbidding new structure as another sign that they lived in a company town where Seibu usually monopolized train, bus, and cab service, invested little in improving stations, and often built the housing they lived in (Tsutsumi is thought to own at least 5 percent of Tokorozawa's considerable land area).[10]

The railway's momentum toward diversification was slowed in late 1979 when Vice President Nisugi Iwao, a career Japan National Railways bureaucrat who had "descended from heaven" (*amakudari*) to join Seibu in 1971, became a rare example of reascension (*amaagari*) by becoming chief of the Railway Construction Public Corporation and then, in December 1983, head of the national railways. After nineteen months at Japan National Railways he was removed for factional reasons by Prime Minister Nakasone Yasuhiro, returning to Seibu in August 1985 and taking over from Tsutsumi as president in January 1989.[11] He pressed forward with express tracking on the Ikebukuro line as well as engineering studies for a 12.8-kilometer tunnel from Kamishakujii to Takadanobaba and Shinjuku. This 40-meter-deep subway, with double tracks, will cut eight minutes from the present twenty-six-minute trip from Tanashi to Shinjuku when it is completed in 2000, at an estimated cost of $1.1 billion in 1990 prices.[12] These improvements, plus the 1997 link between the Ikebukuro line and the Yūrakuchō subway, will finally reduce highway backups at grade crossings, cut congestion on Tokyo's most overcrowded commuter trains, and increase the company's passenger capacity. At the same time Nisugi's main railway-related project to bring in added revenues was to pump new life into the Seibu Trading Company by constructing shopping and restaurant buildings at the biggest of Seibu's 101 stations.

Seibu Trading was created in 1974 to operate the 7,800-square-meter PePe shopping complex beneath the Shinjuku Prince Hotel, opened in early 1977 with ninety stores mainly selling women's wear. Thanks to the two brothers' compact of 1970, Seibu was the only private railroad in Tokyo without a department store, and apart from PePe its only other retailing properties of any size were the Big Box Sports Plaza at Takadanobaba and station buildings leased to restaurants and shops at Sayama and Tanashi. Smaller buildings controlled by Tsutsumi Yoshiaki near stations included Denmark bakeries, Seibu photofinishing centers, Lions' souvenir corners, and gift shops, but these generated relatively little income. The company's annual sales as of March 1990 were estimated at $209.8 million, perhaps 70 percent of it rental income from tenants.[13] Tsutsumi and Nisugi began putting up new stationside shopping centers at Honkawagoe and Hannō, both major terminals, and laid plans for sixteen others—all but Ikebukuro and Nerima located outside the ward area of Tokyo,[14] a sure mark of how tardy Seibu Trading was in entering the field.

Even though real-estate operations accounted for a steady rather than a growing share of the railway's sales in the 1980s, their composition shifted away from housing toward business properties. Paradoxically, among the fourteen major private rail companies in Japan Seibu had the least land for sale (173.7 hectares in 1989) but by far the largest area already in commercial use (5,732.8 hectares, five times the size of Tokyo's Chiyoda Ward)—mainly rental properties, Prince Hotels whose land it still owned, amusement parks, and golf courses operated by Seibu Golf. Just 369.7 hectares were used for railroad operations, including its Tokorozawa foundry for building new rolling stock.[15] These figures, reported semiannually to the Ministry of Finance, exclude the far more extensive real-estate holdings of Kokudo Keikaku. Still Seibu Real Estate's operating income slipped from ¥87.3 billion in the fiscal year ending March 1985 to ¥59 billion ($427.6 million) four years later; net profits were up 4.4 percent in the same period to $1.2 million.[16] Yet because sales of the real-estate divisions of Seibu Trading and other subsidiaries increased, real-estate operations overall claimed roughly the same share of the railway's total sales in 1990 as in 1980.

The true impact of diversification in the 1980s was felt in tourism, although details are elusive because the company reported the performance of unlisted subsidiaries only in cryptic terms. Tourism in the aggregate accounted for $121.2 million in sales in 1980 and $565.8 million ten years later, up 194 percent in yen terms (versus 117 percent for the railway as a whole).[17] Much of the growth came from operating golf courses; a good deal came in the form of rentals from Prince Hotel properties it owned, even though it transferred its Prince shares to Kokudo Keikaku in 1986. The railroad also owned hotels, tennis courts, and bowling centers along its tracks that contributed to the rise in revenues. So did Seibu Construction, which the railway owned jointly with Kokudo Keikaku, inasmuch as a good deal of the construction was golf links, tennis courts, hotels, ice arenas, ski slopes and other leisure facilities. Seibu Construction, which ranks about thirty-fifth in revenues among Japanese builders, increased its sales between 1984 and 1988 by 46.1 percent, to $983.6 million as of March 1989, and its after-tax profits by 288 percent to $9.3 million.[18] Its chief subsidiary, Seibu Construction Materials Company (Seibu Kenzai), added another $160.5 million in sales and $1.5 million in net profits in the year ending March 1989.[19] The railway's tourism revenues also swelled from operating Lions Stadium in Tokorozawa, although the franchise itself belonged to Kokudo Keikaku; about three dozen concerts a year augmented the income from home baseball games, and often playoffs, each year.[20]

Through solid real-estate revenues and energetic growth in the tourism sector, Seibu ended the decade as it began, the second most profitable private railway in the country, with after-tax gains of $17.5 million for the year ending March 1990.[21] Then as interest rates rose in several stages during 1990, the company's current profits were trimmed by the costs of debt service, despite thriving real-estate and hotel revenues. A new tennis park in Chichibu, opened in April 1991, and a joint venture with the Burger King Corporation to bring the restaurant chain to Japan, starting in September 1993, were expected to enrich the railroad still further.[22] The company's assets in 1990, including 5,705 hectares of land, were valued for tax purposes at $1.8 billion, almost evenly divided between the railway and its subsidiaries.[23] But at market values that same year, the 695 hectares of golf courses owned by the railway group at Karuizawa alone were thought to be worth more than eight times that total, or $14.7 billion[24]—an example of just how unrealistic official valuations can be and a clear indicator of why Tsutsumi and Nisugi have led the railroad toward recreation, with its immense promise for future assets and profits.

LEISURE AS TIME IN

Entertainment in Japan for many decades provided salaried employees with socially sanctioned time out from the pressures of corporate performance by temporarily creating an alternative form of community in a favorite coffee shop, bar, or restaurant where middle-class

workers could lampoon, without rejecting, the values of the worka-
day social system. By stepping out of ordinary roles for a short time
in a defined amusement quarter of a big city, company employees re-
affirmed the established structure even while letting down their hair
a bit to escape its relentless demands. Entertainment modulated the
responsibilities of everyday role fulfillment in the Japanese corporation or public agency during the era of high-speed growth, reducing
the likelihood of conflict between personal desires and role assign-
ments. In that phase of Japan's development the very nature of entertainment for small groups in districts like Shinjuku's Kabukichō, as
Tobit B. Morral has written, was consciously to release inhibitions
and embrace "non-ordinary social conduct that acts to bolster the self
and reaffirm the structure as a whole"[25]—in short, re-creation of the
corporate personality.

Leisure, by contrast, evolved in the period of mature, lower-speed
growth after the mid-1970s to fulfill the need for time and space for personal renewal, both individually and in family units, as middle-class
Japanese increasingly prized self-expression and the distinctiveness of
their immediate families rather than the collective ethos of the workplace. The growing focus on self and loved ones, often called my-
homeism, coincided exactly with the emergence of leisure-time activities as part of the weekly or seasonal routine—no longer stepping
aside for time out but integrating leisure into people's increasingly
flexible schedules as time in, a normal and regular period of self-indulgence and self-renewal (what Tsutsumi Yoshiaki calls "luxury" and "recreation"). In this new era of leisure the social unit was no longer the
company work group but the family or close friends, the locale was
no longer a big-city entertainment quarter but a mountain or seaside
resort, and the activity was no longer so likely to be alcoholic as
fitness-centered. Entertainment suspended the everyday rules, but leisure created new ones as individuals and families found their own
paths to personhood.

Once their material needs were more nearly satisfied in the late
1970s compared with earlier decades, more and more Japanese turned
to leisure as a third space, in addition to home and workplace. They
also began pursuing more personally fulfilling activities known as the
three S's: study, sports, and social life.[26] The goods people selected
were less often standardized; instead they more and more fitted the par-

ticular lifestyles buyers chose, with leisure an integrated part rather than something exceptional. Government responded by identifying goals for a leisure (*yutori*)-type society, even if many of the specifics addressed Japan's ever-larger numbers of elderly people. A typical statement came from the Tokyo prefectural authorities in November 1989: "A Yutori-type society refers to a society which attaches greater importance to better social quality than to quantitative economic expansion . . . it is a society in which every person can be assured of time, space and information to enjoy his or her life."[27] As a third space, the statement concluded, leisure-time activity was meant to be regularized into personal routines to help attain dignity, foster independence and self-help, and thus reinforce social solidarity.

Japan's most widely used statistics on the subject are generated by the Leisure Development Center, established as a nonprofit organization by the Ministry of International Trade and Industry in 1973. This group's definition of what constitutes leisure-time activity is too all-embracing to be a precise guide to trends in the markets exploited by the Seibu Railway Group, but its data show an average annual increase in leisure spending of about 7 percent during the latter half of the 1980s, to $443.7 billion in the year ending March 1990. This is about 15 percent of GNP and nearly 29 percent of private consumption (up from 26.2 percent in fiscal year 1985).[28] Spending on sports in fiscal year 1989 rose the fastest (11.6 percent over the year before) of the categories glossed by the center, but its absolute level, $31.16 billion, was still low if one considers that the annual per-capita outlay for sports ($245) was about the same as the greens fee for a round of golf at Karuizawa 72.[29]

Just as important as having cash is finding the time to spend it; there is no doubt that Japanese are finally moving toward more and longer holidays, after many years of official pronouncements in favor of vacations and much unofficial foot-dragging by employers. A virtually full-employment economy during 1987–1992, together with a shrinking pool of young workers, created contrary tugs: employees were asked to put in much lucrative overtime, yet the labor shortage forced businesses to grant more days off. Naturally the rising demand for leisure activities made work busier than ever for employees in the service industries. Ministry of Labor surveys showed that companies gave more vacation days each year starting in 1984—and that workers shunned taking all the time due them, whether because of subtle pressures from their bosses or the lure of overtime pay.[30] Still the decisive benchmark was clear: the annual number of regular and overtime hours worked fell for the third straight year to 2,044 in fiscal year 1990, down 32 hours from 1989.[31] Government offices, banks, and many private companies were routinely closed on Saturdays and Sundays, and neighborhood shopkeepers often began shutting down en masse one day a week. Perhaps the most sensitive indicator of all was that in early 1991 the Seibu Railway finally began running its Saturday trains on holiday rather than weekday schedules.

PRINCES BEYOND TOKYO

Tsutsumi Yoshiaki's slice of the total leisure industry—hotels, resorts, amusement parks, and sports facilities—requires a high level of know-how, skilled service, and huge investments in staff and equipment, meaning that productivity is low. Demand depends on the season or day of the week, causing employees to snarl about their work schedules.[32] Regardless of such exacting requirements, Prince Hotels and the group's other lodgings benefited from a boom market in the 1980s: occupancy rates in city hotels nationwide were 77.2 percent in the year ending March 1990, and those in resort hotels were 60.9 percent—both the highest in a decade.[33] Thanks to strong growth in the overall economy, occupancy rates in Tokyo's fourteen major hotels during the summer and fall of 1990 were close to 90 percent, also the best in ten years.[34] When Tsutsumi launched the new wing of the Akasaka Prince in 1983, the number of rooms in the Prince chain surpassed 10,000. The company touched off a new round of expansion the next year that sent the figure past 20,000 when the Makuhari Prince, New Yokohama Prince, and Hiroshima Prince became operational in the early 1990s.

One area Tsutsumi finally tapped was Kyoto. "When Kansai people come to Kantō they succeed," he noted in 1982, "but when Kantō people try to sell in Kansai, many times they fail."[35] In fact Seibu already had four locations in Kansai when it joined the Kyoto hotel splurge of the mid-1980s by opening the stunning Takaragaike Prince in October 1986. Tsutsumi managed to overcome site restrictions (the hotel was built in a historical-preservation zone) and high land values (he reportedly paid $375 per square meter for land said to be worth $1,270) in order to build the 332-room luxury hotel in time for a proposed May 1986 summit of world leaders at the nearby Kyoto International Conference Hall.[36] The summit was held in Tokyo instead, the hotel opened five months behind schedule, and the city authorities who had approved the project endured a good deal of criticism for granting exceptions to Prince.[37] The thirty-eight-story Ōtsu Prince, opened two years later immediately adjacent to Kyoto, encountered fierce opposition during the planning stages as too grandiose because of its 136-meter height and 540 rooms in a small city of 240,000 with no tall buildings. But guests found it an architectural success, with every room in the hemispherical tower affording a view of Lake Biwa to the northeast, and it has apparently operated in the black almost from the start.[38]

The Takaragaike and Ōtsu buildings were part of the rush of new Princes that appeared during the peak years 1986–1989, centerpieces of the railway group's estimated annual investments of $400 million at this time.[39] This latest wave of expansion was partly defensive, responding to new hotels by the Ōkura and the New Ōtani in Kansai as well as to new concepts in Tokyo hotel keeping, like the computerized Washington Hotels and the ultra-luxury suites at the intimate Seiyō Ginza. Prince scored a coup of prestige, or at least political pull, when it was designated sole caterer of functions at the Akasaka State Guest House in April 1987, an honor long rotated among the Imperial, Ōkura, and New Ōtani. Three years later Tsutsumi opened the totally rebuilt Yokohama Prince with 441 oceanfront rooms and began construction of the 885-room New Yokohama Prince, which he christened in 1992 as part of an urban resort and giant convention center.[40]

Nonetheless the greatest cluster of new Princes sprang up in resort areas, including renovations and additions to the posh Hakone Prince Hotel such as a lakeside lodge and cottages to attract younger guests. Although Tsutsumi said in an interview published in 1984 that because of the off-season "a 50 percent occupancy rate is ideal,"[41] the hotel is thought to run in the red—balanced by at least $3.5 million a year in net profits from the nearby Dai Hakone Country Club,[42] next to which the company opened the 96-room Hakone Sengokuhara Prince in 1987 to capitalize on the increasing popularity of golf. That same year the chain made an instant success of the Gamagōri Prince on Atsumi Bay, purchased as Tsutsumi has admitted for about $2 million less than its market value of $4.7 million from the city of Gamagōri, which was eager to see the bankrupt 27-room hotel restored to its 1930s opulence.[43] Prince's main resort operations abroad were concentrated in Hawaii, where the 300-room Maui Prince, opened in 1986, was joined by the twin-towered 521-room Hawaii Prince Waikiki in 1989, a year after the chain bought the Westin Mauna Kea Beach hotel on the big island. This hotel, built by Laurence S. Rockefeller in 1965 and later owned by United Air Lines, has long been considered the premier resort in the state, where Seibu also operates two golf courses.[44]

Virtually all the expansion at home and abroad in the 1980s was a result of Tsutsumi's personal leadership of Prince Hotels. His brother Yūji (the youngest of Yasujirō's sons with Ishizuka Tsuneko) had served as president from the company's start in 1970 until Yoshiaki demoted him in 1976 to vice president, assuming the presidency himself. Yūji, a 1965 graduate of UCLA, was trained in the latest American management techniques; his progressive views apparently clashed with Yoshiaki's, even though in 1986 the latter denied that he and Yūji had ever quarreled.[45] Yoshiaki also opposed his brother's marriage to a Canadian, Lynette Himmelman, whose father chaired the Western International Hotels. Yūji quit the Prince Hotels in January 1985, operated a restaurant in Canada, and then stunned the Japanese hotel industry late the next year by joining Tsutsumi Seiji's Saison Group to help run the Hotel Seiyō Ginza when this trend-setting small building opened in March 1987—ratcheting up the rivalry in leisure services between Seiji and Yoshiaki by several notches.[46] Having pushed Yūji aside in 1976, Yoshiaki guided the company through its greatest wave of urban construction and planned much of the resort expansion of the late 1980s before stepping up to become board chair in June 1987. His pretext for turning operations over to subordinates was that he had "no time" for the chain any longer, but the impression was strong that he did so to skirt future conflicts of interest with the various athletic federations and committees he led.[47]

Just after Prince had brightened its image by taking over as caterer at the State Guest House, its reputation was damaged by an episode of food poisoning affecting 194 guests at the Akasaka Prince Hotel during the summer of 1987. Tsutsumi acknowledged the following year that "it's much worse in the service industry to lower your level of service than to run a deficit. You can make up deficits, but once you get a reputation for bad service, you can never recover from it."[48] In fact there were persistent complaints by then about attitude and service throughout the chain, apparently catalyzed by Yūji's departure in 1985. One unsystematic but widely remarked survey, published in *Shūkan bunshun* on July 5, 1990, chagrined the company by criticizing the equipment and facilities at the Akasaka, Takanawa, and Tokyo Princes while awarding five stars to the Imperial, Ōkura, and, most embarrassing of all, Seiji's Seiyō Ginza.[49]

Although the top-line hotels in Tokyo did very handsomely in the late 1980s, competition among them kept room charges lower than those in resorts where the railway group had a monopoly. Tacitly acknowledging the dissatisfaction with service, Tsutsumi wrote in 1988 that "this is now the time for Prince to build trust, since it's not profitable."[50] The company shields its financial reports from outsiders; but it is safe to assume that if the chain was not profitable, the reason was high interest payments on loans to finance expansion, keeping taxes low. The owner referred to the railway group's overall hotel business as a $1.6 billion enterprise in 1988, but this sum presumably included auxiliary tourism revenues not directly connected with either Prince or other hotels and inns belonging to the group. The most well-informed estimates were that Prince itself enjoyed a 66.7 percent increase in sales to $652.2 million between 1983 and 1988, much of it attributable to newly opened buildings for middle-class families in search of recreation as well as a place to stay.[51]

THE BLOSSOMING OF INTEGRATED RESORTS

Recreation complexes beyond hotels themselves were where the Seibu Railway Group showed the most vigorous leisure-related activity during the 1980s, in line with Tsutsumi's rather arid 1987 assertion that "recreation is as important as food, clothing, and shelter."[52] In addition to its longtime bastions in Nagano, Hakone, and Izu, Kokudo Keikaku was busiest in Hokkaido and northeastern Japan, although in the late 1980s it also opened new resorts at two sites in Kyushu. Hokkaido is interesting because it took Tsutsumi so long to challenge the Gotō family's Tōkyū enterprises as the main developer of the island's tourism opportunities. Tōkyū first arrived there in 1957, eight years before Seibu's small start with a golf course at Ōnuma. By the time Tsutsumi opened the Sapporo Prince and started bulldozing Furano into an enormous recreation complex in 1972, Hokkaido was almost a Tōkyū fiefdom under the leadership of Gotō Noboru, son of Yasujirō's lifelong rival, Gotō Keita. But Yoshiaki foresaw much potential in integrated resorts at a time when Tōkyū was still heavily invested in suburban housing development outside Tokyo, a market Kokudo Keikaku by then eschewed for the most part. Shortly after this time the combined earnings of the Seibu railway and retailing groups surpassed those of the Tōkyū enterprises, which have remained in Seibu's shadow since.[53] The overall leisure industry grew so fast by the time Tsutsumi's resorts were ready that there proved to be plenty of business for both Tōkyū and the railway group in the prefecture. Indeed the two became so cooperative that Gotō Noboru asked Tsutsumi to rent him a golf course at Karuizawa 72 for the first annual Tōkyū Ladies Open tournament in August 1987, an event that has been held there each year since.[54]

Furano was a dying town of twenty thousand in the center of Hokkaido when Kokudo Keikaku began sculpting ski slopes and putting up a chalet-style Prince with 144 rooms, ready in 1974 at the foot of a course now used regularly for World Cup races. Tsutsumi's incrementalist strategy of plowing cash flow back into additional facilities via loans meant a steady expansion of lifts and gondolas, restaurants, and tennis courts as well as an indoor swimming pool. Furano was so glad for new jobs and local purchasing, with a combined value by today of $23.4 million a year,[55] that it helped the developers clear the way for a hillside golf course downslope from the 407-room New Furano Prince, both opened in 1988. More than 1.5 million skiers are drawn to this "Switzerland of Japan" each season, and hundreds of thousands more in summers.[56] Among the company's five other recreation zones in the prefecture, Niseko attracted Tsutsumi's special attention in the 1980s in an effort to replicate the success of Furano on a smaller scale. The Niseko Higashiyama Prince, completed in 1982, was surrounded by ski slopes with a gondola and seven lifts, twenty-three tennis courts, an equestrian facility, and soon thereafter a golf course on land the Seibu Real Estate Company took over in 1978 from Tōa Sōgo Kigyō, a failed development firm with apparent underworld links.[57] Niseko and Furano are the most ambitious of Tsutsumi's many projects in Hokkaido, where the railway group currently operates seven hotels, six ski areas, five golf courses, and a variety of restaurants.

Kokudo Keikaku's principal task in the Tōhoku district of northeastern Honshu was to overcome the head start in tourism made by a notable rival developer, Kokusai Kōgyō. Osano Kenji, its president as well as the largest shareholder of Tōkyū until his death in 1986, first invested in the region in 1962 and eventually rose to the peak of the hotel world by becoming owner of the Imperial in Tokyo.[58] In the cushy realm of Japanese construction there is a slice of business for everyone, but newcomers must be especially decorous in avoiding direct confrontations with powerful elder figures like Osano, who was also the largest individual shareholder in Japan Air Lines and a principal in the Lockheed scandal of 1976.

Tsutsumi was scrupulously deferential to Osano, seventeen years his senior, but at the same time began to compete with Kokusai Kōgyō when he opened the Towada Prince in 1977 and started building ski facilities in five locations around Tōhoku. A Prince was added in 1984 at the region's other large lake, Tazawako, and Seibu Golf installed three courses during that decade. By far the largest Tsutsumi development in the area sprouted at Shizukuishi, just west of the Tōhoku Shinkansen train terminal at Morioka. First came a widely praised ski area, opened in 1980, that now offers two gondolas and thirteen lifts; the world Alpine ski championships, plagued by dreadful weather, were held there in February 1993. A thirty-six-hole golf course opened in 1984, and the 266-room Shizukuishi Prince soon followed. Although Seibu was well established in the region by the time Osano died in October 1986, Tsutsumi showed no interest in taking over his resort empire in either Tōhoku or Hawaii, and Osano's brother Masakuni stepped in to lead Kokusai Kōgyō without incident.[59]

Of the many other Kokudo Keikaku resort projects in the 1980s, three illustrate the complexities the company faced when it operated outside its traditional zones of influence near Karuizawa, Hakone, and Izu. One was the integrated recreation complex at Minakami Kōgen, a high plateau in Gunma Prefecture surrounded by tall peaks and relatively undeveloped timberland. The company bought 308 hectares there in the late 1960s but ran into fierce trouble before winning local approval for its plans. Unlike other major resorts that evolved incrementally, Minakami Kōgen's facilities became backed up because of tangled local clearances and finally opened all at once in 1986: a 212-room Prince, twenty tennis courts, a thirty-six-hole golf links, and a small ski area with three lifts.[60] Two years later the Myōkō Pine Valley facility opened north of Lake Nojiri in Niigata Prefecture with a Prince Hotel, twenty-seven-hole golf course, tennis courts, gymnasiums, pool, equestrian club, and modest ski slope. Two big Kokudo Keikaku ski areas were nearby. The Myōkō Pine Valley resort was actually built and owned by the Matsushita enterprises but operated under contract by Kokudo Keikaku, apparently because of Tsutsumi's amicable relationship with Matsushita Kōnosuke, the Panasonic baron (Prince's other operating contract was for the Moriguchi Prince in Osaka).[61] The Kitakyūshū Prince, also dating to 1988, was the keystone of a new urban resort foreshadowing the railway group's likely projects in the 1990s. It included a 220-room hotel with the usual restaurants and banquet halls, a PePe shopping arcade and delicatessen, a gym, an ice arena, a pool, and tennis courts, as well as a multipurpose hall for trade shows.[62] Essentially an updated version of the hugely profitable Shinagawa sports complex, this city recreation zone contained more retailing outlets than other developments by the railway group and represented its biggest foray thus far into urban planning on recently acquired land. It was also unusual in that it was developed as a joint venture with Mitsubishi Kasei, which was a 60-percent participant.[63]

THE RESORT LAW AND THE ANTI-GOLF MOVEMENT

A new set of rules came into play in May 1987 when the Diet passed the so-called Resort Law (Sōgō Hoyō Chiiki Seibihō) as a part of Prime Minister Nakasone's broad program of privatization and deregulation. The new law, for which both Tsutsumi Seiji and Tsutsumi Yoshiaki lobbied, allowed local and prefectural governments to issue bonds to finance infrastructure for resort projects in a thousand locations covering nearly a third of the nation's territory. It gave developers ways to obtain land cheaply, including large tax breaks, and provided for $69 billion in public funds during 1987–1997 to advance resort construction.[64] Such largess was popular not merely among entrepreneurs but also in rural prefectures that had steadily lost population since the 1950s. Resorts were expected to be in the 1990s what prefectural industrial cities were supposed to have been in the 1960s: heavily subsidized magnets of capital and employment to perk up declining areas of the country.[65] No act of legislation more aptly symbolized Japan's transition from manufacturing to the service sector than this introit to the age of leisure.

The Resort Law posited that $828 billion would be invested by public and private sources in the designated recreation zones by the start of the next century.[66] It also assumed no significant opposition from environmentalists or other local groups, a far cry from reality in the interval since it was enacted in 1987. The legislation seemed almost handmade for both Seibu's and Saison's interests: of the first eighteen projects to be approved, Saison was listed as a codeveloper of three and the railway group of three others.[67] The law effectively confirmed the triumph of Tsutsumi Yoshiaki's longtime method of awaiting an invitation from local authorities, relying on them for regulatory clearances, and expecting that land would be made available cheaply to Seibu.[68]

Environmental concerns have been an issue in urban politics in Japan since the late 1960s, but not until twenty years later did they become sharply focused on rural resort development. The most inviting target was not mountainsides disfigured for ski slopes or pollution from cars on clogged country roadways but verdant golf courses, including a new one Tsutsumi proposed to build in Karuizawa but was forced to abandon in 1990. Most of the railway group's nearly three dozen golf courses around the country were built after 1970, when the sport suddenly acquired the wide middle-class following that Tsutsumi Yasujirō anticipated for it when he arrived in Karuizawa a half-century earlier. By 1986 the Leisure Development Center found that Japan had 7.5 million active golfers, 10 percent of them women, and that expenditures for equipment, golf schools, greens fees, memberships, and driving ranges totaled $8.4 billion a year, greater than for any other sport. (Japanese also spent $14.2 billion that year betting on horse races and an astounding $60 billion on pachinko.)[69] The nationwide anti–golf course movement of the 1980s meant to put a halt to what it saw as the malevolent side effects of the ever more popular game.

As Japan's largest operator of golf courses, with another half-dozen designed by Arnold Palmer and Robert Trent Jones in the works, Seibu Golf was a natural focus for resentments harbored by Karuizawa residents who thought that Tsutsumi had already overdeveloped their village to his own advantage, by friends of nature who thought forests enjoyed by all were being sacrificed to a sport for the privileged few, and by safety-conscious citizens who were convinced that herbicides applied to the fairways were polluting community aquifers. The Karuizawa protesters, led by Iwata Kaoru and backed by such famous vacation residents as the novelists Niwa Fumio and Endō Shūsaku, presented petitions, fanned misgivings about Seibu's domination of local politics, sent delegations to Kokudo Keikaku's offices, and finally filed a complaint with the Tokyo district prosecutor in 1990 charging that the firm had violated certain provisions of the National Land-use Planning Law. At this point Tsutsumi withdrew from the project with the understated comment, "It was difficult to obtain unanimous consent from landowners in the area,"[70] a condition he insisted on for all his ventures. The episode touched off a storm of criticism over his allegedly cavalier disregard of both regulatory procedures and common sense.[71]

The rumpus in Karuizawa was the most widely publicized incident in a surprisingly stubborn movement to restrict further building of courses around the country. In 1990 more than 1,700 golf courses were in operation in Japan, with another 300 under construction and 900 being planned.[72] Opponents were not mollified when the government's Environmental Agency, after much testing, reported that 94 percent of water samples taken near 394 courses were free of herbicides and that the rest contained an average of one milligram per ton, which the agency declared to be safe.[73] The real problem, according to Fujiwara Makoto of Utsunomiya University, seemed to be that "we are consuming the resources of future generations by turning forests into entertainment facilities for immediate profits."[74] The issue became so heated that Kobe placed a year-long moratorium on building new courses in early 1990, six prefectures imposed stiff restrictions on their construction or banned it outright, and voters in a town in Ibaraki Prefecture turned out in record numbers in November 1990 to oust Mayor Matsuzaki Tatsuo largely because he had approved ten new golf courses around the community.[75] It is hardly surprising that Tsutsumi and other resort operators drew the ire of citizens upset when sudden wealth transformed the Japanese countryside.

Even more humiliating than the Karuizawa fiasco was Tsutsumi's resignation on April 12, 1990, as head of the Japan Olympic Committee after just eight months in office. The committee favored building a new ski slope for Japan's bid to host the 1998 winter Olympic Games very near Seibu's existing hotels and ski facilities at Shiga Kōgen, Nagano Prefecture. But local opponents criticized the proposed skiing course as environmentally destructive to Mount Iwasuge, and Tsutsumi resigned to avoid suggestions of conflict of interest if his companies should end up benefiting from the event.[76] At length an alternate site owned by a rival operator was selected as the ski venue for Nagano's successful Olympic proposal.

The Resort Law of 1987 and subsequent vicissitudes led Tsutsumi to refocus the group's goals for the 1990s somewhat, without abandoning the relentless demand for recreation and luxury which led him to note several years ago that the weekend and holiday "rush for leisure activities is now even more amazing than the commute to work and school"[77] on weekdays. Kokudo Keikaku continued to receive nearly a hundred requests a year to build resorts from local governments clamoring for development, and the group had projects under way in half of the forty-seven prefectures in the early 1990s. Nonetheless Tsutsumi said in 1990 that "I have utterly no interest in buying more hotels abroad,"[78] apparently closing that chapter of corporate history. More arresting was the statement he made in the next breath: "Now that the Resort Law is completed, I believe my resort developing is finished. When others start wanting to try it, it's no longer my turn. I'm heading into areas others won't do."[79] This echo of his father's business philosophy is probably worth taking seriously if one recalls that Tsutsumi also withdrew from urban land purchases in 1972 just before the peak of a huge run-up in real-estate values. Without predicting a slowdown in the resort industry, he said in 1990 that the railway group during the next decade would move increasingly into urban development and suburban shopping centers, anchored by small hotels rather than department stores, "because we'd rather not get involved in retailing."[80] In this way Tsutsumi proposed to direct Kokudo Keikaku's future investments where his father began them seventy years before, in the residential suburbs as well as mountain retreats for middle-class consumers.

ONE-PERSON LEADERSHIP AND LOW-PROFIT ENTERPRISES

"I don't like to work with others, no matter who they are. I work by myself,"[81] Tsutsumi Yoshiaki said in 1984, dismissing the need for committee meetings, wide consultation, or group consensus in running his businesses. Tsutsumi, who plays tennis but prefers singles to doubles, helicopters to construction projects for hands-on supervision: "On the site there must always be a single system of command."[82] He is able personally to oversee every new hotel, golf course, and ski slope to an almost unimaginable level of detail because he owns the construction companies that build them. "But once they are weaned," he has claimed, "they are independent. Once they are launched into orbit, we don't interfere with them at all but leave them entirely to the discretion of the people in charge."[83] This all-or-nothing approach assumes that subordinates are talented professionals—or else loyal yes-persons who would never provoke the need for intervention from headquarters.

Unlike his brother Seiji, who is fond of ideas about "the logic of capitalism" and "the logic of humanity," Tsutsumi Yoshiaki says that "I have no theory of management." Instead he has a theory of people centered on hiring loyal junior- or senior-high-school graduates: "In my company we don't need people any brighter than I."[84] This is because "I am the only person who needs to use his head." What the company needs is sincere employees: "Sincerity can't be bought with money,"[85] whereas expertise can. Naturally this highly conservative, patently arrogant view rankled the Seibu Railway Group's college-educated managers, above all when *Asahi shinbun* quoted Tsutsumi in 1987 as saying "university graduates don't meet our needs"[86]—a moment of candor Kokudo Keikaku tried to soft-pedal for public-relations purposes. Apart from hockey and baseball players for the company teams, the group hires relatively few university graduates (perhaps 5 percent).[87] Tsutsumi says that "the number-one defect in university education today is the problem of discipline";[88] consequently he forces those few graduates the group does enroll to undergo a harshly regimented year-long training program to teach them the company motto of "thanks and service"—and, one suspects, humility as well. After a year as waiters, ticket punchers, golf caddies, and toilet cleaners, they meet the owner and become full members of the companies to which they are posted. All new employees are subjected to stiff discipline and are forbidden to smoke, as is everyone in the Kokudo Keikaku head office.[89]

Once they complete their probation, newcomers quickly discover that the group rarely uses policy documents (*ringisho*) signed by middle managers but instead relies on the owner's judgment. Tsutsumi says he expects every subordinate involved in a decision to read all the relevant paperwork and face questioning by the boss.[90] He tells all staff members to state their own opinions, regardless of what others may think or wish to hear, after which he settles the matter.[91] "You can never progress if you are afraid of failure," Tsutsumi has said. "The important thing is to make an effort to recover what was lost in the failure."[92] It is easy to imagine that this one-on-one leadership style cows all but the hardiest employees into virtual silence. Yet the owner is outspoken in rejecting consensus: "When a group does this, it's really dangerous. Group decisions are like the Nazis."[93] To avoid mass consent among his underlings, therefore, he shirks seeking the collective will and instead resolves issues himself.

The railway group is well known for operating its facilities without days off and for requiring that an official always be present to deal with the unexpected. The nature of the service industry, Tsutsumi says, means that "managers by virtue of their positions don't take vacations."[94] Like his father, he rewards hard work, promotes promising cooks and ski instructors to managerial rank, and keeps employees at their jobs long enough to teach them well rather than rotating them frequently. Tsutsumi claimed rather formulaically in 1984 that "we don't build the organization and fit people to it, we start with people and build an organization that fits them."[95] The avowed intent, he said, was to avoid bureaucratism. Under his one-person rule the group for many years had the most skeletal management structure imaginable: only at the end of the 1980s did either the railway or Kokudo Keikaku modernize by appointing a full complement of representative, senior, managing, and regular directors.[96] The motive may have been to blunt criticism of his leadership after the botched episodes with Lion Manager Mori, anti-golf environmentalists, and the Japan Olympic Committee; but it is also true that he has frequently paid lip service to making Seibu "an organization like Mitsubishi"—one strong enough "to be operated by anybody."[97] If the group is to emulate Mitsubishi, it will have to list its subsidiaries on the stock exchange, expand its capital, open itself to outside investors and scrutiny, and give up its character as a closely guarded family enterprise run by an authoritarian owner-president.

Doing so would shake Tsutsumi's empire to its roots and obliterate his strategy of building assets, not profits, by keeping earnings so low that the railway pays only modest taxes and Kokudo Keikaku almost none at all. This technique, dubbed *zeitekku* (tax manipulation) by financial wags, is the Seibu Railway Group's alternative to running up big profits, paying the corporate-profits tax of 52 percent, and using retained earnings for further expansion. Tsutsumi instead follows his father's method of borrowing extensively on the hidden value of the land he controls and making huge interest payments to his creditors, which keeps profits low, minimizes current taxes, depresses the value of shares since few dividends are paid, reduces potential inheritance taxes, and keeps control within the family by avoiding equity markets. Banks are happy to lend without seeking seats on the board of directors. In 1982 Tsutsumi told would-be investors in the railway, which is traded, "If you want a big dividend, don't own our stock."[98] A few years later he told a press conference, "The reason Kokudo Keikaku doesn't pay taxes? That's simple. We have no profits."[99] "If we stopped building new enterprises, we'd earn greater profits," he added in an interview published in 1990, "but actually we have a mountain of businesses we want to try and a full roster of ones to expand, so no matter what we do, we'll not earn bigger profits."[100] Words like these push the Mitsubishi model to the remote horizon at best.

Nikkei bijinesu in June 1984 declared that the Tsutsumi motto should be "land rather than profits" and added, "Perhaps in this sense Seibu is the most difficult enterprise for foreign businesspeople to understand."[101] Actually his realm seems remarkably like a set of modern commercial services bestriding a foundation of late Tokugawa landlordism, in which family property is kept intact across generations and expanded through revenues from trade. Because its shares are unlisted, Kokudo Keikaku's value must be estimated for inheritance-tax purposes; with low profits, few corporate taxes, minimal dividends, and archaic book values of its assets, the assessment is likely to be low, enabling the family to pay its tax and retain control.[102] Thanks to its *zeitekku* methods, Kokudo Keikaku owed no corporate-profits tax at all in 1979–1981 and only very low taxes thereafter. According to a balance sheet leaked to the press in mid-1990, it paid just $83,916 in corporate-profits taxes on sales of $713.3 million for the fiscal year ending March 1990 because of interest payments that year of $83.9 million. Its net profits were $1.7 million.[103] In effect, by paying interest instead of taxes the company was adding to its asset base, but only because banks remained willing to lend against the collateral of Kokudo Keikaku's land. Throughout the 1980s the firm maintained an extremely high debt-to-asset ratio. In March 1990 its loans were $1.45 billion and its total assets were $1.64 billion, a ratio of 87.6 percent. For most businesses such figures would mean peril, but listed among the assets is just $128.2 million in land—clearly worth vastly more in the eyes of bankers if it secures eleven times this amount in borrowings.[104] The company's loans more than doubled in the 1980s as its assets grew and new cash-thirsty projects took shape in nearly every part of the country. All of this has been built on a paid-in capital base of just $733,000, a figure that has not changed in yen terms since 1973.[105]

Kokudo Keikaku's sales rose 191 percent during the 1980s, even faster than its borrowings, according to evaluations by the financial community based on fragmentary information made available to it. At the same time, higher interest rates and other nonoperating costs cut back on net profits as a percentage of sales by the end of the decade.[106] In the year ending March 1990, hotels accounted for 46 percent of the company's sales, golf and skiing 20 percent each, and sports facilities almost all the rest[107]—a near-total transformation of a one-time real-estate concern during the seventy years since it began. Sales figures for the group as a whole, with seventy-four unlisted companies whose financial statements are rarely seen by outsiders, are fragmentary and inexact. Overall sales were estimated at $2.9 billion in 1985[108] and $7.2 billion five years later, up 42.9 percent in yen terms.[109] The group's borrowings began to catch up with sales at the end of the decade: they were estimated at $1.4 billion in 1987[110] and $4.9 billion in 1990, up 250.5 percent in yen terms.[111] Profits for the group were thought to be about $130 million in the year ending March 1990.

According to *Shūkan daiyamondo,* the sales leaders were the railway (22 percent of the group's total), Seibu Construction (20.6 percent), Kokudo Keikaku (13.7 percent), Seibu Motor Freight (12.8 percent), and Prince Hotels (11.5 percent). The railroad, construction company, and Seibu Motor Freight were easily the most profitable, accounting for 74.2 percent of the group's total profits as calculated from rather sketchy statistics.[112]

Even though its sales represent less than a seventh of the group's total turnover, Kokudo Keikaku is the nerve center for controlling the other companies and is kept tightly within the family's grasp. When the speculator Yokoi Hideki began buying up Seibu Railway shares in 1969–1970, Tsutsumi quickly gave in to his demand for greenmail and paid $6.9 million for a position that had cost Yokoi $4.1 million.[113] The owner then steadily increased Kokudo Keikaku's proportion of the railway's stock and the family's percentage of Kokudo Keikaku shares, blocking outsiders through what amounted to a management buyout.[114] The railway group was such a prize because its landholdings greatly exceeded those of any competitor in estimated market value. According to calculations by a major bank in 1984, Seibu's assets had a book value of $840.3 million but a market worth of $50.4 billion, whereas Mitsubishi Estate Company, with much commercial land in central Tokyo, had properties with a book value of $1.3 billion but a market value of just $8.4 billion. The holdings of Mitsui Real Estate Development, Tōkyū, and Ōji Seishi were put at roughly $4.2 billion each.[115]

The financial press has endlessly repeated the figure 14,895 hectares as the approximate extent of the railway group's real-estate holdings, about two-thirds of it owned by Kokudo Keikaku. This estimate is impossible to verify, although Tsutsumi confirmed that Kokudo Keikaku had about 9,930 hectares in 1970,[116] a figure that has probably not contracted since then. Another comprehensive inventory of the group's worth occurred in 1987, when a large securities house took rising land values into account in arriving at the sum of $120.7 billion, an increase of 45.8 percent in yen terms over the 1984 calculation.[117] An even more detailed investigation by *Shūkan daiyamondo* in July 1990 acknowledged further leaps in real-estate prices by fixing the railway group's value at $279.7 billion, a 128.5 percent jump in yen terms over the 1987 assessment.[118] This figure is almost quadruple the listed assets of Nippon Telegraph and Telephone Corporation, Japan's richest publicly traded company.[119] Since no one is about to purchase Tsutsumi's realm at a stroke, such estimates are hypothetical and probably misleading measures of worth because his land could be converted to cash only on a piecemeal basis. But they benefit Seibu psychologically by making bankers more cooperative, competitors more wary, and the public more awed by the power that lies in the hands of a company so rich.

What is intriguing is how Tsutsumi Yoshiaki controls so much wealth with such a relatively small stake. Before the Nikkei market index tumbled in mid-1990, a share of Kokudo Keikaku based on those of similar companies was estimated to be worth about $38. Tsutsumi owned 40 percent of the company's shares, with loyal senior managers and affiliated companies accounting for a good deal of the rest. His 828,000 shares had a value of $31.5 million,[120] an impressive sum but only 15 percent the estimated worth of Nakauchi Isao, the president of Daiei,[121] and far below Japan's truly rich. His family should have no trouble paying the inheritance tax on $31.5 million, keeping the property intact. Kokudo Keikaku owned 100 percent of the Prince Hotels, 50 percent of Seibu Construction, and 48.7 percent of the Seibu Railway and, through the latter, scores of subsidiaries besides. This meant that as of 1990 Tsutsumi's $31.5 million holdings gave him control of a group with a book value of roughly $1.8 billion (a ratio of 1:57) and an estimated market worth of $279.7 billion (a ratio of 1:8,890).[122] Lewis Carroll might like the ingenious way Tsutsumi's $31.5 million became $111.8 billion—the putative value of the 40 percent of the empire he "owns."

Not even *Forbes*, which since 1987 has ranked Tsutsumi as one of the world's richest private citizens, contends that his personal worth approaches this astronomical sum—the more so because he does not even own his principal residence, an unprepossessing two-story house in tan brick with eaves that almost touch his neighbors' in Nishi Azabu, situated on 900 square meters of company-owned land worth $9.6 million in 1987.[123] *Forbes* as of 1990 put his wealth at $16 billion, a bit ahead of Mori Taikichirō, another land magnate who, before his death in 1993, presumably directly owned more of his companies than did Tsutsumi; in 1993 the magazine placed Tsutsumi's holdings at least as high as $9 billion, and quite possibly $22.5 billion, depending on the basis of calculation.[124] Most Japanese financial commentators say that all the *Forbes* estimates seem low, but how low is guesswork and probably unimportant. Tsutsumi's 40 percent holdings in Kokudo Keikaku translate into 84.2 million shares of the Seibu Railway, with a mid-1990 value of $2.9 billion;[125] all reckonings beyond this point are based on assumptions that cannot be fully corroborated. Whatever his potential worth, Tsutsumi's personal income taxes are sizable (a bit under $1.6 million a year) but not enough to place him among the top 100 taxpayers in Japan, 60 of whom on the 1990 list made their money in land transactions.[126] Still the scope and wealth of the businesses he commands make him Japan's lion of leisure, dating back to his oceanside swimming pools, mountain skate centers, and artificial ski runs as an undergraduate in the 1950s—like his father's career, a record of learning and labor across many years before he helped to establish leisure as a routine part of Japanese life and finally realized king-size financial returns from it in the 1980s.

CHAPTER TEN

LEISURE AS AMENITIES: THE SEIBU SAISON GROUP IN THE 1980s

Leisure became a regular part of daily or weekly schedules for most people in Japan during the 1980s, even if they did not have much time for it or ended up doing little more than watching television, at which the Japanese outdo all other nations. Despite the thirst for overtime in an expanding economy after 1986, the number of hours worked in manufacturing fell off gradually to 42.3 per week in 1990, even though the average Japanese employee still put in 168 extra hours a year as of 1991, comparable to the 164 hours of paid overtime for workers in the United States that same year.[1] In both countries two-income families faced what Juliet B. Schor calls "a profound structural crisis of time,"[2] in which couples had to plan carefully for both personal relaxation and civic activities. This crisis may be recent and unexpected in the United States, but Japanese have long since learned to budget their free hours carefully as they move toward a *yutori*-type society. Still, old habits die hard: the Japan Recreation Association offered a course in September 1991 on how to use leisure time and was swamped with three times the expected number of applicants willing to pay for the chance to study how to relax.[3]

The Seibu Saison Group reconnoitered the growing leisure market in the 1980s by ferreting out niches among the clientele it already served, not by a massive, capital-intensive assault like the railway group. Even its expeditions into the $31.16 billion sports industry, which the Ministry of International Trade and Industry predicts will grow five-fold by 2000,[4] were selective and narrowly slotted, like the Club Med resort in Sahoro or the Seabornia Marina at Miura. Saison's strategy was targeted especially at the 38 percent of women in their twenties who by 1992 said they "enjoy leisure as much as possible" (only 3 percent in the same survey said "work is important").[5]

But the proper tactics for exploiting this market proved to be surprisingly slippery. As Egashira Keisuke, president of the Osawa trading company, pointed out in late 1990:

> It's easy to conceptualize leisure in the abstract but hard to think about it in practical marketing terms. It's not like the 1960s, when everybody wanted a car, a color TV, and an air conditioner. Is leisure a shirt? A trip somewhere? A set of golf clubs? This is a real problem for planning a marketing strategy. Japanese are more diverse and individualistic than they were twenty years ago, but they pursue leisure in groups far more than Americans and Europeans. Our marketing is based on the assumption that leisure lifestyles are very diverse, but this is difficult to pinpoint.[6]

Keeping up with this diversity is the challenge of Tsutsumi Seiji's dictum that "management is an eternal revolution," part of his campaign to force his employees to stay abreast of changes in politics, society, lifestyles, and consumer values by trying to imagine what fashions and leisure modes would please shoppers of the future.[7]

Leisure was a mainline component of the mature consumer economy, Tsutsumi noted in 1991, insofar as individuals sought psychological and sensual satisfaction as well as functional utility from their purchases.[8] Saison confirmed that "the self" (*watakushi*) was an ever more critical marketing focus that year. President Mizuno Seiichi of Seibu Department Stores noted that "*Watakushi* means both individuality and selfishness. Until recently there has been a single market of people who are more or less equal. Nowadays the self has become a firm part of people's sense of values. The result is that we face a very difficult market, because people are so individualized and because there is such a fine line between individuality and selfishness."[9] This fine line was especially hard to draw in the growing leisure market, Mizuno said: "How to respond to it is a question not just for the department store but also for the group as a whole."[10] First Seibu developed recreational products for its stores, then spun off small subsidiary companies as demand grew, and eventually drew them back together under the rubric of "leisure life products" to take advantage of the supposed synergy effect. "The total power of the group is what counts, not just what the department store does. The department store's part is relatively modest, but it ties in with what the group as a whole does with hotels, tourism, golf, and other leisure activities, including culture"[11]—exactly the market slots Saison carved out among its well-to-do, predominantly female customers as they turned more and more to leisure for self-expression in the later 1980s.

VACATIONS AND HOUSING FOR HAND-PICKED CLIENTELES

Like his brother Yoshiaki, Tsutsumi Seiji used a mainstream real-estate company within his own enterprise group as the fastest route to the upscale leisure market in the 1980s. His Seibu Urban Development Company, after suffering deep losses a decade earlier, transformed itself by degrees into a mildly profitable and much-discussed developer of hotels, sports facilities, and urban properties that today produce almost as much revenue for the group as its well-established housing business.[12] Two decades earlier Tsutsumi had predicted in *Rejā no kagaku* (Science of leisure, 1962) that the field would be defined more and more broadly in the decades ahead.[13] The way to exploit it, he decided soon thereafter, was to work with partners and build imaginative projects on leased property rather than to become a large landowner himself (he said that "landlords are very conservative and exclusive"[14]). His strategy ever since had been to make money by adding prestige value to a building through function, style, and environment—as in Europe or the United States—rather than the usual Japanese practice of land speculation.[15] To be sure, Tsutsumi lacked the resources to buy real estate in a big way. His use of partners was driven by necessity, whereas Yoshiaki turned down a chance to buy the Inter-Continental Hotel chain before Seiji acquired it in 1988 because "I don't believe in joint management in principle."[16]

The Seibu Retailing Group bought into the resort industry in

December 1982 by forging a management and capital linkup with Taiyō Real Estate Industries (Taiyō Fudōsan Kōgyō), a Yokohama firm with annual sales of $60.2 million but debts reportedly twice that size.[17] Tsutsumi Seiji became its board chair the following July and soon obtained loans from Mitsubishi Trust Bank that allowed him to merge Taiyō with Seibu Urban Development in January 1986, forming the Seiyō Corporation. At that point the new company had more than 3,000 hectares under development.[18] Tsutsumi welcomed Taiyō because of its hotels, golf courses, marinas, and housing complexes as well as its commercial properties throughout Japan. Many of its leisure investments were located near resorts owned by the Seibu Railway Group, stirring much speculation about rivalry between siblings that Seiji tried to parry with indirection: "A lot is said about us brothers, but relations are neither good nor bad."[19]

Taiyō brought with it 1,254 hectares of real estate, including 594 at Ōnuma in Hokkaido, where its hotel and country club competed directly with facilities owned by Kokudo Keikaku.[20] Even though Arai Minoru, the president of Seiyō, plunged into new golf and ski projects on former Taiyō land from Hokkaido to Okinawa, by 1990 it was clear that Tsutsumi Seiji was turning into the prince of marine sports, as Yoshiaki was of those on grass and snow. Thanks to its acquisition of Taiyō, Seibu Saison dominated the marinas in Shōnan and Izu, the country's richest markets for boating. The company used its Taiyō connections to set up joint ventures with the Yamaha Corporation, whose yachts and motorboats gave it a 70 percent share of the marine-sports industry in Japan.[21] Eventually Seiji hoped to create a nationwide boating network tying Hokkaido, Shōnan, and the Shima Peninsula with Kyushu and Okinawa for an annual series of yacht races.[22]

Although they sometimes competed with Yoshiaki's facilities, these leisure-time investments were natural choices for Seiji in the economic run-up of the 1980s. Nor were they unprecedented for Seibu Saison, which had opened a resort lodge at Yatsugatake for golf and skiing in 1975, then later added tennis courts, 700 mountainside cottages, a crafts studio, and a chamber-concert hall (opened in August 1988).[23] The Resort Law of 1987 smoothed the group's efforts by encouraging cooperation with prefectures and localities eager for tourists, but the countervailing force of environmentalism led Arai to declare that "the point of a resort is that it is meant to harmonize with nature. If it ends up destroying it, it's worthless."[24] It is easy to imagine that market demand from well-to-do home seekers who valued parks and green zones, not an abstract commitment to conservation, led Seiyō to use just 22 percent of the land area at its luxury development in Senri New Town for housing[25] and to locate its exclusive home sites at Katsurazaka next to Kyoto's highly prized bird sanctuary.

Reasoning that resorts in the 1980s had to provide a relaxing atmosphere and plenty of sports for customers who took travel for granted, Seibu Saison unveiled Club Med Sahoro at Karikachi Highlands in Hokkaido in December 1987, a joint venture with the Paris-based chain of vacation villages. This relatively limited facility, Club Med's first in Japan, offered skiing, golf, tennis, and commodious temporary living space on forested mountainsides for urban families who had little room or greenery back in the city. Seibu Saison invested $248.3 million at Sahoro,[26] but as a members-only vacation resort it posed little threat to high-volume, high-turnover sites operated nearby at Furano by Kokudo Keikaku or outside Sapporo by Tōkyū. So small was this resort that fewer than 10,000 guests stayed at Sahoro in an entire season, yet by 1990 the club was running at 90 percent of capacity.[27] Most important to Tsutsumi, the joint venture gave Seibu Saison's travel agencies entrée to the worldwide skein of Club Med locations and formed the basis for Tsutsumi's planned Pacific Rim resort group, which by 1990 included a fisherman's wharf elsewhere in Hokkaido with the improbable name of Moo Kushiro.[28]

Seiyō's cooperative agreement with the Yamaha Corporation after 1984 centered on the Ise Shima Peninsula in Mie Prefecture, where Seiyō was also the lead developer of a composite resort that included a $200 million colony for artists in Toba, opened in 1993.[29] In addition to investing in marinas and waterfront commercial projects, the company signed a contract with Accor S.A. of France in February 1988 to introduce thalassotherapy to Japan, a set of ocean-derived treatments for ailments such as gout, eczema, and rheumatism. In 1992 Seiyō inaugurated a five-story hotel in Shima to house 250 long-term guests, some of whom evidently came for the cosmetic effects of saltwater showers and seaweed-and-mud facial packs.[30] Further west the company began building Japan's first full-fledged waterfront park, known as Water Wonderland, on Rokkō Island off Kobe, starting in March 1990. Seiyō's reach extended even to Scotland, where it joined several other international partners in early 1988 to buy the historic 125-room St. Andrew's Old Course Hotel, a monument among golfers from Japan no less than from elsewhere. By the end of the decade the Seiyō group's resorts, sports facilities, and waterside developments had grown to 15 percent of its total sales, and its equally upstart hotel business accounted for another 10 percent.[31]

Seibu Saison crafted its hotel strategy to fit many of the same monied niches as its leisure-time marketing in the 1980s. Although Seibu Urban Development operated the Seibu Orion in Okinawa after 1975 and inherited a string of inns in Izu when it merged with Taiyō, the company's first major venture of the 1980s was the $54.4 million Hotel Edmont, opened in June 1985 at Iidabashi, Tokyo, with Japan National Railways as majority partner. The Edmont, intended for businesspeople, covered its construction costs by selling memberships like a golf club.[32] The luxurious 450-room building drew 600,000 visitors during its first year to a site that was once a freight yard—the first of several former national-railways properties that Tsutsumi managed to convert to commercial use. Even though this move into hotels seemed an even greater threat to Tsutsumi Yoshiaki's Princes than were Seiyō's resorts, Yoshiaki quickly concluded that a business-oriented membership hotel posed little real challenge to his tourism empire.[33] The same silent treatment could scarcely be expected, however, when Seiyō bought a 70 percent stake in the pretentious but unprofitable Kyoto Royal Hotel in August 1986, just two months before Yoshiaki unveiled the sumptuous Takaragaike Prince a few kilometers to the north. He was clearly embarrassed and irritated by Seiji's last-minute intrusion in a market each had long coveted for prestige as well as for profit.[34]

Much like the showcase Seibu department store at Yūrakuchō, cachet also explained Tsutsumi Seiji's ambition to build a small, elegant hotel with superb services for rich European and American travelers on the main street of Ginza. Modeled after the Waldorf Towers, whose manager Tsutsumi stole away, the Hotel Seiyō Ginza opened in March 1987 with just eighty guest suites costing an average of $550 per day.[35] The property was owned by Tōhō Life Insurance Company and Tokyo Theatre, a film distributor of which Seiyō is currently the top shareholder; Seibu Saison's investment in the building was $69 million.[36] Whereas other five-star hotels in Japan routinely contained lucrative wedding halls and banquet facilities, the Seiyō

Ginza reflected Tsutsumi's passion for the arts: attached were a small Seiyū cinema showing highbrow movies and a 774-seat Saison theater for professional drama.[37]

A few skeptics dismissed the inconspicuous edifice as a vanity ploy to feed "the Seibu Saison Group myth" and scoffed at the Seiyō Ginza's plan to operate in the black within nine years as "naive rubbish."[38] With an annual rent of nearly $3 million to pay, the building required at least the 60 percent occupancy rate that was sine qua non, as Tsutsumi Yoshiaki noted, for hotels that did not already possess their own land.[39] Since most wealthy foreigners stayed at the Ōkura, Imperial, or Palace, where the room charges were less than half the Seiyō Ginza's, it was far from clear that Tsutsumi Seiji could cull enough visitors from his target audience to make the venture fly. But no one doubted his assertion that "we're aiming at a different clientele from the Prince Hotel chain,"[40] which mainly attracted Japanese businesspeople.

Personal rather than commercial rivalry led to friction among the Tsutsumis when Yūji, Yoshiaki's full brother who quit as vice president of the Prince Hotels in January 1985, joined Seiji in mid-1986 to help run the Seiyō Ginza and later became board chair of Inter-Continental Hotels after Saison acquired the chain in September 1988. Yūji was also named chair of Tōkai Kankō, a major tourism company, in March 1990. Its marquee property, the Takanawa Hotel, had been managed by Seiyō since 1985 and completely renovated during 1987–1990 at a cost of $22 million.[41] By then Saison owned or operated nearly two dozen hotels, as well as inns in Izu and lodges in the mountains. None of them seemed so audacious to the railway group as the Takanawa, perched a stone's throw from Yoshiaki's citadel of Princes at Shinagawa.

No enterprise better illustrated Seiyō's boutique approach to marketing in the 1980s than housing, which continued to generate slightly more than half the company's consolidated revenues at the end of the decade. Of its many luxury developments, the most spectacular was a 3,000-unit venture on 130 hectares of choice Kyoto hillside at Katsurazaka, arguably the most exclusive address for new homes in the Kansai region. For many years Seibu Urban Development stockpiled parcels of land in Katsurazaka. Local clearances came through in March 1983, when construction began in earnest. The company touted its project by appealing to customers' desire for nature (Japan's largest bird sanctuary nearby), culture (the new International Research Center for Japanese Studies), and safety (the Woonerf design from Holland, separating cars from pedestrians). Posh residences were built on meticulously landscaped sites overlooking a 3.5-hectare historical park that preserved ancient burial mounds (*kofun*) and other archaeological locations. In 1985 Seiyō projected a total outlay of $418.4 million at Katsurazaka and expected to recoup its investment within ten years.[42]

The company built other paragons of city comfort with names like Ville Saison and Cité Neuve in the Tokyo suburbs during the 1980s, most of them high-tech condominiums wired for office automation and served by concierges and twenty-four-hour room service. Seiyō sold out a half-dozen of these information-intensive structures, each with several hundred units, as soon as they went on the market—the most swank of the seventy-eight apartment buildings it constructed between 1972 and 1990.[43] Altogether the firm sold more than 8,000 condominiums, 3,000 resort homes, and 13,000 residential lots, most of them with houses developed by Seiyō, during this period.[44] It also engaged in leasing homes to corporations for temporary use by their employees, starting in 1983; and it moved increasingly into brokering real estate at home and abroad through Houseport Seiyō,[45] a franchised subsidiary established in 1987 to cater to the New Rich. These diverse ventures allowed the company to recover from several unprofitable years during the real-estate slump of the early 1980s, so that pretax profits reached $10 million by March 1989, on annual operating revenues of $583.6 million. For the Seiyō group as a whole, including resort subsidiaries, total operating income at that point amounted to $949.3 million, up 325 percent in yen terms since the tie-up with Taiyō in 1982. By March 1992 the group's operating income stood at $1.37 billion a year.[46]

Even though housing remained its bedrock, Seiyō began the 1990s by joining with the Seibu department store, Seiyū, Parco, and Credit Saison to set up Seiyō Land Systems, Ltd., for developing and operating integrated shopping centers and urban leisure facilities from Hokkaido to Okinawa. Because Seiyō Land Systems was no match for giant entrepreneurs like Daiei and Mitsui Fudōsan in capital or land assets, it focused on carefully selected projects where it was explicitly invited by local agencies, such as shopping plazas at Shin Yurigaoka and Hiroshima, both ready in 1993. Among its most spectacular ventures was an amusement fortress called Osaka Paradiso, opened in July 1990 at Bentenchō, boasting four swimming pools (including Japan's largest indoors), space simulators providing tours of the universe, and eight floors of other diversions as well as restaurants, medical offices, hotels, and condominiums. Seiyō developed and operated this futuristic facility on public lands leased to a consortium headed by Sumitomo Trust Bank. An unintended irony was that one of its biggest draws was the thirty-eight lane bowling alley[47]—a business that had nearly bankrupted the company two decades earlier.

DINING AND TRAVEL À LA SAISON

Just as personalized fashions and individualized lifestyles revolutionized Japanese retailing after the mid-1970s, indulging one's own tastes in food and preferences in travel created a huge demand for greater variety among affluent customers in the 1980s, above all single young women. Saison was a latecomer to both the restaurant and the overseas travel business; but by the end of the decade the group was taking in more than $1 billion a year from dining services and an even greater amount from travel operations, including its crown jewel, the Inter-Continental Hotel chain. Meals at restaurants and trips abroad became familiar amenities for more and more of the affluent who formed Seibu's and Parco's customer base.

Restaurant Seibu was tenth in its industry, with yearly sales of $214.3 million, when Wada Shigeaki from the department store succeeded Takeuchi Toshio as president in 1983.[48] Ever longer commutes and greater employment of females boosted spending at restaurants in Japan from 13.9 percent of total household food costs in 1983 to 15.8 percent in 1988,[49] and well-off patrons were increasingly lured by more comfortable surroundings as well as by high-quality food in an extraordinary variety of national cuisines. Japanese who might once have been indifferent to the art of fine dining became appreciative customers, and sometimes gourmets, in the newfound passion for restaurants in the later 1980s. The unceasing quest for variety and novelty on the dinner plate had its costs, both for exotic ingredients and scarce labor: by March 1992 college students, who made up a large share of food-service workers, averaged $8.50 an hour for part-time work, and

Kentucky Fried Chicken Japan offered overseas trips to its part-time employees for staying on the job just six months.[50]

The key to profitability in Seibu's restaurant chains turned out to be standardization of operations (training, purchasing, recipes, layout) and diversification of cuisines (Italian, French, Portuguese, and American tastes as well as Chinese and Japanese). Saison credits Wada with revitalizing and expanding Restaurant Seibu after 1983 by closing money-losing branches and slotting each of the company's chains for a different traffic flow: Casa for suburban roadside locations, Shōchibō for city customers eager for Chinese food, Itoguruma for young women who liked noodles and tea in the Kyoto manner, and Han near railway stations for men fond of country cooking. Wada further modernized the company in April 1985 when he merged it with the department store's dining-out division, known as Semica, and he increased the number of Casa family restaurants from 9 to 114 within six years.[51]

Restaurant Seibu, which was promoted to the first section of the Tokyo Stock Exchange in October 1983, doubled the number of customers served at its group's outlets between then and 1989, to 171 million. In the latter year restaurants accounted for 43 percent of sales, fast food such as doughnuts and beef-in-a-bowl another 37 percent, and catering and packaged-food sales the rest.[52] After just four years of Wada's leadership, Restaurant Seibu had by 1987 surpassed Daiei and risen from tenth to third place among Japanese restaurant enterprises, a rank it retained in March 1990 with annual sales of $1.03 billion at its 1,404 locations, compared with $1.18 billion for Japan McDonald's and $1.12 billion for Skylark family restaurants.[53] As a publicly traded concern, its equity ratio was higher (51.7 percent in March 1990) and long-term borrowings ($209.4 million) proportionately lower in relation to sales than many other Saison businesses, allowing the company and affiliates to show estimated pretax profits of $74.9 million, an increase of nearly 600 percent since Wada took over in 1983.[54] Riding the crest of diversification and growth, Restaurant Seibu changed its name in October 1989 to Seiyō Food Systems, Inc., to cement its affinity with other Saison companies engaged in travel and leisure services under the Seiyō name.

One major exception that kept its own identity was Inter-Continental Hotels, which Saison and other investors acquired in September

1988 from Grand Metropolitan PLC of Great Britain for $2.27 billion in a takeover less widely noted than Matsushita's 1990 purchase of MCA ($6.06 billion), Sony's acquisition of Columbia Pictures in 1989 ($5 billion), or Bridgestone's $2.65 billion payment for Firestone Tire and Rubber in 1988.[55] Founded in 1946 by Pan American World Airways, Inter-Continental passed into Grand Met's hands for $500 million in 1981 and grew to 100 hotels around the world with annual operating revenues of $542.7 million by the time Saison bought it. Tsutsumi Seiji sold a 40 percent stake in the chain to Scandinavian Airlines System in May 1989 for $500 million and access to Scandinavian's computerized reservation network, so that Saison could build "a total travel service organization"[56] tailored to individuals' own preferences, not conventional tours by Japanese groups. After Inter-Continental lost money in both 1990 and 1991, Scandinavian sold back its investment to Saison in May 1992 for as little as $167 million plus 3 of the chain's most desirable hotels.[57]

Even though Tsutsumi took over Inter-Continental on the eve of a worldwide business slowdown, the purchase brought Saison such prestigious locations as the Mark Hopkins in San Francisco, the Barclay in New York, the Mayfair in London, and the Carleton in Cannes. To these Tsutsumi added the gull-like Yokohama Grand Inter-Continental Hotel, a pet project he opened in July 1991 as the first directly owned and operated member of the chain in Japan (the Keiō Plaza participated in Inter-Continental's reservations system).[58] Soon after initiating Inter-Continental as a core company in the Saison Group, Tsutsumi established a separate firm under his half brother Yūji's leadership, Seiyō Continental Hotels, Ltd., to manage Seiyō's hotels within Japan and develop new ones both at home and elsewhere in Asia.[59] Because Inter-Continental provided the breakthrough that Tsutsumi Seiji needed to compete in overseas travel, he called it the "final step in the process of forming the Saison Group."[60] Tsutsumi Yoshiaki, in a classic parable of avoidance, denied that the Inter-Continental purchase was a significant challenge. "It's no use comparing us," he told a reporter in 1988. "Our philosophies are different, and we are in different lines of business"[61] — a distinction that grew finer with each new venture by Seiji.

Both Saison and Scandinavian Airlines almost certainly paid too much for their shares in Inter-Continental during the boom of 1988–

1989, but Tsutsumi Seiji hoped to blot away the chain's red ink by funneling travelers to its hotels through Vivre, the travel arm of the Saison Group that was reorganized in September 1990 under Tsutsumi Yūji as board chair. Originally a subsidiary of Seibu Urban Development, Vivre began as a package-tour wholesaler for exotic forays to the South Pole and African game lands. With operating revenues of $437 million in the year ending March 1990, this company was a perennial also-ran in the $70 billion Japanese travel industry,[62] probably because Saison allowed it to flounder for many years out of deference to Seibu Travel, owned by the railway group.[63]

Saison finally decided in 1990 to consolidate all its travel operations in Vivre because "you have to have a travel agency" to promote your hotels and leisure facilities, "even if it earns just the standard 7 percent commission."[64] That same year the group bought a 10 percent position in Virgin Travel Holding Company of London and established a joint venture between Vivre and Thomas Cook, Britain's largest travel agency. Vivre hoped to promote shopping tours for wealthy women but also to handcraft overseas trips for individuals and small groups of unmarried female office workers, exactly like Japan Air Lines' travel promotion, "I'll," which was adopted in 1991 to replace its twenty-six-year-old group tours known as JALPAK. Vivre established a separate retail travel company, Pacific Tour Systems Corporation, in 1992, so that Vivre could concentrate on wholesaling of travel packages. Saison was so confident of its new initiatives that it predicted its travel businesses would rise to seventh or eighth largest among Japanese agencies by 1994.[65]

ARTS AND COMMERCE

"Saison culture" became one of the group's buzzwords when the age of leisure arrived in Japan in the 1980s. Like dining, sports, vacations, or travel, the arts turned into a prized medium of self-expression and locus of individual value to more and more consumers who could afford cultural activities. Along with other retailers, the Seibu Saison Group had for many years sponsored arts events for reasons of prestige as well as publicity and profit, but in the case of Tsutsumi Seiji the motives included patronage as well. Even though Saison has not yet erected a landmark facility comparable to Suntory Hall or the Tōkyū

Culture Village, no other conglomerate in Japan has matched the variety or impact of its activity in the contemporary arts, ranging from culture as a consumer commodity for the newly leisured middle class to money-losing but image-building exhibitions and outright advocacy of the avant-garde.

Tsutsumi began his career as a sales clerk in the book section at the Ikebukuro Seibu and by 1980 turned its eleventh-floor bookshop, called Libro Porto, into one of the largest in the country, with more than 400,000 titles. In 1989 Libro Porto moved to the basement of the new Sezon Museum of Art nearby (now operated by Seiyū); by then it was the anchor of Japan's fourth-largest chain of bookstores, with thirty-three locations, annual sales of $129.7 million, and its own publishing imprint starting that year. Sales rose to $170.9 million in the year ending March 1992.[66] Both Seibu and Seiyū began sponsoring young painters, sculptors, and printmakers in the 1980s by holding exhibitions and sales aimed at people in their twenties and thirties who were just establishing homes. Seiyū, which priced original works at $70–210, installed Art & You galleries in ten of its stores during 1990 and mini art shops in fifty others, hoping for sales of $70 million within five years.[67] At the top end of the market, Seibu Department Stores began holding highly successful auctions of nineteenth- and twentieth-century Western prints and contemporary works in conjunction with Sotheby's. Through 1991 the first three sales brought in $25.9 million and left only 8 percent of the offerings unclaimed.[68] Culture with greater mass appeal received its due when the newly established Seibu Saison Productions engineered a nine-concert tour by Madonna that drew 300,000 fans in April 1990.[69]

Nearly all Japanese department stores emulated the great newspaper companies by offering noncredit classes on middlebrow topics for female audiences in the 1970s, but Seibu was the first retailer to establish a real culture center when it opened Ikebukuro Community College in 1979. This enterprise soon grew to 700 courses with 35,000 members, said to be the largest in the country, on such topics as English conversation, dance, glass blowing, sports, yoga, cooking, and the polite arts.[70] The idea was popular among women who lacked or disliked the conventional group solidarity of family, neighbors, and PTA. The community college gave them freedom to choose their own subjects, not the routinized piano or ballet of their childhoods, and make new friends on their own in an age of greater individual choice about how to lead one's life. Yokogoshi Yūichirō, the college's head, noted that its purpose was to improve the Saison Group's reputation and that it attracted 2,000 students a day, 80 percent of whom said they shopped in the department store after class.[71] Even though Tsutsumi insisted that even the famous instructors show up for every class and that courses be kept small like seminars, competition for students was too severe to allow Yokogoshi to raise tuition charges to cover his costs, and Seibu gradually scaled back its offerings.[72]

Apart from these forays into merchandising culture, most of Saison's arts activity in the 1980s helped to elevate audience tastes as well as the corporate image of cultivated benefactor. Partly because Tsutsumi's eldest son Kōji was a film director, the group took up cinema as a serious endeavor well beyond its obvious appeal to shoppers who were drawn to theaters at Seibu and Seiyū for movies distributed by Ciné Saison.[73] As a part of its quality campaign in the early 1980s, Seiyū became the first Saison company to produce its own film when it completed Nakagami Kenji's *Hi matsuri* (*Fire Festival*, 1985). Ciné Saison, which was established in 1984 to pool the group's movie activities, released about one film per year in the later 1980s, including *Sen no Rikyū* (*Death of a Tea Master*, 1989) and *Shikibu monogatari* (*Tale of Shikibu*, 1990), both directed by Kumai Ken and both awarded prizes at international festivals in Venice.[74]

Ciné Saison distributed some of these works to national theater chains and drew more than a million viewers to two of them.[75] In addition to in-store theaters, the Saison Group opened the Ginza Teatoru Seiyū next to the Hotel Seiyō Ginza in 1987 and Kineka Kinshichō, specializing in Russian movies, in 1990. By this point Saison operated twenty-two theaters with thirty-two screens, but the high costs and slender returns from making art films posed a corporate dilemma for a group hard-pressed to improve its profitability. Sources inside and outside the company agreed that polishing Saison's luster via high-quality productions took precedence, ruling out cartoons or other moneymaking genres, but directors faced much pressure to seek earnings whenever possible.[76]

The art versus profit conundrum bedevils corporate arts committees everywhere, but Tsutsumi Seiji made it clear on many occasions that he assumed costs would outrun income for Saison's events in dance, classical music, theater, and the visual arts as well as all forms of the avant-garde.[77] The group estimated in 1990 that it recovered about 45 percent of its expenses on cultural events and considered the rest a combination of public relations and philanthropy.[78] No one denied the entrepreneurial advantages, including free publicity, that accrued from holding art shows at a nominal loss in order to mobilize customers for the department store. Many of the million or more who attended exhibitions at the Sezon Museum of Art each year stepped next door to shop at Seibu, and presumably most of them thought the better of Saison for putting art works on display.[79] As an official of the Seibu Museum of Art (succeeded by the Sezon in 1989) put it, "holding the shows casts a certain subtle image on the goods we sell. Our emphasis on contemporary art helps establish a very contemporary image in the minds of the modern young women who shop here."[80]

But Saison also became benefactor as well as producer for serious artists with limited commercial appeal. Tsutsumi wrote in 1987 that business should "provide artists with a place for their work" and "arrange the proper conditions for artistic activity. Artistic activity itself is something carried out independently by artists, quite apart from business."[81] Cultural events that were not economically viable, he told a group of arts leaders that summer, should properly be sponsored by companies, although "all the corporation can do is provide the stage, the theater, the art museum . . . what should be seen or heard there is for you to select; the company should not interfere."[82] Tsutsumi evidently recognized that supporting art critical of consumer society and the business establishment might seem counter to Saison's interests; of course it is also true that the criticism might serve as a safety valve for dissent and end up strengthening corporate culture.[83]

Whether the arts could serve purely mercenary aims was another matter: "It is wrong to use artistic culture merely for corporate public relations," Tsutsumi wrote in 1987. "Such artistic culture contributes nothing to society."[84] Three years later he added, "Cultural and artistic activities that are not consistent with corporate culture will not help improve corporate identity."[85] Whatever the pull of exhibitions and concerts in luring shoppers to its stores, Saison clearly went beyond its middle-class customer base in patronizing the avant-garde. Not all the shows at the Sezon Museum of Art catered to the tastes of female audiences; some were very unappealing—yet much appreciated by the artists represented.[86]

Image, commerce, and patronage all help to explain why the Seibu/ Sezon museum became the major locale for exhibitions of current visual art in nearly every conceivable style, both foreign and Japanese, carefully interspersed with retrospectives of twentieth-century masters like Miró, Munch, Ernst, and Henry Moore. Kinokuni Ken'ichi, the former advertising executive and Seibu Department Stores director who headed the museum from its start in 1975, candidly characterized its purpose as "selling cultural information,"[87] especially through monster shows of Renoir or Millet that drew a half-million customers each.[88] But Tsutsumi also encouraged concerts, lectures, flower and fashion exhibits, poetry readings, and multimedia events in the museums, as well as experimental films and panel discussions in Studio 200 next to the Seibu Museum of Art. Whatever they think of Tsutsumi's own novels and poems, most critics agree that no other alternative space in Japan had such a big effect on the avant-garde arts in the later 1970s and 1980s as Seibu.[89]

These happenings at Ikebukuro formed the core of "Seibu culture," an ill-defined but well-known term used by both artists and audiences in the 1980s. Tsutsumi also gradually transformed the Takanawa Museum of Art, founded in 1960 to house his father's collection of Japanese works, into the Saison Museum of Modern Art after moving it in 1981 to a striking building in Karuizawa designed by Kikutake Kiyonori. There he exhibited mainly contemporary art and provided an experimental laboratory for creative works in film, photography, music, theater, and dance.[90] As with Art Today, the Sezon's annual display of fresh Japanese artists, Tsutsumi sponsored Music Today to spotlight contemporary works by Japanese and foreign composers. The classics received attention at the music hall opened in August 1988 at the Seiyō Yatsugatake Highlands resort. Seiyū underwrote touring productions of Broadway musicals between 1973 and 1988, then switched to another level of taste the following year when it opened the Soviet Ballet Institute in Shibuya, in association with the since-renamed Soviet National Ballet.[91]

Tsutsumi gave particular sustenance to contemporary theater in the late 1980s, mainly through performances at the stunning 774-seat Ginza Saison Theater next to the Hotel Seiyō on the central Ginza avenue, opened in March 1987. Japanese department stores have had stages at least since Mitsukoshi rebuilt its Nihonbashi headquarters after the September 1923 Kantō earthquake and fires. Indeed, despite Tōkyū's splendid Culture Village (opened in 1989) and a notorious episode of forgery in its own art department, Mitsukoshi was Seibu's main competitor among retailers in hosting arts events during the 1970s and 1980s. Parco has had a 478-seat theater at Shibuya since 1973, originally called the Seibu Theater, but its purpose has been to create a fashion environment more than to develop serious dramatic art. Parco's Space Part III, a mini-theater opened in 1981 just off Park Avenue, presented a good deal of experimental drama and, in March 1992, sponsored Japan's first gay and lesbian film festival. Still the not-for-profit Ginza Saison overshadowed every other stage in Tokyo in the late 1980s with its high-quality performances of new work by both Japanese and foreign playwrights, produced and directed by professionals on Saison's payroll. This superb facility had already drawn 500,000 patrons by December 1989, but in spite of big crowds, it was unlikely ever to pay for itself.[92]

More flexible tax regulations since the late 1980s made it easier for Tsutsumi and other corporate patrons to underwrite the arts through charitable foundations. Even before the changes took effect, Tsutsumi donated $4.2 million of his own money to the Asian Cultural Council in New York to endow a Japan-United States Arts Program in 1984. Three years later he used $18.2 million of his personal fortune to establish the Saison Fund (Sezon Bunka Zaidan) to promote creative work through the exchange of artists and overseas study opportunities.[93] Tsutsumi said in late 1991, "I expect that even the Japanese government will recognize the need to promote more cultural activity. The tax system has been changed a little bit to help in this regard. Mr. Nishio of Daiichi Seimei, who is the head of the cultural division of Keidanren, has been leading the effort for corporations to give 1 percent of net profits to promote culture."[94] Another movement in which Tsutsumi was a leader was the Association for Corporate Support of the Arts (Mecenat Council), founded in February 1990 by 130 companies to increase the estimated $290 million business contributed to the arts each year (national government aid in 1990 was about $90 million).[95]

Assisting the arts unquestionably has great commercial advantage for Saison, even if much of the benefit is indirect. In this respect the company treats art like a commodity with ever greater éclat in the age of leisure. In a broader sense the arts may be a metaphor for the fate of the entire Saison Group. As Egashira of Osawa notes, "A real question for the group is how to balance Mr. Tsutsumi's investments in future experiments with current business operations. How far can we support arts ventures like the Shima colony or the Ginza Saison Theater when doing so means increasing the group's borrowings? . . . We knew from the start that serious theater would not earn its way. The Yatsugatake music hall is beautiful. If it were booked two hundred days a year, instead of a week here and a few days there during the summer, it might—only might—have a chance of commercial success."[96] Expensive as art may be, without it Saison would be just another retailer and leisure-services operator, not the considerable cultural phenomenon it has become among the avant-garde as well as the broader public.

CHAPTER ELEVEN

ARCHITECTS OF AFFLUENCE

Tsutsumi Seiji surprised the Japanese business world on January 12, 1991, by revealing his intent to step down as head of the Saison Group just when the country was entering the peak year of postwar prosperity. By then both Saison and the Seibu Railway Group had long since outgrown their humble beginnings and ascended to the top echelons of retailing, transportation, and leisure services, with estimated 1990 revenues of $32.7 billion and $7.2 billion, respectively.[1] The Tsutsumi brothers were just as famous within Japan as Matsushita Kōnosuke of Panasonic or Morita Akio of Sony, and their realms were more diverse than was the case with either of these electronics celebrities of the 1980s. Although their enterprise entente of 1970 had marked out separate spheres of activity for Seiji and Yoshiaki within the empire bequeathed by their father, further economic growth and the advent of leisure as a widely accepted aspect of Japanese society brought their endeavors back almost full circle by 1990: travel, recreation, and vacation services for millions of consumers who once regarded these as unattainable luxuries. Despite a substantial recession in 1992–1993, there was every likelihood that the services for sale by these architects of Japan's affluence would keep on expanding as society grew more diverse and more individualized in its self-proclaimed age of maturity and personal fulfillment.

THE SAISON CORPORATION

Tsutsumi Seiji's departure as chief of his conglomerate at age sixty-three was more nominal than real: no one succeeded him (henceforth the group would practice "collective management"), and he took up the new position of chair of the Saison Corporation, a concept company established in October 1987 to coordinate group policy, develop large-scale projects, and serve as a steering committee for the core firms. This new entity supposedly would supplant Tsutsumi himself as the glue holding the group together. Creating this new body reemphasized the point that the era of retailing was at an end, because Tsutsumi thereby reduced the role of the department store in speaking for the group—and in raising funds for it.[2]

Since holding companies were illegal in Japan, Tsutsumi intended that Saison Corporation rule by coordinating a network of information, not one of financial instruments. In essence, he wanted the corporation to become an agglomeration of ideas, not of capital as in the old *zaibatsu.* Tsutsumi called it a rhizome, the horizontal underground plant stem for the core-company shoots above,[3] as opposed to a nested hierarchy of vertically arranged enterprises. He hoped, in effect, that his ideology of management republicanism (a federation of ostensibly equal firms) and comprehensive lifestyle industry (selling services as well as goods) would surmount conventional corporate structures and form a new organization of its own, through the synergy effects of combined performance by member firms. Tsutsumi explained his goal on September 6, 1989: "sharing experience, facilities, and equipment" as well as "sharing capital, technology, and know-how with other departments—i.e., management activity that increases productivity as much as possible by transcending departmental and companywide restrictions."[4]

As an ideological gemeinschaft the Saison Corporation pulled together the strategic-planning functions that for many years had been scattered among the constituent companies, whose managers were often addled by the complexity or even opaqueness of Tsutsumi's projections for the future. The Saison Corporation consisted of a dozen top executives supported by thirty-person project teams assembled ad hoc. One big task was to reconstitute the two hundred companies of the Saison Group into seven enterprise clusters, proclaimed on March

1, 1991: retailing, distribution, real estate, hotels and travel, finance, food service, and marketing and communications. This action supposedly trimmed retailing's sails within the group, but no amount of ideological deflection could mask Saison's continuing reliance on Seiyū and the Seibu Department Stores for cash flow.[5]

Another goal of the new entity was to coordinate the core companies' strategies abroad. Saison had long been active overseas, but mainly by scouring the continents for raiment and comestibles to suit discriminating tastes at home. The new corporation, in keeping with the national vogue in the late 1980s, plumped for "internationalization" by encouraging Seiyū and FamilyMart, in particular, to invest in joint ventures in Korea, Taiwan, Hong Kong, and Southeast Asia.[6] Seiyū paid $46.7 million in 1989 to acquire 40 percent of Wing On, the operator of nine department stores in Hong Kong, and Seibu Department Stores belatedly opened a small outlet in that city on November 23, 1990, many years after other Japanese retailers had established themselves there.[7] Seiyū and its affiliate Tokyo City Finance also greased their skids for the economic unification of Europe by setting up Seiyu Netherlands BV in February 1990 to supply funds to the continent.[8] Although the purchase of Inter-Continental Hotels in September 1988 stretched Saison's resources to the limit, the group managed to construct a joint company in April 1990 with Hermès, the French fashion house, to buy Jean-Louis Scherrer's haute couture business[9]—a trophy with even greater sheen in Tokyo than in Paris.

However much Saison may have resembled the conglomerates of other countries structurally, in advertising and sales techniques it remained very sensitive to different consumer cultures. Tsutsumi said in 1990 that his group had no global strategy, "only a market strategy. Today this means going abroad by definition."[10] He elaborated in late 1991: "Each country has a different market. Even within Japan each district has its distinctive market. We have to adjust our sales activity according to the particular market, but we have no rigid method—we use very elastic approaches, both in the domestic market and abroad. . . . Still, even though we choose different words for marketing in different areas, the underlying method is the same."[11] Nakauchi Isao and many other retailers have echoed this view that foreign goods must be adapted to Japanese needs and vice versa, if only because semidurables like automobiles and electronics are more culturally neutral than most foods, apparel items, and services available from department stores.[12]

These Saison Corporation functions at home and abroad are reminders that Tsutsumi's rhizome sprouted as a new leadership model at a time when the basic concepts of company, industry, and even national economy were atrophying in Japan. The company no longer meant a stable group of member-workers adept at multiple tasks, now that employee turnover was considerable and specialized functions were increasingly contracted out to consultants, fee-for-service vendors, and many other temporaries. All sorts of businesses in the late 1980s diversified beyond their usual industrial boundaries into unrelated fields, so that oil companies and steel manufacturers began investing in sports, amusement parks, and other leisure services which had been left to others before. Just as dividing lines between individual industries were growing obsolete because now single enterprises typically performed complex functions, national borders took on somewhat different meanings in an era of multinational symbiosis (kyō-sei)—a business watchword in the early 1990s.

ELEMENTS OF STRENGTH

The Seibu-Saison story is an ongoing chronicle of careful planning and calculated investment in the future, tracing back to Tsutsumi Yasujirō's earliest real-estate developments in the 1910s. The greatest reason for Yoshiaki's and Seiji's prosperity was their priceless inheritance in land, not merely the railway group's vast holdings but also the unspoken backing its properties conferred on the retailing group, even after the brothers uncoupled their businesses in 1970. Another reason was their single-minded focus on lucrative wedges of the service sector as consumerism matured in the 1970s and 1980s: Yoshiaki in sports, leisure, and tourism, Seiji in information, finance, vacations, and dining out. Fortuitous circumstance also played a part: the brothers launched their diversified businesses during a time of almost unremitting prosperity for Japan, tapping new markets as soon as they appeared and giving considerable direction to middle-class spending habits.

Tsutsumi Yoshiaki relentlessly built Kokudo Keikaku's asset base through long-range planning based on high sales volume, heavy borrowing, slender profits, and low taxes. His strategy of incremental development took shape in enterprise zones like the Shinagawa complex, Lions Stadium, and the recent integrated resorts in the mountains. Through unceasing micromanagement and vigor of personality he created a corporate identity for the railway group as a variegated leisure-services operator driven by family-like devotion to its autocratic leader. The retailing group showed comparable determination but greater flexibility in reacting to social changes (my-homeism, the New Self, the New Breed) with niche marketing, selling experiences as well as goods, and developing concept stores where people could create their own lifestyles. The personal factor was also crucial: without the ambition, acumen, and consumer sophistication of Tsutsumi Seiji, there would have been no such marketing phenomenon as Seibu.

These elements helped both groups confront national economic adversity after 1991 from a reasonably stable position. The world.wide recession that struck Japan most severely in 1992–1993 reduced the country's growth to a crawl. Commercial banks, beset with tens of billions of dollars in bad loans, faced unprecedented dangers that sliced stock-market values to half their December 1989 values. The Economic Planning Agency estimated that the hidden assets of nonfinancial corporations as of June 1992 had fallen 30 percent from their 1989 peak of $5.2 trillion,[13] although the types of assets controlled by the Seibu Railway Group and Saison Group were presumably less vulnerable than commercial office properties in the biggest cities. Three public-works packages worth $280 billion, together with a bank bailout, revisions in the tax code, and government efforts to boost the stock market in 1993, were intended to restore business confidence and stem criticism from abroad regarding the record $136.2 billion trade surplus Japan ran up in 1992.[14] Nissan shocked the corporate world by announcing the closing of its Zama plant in February 1993, the most stunning but far from the largest of the layoffs announced by big business that winter.[15]

The slowdown, as Karel van Wolferen noted, provided "an opportunity for long-term economic strengthening through this further consolidation and for tackling a much needed overhaul of the financial system."[16] Apart from a drop in life-insurance revenues, Saison seemed relatively well equipped to ride out the recession. Unlike companies that were deeply committed to corporate finance and real-estate lending, Credit Saison's consumer orientation meant that it suffered relatively little when the bubble sagged. As an importer of luxury goods, the Osawa trading company seemed almost immune to recession (sales of jewelry and gourmet foods continued to be strong); but the firm chose the occasion to shift increasingly to functional, affordable products as personal spending dipped in 1992—although independent estimates predicted a rise in consumer outlays of $2.6 billion in 1993.[17] The Saison Group as a whole maximized its financing and leasing businesses during the downturn because consumers found it harder to afford expensive durables—even though its reputation was tarnished in June 1992 when two former employees of Seibu Department Stores were arrested for allegedly swindling $114.5 million from a leasing company the previous August.[18] Both the railway and Saison groups, which depended very little on the slumping stock market for funds, could count on cash flow to bear up; each expected the demand curve for leisure to moderate during the recession and then resume its steep incline later in the decade, as Japan continued to catch up to other countries in recreational amenities.

SEIJI AND YOSHIAKI

In many ways Tsutsumi Seiji was a bellwether of structural change in the Japanese business world, whereas his brother Yoshiaki fervidly defended tradition, even if he did not always hew to it. Yoshiaki presumably meant to send Seiji a message when he said in 1982, "Lately what I've noticed about instances of successful people who later fail is that after succeeding with one enterprise, they get sidetracked by something else."[19] Two years later he observed that "what made the American economy go bad was conglomerates."[20] Yoshiaki did not literally obey his father's injunction to "do nothing for ten years" after inheriting the railway group in 1964; the stagnancy of rail transport after the 1960s forced him to branch out further into tourism and recreation. Certainly by the 1980s Yoshiaki was archon of a vast leisure-services conglomerate, but he assembled it cautiously, rarely risking the company's fate and sticking to industries familiar to him—sports and hotels.

Where Yoshiaki upheld tradition with special vigor was in his one-person leadership, refusing to delegate much responsibility, seldom working with partners, and surveying his fiefdom by helicopter—whereas Seiji often drove his own Saab or "put on a raincoat like Colombo in the old TV series and rode the subways to visit his stores incognito,"[21] as a close confidant has noted. Yoshiaki's overlordship was a matter of personal style as well corporate culture within the railway group, dating to Yasujirō's time. Autocratic rule was all the easier for him because he had access to the overwhelming borrowing power of Kokudo Keikaku's land. Seiji depended instead on ingenuity and perceptiveness about consumer trends, assets just as vital to the Saison enterprises as real estate was to the railway group's. Seiji's preference for management republicanism was neither categorical nor derived mainly from theory; instead it was largely a nod to the objective reality that his companies were too variegated and far-flung, and probably too driven by subjective judgments about shoppers' tastes that had to be reached on the spot, to be operated from a single suite in Ikebukuro.

The greatest contrast between the brothers involved values, attitudes, and how workers related to the company as a social organization. Like his father, Yoshiaki idealized the paternalistic bond between owner and worker that was supposed to characterize modern Japanese labor relations since early in the twentieth century. He expected his employees to exemplify such conventional traits as cooperation, perseverance, patience, and loyalty to Seibu. He prized sincerity, simplicity, and humility—virtues especially hard to impart to the Lions of Tokorozawa. The only outright ideology he upheld was patriolatry, through graveside vigils and annual pilgrimages to Kamakura to honor the memory of his father. In effect, as the forced-march cheering sections for company ice-hockey games show, the organization became its own ideology—yet the organization transparently suffered from truncated growth because of its autocephalism.

Seiji, too, was sometimes portrayed as "very much a dictator," despite his "gentle and courteous image in public,"[22] but most writers called him democratic rather than authoritarian or laissez-faire as a manager. He encouraged discussion at policy conferences and listened carefully, but he expected debate to take place within the policy framework he set out.[23] Throughout his career he stayed several steps ahead of the competition, partly by studying his rivals thoroughly, so as to retain the image of freshness that animated all his enterprises. This foresight and conceptual skill may be difficult to impart to the next generation of Saison leaders. In contrast to Yoshiaki, Seiji believed in the transformative power of corporate ideology (the consumer industry, the integrated lifestyle industry, management republicanism, synergy, rhizome) and placed correspondingly less weight on upholding customary values among his employees. He minimized the importance of sincerity, earnestness, and hard work, seeking quickness and inventiveness instead; and he recognized earlier than any other Japanese retailer that individualism, self-expression, and the New Breed were corroding the notion of company loyalty at its core. Rather than resisting this trend, he redefined the connection between worker and company by establishing shopmasters, specialists, women licensees, and the Order Entry System for training, each of which put the employee in a one-to-one relationship with the job, not the company as a whole.

These differences between Tsutsumi Seiji and Tsutsumi Yoshiaki in managerial outlook, leadership style, and corporate conception were fundamental, yet many other aspects of their business careers possessed sympathy of character. In contrast with competitors like Gotō Noboru of Tōkyū, neither brother behaved like a timid second-generation manager of inherited firms but instead acted boldly, like first-generation entrepreneurs. Like Tsutsumi Yasujirō, each eschewed manufacturing except as something ancillary (tofu, rolling stock) to a mainline service business. All three Tsutsumis were twenty or more years ahead of their times—Yasujirō in building housing and resorts, Yoshiaki in shifting from land to leisure, Seiji in trumpeting the age of information—and each designed his enterprises in defiance of the prevailing official policy favoring production over consumption and thrift over spending. Both brothers ended up as princes of leisure in clearly differentiated segments of that recent market, one the government belatedly discovered and approved when it became clear that the number of retirees was rising dramatically. Each took part in the business establishment primarily through his avocation: Seiji by patronizing the arts, Yoshiaki through sports federations. Both were well connected politically but avoided electoral politics, even though Yoshiaki's influence was strongly felt in the Liberal Democratic Party.

Tsutsumi Seiji and Tsutsumi Yoshiaki came of age during the first and greatest wave of postwar entrepreneurship (the 1950s), when bold reorganizers of existing companies and founders of new ones quickly challenged the cautious managers of the former *zaibatsu* firms for leadership of Japanese business innovation. The most famous reorganizers included Ishibashi Shōjirō of Bridgestone Tire, Matsushita Kōnosuke of National Panasonic, and Dokō Toshio of Ishikawajima Heavy Industries, none of whom was beholden to the postwar corporate linkages known as *keiretsu*. Tsutsumi Yoshiaki's career lies between this cohort and upstarts like Ibuka Masaru of Sony, Mitarai Tsuyoshi of Canon, and Honda Sōichirō of Honda Motor: although Tsutsumi inherited the Seibu Railway and Kokudo Keikaku, he transformed the former and virtually revolutionized the latter into a leisure-services firm that now takes in almost no revenue from its prewar land holdings. Spiritually he was probably most akin to Matsushita, whose familism and company loyalties he greatly admired, whereas Tsutsumi Seiji—unmistakably a new-generation entrepreneur—identified closely with Ibuka's and Honda's emphases on rational management techniques, research and development, and results-oriented leadership rather than punctilio or academic pedigrees (Yoshiaki had even less use for the latter).[24]

The Tsutsumi brothers were heirs to a minority tradition in modern Japanese business history, the owner as entrepreneur. Most Japanese corporations before World War II derived their capital either from their origins as merchant houses dating to the Edo period or, more commonly, from new money raised through equities and bank loans. Japan's rapid industrialization crowded out most owner-entrepreneurs because they were unable to expand quickly enough through retained earnings to compete with larger companies that had many investors, bankers at the ready, and university-educated managers to operate them. Nor did Tsutsumi Yasujirō, a son of the soil, have family resources to fall back on, else he might have been able to forge links with a bank and mimic the *zaibatsu* pattern of controlling multiple companies through kinship.

Tsutsumi was one of relatively few owner-entrepreneurs who survived, but only because, after much trial and error, he ended up buying land that no one else wanted—and because that land appreciated considerably during the last decade of his life. His firms were finally able to prosper outside the *zaibatsu-keiretsu* continuum mainly because real-estate values kept on rising in the 1960s and 1970s, making it possible for both the Seibu Railway and Seibu Retailing groups to borrow liberally against the growing worth of their properties and assemble new businesses that were heavily leveraged but held great potential for the future. Each group contained a few companies that were listed on the stock exchanges; but on the whole neither faced strong shareholder pressure for dividends, and consequently each could sacrifice current profits in favor of heavy interest payments on borrowings to finance expansion. In effect, as Tsutsumi Seiji was fond of saying, "Our loans are our future assets."[25]

If so, each group will carry a resplendent patrimony into the next century, inasmuch as the railway group began the 1990s with an estimated $4.90 billion in borrowings[26] and Saison with a reported $9.16 billion.[27] Many of the Saison companies were acquired or rebuilt when money was cheap in the late 1980s, but the burden of debt service became incomparably heavier as the Bank of Japan discount rate doubled between mid-1989 and late 1990 (it then tumbled to a record low of 2.5 percent in February 1993). As in other countries, quality replaced growth as the catchword of the 1990s, yet only if a financial cataclysm struck Japan would Saison's new businesses be likely to face peril.

No one thinks that the railway group, with loans little more than half of Saison's and Japan's richest commercial land holdings to back them, could be menaced by anything short of national economic catastrophe. For this reason it is likely that Tsutsumi Yoshiaki will plow forward ceaselessly into urban development, suburban shopping centers, and small hotels as well as leisure services for the rest of the century. But given its enormous borrowings and relatively modest properties securing them, why does Saison continue to live so close to the edge?

Egashira Keisuke, president of Osawa, provides an answer in tones that evoke the founder's philosophy of "thanks and service": "Saison could be profitable, very profitable, if it ran only its Ikebukuro and Shibuya department stores and a dozen large-scale Seiyūs. Instead, Mr. Tsutsumi prefers to do two things that reduce profitability but have social benefits. One is to provide a full range of services to consumers—what he likes to call the consumer industry—which means responding to people's changing lifestyles. The second is to do things that are experimental, anticipating future developments."[28] The latter include both high-information demonstrations such as mechatronics at Seiyū or robots at Tsukuba and support for artists at Shima and the Sezon. It is easy to see the business advantage of much of this strategy. Although they may not be currently profitable, both consumer services and high-tech stores have the potential for great future earnings and are unmistakably part of a corporate blueprint predicated on capitalist principles, however inept Saison may sometimes seem in following out that blueprint. Nonetheless Egashira contends that more than the pursuit of profit motivates Tsutsumi Seiji: "He wants to experiment in these ways out of a genuine sense of serving society—in this sense he is still a socialist." And a gambler, too: "Mr. Tsutsumi is not afraid to put his ideas about the future into practice."[29]

Remarkable though the railway group was in influencing how people used their leisure time, Tsutsumi Yoshiaki was far abler at anticipating business developments than social trends in the 1970s and 1980s. By most orthodox reckonings, Seiji was a less gifted business executive than Yoshiaki and made a number of costly mistakes that wounded his companies deeply. His chief contribution was not financial but conceptual: he more often than not perceived subtle changes in consumer behavior and intuited shoppers' desires for psychological as well as material satisfaction faster than anyone else in his field. In good part because of Seiji's sensitivity to social as well as economic changes, Saison was frequently able to foretell—and profit from—fundamental shifts from sameness to selfhood (prêt-à-porter to individuality), from goods to services (material artifacts to information and experiences), from living to lifestyles (food, clothing, and shelter to amenities), and from a focus on working to leading the good life (entertainment to leisure).

NOTES

SOURCES CITED

<u>INDEX</u>

Notes

INTRODUCTION

1. Reprinted in Tsukui Masayoshi, *Tsutsumi Yasujirōden* (Tokyo: Tōyō Shokan, 1955), p. 113.

2. Tsutsumi Yasujirō, *Kutō sanjūnen* (Tokyo: Sankō Bunka Kenkyūjo, 1962), p. 49. See Tsukui, pp. 113–117; Tomizawa Uio, *Raitei Tsutsumi Yasujirō* (Tokyo: Arupusu, 1962), pp. 176, 189–190; Atsuta Masanori, *Tsutsumi Yoshiaki no 10nengo hassō* (Tokyo: Yumanite, 1983), pp. 119–120.

3. "Hadō kara ōdō e," *Heisei gijuku*, September 1990, p. 38; "Seibu Tetsudō Gurūpu 'LBO keiei' no kakushin," *Shūkan daiyamondo*, July 21, 1990, pp. 41–42.

4. *Saison Group 1992* (Tokyo: Saison Group, 1992), pp. 5–8; Keizai Koho Center, *Japan 1993: An International Comparison* (Tokyo, 1992), p. 23. Sales figures are for fiscal year 1991 ending March 31, 1992.

5. Nagai Michio, telephone interview, December 4, 1990.

6. Nagai interview, July 23, 1986.

7. Seibu Tetsudō, *Tsutsumi Yasujirō kaichō no shōgai* (Tokyo, 1973), p. 76. See also Karuizawa-machi, *Ko Tsutsumi Yasujirō sensei o shinobu* (Karuizawa-machi, 1964); Sezon Gurūpu Gesuto Hausu, *Tsutsumi Yasujirō* (Tokyo, 1991), p. B.

8. Quoted in Manabe Shigeki, *Tsutsumi Yoshiaki no keiei tama: "Jūnen saki ni katsu"* (Tokyo: Kōdansha, 1986), p. 122.

9. *Sezon no rekishi*, ed. Yui Tsunehiko (Tokyo: Riburopōto, 1991) vol. 1, p. 71; Gendai Kigyō Kenkyūkai, *Seibu* (Tokyo, 1964), p. 13; Matsueda Fumiaki, *Tsutsumi Seiji no kenkyū* (Tokyo: Tōkyō Keizai, 1982), p. 56.

10. Tsukui, p. 80.

11. Ishikawa Tatsuzō, *Kizudarake no sanga* (Tokyo: Shinchō Bunko, 1964); Kajiyama Toshiyuki, *Akunin shigan*, vol. 11 of *Kajiyama Toshiyuki jisen sakuhinshū* (Tokyo: Shūeisha, 1972). See Hayakawa Kazuhiro, *Tsutsumi Yoshiaki: Aku no teiōgaku* (Tokyo: Ēru Shuppansha, 1981), pp. 83, 162; Kosakai Shōzō, "Gotō Noboru, Tsutsumi Seiji, Tsutsumi Yoshiaki: Mitsudomoe no seizetsu osero gēmu," *Gendai*, March 1987, p. 255; Yasuda Shinji, *Tsutsumi Seiji* (Tokyo: Paru Shuppan, 1985), p. 66.

12. The Ōya Sōichi Bunko catalogue, which focuses on periodicals in the contemporary social sciences, contains far more entries for Seibu and Saison in the period 1980–1990 than for any other enterprise group.

13. Eikawa Kōki, *Tsutsumi Seiji: Keiei wa eikyū kakumei da* (Tokyo: Daiichi Kikaku Shuppan, 1988), pp. 51–52, 216–217; Yasuda, p. 149.

14. Eikawa, pp. 216–217; *New York Times*, December 23, 1990, p. III:1.

15. *Daiyamondo kigyō rankingu '90* (Tokyo: Daiyamondosha, 1990), p. 158.

16. Hayakawa Kazuhiro, *Tsutsumi Yoshiakishiki keiei no shippai* (Tokyo: Ēru Shuppansha, 1990), p. 22.

17. The 1990 report shows that Tsutsumi Yoshiaki paid taxes of $1.59 million in 1989, ninth among corporate officials. Tsutsumi Seiji paid $954,928 for the same year, twenty-third among corporate taxpayers. Corporate leaders as a group are not well represented among the highest taxpayers. *Kōgaku nōzeisha meibo 1990* (Tokyo: Teikoku Dēta Banku, 1990), East Japan vol., p. 669; *Daiyamondo kigyō rankingu '90*, p. 162. See Kosakai Shōzō, "Tsutsumi Yoshiaki—tochi o seishi, seikai o ugokasu," *Hōseki*, April 1988, p. 165; Eikawa Kōki, *Jūnengo no Tsutsumi Seiji to Tsutsumi Yoshiaki* (Tokyo: Daiichi Kikaku Shuppan, 1987), pp. 218–220; Hayakawa, *Tsutsumi Yoshiakishiki*, p. 24; Noda Mineo and Koyama Tadashi, "Futatsu no Seibu o eguru!," *Hōseki*, October 1986, p. 85.

18. E.g. the Economic Planning Agency's April 1989 report on new social indicators. See *Japan Report* (Consul General, New York), July 1989, p. 4.

19. Gary R. Saxonhouse, "Services in the Japanese Economy," in Robert P. Inman, ed., *Managing the Service Economy* (New York: Cambridge University Press, 1985), pp. 54–58, 77. See Yuichiro Nagatomi, "The Dynamics of Service-Sector Growth," *Economic Eye*, vol. 4, no. 4, pp. 4–7 (1983).

20. Tsutsumi Seiji, *Henkaku no tōshizu* (Tokyo: Torebiru, 1986), pp. 224–225.

21. "Japan's Service Industry and Service Trade: An Overview," *Japan Economic Institute Report*, November 8, 1985 (Washington, D.C.), pp. 1–3; Nagatomi, pp. 4–5; Mitsuru Miyata, "Problem Points in a Services-Oriented Economy," *Economic Eye*, vol. 4, no. 4, p. 15 (1983).

22. "Distribution Moves Toward the Information Age," *KKC Brief*, no. 34, p. 2 (April 1986).

23. Keizai Koho Center, *Japan 1991*, p. 21. The employment figure is for FY 1989 and the GDP figure is for FY 1988. International comparisons are imprecise because of differing sectoral definitions; Japan lags the United States by perhaps 10 percent and is roughly comparable for these years to the United Kingdom, France, and the former Federal Republic of Germany. See Yoko Sazanami, "Japan's Trade and Investment in Finance, Information, Communications, and Business Services," in Chung H. Lee and Seiji Naya, eds., *Trade and Investment in the Asia Pacific Region* (Boulder, Colo.: Westview, 1988), pp. 153–156; Nagatomi, p. 4; "At Your Service," *Look Japan*, December 10, 1985, p. 28; "Japan's Service," pp. 1–7; *Japan Times*, June 8, 1988, p. 10; Nakamura Takafusa, "What the Strong Yen Wrought: The Japanese Economy Yesterday and Today," *Japan Foundation Newsletter*, May 1990, pp. 3–4; Yoshihiko Miyauchi, "Sunrise, Sunset: Japan's Transformation into a Service Economy," *Speaking of Japan*, October 1987, pp. 16–17.

24. Miyata, p. 15; Sazanami, pp. 155–156; Nagatomi, pp. 5–6.

25. Asō Kunio, *Sezon Gurūpu no subete* (Tokyo: Nihon Jitsugyō Shuppansha, 1991), p. 267; Asō Kunio, *Seibu Sezon Gurūpu* (Tokyo: Nihon Jitsugyō Shuppansha, 1985), p. 89.

26. *Japan Report*, June 1992, p. 4; January 1993, p. 4.

27. Yui Tsunehiko interview, July 1, 1986. See Shin-ichi Yonekawa, "Recent Writing on Japanese Economic and Social History," *Economic History Review*, 2nd ser., vol. 38, no. 1, pp. 107–108, 117 (1985).

CHAPTER ONE: THE LURE OF LAND

1. Tsukui, p. 139.

2. *Sezon no rekishi*, vol. 1, p. 12; Tsutsumi Yasujirō, "Watakushi no rirekisho," in Nihon Keizai Shinbunsha, ed., *Watakushi no rirekisho, keizaijin* 1 (Tokyo, 1980), p. 58.

3. *Sezon no rekishi*, vol. 1, p. 12; Seibu Tetsudō, *Tsutsumi Yasujirō*, p. 4; Kamibayashi Kunio, "Waga Tsutsumi ichizoku chi no himitsu," *Bungei shunjū*, p. 176 (August 1987); Tsukui, p. 15.

4. Tsutsumi Yasujirō, "Watakushi no rirekisho," p. 55; Sezon Gurūpu Gesuto Hausu, p. B.

5. Tsutsumi Yasujirō, "Watakushi no rirekisho," p. 55.

6. Hongō Kan'ichirō, *Mokka funtōchū* (Tokyo: Tokuma Shoten, 1963), pp. 15–16; Noda Kazuo interview, July 11, 1986; Inose Naoki, *Mikado no*

shōzō (Tokyo: Shōgakkan, 1986), p. 565. In an interview on November 11, 1991, Tsutsumi Seiji speculated that his father's motto, "thanks and service," may be "connected with the teachings of Nakae Tōju and Ishida Baigan."

7. Tsutsumi Yasujirō, "Watakushi no rirekisho," p. 58; Tsukui, pp. 20–25, 32; *Zaikai kakushin no shidōsha* (Tokyo: TBS Buritanika, 1983), p. 278.

8. Tsutsumi Yasujirō, "Watakushi no rirekisho," p. 58.

9. *Sezon no rekishi,* vol. 1, p. 13; Kamibayashi, p. 160; Inose, p. 218.

10. Nagai interview, July 23, 1986. See Tsukui, p. 199.

11. Tsutsumi Yasujirō, "Watakushi no keiei tetsugaku," in Ōya Sōichi et al., eds., *Watakushi no keiei tetsugaku* (Tokyo: Chikuma Shobō, 1964), p. 163; Tsutsumi Yasujirō, "Watakushi no rirekisho," p. 59; *Sezon no rekishi,* vol. 1, p. 14.

12. Tsutsumi Yasujirō, "Watakushi no rirekisho," p. 62.

13. Seibu Tetsudō, *Tsutsumi Yasujirō,* p. 20; Kamibayashi, p. 169. Kamibayashi is Tsutsumi Yasujirō's first cousin and a long-time Seibu employee. By his account, Tsutsumi Kiyoshi was reared by a family named Takahashi, took that surname, and then at age seventeen was adopted back into the Tsutsumi family. He graduated from high school in Shizuoka and then from Tokyo Imperial University, spending his business career with the Ōmi Railway and other Seibu companies. He was eventually disinherited by his father. Tsutsumi Seiji's autobiographical novel, *Hōkō no kisetsu no naka de,* under the penname Tsujii Takashi (Tokyo: Shinchōsha, 1969), contains colorful descriptions of Kiyoshi's childhood. See also Inose, p. 223; Eikawa Kōki, *Yabō to kyōki* (Tokyo: Keizaikai, 1988), pp. 88–93.

14. Tsutsumi Yasujirō, "Watakushi no rirekisho," p. 62; Yasuda, p. 43; Kamibayashi, p. 162.

15. Yasujiro Tsutsumi, *Bridge Across the Pacific* (Tokyo: Sanko Cultural Research Institute, 1963), pp. 195, 198–206; Tsukui, pp. 45–46, *Sezon no rekishi,* vol. 1, p. 13; Nagai interview, July 23, 1986; Seibu Tetsudō, *Tsutsumi Yasujirō,* pp. 18, 22–23.

16. *Sezon no rekishi,* vol. 1, pp. 14–15; Tsutsumi Yasujirō, "Watakushi no keiei," pp. 164–165; Natsubori Seigen, "Tsutsumi Yasujirō," *Purejidento,* February 1989, p. 113; Tsukui, pp. 39–41.

17. Quoted in Narushima Tadaaki, *Seibu no subete,* rev. ed. (Tokyo: Nihon Jitsugyō Shuppansha, 1989), p. 287. See Tsukui, p. 50; Eikawa, *Yabō,* pp. 162–163; Kobayashi Kichiya, *Tsutsumi Yoshiaki no keieijutsu zenmanyuaru* (Tokyo: Paru Shuppan, 1988), p. 16.

18. Yasujiro Tsutsumi, *Bridge*, p. 201; Tsukui, p. 43; Sugiyama Katsuhiko interview, August 6, 1986; Seibu Tetsudō, *Tsutsumi Yasujirō*, p. 24. Seibu Polymer Chemical Industries today is a sister company but not a member of the Seibu Railway Group.

19. Tsutsumi Yasujirō, "Watakushi no keiei," pp. 167–168. See also pp. 164–166; Seibu Tetsudō, *Tsutsumi Yasujirō*, pp. 24–25.

20. Quoted in Tsukui, p. 128.

21. *Nihon chimei daijiten* (Tokyo: Asakura Shoten, 1968), vol. 4, p. 143; *Japan Times*, July 10, 1986, p. 7; Inose, p. 182; Karuizawa-machi, p. 5.

22. Tsutsumi Yasujirō, *Shikaru* (Tokyo: Yūki Shobō, 1964), p. 32.

23. Inose, p. 125.

24. "Tsuyosa no kenkyū: Seibu Tetsudō Gurūpu," *Nikkei bijinesu*, June 25, 1984, p. 31; Inose, p. 209; "Curbing Land Prices in Tokyo: Causes and Effects of the New Land Tax," *Tokyo Business Today* (January 1991), p. 12; Keizai Koho Center, *Japan 1991*, p. 87.

25. Quoted in Eikawa, *Yabō*, p. 106. See Yasujiro Tsutsumi, *Bridge*, p. 203.

26. Kaminogō Toshiaki, *Seibu ōkoku* (Tokyo: Kōdansha, 1982), p. 89. See also pp. 90–91.

27. Kamibayashi, p. 163.

28. Seibu Tetsudō, *Tsutsumi Yasujirō*, p. 28; Natsubori, p. 115.

29. Yasujiro Tsutsumi, *Bridge*, p. 205; Karuizawa-machi, p. 2; Natsubori, p. 115.

30. Yasujiro Tsutsumi, *Bridge*, pp. 205–206; Tsutsumi Yasujirō, "Watakushi no keiei," p. 168; *Sezon no rekishi*, vol. 1, p. 16; Inose, p. 137.

31. *Sezon no rekishi*, vol. 1, p. 16.

32. Tsutsumi Yasujirō, "Watakushi no keiei," p. 169. See Karuizawa-machi, p. 2; Tsukui, p. 72.

33. Karuizawa-machi, pp. 2–3; Nagai interview, July 23, 1986; *Sezon no rekishi*, vol. 1, p. 21; Inose, pp. 139, 159, 565.

34. Quoted in Eikawa, *Yabō*, p. 115.

35. *Sezon no rekishi*, vol. 1, pp. 16–17. See Tsukui, pp. 55–56; Seibu Tetsudō, *Tsutsumi Yasujirō*, p. 28.

36. Discussed more fully in Yasuda, p. 67.

37. Inose, p. 224. See *Sezon no rekishi*, vol. 1, p. 17.

38. Tsukui, p. 57.

39. Seibu Tetsudō, *Tsutsumi Yasujirō*, p. 31; Gendai, pp. 13–14; Tsukui, pp. 59–60, 75.

40. See Tsukui, pp. 75–77. For other versions, see Kamibayashi, p. 157; Natsubori, p. 117.
41. Tsutsumi Yasujirō, "Watakushi no keiei," p. 171. See *Sezon no rekishi*, vol. 1, p. 21.
42. *Sezon no rekishi*, vol. 1, pp. 21–22; Tsukui, pp. 60–65; *Zaikai kakushin*, pp. 278–279; Atsuta Masanori, *Seibu Gurūpu Tsutsumike no hassō* (Tokyo: Tokuma Shoten, 1979), pp. 152–153.
43. *Sezon no rekishi*, vol. 1, p. 22.
44. Ibid., vol. 1, p. 36.
45. The conflict is discussed in Kosakai, "Gotō," pp. 246–248. Other accounts are found in Eikawa, *Yabō*, pp. 123–129; Kaminogō, *Seibu*, pp. 96–98; Natsubori, pp. 118–119.
46. Edward Seidensticker, *Tokyo Rising: The City Since the Great Earthquake* (New York: Knopf, 1990), pp. 43, 93–96.
47. Kamibayashi, p. 173; Eikawa, *Yabō*, pp. 131–135.
48. *Sezon no rekishi*, vol. 1, p. 17; Fujiya Yōetsu, "Mejiro Bunkamura," in Yamaguchi Hiroshi, ed., *Kōgai jūtakuchi no keifu* (Tokyo: Kajima Shuppankai, 1987), pp. 158–165, 172; Yamaguchi Hiroshi, "Kaisetsu," in Yamaguchi, ed., *Kōgai*, pp. 45–55.
49. Seibu Tetsudō, *Tsutsumi Yasujirō*, p. 32; Matsui Haruko, "Hakone Tochi no Ōizumi, Kodaira, Kunitachi no kōgai jūtakuchi kaihatsu," in Yamaguchi, ed., *Kōgai*, p. 222; Hayabusa Nagaharu, "The Tsutsumi Brothers, Feuding Magnates," *Japan Quarterly*, vol. 35, no. 2, p. 193 (1988).
50. Eikawa, *Yabō*, p. 143. For debt figures, see p. 144.
51. Matsui, p. 222; Eikawa, *Yabō*, pp. 144–145.
52. Hayakawa Kazuhiro, *Tsutsumi Yoshiaki: Aku no teiōgaku* (Tokyo: Ēru Shuppansha, 1981), p. 89; Atsuta, *Seibu*, p. 149.
53. Matsui, p. 224; Tsukui, p. 69.
54. Matsui, pp. 224–226; Seibu Tetsudō, *Tsutsumi Yasujirō*, p. 94.
55. Matsui, pp. 224–226.
56. Tsutsumi Yasujirō, "Watakushi no keiei," p. 170; Matsui, pp. 226–228; *Zaikai kakushin*, p. 279.
57. Matsui, pp. 227–231.
58. Eikawa, *Yabō*, pp. 141–142; Matsui, pp. 226, 234; Kosakai, "Gotō," pp. 245–246.
59. "Tsuyosa," p. 30.
60. Narushima, p. 292.

61. Seibu Tetsudō, *Tsutsumi Yasujirō*, p. 74.
62. Tsutsumi Yasujirō, "Watakushi no keiei," p. 171.
63. Seiji Tsutsumi and Foumiko Kometani, "The Conversation," *Tokyo Journal*, January 1991, p. 22.
64. Tsukui, p. 162; Sakaguchi Yoshihiro, *Tsutsumi Seiji no sōdai na yabō* (Tokyo: Seinen Shokan, 1990), pp. 75, 82; Natsubori, p. 114; Nagai interview, July 23, 1986. See Seibu Gurūpu Gesuto Hausu, p. E.
65. Tsutsumi Yasujirō, "Watakushi no keiei," p. 172.
66. Eikawa, *Yabō*, pp. 176–178; Natsubori, p. 114; Tsukui, pp. 180–181.
67. Kamibayashi, pp. 158–163. Kamibayashi worked for Tsutsumi on Aoyama's business and was frequently present at the Aoyama household. His account has not been denied. See also Yamakawa Sanpei, *Gotō Tsutsumi fūunroku* (Tokyo: Zaikai Tsūshinsha, 1959), p. 99; Eikawa, *Yabō*, p. 191.
68. Kamibayashi, pp. 158–159, 166–167; Tsukui, pp. 255–262; Eikawa, *Yabō*, pp. 188–196; Hayabusa, p. 195; Atsuta, *Seibu*, p. 118.
69. Tsukui, p. 182.
70. Ibid., pp. 189–194. See Tsutsumi Yasujirō, "Watakushi no rirekisho," p. 72; Tomizawa, pp. 149–150.
71. Kamibayashi, p. 170; Kaminogō, *Seibu*, pp. 179–197; *Friday*, December 14, 1984, p. 69.

CHAPTER TWO: THE FAST TRACK

1. "Seibu teikoku," *Shūkan hōseki*, November 13, 1987, pp. 62–63.
2. Tomizawa, pp. 36, 144–145, 149, 168–169; Tsutsumi Yasujirō, "Watakushi no keiei," p. 173; Tsukui, pp. 103–107.
3. *Sezon no rekishi*, vol. 1, p. 23. See vol. 1, pp. 10–11; Tsukui, pp. 84–85, 87–91; Tomizawa, pp. 146–148; Ukaji Kiyoshi, ed., *Nihon no kaisha 100nenshi* (Tokyo: Tōyō Keizai Shinpōsha, 1975), vol. 1, p. 870.
4. Tsukui, p. 100. See also pp. 91–99; Tomizawa, pp. 150–159; Seibu Tetsudō, *Tsutsumi Yasujirō*, pp. 34–35.
5. Yamakawa, p. 83; Kosakai, "Gotō," p. 246; Tomizawa, pp. 158, 195.
6. Tsutsumi Yasujirō, "Watakushi no keiei," pp. 173–174; Seibu Tetsudō, *Tsutsumi Yasujirō*, p. 35; Tsukui, pp. 100–103; Tomizawa, p. 159.
7. *Sezon no rekishi*, vol. 1, pp. 23–24.
8. Seibu Tetsudō, *Tsutsumi Yasujirō*, p. 39; Tsukui, pp. 141–142.
9. Ukaji, vol. 1, p. 870; Tōkyōto, *Tōkyō hyakunenshi* (Tokyo: Gyōsei,

1972–1979), vol. 3, p. 430, vol. 4, p. 756; Nishio Keisuke and Inoue Hiro-kazu, *Nihon no shitetsu 2 Seibu* (Osaka: Hoikusha,1980), pp. 101, 150; Sei-densticker, p. 318; Tsukui, pp. 107–109; Seibu Tetsudō, *Tsutsumi Yasujirō,* pp. 36–37; Tomizawa, pp. 161–162.

10. Tsutsumi Yasujirō, "Watakushi no keiei," p. 174.

11. Ibid., p. 175; Tsukui, p. 110; Tomizawa, pp. 161–168; Seibu Tetsudō, *Tsutsumi Yasujirō,* pp. 36–37; Tsutsumi Yasujirō, *Kutō,* pp. 36–40; Yama-kawa, p. 42.

12. Yamakawa, pp. 38–39; Kosakai, "Gotō," p. 246. See also Ukaji, vol. 1, p. 870; *Sezon no rekishi,* vol. 1, pp. 35–36.

13. Quoted in Yamakawa, p. 39.

14. Yamakawa, pp. 39–40; *Sezon no rekishi,* vol. 1, p. 36; Tsukui, pp. 119–120.

15. Yasujiro Tsutsumi, *Bridge,* p. 161.

16. Tsukui, p. 201. See Yasujiro Tsutsumi, *Bridge,* pp. 161–183.

17. Tsukui, p. 201.

18. Ibid., pp. 200–203; Tomizawa, p. 200; Yasujiro Tsutsumi, *Bridge,* p. 215.

19. Tsukui, p. 203; Eikawa, *Yabō,* p. 183.

20. Nagai interview, July 23, 1986.

21. Yasujiro Tsutsumi, *Bridge,* p. 184.

22. Idem.

23. Tsukui, pp. 207–213; Yamakawa, p. 47; Yasujiro Tsutsumi, *Bridge,* pp. 186–188.

24. Tsutsumi Seiji portrays Tsutsumi Yasujirō, Tsutsumi Kiyoshi, and Tsu-tsumi Yoshiko in Tsujii, *Hōkō.* See Kamibayashi, pp. 160–166, 169–170; Tomizawa, pp. 171–174; Tsukui, pp. 150–154; Imaoka Kazuhiko, *Tsutsumi Seiji no kigyōka seishin* (Kyoto: PHP Kenkyūjo, 1985), pp. 85–86; Sakagu-chi, *Tsutsumi Seiji,* p. 89; Atsuta, *Seibu,* pp. 169–170; "Tsutsumi Yoshiaki-shi no 12chōen 'shisan' to 'ketsuzoku' kōsō no akirakasarenai bubun," *Shūkan gendai,* August 1, 1987, p. 29; Eikawa, *Yabō,* pp. 189, 203–209; Yamakawa, p. 50.

25. Kamibayashi, p. 161; Natsubori, p. 112; Atsuta, *Tsutsumi,* p. 115; Tsukui, pp. 1–2.

26. Inose, p. 126.

27. Ibid., p. 204.

28. *Sezon no rekishi,* vol. 1, p. 43; Tsutsumi Yasujirō, "Watakushi no keiei," p. 176; Seibu Tetsudō, *Tsutsumi Yasujirō,* pp. 51–52; Tsukui, pp. 123–124, 128.

29. Yasujiro Tsutsumi, *Bridge,* p. 188; Tomizawa, p. 169; Seibu Tetsudō, *Tsutsumi Yasujirō,* p. 40; Hirose Yoshinori, "Tsutsumi Seiji Yoshiaki kyōdai—Seibu ōkoku 'bunkatsu tōchi' no uchigawa," *Hōseki,* December 1978, p. 77; Sakaguchi, *Tsutsumi,* p. 77.

30. Tsujii Takashi, "Yoshida Shigeru to chichi Tsutsumi Yasujirō no tegami," *Shinchō,* no. 45, p. 94 (August 1987).

31. Hotta Masayuki, *Seibu Ryūtsū Gurūpu* (Tokyo: Asahi Sonorama, 1981), p. 55; Tomizawa, pp. 193–197; Tsukui, pp. 121–122; Nishio and Inoue, pp. 110–112.

32. Tsukui, pp. 131–134; Tomizawa, pp. 198–199; Eikawa, *Yabō,* p. 221; Sataka Makoto, "Seibu Tetsudō Gurūpu—hadaka no ōsama," *Asahi jānaru,* May 2, 1986, p. 104; Kamiya Yūji, *Tsutsumi Yoshiaki to Kokudo Keikaku* (Tokyo: Paru Shuppan, 1987), p. 160; Atsuta, *Seibu,* p. 187.

33. Seibu Tetsudō, *Tsutsumi Yasujirō,* p. 70.

34. Seibu Hyakkaten, *Kurashi no yume no furonteia* (Tokyo: Fuji Intānashonaru Konsarutanto Shuppanbu, 1962), pp. 25–26; Seibu Tetsudō, *Tsutsumi Yasujirō,* pp. 70–71.

35. Seibu Tetsudō, *Tsutsumi Yasujirō,* pp. 53, 71; Tsukui, pp. 129–131; Yamakawa, pp. 45–46; *Sezon no rekishi,* vol. 1, p. 93.

36. *Sezon no rekishi,* vol. 1, p. 94; Seibu Tetsudō, *Tsutsumi Yasujirō,* p. 40; Tsukui, pp. 143–146.

37. *Sezon no rekishi,* vol. 1, pp. 94–95; Tsukui, p. 146.

38. Seibu Hyakkaten, *Kurashi,* p. 24; *Sezon no rekishi,* vol. 1, pp. 93–96; Ukaji, vol. 1, p. 870.

39. *Sezon no rekishi,* vol. 1, p. 93.

40. Seibu Tetsudō, *Tsutsumi Yasujirō,* p. 73; Atsuta, *Tsutsumi,* pp. 121–124.

41. Inose, p. 125.

42. Ibid., pp. 50–51, 62–67, 226; Kamiya, p. 195.

43. "Tsuyosa," pp. 32–33. See Inose, pp. 61–62, 67–68 for details of the land purchases.

44. Kusano Hiroshi, *Seibu shōhō—aku no kōzu* (Tokyo: Ēru Shuppansha, 1983), pp. 85–86; Inose, pp. 102–105.

45. Inose, p. 89.

46. "Tsuyosa," p. 32; Hayakawa, *Tsutsumi Yoshiaki: Aku,* p. 94; Kusano, pp. 84–85; Inose, pp. 79–80, 86–89, 91, 97–100. Unofficially the Kitashirakawa property may have appreciated three hundred times. Inose, p. 100.

47. Inose, pp. 88, 100.

48. Kusano, pp. 82–85; Inose, p. 95. See also Inose, pp. 79–80, 87–88, 91–96.

49. Kusano, p. 83; "Tsuyosa," p. 32; Inose, pp. 79–80, 97–99.

50. See "Tsuyosa," p. 32.

51. Atsuta, *Seibu,* p. 214; Ukaji, vol. 1, p. 871; Sataka, p. 102; Inose, pp. 81, 101, 106.

52. Kusano, p. 83; Inose, pp. 106, 125.

53. *Sezon no rekishi,* vol. 1, p. 94. See Gendai, pp. 9–10; Hariki Yasuo, *"Wakaki teiō" Tsutsumi Yoshiaki ga yuku* (Tokyo: Kou Shobō, 1984), pp. 98–99; Atsuta, *Seibu,* pp. 138–139; Inose, p. 140.

54. *Sezon no rekishi,* vol. 1, pp. 5–8, 38.

55. *Sezon no rekishi,* vol. 1, pp. 38–39. See Seibu Hyakkaten, *Kurashi,* p. 42; *Sezon no rekishi,* vol. 1, pp. 8–9, 25–26.

56. Seibu Hyakkaten, *Kurashi,* p. 42; *Sezon no rekishi,* vol. 1, pp. 27–35; Tsukui, p. 125; Ukaji, vol. 1, p. 702.

57. Hayashi Fumiko, *Ukigumo* (Tokyo: Shinchōsha, 1951); translated as *Floating Clouds* by Yoshiyuki Koitabayashi and Martin C. Collcutt (Tokyo: Hara Shobō, 1965).

58. Seibu Hyakkaten, *Kurashi,* pp. 38–41, 48–49, 174–177, 206; *Sezon no rekishi,* vol. 1, p. 54; Kaminogō, *Seibu,* pp. 162–163; Tsukui, pp. 125–126.

59. E.g. Tsukui, p. 127.

60. Tsutsumi Yasujirō and Tsutsumi Seiji, "Jigyō wa hōshi nari," *Chūō kōron,* December 1961, p. 158. See Tsutsumi Yasujirō, "Watakushi no keiei," pp. 175–176; Tsukui, p. 127; Gendai, p. 7.

61. *Sezon no rekishi,* vol. 1, pp. 38–39; Seibu Hyakkaten, *Kurashi,* p. 24. See Atsuta, *Seibu,* p. 137; Seibu Hyakkaten, *Kurashi,* p. 44; *Sezon no rekishi,* vol. 1, pp. 54–55.

62. Seibu Hyakkaten, *Kurashi,* p. 50.

63. *Sezon no rekishi,* vol. 1, p. 50. See vol. 1, pp. 58–60; Seibu Hyakkaten, *Kurashi,* pp. 50–51.

64. Hongō, p. 13; Yamakawa, p. 45; Hotta, p. 44.

65. *Sezon no rekishi,* vol. 1, pp. 59–62; Seidensticker, p. 162; Matsueda, p. 55.

66. *Sezon no rekishi,* vol. 1, p. 65.

67. Seibu Hyakkaten, *Kurashi,* p. 52; Tsukui, p. 126.

68. Seibu Hyakkaten, *Kurashi,* pp. 54–56, 145; *Sezon no rekishi,* vol. 1, pp. 65–69.

69. *Sezon no rekishi,* vol. 1, p. 69.

70. Ibid., vol. 1, pp. 93, 206.

71. Yasujiro Tsutsumi, *Bridge,* p. xvi; Seibu Tetsudō, *Tsutsumi Yasujirō,* p. 91;

Tsukui, pp. 12–13. See Hariki Yasuo, *Netsujō no kenjitsu keiei: Tsutsumi Yoshiaki* (Tokyo: Kōdansha, 1987), p. 130.

72. Yasujiro Tsutsumi, *Bridge,* pp. 30, xvi. See Tsukui, pp. 11, 220–237.

73. Yasujiro Tsutsumi, *Bridge,* pp. xvii, 10–25, 35.

74. Nagai interview, July 23, 1986.

75. Tsukui, pp. 247–249; Eikawa, *Yabō,* p. 39; Yasujiro Tsutsumi, *Bridge,* pp. xvii, 44, 47.

76. Hayakawa, *Tsutsumi Yoshiaki: Aku,* pp. 80–82, 95–98; Kaminogō, *Seibu,* p. 168.

77. Kaminogō, *Seibu,* pp. 167–168.

78. Tsukui, pp. 262–263; Yasujiro Tsutsumi, *Bridge,* pp. 64, 77; Sakaguchi, *Tsutsumi,* pp. 80–81.

79. Hayakawa, *Tsutsumi Yoshiaki: Aku,* pp. 98–101.

80. Miki Yōnosuke, "Zaikai saigo kaibutsu no shi," *Zaikai,* June 1, 1964, p. 11; Yasuda, p. 100; Sakaguchi, *Tsutsumi,* pp. 79–80; Kusano, pp. 18–19; Kaminogō, *Seibu,* pp. 36–40; Miyashita Hiroyuki and Shūdan Topura, *Tsutsumi Yoshiaki no gekirin ni fureta Seiji no yabō* (Tokyo: Appuru Shuppansha, 1988), p. 84; Kobayashi Kazunari, *Tsutsumi Yoshiaki* (Tokyo: Paru Shuppan, 1985), p. 87.

81. Tomizawa, p. 200.

82. Natsubori, p. 119. Gotō Keita reported income for 1958 of $63,416 and Osano Kenji, president of Kokusai Kōgyō, reported income of $158,694. Atsuta, *Tsutsumi,* pp. 120–121. See Miki, "Zaikai saigo," p. 9.

83. Atsuta, *Tsutsumi,* p. 120. See Miki, "Zaikai saigo," p. 9.

84. Quoted in Atsuta, *Seibu,* p. 145.

85. Gendai, pp. 18–19.

86. Ibid., pp. 17–18; Tsukui, p. 163; Atsuta, *Seibu,* p. 169; Hariki, *Netsujō,* p. 105; Yasuda, pp. 102–111.

87. Gendai, pp. 118–120.

88. Quoted in Hariki, *Netsujō,* p. 98.

89. Atsuta, *Seibu,* pp. 173–174.

90. Kaminogō Toshiaki, ed., *Tsutsumi Yoshiaki wa kataru* (Tokyo: Kōdansha, 1984), p. 133; Eikawa, *Yabō,* p. 14. On Misao's role, see Kaminogō, *Seibu,* pp. 24–27; Kamibayashi, p. 170; Kikuchi Hisashi, *Shura no gun'yū* (Tokyo: Besuto Bukku, 1985), pp. 38–40; Sakaguchi, *Tsutsumi,* pp. 99–100.

91. *Sezon no rekishi,* vol. 1, pp. 253–254; Kaminogō, *Seibu,* pp. 24–27.

92. Seibu Tetsudō, *Tsutsumi Yasujirō,* p. 74; Narushima, p. 292.

93. Seibu Gurūpu Gesuto Hausu, p. E; Eikawa, *Yabō*, p. 12; Hariki, *Netsujō*, pp. 108–111; Kaminogō, *Seibu*, p. 77; Miki Yōnosuke, *Gekidōki no keieisha* (Tokyo: Sekkasha, 1965), p. 27.

CHAPTER THREE: THE RETAILING REVOLUTION

1. Tsutsumi Seiji, *Henkaku*, pp. 107–108, 145.

2. E.g. Yamanaka Takahashi, former president of Matsuya. See Umemoto Katsushi, "Gekitotsu! Sakakura Mitsukoshi vs. Tsutsumi Seibu," *Hōseki*, June 1986, p. 81.

3. Shin'ya Nakata, "Retailing: Variety of Means and the Conglo-merchants," *Japan Update*, no. 8, p. 19 (summer 1988); Yutaka Kosai, *The Era of High-Speed Growth: Notes on the Postwar Japanese Economy*, Jacqueline Kaminski, tr. (Tokyo: University of Tokyo Press, 1986), p. 151; Sasaki Fumie, *Depāto sensō* (Tokyo: Keirin Shobō, 1985), p. 65; Okada Yasushi, *Hyakkaten gyōkai* (Tokyo: Kyōikusha, 1985), pp. 38–39.

4. Kazutoshi Maeda, "The Evolution of Retailing Industries in Japan," in Akio Okochi and Koichi Shimokawa, eds., *Development of Mass Marketing: The Automobile and Retailing Industries* (Tokyo: University of Tokyo Press, 1981), p. 270.

5. *Saison Journal*, August 17, 1990, p. 5; Okada, p. 9; Seidensticker, p. 30.

6. Okada, p. 12; Yamaichi Shōken Keizai Kenkyūjo, *Sangyō no subete, 1990* (Tokyo, 1990), p. 208; Japan External Trade Organization, *Retailing in the Japanese Consumer Market*, rev. ed. (Tokyo, 1979), p. 17; Shiizuka Takeshi, *Kōkando shōnin shūdan: Marui, Seibu ni miru "datsuryūtsū" senryaku* (Tokyo: Jatekku Shuppan, 1986), pp. 186–187.

7. Japan External, *Retailing*, p. 15.

8. Okada, pp. 218, 26–27; Toba Kin'ichirō, *Nihon no ryūtsū kakushin* (Tokyo: Nihon Keizai Shinbunsha, 1979), pp. 45–55, 75–81; Matsueda, p. 69; Maeda, p. 272; Noda interview, July 11, 1986.

9. Toba, pp. 87–89; Okada, pp. 27–29; Thomas K. McCraw and Patricia A. O'Brien, "Production and Distribution: Competition Policy and Industry Structure," in Thomas K. McCraw, ed., *America versus Japan* (Boston: Harvard Business School Press, 1986), p. 108.

10. *Sezon no rekishi*, vol. 1, pp. 79–80; Toba, pp. 126–127; Okada, pp. 29–36; Tsutsumi Seiji, *Henkaku*, p. 145.

11. Maeda, p. 277; Okada, p. 39. Small-store retail sales leaped from $10.8 billion in 1960 to $60.4 billion in 1972, even though their share of total retail sales fell from 90.7 to 79.1 percent during the same period. Kosai, p. 151.

12. Nakamura Kōhei, "Seibu Gurūpu o meguru sōkoku no kōzu," *Rekishi tokuhon,* summer 1987, p. 131; Tsutsumi Seiji and Kometani, p. 22; Kaminogō Toshiaki, *Tsutsumi Seiji ga Yoshiaki ni atama ga agaranai riyū* (Tokyo: Kōbunsha, 1985), p. 89; Imaoka, *Tsutsumi,* p. 142.

13. Tsutsumi Seiji and Kometani, p. 22.

14. Imaoka, *Tsutsumi,* pp. 11–12; Takabatake Michitoshi interview, July 1, 1986.

15. Kaminogō, *Seibu,* p. 150; "Henka no jidai ni shinayaka ni taiō seyo," *Hōseki,* March 1985, p. 333; *Sezon no rekishi,* vol. 1, p. 98.

16. "Henka," p. 334. See Imaoka, *Tsutsumi,* pp. 38–47; Hongō, p. 17; Hariki, *Netsujō,* p. 104.

17. *Sezon no rekishi,* vol. 1, p. 98; Kaminogō, *Tsutsumi Seiji ga,* p. 89; Imaoka, *Tsutsumi,* pp. 137–138, 170; Sakaguchi, *Tsutsumi,* p. 97; Nijūisseiki Kigyō Kenkyū Gurūpu, *Shin Seibu vs. Tōkyū aratanaru kōsō* (Tokyo: Yamanote Shobō, 1984), pp. 136–137; *Shūkan bunshun,* November 21, 1985, p. 18; Kaminogō, *Seibu,* p. 142.

18. Tsutsumi Seiji and Kometani, p. 24.

19. Tsujii Takashi, *Itsumo to onaji haru* (Tokyo: Kawade Shobō Shinsha, 1983); translated as *A Spring Like Any Other* by Beth Cary (Tokyo: Kodansha, 1992).

20. Takashi Tsujii, *A Stone Monument on a Fine Day: Selected Poems,* Hisao Kanaseki and Timothy Harris, trs. (Tokyo: Libro Port Publishing Company, 1990).

21. Tsutsumi Seiji and Kometani, p. 24. See Atsuta, *Seibu,* p. 205.

22. Matsunobu Hiromasa, *Dainiji ryūtsū kakumei* (Tokyo: Kyōikusha, 1986), p. 15; Yohei Mimura, "Expert Consumers: Trends in Japanese Purchasing and Lifestyles," *Speaking of Japan,* no. 96, p. 8 (December 1988); Okada, p. 18; Sasaki, pp. 65–67.

23. Seibu Department Stores, Ltd., *Seibu Department Stores Group 1990–91,* p. 4. See Sasaki, p. 65; Mimura, p. 8; Matsunobu, pp. 15–16.

24. Quoted in Kaminogō, *Seibu,* p. 166.

25. Esaka Akira, "Tsutsumi Seiji: Risuku osorenu 'keiei wa eikyū kakumei' shugi," *Purejidento,* vol. 26, no. 1, p. 100 (January 1988); Kaminogō Toshiaki, *Ginza ryūtsū sensō* (Tokyo: Kōdansha, 1985), p. 118.

26. Asō, *Seibu,* p. 36; Imaoka, *Tsutsumi,* p. 153; *Sezon no rekishi,* vol. 1, p. 92.

27. Tsutsumi Yasujirō and Tsutsumi Seiji, "Jigyō," p. 155.

28. Matsueda, p. 55. See *Sezon no rekishi,* vol. 1, p. 105.

29. Sugiyama interview, August 6, 1986.

30. Seibu Hyakkaten, *Kurashi*, pp. 60–61, 222; Seibu Hyakkaten Ikebukuro Komyunitei Karejji and Ryūtsū Sangyō Kenkyūjo, *Kansei jidai no jinji senryaku* (Tokyo: Daiyamondosha, 1985), pp. 51–56, 59; Miyashita Hiroyuki and Shūdan Topura, *Seibu Sezon zankoku monogatari* (Tokyo: Ēru Bukkusu, 1987), p. 103; Sakaguchi Yoshihiro, *Seibu zankoku monogatari* (Tokyo: Ēru Shuppansha, 1979), p. 88; Kusano, pp. 51–53.

31. *Sezon no rekishi*, vol. 1, p. 103. See Atsuta, *Seibu*, pp. 79–81; Yasuda, p. 85.

32. Seibu Hyakkaten, *Kurashi*, p. 96. See Hongō, p. 21.

33. Seibu Hyakkaten, *Kurashi*, p. 222.

34. Tsutsumi interview, November 11, 1991. Kusano, pp. 48–51, suggests an antileftist bias in Saison's hiring over the years. In an interview on December 8, 1990, Egashira Keisuke said discrimination was implausible, given Tsutsumi's well-known liberalism.

35. Seibu Hyakkaten, *Kurashi*, pp. 58–60, 79–80.

36. Ibid., p. 211; *Sezon no rekishi*, vol. 1, pp. 85, 179.

37. Seibu Hyakkaten, *Kurashi*, pp. 206, 219.

38. Ibid., pp. 62, 222; *Sezon no rekishi*, vol. 1, pp. 81, 119.

39. Seibu Hyakkaten, *Kurashi*, p. 223.

40. Ibid., p. 225. See also pp. 63–64; Asō, *Seibu*, pp. 39–40.

41. *Sezon no rekishi*, vol. 1, p. 90.

42. Idem.

43. Ibid., vol. 1, p. 82.

44. Quoted in Hariki, *"Wakaki,"* pp. 42–43.

45. Seibu Hyakkaten, *Kurashi*, p. 212; *Sezon no rekishi*, vol. 1, pp. 134–140; Asō, *Seibu*, p. 41.

46. *Sezon no rekishi*, vol. 1, pp. 81, 128.

47. Long-term borrowings rose from $2.8 million in 1960 to $7.8 million in 1961. *Sezon no rekishi*, vol. 1, p. 128.

48. Ibid., vol. 1, p. 167. See pp. 165–166; Seibu Hyakkaten, *Kurashi*, pp. 221–222.

49. Seibu Hyakkaten, *Kurashi*, p. 65–66, 144–152; *Sezon no rekishi*, vol. 1, pp. 207–217; Asō, *Sezon*, pp. 104–107; *Tsutsumi Kuniko rirekisho* (mimeo, 1990), p. 1.

50. Seibu Hyakkaten, *Kurashi*, p. 97.

51. *Sezon no rekishi*, vol. 1, pp. 126, 188–190.

52. Ibid., vol. 1, p. 176.

53. Ibid., vol. 1, pp. 193–201; Seibu Hyakkaten, *Kurashi*, pp. 69–70.

54. Shiizuka, pp. 92–93.

55. Seibu Hyakkaten, *Kurashi,* p. 96.

56. *Sezon no rekishi,* vol. 1, p. 155; Seibu Hyakkaten, *Kurashi,* pp. 88, 92; Tsutsumi Seiji, *Hatsugen shirīzu,* vol. 14, p. 51 (1982); Shiizuka, p. 181; Miyashita and Shūdan, *Seibu,* p. 106.

57. Seibu Hyakkaten, *Kurashi,* p. 68; *Sezon no rekishi,* vol 1, pp. 329–338; Shiizuka, pp. 104–105.

58. *Sezon no rekishi,* vol. 1, p. 202.

59. Ibid., vol. 1, pp. 99–101, 120; Yasuda, p. 126; Matsueda, pp. 64–65; Kaminogō, *Seibu,* pp. 171–172; Hariki, *Netsujō,* pp. 99–101.

60. *Sezon no rekishi,* vol. 1, p. 220.

61. Ibid., vol. 1, pp. 218–222; Seibu Hyakkaten, *Kurashi,* pp. 66–67, 207.

62. Seibu Hyakkaten, *Kurashi,* pp. 139, 142.

63. Atsuta, *Seibu,* p. 197; Yasuda, p. 127.

64. Quoted in Asō, *Seibu,* pp. 42–43. Yasuda, p. 122, contains a similar statement from Tsutsumi.

65. See Imaoka, *Tsutsumi,* p. 159; Asō, *Seibu,* pp. 47, 118–119.

66. Orihashi Seisuke, *Sūpā gyōkai,* rev. ed. (Tokyo: Kyōikusha, 1988), p. 70.

67. Tsutsumi Seiji, *Henkaku,* pp. 106, 109; Toba, pp. 131–136, 142; Orihashi, p. 70; Hayashi Kaoru, *Ryūtsū biggu san no gyōmu kaikaku* (Tokyo: Paru Shuppan, 1986), pp. 18–19; Hotta, pp. 153–155.

68. Seibu Hyakkaten, *Kurashi,* p. 215; Sasaki, pp. 63–65; Toba, pp. 134, 142.

69. Takaoka Sueaki, *Seiyū Sutoā no ryūtsū shihai senryaku* (Tokyo: Nihon Jitsugyō Shuppansha, 1970), p. 21; Yoshida Sadao, ed., *Kimi wa eien no teki da* (Tokyo: Chūkei Shuppan, 1984), p. 34.

70. Takaoka, pp. 27–40.

71. Yasuda, p. 135; Matsueda, p. 149.

72. Quoted in Tominaga Masabumi, *Seiyū Sutoā no keiei* (Tokyo: Nihon Jitsugyō Shuppansha, 1978), p. 39. See *Sezon no rekishi,* vol. 1, p. 382.

73. Tominaga, p. 39; Yasuda, p. 134; Toba, p. 137.

74. *Sezon no rekishi,* vol. 1, pp. 382–384, 390–391; Asō, *Sezon,* p. 52; Asō, *Seibu,* p. 14; Yoshida, p. 26.

75. *Sezon no rekishi,* vol. 1, pp. 391–395.

76. Ibid., vol. 1, pp. 423–425. See vol. 1, pp. 401, 404–413, 423.

77. Sakaguchi, *Tsutsumi,* pp. 131–133; Atsuta, *Seibu,* 151–152.

78. Kishiro Yasuyuki, "Tsutsumi Seiji Yoshiaki no ikon keiei," *Shūkan asahi,* June 13, 1986, p. 22; Asō, *Seibu,* p. 250.

79. *Sezon no rekishi,* vol. 1, pp. 202–203, 375, 378.

80. *Sezon no rekishi,* vol. 1, pp. 428–429. See Asō, *Seibu,* pp. 119, 232; Sakaguchi, *Tsutsumi,* pp. 25–26; Eikawa, *Tsutsumi Seiji,* p. 219; Asō, *Sezon,* p. 263.

81. *Sezon no rekishi,* vol. 1, pp. 376–377; Eikawa, *Tsutsumi Seiji,* p. 220; Asō, *Seibu,* p. 233. See *Japan Company Handbook,* first section, p. 33 (spring 1991) (Tokyo: Tōyō Keizai Shinpōsha, 1991).

82. *Sezon no rekishi,* vol. 1, pp. 355–356. See pp. 275–276, 280–281; Asō, *Seibu,* p. 225.

83. *Sezon no rekishi,* vol 1, p. 358.

84. Ibid., pp. 358–360.

85. Ibid., p. 358.

CHAPTER FOUR: FROM LAND TO LEISURE: THE SEIBU RAILWAY GROUP, 1964–1974

1. Asō, *Seibu,* p. 210. See Matsueda, pp. 121–122; Sataka, pp. 102–103.

2. Sataka, p. 103.

3. Oda Susumu, "Kenryokusha no seishin byōri (14) Tsutsumi Yoshiaki," *Hōseki,* September 1982, p. 106.

4. E.g. Hayakawa, *Tsutsumi Yoshiakishiki,* pp. 121–122.

5. Quoted in Narushima, pp. 288–289.

6. Quoted in Hayakawa, *Tsutsumi Yoshiakishiki,* p. 49.

7. Tsutsumi Yoshiaki and Kaminogō Toshiaki, *Tsutsumi Yoshiaki no ichinichi ikkun* (Tokyo: Rongu Serāzu, 1985), p. 26. Atsuta, *Seibu,* reports a similar statement by Matsushita to Tsutsumi when they first met in June 1978 at Hakone (p. 159).

8. Quoted in Tsutsumi Yoshiaki and Kaminogō, p. 21.

9. Tsutsumi Yoshiaki and Kaminogō, pp. 15–16. Biographical details are taken from Matsueda, p. 100; Kaminogō, *Seibu,* pp. 200–203; Hariki, *"Wakaki,"* p. 17.

10. Quoted in Tsutsumi Yoshiaki and Kaminogō, p. 14. See also p. 13.

11. Yamada Naohiro interview, July 3, 1986; Kaminogō, *Seibu,* pp. 204–205.

12. Tsutsumi Yoshiaki, "Amaenaki kyōiku: seisaku aru seiji o," *Matsushita seikeijuku kōwaroku,* vol. 7 (Kyoto: PHP Kenkyūjo, 1984), pp. 11–12.

13. Quoted in Kaminogō, *Tsutsumi Yoshiaki wa,* pp. 132–133.

14. Tsutsumi Yoshiaki and Kaminogō, p. 238.

15. Kobayashi Kazunari, pp. 86–88; Sakaguchi, *Tsutsumi,* p. 84.

16. Tsutsumi Yoshiaki and Kaminogō, p. 30; Hayakawa, *Tsutsumi Yoshiakishiki,* pp. 152–153; Eikawa, *Jūnengo,* p. 77.

17. *Yūka shōken hōkokusho sōran, Seibu Tetsudō Kabushiki Kaisha* (March 1990) (Tokyo: Ōkurashō Insatsukyoku, 1990), p. 4; Atsuta, *Seibu*, p. 184; Eikawa, *Jūnengo*, p. 77.

18. Quoted in Miyashita, *Tsutsumi Yoshiaki*, p. 56.

19. Wakabayashi Terumitsu, "Shafū wa 'chikara' nari—Tsutsumi Yoshiaki to Kokudo Keikaku," *Will*, December 1983, p. 69.

20. Ukaji, vol. 1, p. 871.

21. Hayakawa, *Tsutsumi Yoshiaki: Aku*, pp. 154–157.

22. Manabe Shigeki, *Tsutsumi Yoshiaki no 21seiki senryaku* (Tokyo: Kōdansha, 1984), pp. 95–102; Kaminogō, *Seibu*, pp. 8–10; Ukaji, vol. 1, p. 871; Manabe, *Tsutsumi Yoshiaki no keiei*, pp. 178–179.

23. Ukaji, vol. 1, p. 871; Kamiya, pp. 162–163.

24. Miyazaki Yoshikazu, *Sengo Nihon no kigyō shūdan* (Tokyo: Nihon Keizai Shinbunsha, 1976), pp. 123, 129, 135.

25. Ukaji, vol. 1, p. 871.

26. *Yūka, Seibu* (March 1990), p. 4; Eikawa, *Jūnengo*, pp. 182–185; Asō, *Seibu*, pp. 216–217.

27. Eikawa Kōki, *Tsutsumike no gokui* (Tokyo: Besuto Serāzu, 1984), p. 79; Kobayashi Kichiya, pp. 166–167.

28. *Yūka, Seibu* (March 1990), p. 4; Kobayashi Kazunari, p.19; Kusano, pp. 69–72; Kaminogō, *Seibu*, pp. 56–57.

29. Fujii Yatarō, ed., *Shitetsu gyōkai* (Tokyo: Kyōikusha, 1985), p. 115. See pp. 112–116.

30. Ibid., p. 117. See Seibu Tetsudō, *Tsutsumi Yasujirō*, p. 21; "Hadō," p. 43; Ukaji, vol. 1, p. 871.

31. Fujii, p. 182.

32. Quoted in Atsuta, *Seibu*, p. 139.

33. Hayakawa, *Tsutsumi Yoshiakishiki*, pp. 50–51; Eikawa, *Tsutsumike*, pp. 69–70.

34. Tsutsumi Yoshiaki and Kaminogō, p. 88. See Kaminogō, *Seibu*, p. 206.

35. Eikawa, *Tsutsumike*, pp. 67–68; Ukaji, vol. 1, p. 871; Hayakawa, *Tsutsumi Yoshiakishiki*, p. 51. Artificial turf was added to the slope in 1987. See Narushima, nenpyō.

36. Ukaji, vol. 1, p. 871; Atsuta, *Seibu*, p. 83; Hariki, "*Wakaki*," p. 13.

37. Tsutsumi Yoshiaki and Kaminogō, p. 222; Hariki, "*Wakaki*," pp. 52–53; Atsuta, *Tsutsumi*, pp. 129–132; Atsuta, *Seibu*, pp. 129, 191–192; Wakabayashi, p. 70; Kobayashi Kichiya, p. 90.

38. Tsutsumi Yoshiaki and Kaminogō, p. 89.

39. Nakayama Hiroto, *Rejā sangyōkai*, rev. ed. (Tokyo: Kyōikusha, 1988), pp. 69–70. See Ukaji, vol. 1, p. 871; Narushima, p. 167; Kobayashi Kazunari, pp. 157–159.

40. Tsutsumi Yoshiaki and Kaminogō, p. 90; Kobayashi Kazunari, p. 158.

41. Tsutsumi Yoshiaki and Kaminogō, p. 81.

42. Ibid., p. 82; Sakai Toshiyuki interview, May 8, 1991; Atsuta, *Seibu*, pp. 51–55.

43. Tsutsumi Yoshiaki and Kaminogō, p. 86.

44. Ibid., pp. 89, 152; Tsutsumi Yoshiaki and Satō Masatada, "Kokudo Keikaku Tsutsumi Yoshiaki shachō ga akasu 'rizōto kaihatsu de seikōsuru hō,'" *Keizaikai*, December 13, 1988, p. 102; Hariki, "*Wakaki*," pp. 76–82, 98; "Tsutsumi Yoshiaki no," p. 30; Atsuta, *Seibu*, pp. 193–194; Narushima, pp. 20–24, 60.

45. Atsuta, *Seibu*, pp. 140, 194.

46. Eikawa, *Tsutsumike*, pp. 33–34, 58; Shigeki Manabe, "Young Dictator Hidden in Veil," *Tokyo Business Today*, July 1986, p. 28.

47. Narushima, pp. 57–58; *Purinsu Hoteru rejā katarogu* (Tokyo: Purinsu Hoteru, 1991), pp. 377–418.

48. "Tsuyosa," p. 30; Narushima, nenpyō.

49. Tsutsumi Yoshiaki and Kaminogō, p. 86.

50. Hariki, *Netsujō*, p. 31; Kobayashi Kichiya, p. 90.

51. Tsutsumi Yoshiaki and Kaminogō, p. 30. See Kobayashi Kichiya, pp. 90–91; Atsuta, *Seibu*, pp. 129, 192.

52. Hariki, *Netsujō*, pp. 130–131; Atsuta, *Seibu*, p. 223; Kosakai Shōzō, "Nihon rettō seiha sensō," *Hōseki*, September 1987, p. 86; Takahashi Kenji, "Tōkyū Gotō Noboru no 'fuzai' de funshutsushita Osano Kenji Tsutsumi Yoshiaki," *Hōseki*, February 1986, p. 178; Kobayashi Kazunari, pp. 227–235; "Tsuyosa," p. 27.

53. Takabatake interview, July 1, 1986.

54. Kusano, p. 27; Takabatake Michitoshi, *Chihō no ōkoku* (Tokyo: Ushio Shuppansha, 1986), pp. 200–201.

55. Kosakai, "Nihon," p. 86; Kusano, pp. 21–22, 32–33; Takabatake, *Chihō*, p. 201.

56. Kusano, pp. 23–24, 42–44, 87–90.

57. Ibid., p. 90; Takabatake interview, July 1, 1986.

58. Suzuki Tōichi, "Misshitsu 'Takeshita' saiteigeki o kimeta Tsutsumi Yoshiaki 'gokuhi jōhō' no iryoku," *Sandē mainichi*, November 8, 1987, p. 28. See Kobayashi Kazunari, p. 17; Satō Tatsuya and Ōtemachi Tada-

shi, "Kokutetsu hyakuchōen riken kara shimedasareta Tsutsumi Yoshi-aki no tai Nakasone, Gotō, soshite ani Seiji e no daihangeki," *Hōseki* (August 1986), p. 143; Eikawa Kōki, *Tsutsumi Yoshiaki to iu otoko no yomi-kata* (Tokyo: Besuto Serāzu, 1984), pp. 169–172; Takabatake interview, July 1, 1986.

59. Quoted in Miyashita, *Tsutsumi*, p. 25.

CHAPTER FIVE: MERCHANTS TO NEW MARKETS: THE SEIBU RETAILING GROUP IN THE 1970S

1. Masuda Tsūji, *Paruko no senden senryaku* (Tokyo: Paruko Shuppan, 1984), p. 63.

2. *Sezon no rekishi*, vol. 1, p. 260. See Miyashita, *Seibu*, p. 151; Asō, *Seibu*, pp. 50, 216; Kaminogō, *Tsutsumi Seiji ga*, pp. 50–53.

3. Tsutsumi Yoshiaki's estimate as given in Kaminogō, *Tsutsumi Seiji ga*, p. 56. See Sakaguchi, *Tsutsumi*, pp. 24, 57; Tawara Sōichirō, "'Shinsōgyō' jidai," *Purejidento*, January 1987, p. 213; Hariki, *Netsujō*, p. 124; Eikawa, *Jūnengo*, pp. 72–73.

4. Quoted in Yasuda, p. 118.

5. Yasuda, p. 118; Atsuta, *Seibu*, pp. 77–78; Asō, *Seibu*, p. 217; Sakaguchi, *Tsu-tsumi*, p. 100; Kishiro, pp. 22–23; *Sezon no rekishi*, vol. 1, p. 255.

6. Egashira Keisuke interview, December 8, 1990. On Seiwa Sangyō, see *Nihon kaisharoku*, 17th ed. (Tokyo: Kōjunsha, 1989), pp. SA530–531; Mi-yashita and Shūdan, *Seibu*, pp. 60–61, 86–88. As of August 1971, Seibu Kagaku Kōgyō's main investors were Seibu Department Stores ($1.7 mil-lion) and Kokudo Keikaku ($1.4 million). At that point Seiwa Sangyō's investment in Seibu Department Stores was $292,000; the next-largest investors were Seiyū ($187,500) and Seibu Railway ($93,750). Seiyū's main investors were Seibu Department Stores ($1.1 million) and Seiwa Sangyō ($555,500). *Sezon no rekishi*, vol. 1, p. 260.

7. *Asahi Kōgyō kaisha annai* (Tokyo: Asahi Kōgyō, 1990), inside front cover; *Saison Group 1992*, p. 5. See *Asahi Industries Co., Ltd.* (Tokyo: Asahi Industries, 1985), inside front cover, pp. 7–8; *Sezon no rekishi*, vol. 1, pp. 453–454, vol. 2, pp. 534–535, 546, 550–552; "Seibu Sezon Gurūpu dai-shakkin hensai sakusen no shingan," *Shūkan daiyamondo*, October 26, 1985, p. 50.

8. *Sezon no rekishi*, vol. 1, pp. 453–454; Tawara, p. 213.

9. Miyashita and Shūdan, *Tsutsumi Yoshiaki*, p. 104; Imaoka Kazuhiko, *Konnichi o kowase* (Tokyo: Parusu Shuppan, 1977), pp. 131–134; Eikawa, *Jūnengo*, p. 138.

10. Miyashita and Shūdan, *Seibu*, p. 80.

11. Asō, *Seibu*, pp. 26, 49–50.

12. *Sezon no rekishi*, vol. 1, p. 251. See pp. 247–248.

13. Ukaji, *Nihon*, vol. 1, p. 702; *Toshimakushi, nenpyōhen* (Tokyo: Toshimaku, 1982), pp. 319, 325; Wada Shigeaki, *Chōsenteki keiei no himitsu* (Tokyo: Jōhō Sentā Shuppankyoku, 1981), p. 103.

14. Okada, pp. 50–51; "Commercial Activities in Tokyo," *Tokyo Municipal News*, vol. 22, no. 4, p. 1 (June 1972). See also Okada, pp. 40–42.

15. Tsutsumi Seiji, *Henkaku*, pp. 228–229. See Sasaki, pp. 68–69; Okada, p. 48.

16. Japan External, *Retailing*, pp. 23, 26.

17. Shuzo Koyama, "The Japanese Distribution System: 'Complex and Incomprehensible'?," *Look Japan*, December 10, 1984, p. 10. See Tsutsumi Seiji, *Henkaku*, pp. 148, 152, 231–233.

18. Japan External, *Retailing*, p. 29.

19. Ibid., p. 36.

20. Yoshida, p. 29; Isao Nakauchi, "The Yoke of Regulation Weighs Down on Distribution," *Economic Eye*, vol. 10, no. 2, p. 18 (summer 1989); *Japan Economic Survey*, vol. 8, no. 11, p. 10 (November 1989).

21. Yamaichi, p. 209.

22. *Japan Economic Survey*, vol. 9, no. 3, pp. 13–14 (March 1990); Nara Chizuko interview, June 22, 1988; *Japan Times*, February 2, 1991, p. 10, May 9, 1991, p. 12.

23. See McCraw and O'Brien, p. 112; *Japan Times*, August 24, 1990, p. 3, October 25, 1990, p. 15.

24. *Sezon no rekishi*, vol. 1, p. 288. See Asō, *Seibu*, p. 46.

25. *Sezon no rekishi*, vol. 1, pp. 288–290.

26. Kaminogō, *Seibu*, p. 177.

27. Kosakai, "Gotō," p. 249.

28. Quoted in Ōtsuka, Hideki, "Tsutsumi Yoshiaki: waga 'jūnen senryaku,'" *Hōseki*, February 1987, p. 139.

29. Quoted in Yoshida, p. 205. See Kamiya, p. 43.

30. *Sezon no rekishi*, vol. 1, pp. 297, vol. 2, pp. 61–64. See Asō, *Sezon*, p. 55; Asō, *Seibu*, p. 200.

31. Wada, *Chōsenteki*, pp. 37–41, 129–131.

32. Kusaka Kimindo, *Hapuningu abenyū "246"* (Tokyo: Taiyō Kigyō Shuppan, 1984), pp. 33, 36; Seibu Hyakkaten Bunka Kyōiku Jigyōbu, *SEED reboryūshon* (Tokyo: Daiyamondosha, 1987), p. 196; Shiizuka, p. 40.

33. Tsutsumi Yoshiaki, in Kaminogō, *Tsutsumi Yoshiaki wa*, p. 196; Tsutsumi Seiji, *Hatsugen shirīzu*, vol. 20, p. 20 (1988).

34. *Sezon no rekishi*, vol. 1, pp. 85, 435–436; *Yūka shōken hōkokusho sōran, Kabushiki Kaisha Paruko* (February 1990) (Tokyo: Ōkurashō Insatsukyoku, 1990), p. 1; Asō, *Seibu*, pp. 75–76, 114; "Paruko 'ryūtsū bunka' o kaeta Masuda Tsūji to iu otoko," *Decide*, May 1987, p. 36.

35. Quoted in Imaoka, *Konnichi*, p. 77.

36. *Sezon no rekishi*, vol. 1, pp. 440–441; Esaka, "Tsutsumi Seiji: Risuku," p. 99; Imaoka, *Konnichi*, p. 78.

37. Masuda, pp. 25–26, 52, 178–180.

38. *Sezon no rekishi*, vol. 1, pp. 437–438. See pp. 440–443; "Paruko 'ryūtsū bunka,'" p. 36; Hotta, p. 70.

39. Seidensticker, p. 301. See Matsueda, pp. 176–177; Katayama Mataichirō, *Tsutsumi Seiji chōjōshiki no keiei* (Tokyo: Keirin Shobō, 1987), pp. 81–82; Wada, *Chōsenteki*, p. 39.

40. "Shinka no kenkyū: Seibu Sezon Gurūpu," *Nikkei bijinesu*, September 28, 1987, p. 11; Masuda, p. 104.

41. Masuda, p. 179.

42. Ibid., pp. 99–100. See pp. 24, 29, 46, 56–57, 64–65.

43. Ibid., pp. 46, 70, 99.

44. Ueno Chizuko, "Imēji no shijō," in Ueno Chizuko et al., *Sezon no hassō: Māketto e no sokyū* (Tokyo: Riburopōto, 1991), p. 83.

45. Ibid., p. 92.

46. Ibid., p. 95.

47. *Sezon no rekishi*, vol. 2, p. 200.

48. Ibid., p. 208; Imaoka, *Konnichi*, p. 74; Masuda, pp. 73, 183, 188.

49. Kosakai, "Nihon," p. 90. See "Paruko 'ryūtsū bunka,'" p. 35.

50. Seibu Hyakkaten, *SEED*, p. 37, 41; Kikuchi, p. 67; James A. Doherty interview, July 30, 1986.

51. Egashira interview, July 19, 1986; Yamashita Takeshi, *Seibu Ryūtsū Gurūpu no subete* (Tokyo: Kokusai Shōgyō Shuppan, 1980), pp. 89–92; Hotta, p. 90.

52. *Yūka shōken hōkokusho sōran, Kabushiki Kaisha Seiyū* (February 1990) (Tokyo: Ōkurashō Insatsukyoku, 1990), p. 3. For agreements between Sears and Seiyū in 1989–1990, see Sakaguchi, *Tsutsumi*, pp. 40–41; *Saison Journal*, December 14, 1990, p. 1.

53. Mizuno Seiichi interview, February 1, 1991. Sales data appear in *Sezon no rekishi*, vol. 2, p. 59.

54. Tsutsumi Seiji, *Hatsugen shirīzu,* vol. 16, p. 72 (1983).

55. *Japan Times,* March 15, 1991, p. 14; *Yoke,* no. 33, p. 6 (January 1989).

56. Ikuno Shigeo interview, August 1, 1986.

57. Idem; *Sezon no rekishi,* vol. 2, pp. 330–335; *Saison Group* (Tokyo: Saison Group, 1990), p. 32, data p. 16; Esaka, "Tsutsumi Seiji: Risuku," pp. 95–97; Miyashita and Shūdan, *Seibu,* p. 127.

58. Quoted in Esaka, "Tsutsumi Seiji: Risuku," p. 95.

59. *Sezon no rekishi,* vol. 1, pp. 171–172, vol. 2, p. 602; Maeda, p. 277; "Seibu Kurejitto Marui ni yabureta geppu hyakkaten no tettei henshin," *Decide* (May 1987), p. 40; Okada, p. 21; Sakaguchi, *Seibu,* p. 136.

60. *Sezon no rekishi,* vol. 2, p. 279.

61. Kawakami Seiji, "Seibu Sezon Gurūpu no kin'yū senryaku no zenbō," *Zaikai,* July 1, 1986, p. 29. See *Sezon no rekishi,* vol. 2, pp. 286–287, 296, 299–300, 602–604; "Seibu Kurejitto," p. 41; Asō, *Seibu,* pp. 78, 115–116; Okada, pp. 22–23.

62. *Pictorial Encyclopedia of Modern Japan* (Tokyo: Gakken, 1986), p. 126. The figure is for 1986.

63. *Hyakkaten no teatsui hogo no moto* (1971), in *Sezon no rekishi,* vol. 2, p. 220.

64. *Sezon no rekishi,* vol. 2, pp. 217–219, 233–234; Imaoka, *Konnichi,* p. 152. See Matsueda, pp. 174–176; "'Aratanaru gurūpu senryaku' no kagi Tsutsumi Seiji no saiken tetsugaku," *Decide,* May 1987, p. 32.

65. *Sezon no rekishi,* vol. 2, p. 524; Asō, *Seibu,* pp. 108–109, 116–117, 159; "Aratanaru," p. 31; Wada, *Chōsenteki,* p. 86.

66. *Sezon no rekishi,* vol. 1, p. 433; Tominaga, pp. 15, 111; Hayashi Kaoru, p. 20.

67. *Sezon no rekishi,* vol. 1, p. 433.

68. Quoted in Eikawa, *Tsutsumi Seiji,* p. 38. See Asō, *Seibu,* pp. 75, 87.

69. Tsutsumi Seiji, "Shinkeiei no shikon shōken," *Jitsugyō no Nihon,* 14-part series (January 1–July 15, 1970).

70. *Sezon no rekishi,* vol. 1, p. 419; Eikawa, *Tsutsumi Seiji,* pp. 42–44.

71. *Sezon no rekishi,* vol. 2, pp. 35, 141, 146.

72. Ibid., p. 35. See *Yūka, Seiyū* (February 1990), p. 5; "Shōbai wa aruku koto kara—Seiyū," *Chūō kōron,* September 1987, p. 111; Sakaguchi, *Tsutsumi,* pp. 131–133; Atsuta, *Seibu,* p. 151–152.

73. *Sezon no rekishi,* vol. 2, p. 142.

74. Quoted in Asō, *Seibu,* p. 162. See pp. 56–57, 158; Tominaga, p. 111.

75. Eikawa, *Tsutsumi Seiji,* pp. 65–66.

76. *Sezon no rekishi,* vol. 1, p. 432, vol. 2, pp. 36, 150, 186–188. See Yoshida, pp. 27–29; Satō Ichidan, *Biggu sutoa doko ga tsuyokute doko ga yowai ka* (Tokyo: Nihon Jitsugyō Shuppansha, 1982), p. 104; Tominaga, pp. 110–111; Asō, *Sezon,* pp. 81–82.

77. *Sezon no rekishi,* vol. 1, p. 433, vol. 2, p. 191. See vol. 2, pp. 156, 186, 189–190; Eikawa, *Tsutsumi Seiji,* pp. 71–73; Yamashita, *Seibu,* pp. 104–105.

78. Tsutsumi Seiji, *Hatsugen shirīzu,* vol. 15, p. 17 (1983); Satō Ichidan, p. 104. In an interview on November 11, 1991, Tsutsumi praised Jewel as "a truly excellent company with excellent leaders."

79. Quoted in Kaminogō, *Tsutsumi Seiji ga,* p. 60. See *Sezon no rekishi,* vol. 2, p. 257.

80. Kaminogō, *Tsutsumi Seiji ga,* pp. 58, 60.

81. Hariki, *Netsujō,* pp. 122–123. See Eikawa, *Jūnengo,* p. 100.

82. See *Sezon no rekishi,* vol. 1, pp. 453–454, vol. 2, pp. 245–246. See also Hayakawa, *Tsutsumi Yoshiakishiki,* p. 54.

83. Murai Hajime interview, May 8, 1991; "Yahari motsurehajimeta Tsutsumi 'shichi kyōdai' shusshō no innen," *Shūkan shinchō,* June 12, 1986, p. 37; Eikawa, *Jūnengo,* p. 201; Hayakawa, *Tsutsumi Yoshiakishiki,* p. 54.

84. *Sezon no rekishi,* vol. 2, p. 245.

85. "Seibu Sezon Gurūpu daishakkin," p. 52; *Sezon no rekishi,* vol. 2, p. 246.

86. *Sezon no rekishi,* vol. 2, p. 4.

87. Quoted in Atsuta, *Seibu,* p. 84.

88. Atsuta, *Seibu,* p. 208.

89. "At Your Service," p. 28.

90. *Sezon no rekishi,* vol. 1, pp. 338–341.

91. Ibid., pp. 26, 302, 308; Ueno, pp. 8, 47–48; Sakaguchi, *Tsutsumi,* pp. 37–38; Asō, *Seibu,* pp. 86–87; Okada, pp. 67–68.

92. Tamura Akira, "'Kabe' e no chōsen," in Ueno Chizuko et al., *Sezon no hassō: Māketto e no sokyū* (Tokyo: Riburopōto, 1991), p. 191.

93. Ueno, pp. 50–52; Tamura Akira, p. 192.

94. Local partners initially held 52.3 percent of Seibu Hyakkaten Kansai. *Sezon no rekishi,* vol. 2, p. 340.

95. Ibid., pp. 343, 347, 360.

96. Ibid., pp. 352–353. For a more sanguine assessment see Atsuta, *Seibu,* p. 143.

97. *Sezon no rekishi,* vol. 2, p. 355.

98. *Saison Journal,* March 16, 1990, p. 1. The group had Kansai sales of nearly $6.9 billion in the year ended March 1990.

99. *Sezon no rekishi,* vol. 2, p. 355.

100. Quoted in Asō, *Sezon,* p. 97.

101. *Sezon no rekishi,* vol. 2, p. 21. See Wada, *Chōsenteki,* pp. 69–70; Ueno, pp. 7, 23–24.

102. Ueno, p. 37; *Sezon no rekishi,* vol. 1, p. 328.

103. Hotta, p. 44; "Hanayakasa no uragawa de aikawarazu no futōmeiburi o hakkisuru Seibu Hyakkaten," *Gekiryū* (April 1979), p. 64.

104. Hotta, pp. 46–47; Matsueda, p. 73; Asō, *Seibu,* p. 55; Wada Shigeaki, "Seibu Hyakkaten no hassō," in Seibu Hyakkaten Ikebukuro Komyunitei Karejji and Ryūtsū Sangyō Kenkyūjo, *Sentan shōgyō no hassō to senryaku* (Tokyo: Daiyamondosha, 1982), p. 124.

105. *Kihonteki kangaekata,* August 28, 1975, quoted in Ueno, p. 23.

106. *Sezon no rekishi,* vol. 2, pp. 18–19.

107. Hotta, pp. 45–46.

108. Ueno, p. 40.

109. Kishima Akihiko, "Tsutsumi Seiji to 'Yūrakuchō Seibu,'" *Purejidento,* January 1985, p. 221; *Sezon no rekishi,* vol. 1, pp. 322, 324; Ueno, pp. 18, 30–34; Wada, "Seibu," p. 119.

110. Wada, *Chōsenteki,* pp. 135–136; Matsunobu, p. 46; Ueno, pp. 27–28.

111. Imaoka, *Konnichi,* p. 117.

112. Quoted in "Seibu Ryūtsū Gurūpu—yume to risuku no 'shingata shōsha' e sōdai na chōsen," *Nikkei bijinesu,* December 24, 1984, p. 40.

113. Eikawa, *Tsutsumi Seiji,* pp. 64–65; *Sezon no rekishi,* vol. 2, pp. 104–106; Wada, *Chōsenteki,* pp. 131–134.

114. "Seibu Ryūtsū Gurūpu," p. 40.

115. Ueno, p. 40. See also ibid., p. 64; Wada, "Seibu," p. 125.

116. Quoted in Tominaga, p. 37.

117. Quoted in Yasuda, p. 155. See Asō, *Sezon,* p. 73; Matsueda, p. 58.

118. Matsueda, p. 187.

119. *Seibu Ryūtsū Gurūpu no keiei kihon rinen* (1973), quoted in Miura Masashi, "Ikeru gyakusetsu," in Ueno et al., *Sezon no hassō: Māketto e no sokyū* (Tokyo: Riburopōto, 1991), p. 396. See Atsuta, *Seibu,* p. 200.

120. Quoted in Matsueda, p. 30. See Hotta, p. 27.

121. Quoted in Asō, *Sezon,* p. 73. See Eikawa, *Tsutsumi Seiji,* pp. 34–36; Katayama, p. 18; Umemoto, p. 82.

122. Quoted in Asō, *Seibu,* p. 55.

123. Quoted in Hotta, p. 11. See also p. 10.

124. *Sezon no rekishi*, vol. 2, pp. 82, 85. See pp. 66–69; Wada, *Chōsenteki*, pp. 99–100.

125. *Sezon no rekishi*, vol. 2, p. 69; Shiizuka, pp. 21, 81; Hotta, pp. 15–18.

126. *Sezon no rekishi*, vol. 2, pp. 71, 74; Seibu Hyakkaten Ikebukuro Komyunitei Karejji and Ryūtsū Sangyō Kenkyūjo, *Hōshoku jidai no shokuhin māketeingu senryaku* (Tokyo: Daiyamondosha, 1983), pp. 130–131.

127. Egashira interview, July 19, 1986. See *Sezon no rekishi*, vol. 2, p. 76.

128. Seibu Hyakkaten, *Kurashi*, p. 161.

129. *Sezon no rekishi*, vol. 1, pp. 366–371, vol. 2, p. 114; Fusako Goto and Hideo Inohara, *From Salary to Quality of Working Life—CASE: Seibu Department Stores*. Sophia University, Institute of Comparative Culture, Business Series no. 88 (Tokyo: 1982), pp. 2–3, 8, 10, 12.

130. Goto and Inohara, pp. 3, 13–14; Asō, *Seibu*, pp. 191–192; *Sezon no rekishi*, vol. 2, p. 114.

131. Millie R. Creighton, "Department Store *Hina* Dolls and Japan's Equal Employment Opportunity Law," seminar paper, New England Japan Seminar, University of Massachusetts, Boston, February 7, 1989, pp. 26–35. See Ueno, p. 29; Miyashita and Shūdan, *Seibu*, p. 104; Matsueda, pp. 74–75; Hotta, pp. 34–36; Asō, *Seibu*, p. 186.

132. Goto and Inohara, pp. 15–16; Matsueda, p. 79; *Sezon no rekishi*, vol. 2, p. 116.

133. Quoted in Katayama, p. 19.

134. Goto and Inohara, p. 15.

135. See Creighton, pp. 3, 11–12; Miyano Tōru, *Onnatachi no chōsen* (Tokyo: Kōdansha, 1985), p. 20; Eikawa, *Tsutsumi Seiji*, pp. 88–91; Asō, *Seibu*, p. 184.

136. Wada, *Chōsenteki*, pp. 74–76.

137. Tsutsumi Seiji and Kometani, p. 25.

138. "Hanayakasa," p. 64; Asō, *Seibu*, pp. 203–204.

139. *Sezon no rekishi*, vol. 2, p. 48; Eikawa, *Jūnengo*, p. 173; Kaminogō, *Seibu*, p. 36; Asō, *Seibu*, p. 202.

140. *Sezon no rekishi*, vol. 2, p. 47; Umemoto, pp. 71–72; Kaminogō, *Seibu*, pp. 17–23; Tominaga, p. 112; Katayama, pp. 92–95; Asō, *Seibu*, pp. 196, 202–205.

141. Kizu Haruhiko interview, August 1, 1986. See Asō, *Seibu*, pp. 201, 204; Eikawa, *Jūnengo*, pp. 174–175.

142. *Sezon no rekishi*, vol. 1, p. 373, vol. 2, p. 135.

143. Ibid., vol. 2, pp. 35, 135.

144. Ibid., vol. 2, p. 136.

145. "Hanayakasa," pp. 62–63. See *Sezon no rekishi*, vol. 2, pp. 111–112.

146. *Sezon no rekishi*, vol. 2, p. 138.

147. Hotta, p. 41. See Takaoka, pp. 10–12.

148. Quoted in "Seibu Sezon Gurūpu daishakkin," p. 51. See *Sezon no rekishi*, vol. 2, pp. 42–43; *Saison Group*, p. 44; Matsueda, pp. 139–140, 143–145; Takaoka, pp. 21–23.

CHAPTER SIX: PRINCES AND LIONS

1. Tsutsumi Yoshiaki, *Tsutsumi Yoshiaki wa kataru—Kyūjitsu ga hoshikereba kanrishoku o yamero*, ed. Kaminogō Toshiaki (Tokyo: Kōdansha, 1984), pp. 33–34.

2. Quoted in Hariki, *Netsujō*, p. 178. See Seibu Tetsudō, *Tsutsumi Yasujirō*, p. 71.

3. Tsutsumi Yoshiaki and Kaminogō, p. 24. See Hariki, *Netsujō*, p. 179; Hariki, *"Wakaki,"* p. 67.

4. Tsutsumi Yoshiaki and Kaminogō, pp. 23–24; Hariki, *"Wakaki,"* pp. 66–67, Ukaji, vol. 1, p. 871.

5. *Purinsu*, passim.

6. Yamaichi, p. 218; Hara Tsutomu, Okamoto Nobuyuki, and Inagaki Tsutomu, *Hoteru sangyōkai* (Tokyo: Kyōikusha, 1988), pp. 40, 50.

7. *Purinsu*, pp. 14–56; Hariki, *Netsujō*, p. 164.

8. Hara, Okamoto, and Inagaki, p. 199; Kamiya, p. 196.

9. *Purinsu*, pp. 260, 293–298, 307; Hariki, *"Wakaki,"* p. 51; Atsuta, *Seibu*, pp. 216–217.

10. Hariki, *Netsujō*, p. 184; *Purinsu*, pp. 162–170.

11. Eikawa, *Tsutsumi Yoshiaki to*, p. 39; "Tsuyosa," p. 32.

12. Quoted in Hariki, *Netsujō*, p. 167.

13. Inose, pp. 77, 79.

14. Kosaki, "Gotō," p. 251.

15. See Tsutsumi Yoshiaki and Kaminogō, p. 97.

16. Narushima, p. 120. See Inose, p. 79.

17. Seibu Tetsudō, *Tsutsumi Yasujirō*, pp. 46–47; Sakai interview, May 8, 1991.

18. Narushima, pp. 120–121; *Purinsu*, p. 231.

19. Narushima, pp. 62, 127–128, 138.

20. Tsutsumi Yoshiaki and Kaminogō, p. 97. See Inose, pp. 108, 120.

21. Kaminogō, *Seibu*, p. 209.

22. *Purinsu*, pp. 40–45; Narushima, p. 62; Hariki, "*Wakaki*," pp. 90–92; Inose, p. 108.

23. *Nihon keizai shinbun*, April 25, 1983, p. 5. See *Purinsu*, pp. 34–39; Inose, pp. 77–79; Hariki, *Netsujō*, pp. 164–167, 170–172; "Tsuyosa," pp. 31–32.

24. Hariki, *Netsujō*, pp. 185–186. See "Tsuyosa," p. 32.

25. Eikawa, *Tsutsumi Yoshiaki to*, p. 39. See pp. 36–37; *Purinsu*, pp. 48–51; Hariki, *Netsujō*, pp. 178–181.

26. Quoted in Hariki, "*Wakaki*," p. 68.

27. Hariki, *Netsujō*, p. 183; Kobayashi Kazunari, p. 93.

28. Tsutsumi Yoshiaki and Kaminogō, pp. 94–95; Narushima, p. 63.

29. Atsuta, *Seibu*, p. 186. See Hariki, *Netsujō*, pp. 174–175, 204; Narushima, pp. 125–127.

30. Hariki, *Netsujō*, p. 186. See also pp. 174–175.

31. Quoted in Kosakai, "Gotō," p. 251.

32. Quoted in Atsuta, *Seibu*, p. 219.

33. Quoted in Inose, p. 124.

34. Tsutsumi Yoshiaki, *Tsutsumi Yoshiaki wa*, p. 34.

35. *Friday*, December 14, 1984, p. 69; *Focus*, December 7, 1984, p. 9; Kikuchi, pp. 40, 43; Miyashita and Shūdan, *Tsutsumi*, p. 76.

36. Tsutsumi Yoshiaki and Kaminogō, p. 170.

37. Ibid., p. 151.

38. Tsutsumi Yoshiaki, *Tsutsumi Yoshiaki wa*, p. 58; Tsutsumi Yoshiaki and Satō, p. 100.

39. Tsutsumi Yoshiaki and Kaminogō, p. 170; Kobayashi Kazunari, pp. 116–117.

40. Kobayashi Kazunari, p. 121. See also ibid., pp. 118–120; Tsutsumi Yoshiaki and Kaminogō, p. 172.

41. Tsutsumi Yoshiaki and Kaminogō, p. 175. See Kaminogō, *Seibu*, p. 42; Kaminogō Toshiaki, *Tsutsumi Yoshiaki hisokanaru ketsudan* (Tokyo: Ushio Shuppansha, 1984), pp. 30–31.

42. Tsutsumi Yoshiaki and Kaminogō, pp. 159, 175. See Kaminogō, *Seibu*, pp. 44–45; Kosakai Shōzō, "Tsutsumi Yoshiaki ga nerau!," *Hōseki*, January 1987, p. 179; Ebisawa Yasuhisa, *Seibu Raionzu: Puro yakyū gurafuitei* (Tokyo: Shinchōsha, 1983), p. 130.

43. Tsutsumi Yoshiaki and Kaminogō, p. 153.

44. Tsutsumi Yoshiaki and Satō, p. 100; Narushima, p. 102.

45. Tsutsumi Yoshiaki and Kaminogō, pp. 151, 173.

46. Ibid., p. 196.

47. See ibid., p. 186.

48. Sugiyama interview, August 6, 1986. See Robert Whiting, *You Gotta Have Wa: When Two Cultures Collide on the Baseball Diamond* (New York: Macmillan, 1989), p. 230.

49. Tsutsumi Yoshiaki and Kaminogō, p. 198.

50. Ibid., p. 174; Murai interview, May 8, 1991. See Atsuta, *Seibu*, p. 221.

51. Quoted in Narushima, p. 95.

52. Tsutsumi Yoshiaki and Kaminogō, p. 158. See pp. 155–156; Narushima, pp. 96–97.

53. Narushima, p. 102.

54. Whiting, pp. 222–224; Ebisawa, frontispiece, p. 66; Tsutsumi Yoshiaki and Kaminogō, p. 207; Eikawa, *Jūnengo*, pp. 95–96.

55. Whiting, p. 236.

56. Narushima, p. 102.

57. Tsumuji Takao, "Itan no tōshō: Seibu ōkoku Tsutsumi Yoshiaki no henshin," *Shūkan asahi*, January 18, 1985, p. 176; Whiting, pp. 74–76, 214–217; Narushima, pp. 76–77.

58. Quoted in *Shūkan posuto*, November 17, 1989, p. 43. See Kosakai, "Tsutsumi Yoshiaki—tochi," p. 168; Whiting, p. 59.

59. Kosakai, "Tsutsumi Yoshiaki—tochi," p. 173. See Kobayashi Kazunari, p. 90; *Asahi Evening News*, August 18, 1987, p. 6.

60. Quoted in Manabe Shigeki, "Tsutsumi Yoshiaki 'boku wa bushi, Seiji-san wa shōnin,'" *Gendai*, April 1986, p. 115.

61. Idem.

CHAPTER SEVEN: FROM ABUNDANCE TO AFFLUENCE

1. Fujioka Wakao, *Sayōnara, taishū* (Kyoto: PHP Kenkyūjo, 1984).

2. Yamazaki Masakazu, *Yawarakai kojinshugi no tanjō* (Tokyo: Chūō Kōronsha, 1984).

3. See Wada, *Chōsenteki*, pp. 45–46, 105; Ueno, pp. 66–68, 79–80; *Sezon no rekishi*, vol. 2, p. 376.

4. Nakamachi Hiroshi, "Ginza Store Wars," *Japan Quarterly*, vol. 33, no. 1, p. 33 (1986). See Seibu Hyakkaten Ikebukuro Komyunitei Karejji and Ryūtsū Sangyō Kenkyūjo, *Yūrakuchō "Marion genshō" o toku* (Tokyo:

Daiyamondosha, 1985), pp. 25–27; *Sezon no rekishi*, vol. 2, pp. 373–376; Matsunobu, p. 16.

5. Ueno, p. 107; *Sezon no rekishi*, vol. 2, p. 380. See Tsutsumi Seiji, *Hatsugen shirīzu*, vol. 15, pp. 3–6, 18 (1983).

6. Sasaki, pp. 73–75; Ueno, pp. 64–66.

7. Tsutsumi Seiji, *Hatsugen shirīzu*, vol. 14, p. 50 (1982). See also p. 104.

8. Quoted in Hotta, pp. 29–30.

9. Quoted in Esaka, "Tsutsumi Seiji: Risuku," pp. 90–91.

10. Wada, "Seibu," p. 128.

11. Idem; Wada, *Chōsenteki*, pp. 105–113; Matsunobu, p.18.

12. Asō, *Sezon*, p. 256.

13. See *Sezon no rekishi*, vol. 2, p. 390; Hotta, pp. 54, 60–62.

14. *Sezon no rekishi*, vol. 2, p. 383. See Asō, *Seibu*, pp. 26–29; Asō, *Sezon*, pp. 256–258.

15. Quoted in Esaka, "Tsutsumi Seiji: Risuku," p. 97. See Eikawa, *Tsutsumi Seiji*, pp. 78–79, 195; Asō, *Seibu*, pp. 29–32.

16. Quoted in *Sezon no rekishi*, vol. 2, p. 372. See Niwa Tetsuo, *Godai kigyō gurūpu no senryaku kakushin* (Tokyo: Tōyō Keizai Shinpōsha, 1992), p. 29; Ueno, p. 104; Nakamura Tatsuya, "Togisumasareta Don Kihōte," in Ueno et al., *Sezon no hassō: Māketto e no sokyū* (Tokyo: Riburopōto, 1991), p. 163.

17. *Sezon no rekishi*, vol. 2, pp. 391–394.

18. Ibid., p. 372.

19. Asō, *Seibu*, p. 15; Asō, *Sezon*, p. 32.

20. Kaminogō, *Tsutsumi Seiji ga*, p. 4.

21. Asō, *Seibu*, p. 83; "Seibu Ryūtsū Gurūpu," p. 39; Kaminogō, *Tsutsumi Seiji ga*, p. 4.

22. "Shinka," p. 16.

23. *Sezon no rekishi*, vol. 2, p. 88. See Asō, *Seibu*, p. 56.

24. Tsutsumi Seiji, 1983, quoted in Yoshida, p. 113. See Ueno, pp. 10, 71–78; Shiizuka, p. 208; Wada, "Seibu," p. 130; *Sezon no rekishi*, vol. 2, p. 90.

25. Ueno, p. 16.

26. Tsutsumi Seiji, *Hatsugen shirīzu*, vol. 15, p. 20 (1983); "Seibu Ryūtsū Gurūpu," p. 41.

27. Quoted in Esaka Akira, "Tsutsumi Seiji keiei to wa 'eikyū kakumei' de aru," *Purejidento*, vol. 24, no. 7, p. 61 (July 1986).

28. Wada, "Seibu," p. 128.

29. Tsutsumi Seiji, *Hatsugen shirīzu,* vol. 15, p. 33 (1983). See Shiizuka, p. 80.

30. M. Ogura, "Japan's Retail Industry in Trouble," *Tokyo Business Today,* February 1986, p. 51. See Wada, *Chōsenteki,* pp. 137–138; "Za raibaru: Seibu Hyakkaten vs. Isetan," *Gekiryū,* December 1987, pp. 18–19.

31. *Sezon no rekishi,* vol. 2, p. 94; *Saison Journal,* September 14, 1990, p. 1; Sasaki, pp. 70–73; Ueno, p. 61; Wada, *Chōsenteki,* pp. 165–170; Yoshida, p. 29; Satō Ichidan, p. 99.

32. *Sezon no rekishi,* vol. 2, pp. 135, 429.

33. Ibid., p. 137.

34. Ibid., p. 419; Kishima, p. 220.

35. Goto and Inohara, p. 20.

36. *Nihon keizai shinbun,* December 25, 1981, quoted ibid., pp. 20–21. See Sezon Gurūpu, *O.E.S.* (Tokyo, 1989), p. 22.

37. *Sezon no rekishi,* vol. 2, p. 444.

38. Shiizuka, p. 202; Miyano, pp. 25–31; Katayama, pp. 21–22.

39. Nihon Keizai Shimbun, *Nikkei Placement/International 1990* (Tokyo, 1989), p. 266.

40. Idem; Sezon, *O.E.S.,* pp. 18–21; *Shūshoku jōhō,* November 1986, p. 149. See Katayama, pp. 13–16; Asō, *Sezon,* p. 225.

41. *Japan Times,* July 3, 1986, p. 3; Sezon, *O.E.S.,* p. 22; Eikawa, *Tsutsumi Seiji,* p. 96.

42. Tada Chiyoko interview, July 17, 1986; Creighton, pp. 9–10.

43. Alice C. L. Lam, *Women and Japanese Management: Discrimination and Reform* (London: Routledge, 1992), pp. 183, 200–201. See Goto and Inohara, p. 22; Matsueda, pp. 83–84; Shiizuka, pp. 205–206; Hotta, p. 126.

44. Tada interview, July 17, 1986; *Saison Journal,* October 5, 1990, p. 3; Tsutsumi Seiji, *Hatsugen shirīzu,* vol. 20, pp. 18–19 (1988). See Sakaguchi, *Seibu,* pp. 89–90; Miyashita and Shūdan, *Seibu,* pp. 90–99, 103–105; Matsueda, p. 121; "Shinka," pp. 18–19.

45. "Tsutsumi Seiji vs. Tawara Sōichirō," *Hōseki,* January 1986, p. 99.

46. Carol Lufty, "Changing Expectations," *Tokyo Business Today,* June 1988, p. 16. See "Mono no ryūtsū kara bunka no ryūtsū e: Tsutsumi Seiji," *Rekishi tokuhon,* autumn 1987, p. 56; Matsueda, pp. 124, 150–151; Tsujii Takashi and Sakaki Jirō, "'Kashibiru' yori mo 'gekijō' o tsukure," *Voice,* March 1987, p. 50.

47. *Shūshoku jōhō,* November 1986, p. 148. See Shiizuka, p. 195; *Zaikai,* May 3, 1988, p. 134.

48. Asō, *Sezon*, p. 218.

49. Tsutsumi Seiji and Kometani, p. 25. On Korean Japanese, see Tsutsumi Seiji, *Tsutsumi Seiji Tsujii Takashi fuīrudo nōto* (Tokyo: Bungei Shunjū, 1986), p. 232; *Sezon no rekishi,* vol. 2, pp. 475–478. The group ran ads in national newspapers on September 23, 1982, expressing contrition for the Yokosuka incident.

50. Mizuno interview, February 1, 1991.

51. Seibu Department Stores, p. 20; *Saison Journal,* April 13, 1990, p. 1; Hotta, pp. 96–99; *Sezon no rekishi,* vol. 2, p. 391; *Saison Group 1992,* p. 4.

52. *Japan Echo,* vol. 17, no. 4, p. 80 (winter 1990).

53. Andō Masasuke, "Igyōshu to no teikei de gyōtai henshin," *Zaikai,* December 20, 1987, p. 33; Hayashi, pp. 12–15; *Sezon no rekishi,* vol. 2, p. 450. See Matsueda, pp. 29, 189; Matsunobu, p. 150.

54. Tsutsumi Seiji, *Hatsugen shirīzu,* vol. 16, pp. 86, 91 (1984); Nakamura Tatsuya, p. 164; Asō, *Sezon,* p. 190. See Herbert Marcuse, *One-Dimensional Man: Studies in the Ideology of Advanced Industrial Society* (Boston: Beacon Press, 1964).

55. *Sezon no rekishi,* vol. 2, p. 447. The term "prosumer" is Nakauchi Isao's, in "The Pursuit of 'Real' Affluence," *Look Japan,* December 10, 1986, p. 4. See Eikawa, *Tsutsumi Seiji,* p. 144; Katayama, pp. 102–103.

56. *Sezon no rekishi,* vol. 2, pp. 158–160, 453–456; Asō, *Sezon,* p. 68.

57. Quoted in Yoshida, p. 54.

58. *Sezon no rekishi,* vol. 2, pp. 478–479; Hashimoto Ryūgō, "Kokunai no saidai Seiyū shokuchūdoku jiken yonenme no shinjijitsu," *Seikai jānaru,* February 1987, pp. 74–76.

59. Asō, *Seibu,* p. 74.

60. *Sezon no rekishi,* vol. 2, p. 173. See Nakamura Tatsuya, p. 165; Eikawa, *Tsutsumi Seiji,* p. 67.

61. Ueno, p. 58; Hotta, p. 147. See Leonard Koren, *Success Stories: How Eleven of Japan's Most Interesting Businesses Came to Be* (San Francisco: Chronicle Books, 1990), p. 130; Tsutsumi Seiji, *Hatsugen shirīzu,* vol. 15, p. 105 (1983).

62. Matsunobu, p. 47; Koren, p. 132.

63. Tsutsumi Seiji, *Hatsugen shirīzu,* vol. 16, p. 117 (1984); Eikawa, *Tsutsumi Seiji,* p. 48; Asō, *Seibu,* p. 151.

64. Tsutsumi Seiji, *Hatsugen shirīzu,* vol. 16, p. 19 (1984); *The Seiyu, Ltd. 1990 Annual Report* (Tokyo, 1990), p. 13; Asō, *Sezon,* p. 182; *Sezon no rekishi,* vol. 2, pp. 160–168; *Japan Times,* May 11, 1991, p. 7.

65. *Sezon Gurūpu 1989–'90* (Tokyo, 1990), p. 60; *Sezon no rekishi,* vol. 2, p. 464. See Asō, *Seibu,* pp. 154–155.

66. *Sezon no rekishi,* vol. 2, pp. 466, 485; Matsunobu, pp. 73–78; Sakaguchi, *Tsutsumi,* pp. 64–65; Asō, *Sezon,* pp. 88–89; Yamashita Takeshi, *Fuamirī-Māto–yakushin no himitsu* (Tokyo: TBS Buritanika, 1990), pp. 48–50; *Saison Journal,* January 26, 1990, p. 2.

67. *Sezon no rekishi,* vol. 2, p. 482.

68. *FamilyMart Co., Ltd. Annual Report 1990* (Tokyo, 1990), p. 12; *Fuamirī-Māto anyuaru ripōto '90* (Tokyo, 1990), p. 8; *Saison Group,* p. 24; Gotō Ryūichi interview, December 6, 1990; *Sezon no rekishi,* vol. 2, pp. 482–483. See Asō, *Sezon,* pp. 88–89; Yamashita, *FuamirīMāto,* p. 22.

69. *Sezon no rekishi,* vol. 2, p. 487; *FamilyMart,* p. 10; *Saison Group,* p. 24; Yamashita, *FuamirīMāto,* pp. 28, 40, 87, 89, 100–101; *Saison Journal,* February 23, 1990, p. 2, April 13, 1990, p. 1.

70. *FamilyMart,* p. 1; Yamashita, *FuamirīMāto,* pp. 53–54; *Saison Journal,* January 26, 1990, p. 2.

71. *FamilyMart,* p. 1; *Japan Company,* p. 883; *Sezon no rekishi,* vol. 2, p. 492; *Saison Group 1992,* pp. 4–7.

72. Sakaguchi, *Tsutsumi,* p. 64; Yamashita, *FuamirīMāto,* p. 51.

73. Asō, *Seibu,* p. 229.

74. *Sezon no rekishi,* vol. 2, p. 191; Hotta, pp. 77–78; Hayashi, p. 121.

75. *Sezon no rekishi,* vol. 2, p. 185.

76. Ibid., pp. 188–189; Egashira interview, December 8, 1990; *Yūka, Seibu* (March 1990), p. 20.

77. Quoted in Eikawa, *Yabō,* p. 115.

78. *Sezon no rekishi,* vol. 2, p. 600. See also pp. 589–601. See Asahi Kōyō Kabushiki Kaisha, *Keirekisho* (Tokyo, 1989), pp. 12–13; "Aratanaru," p. 30.

79. *Sezon no rekishi,* vol. 2, p. 594; *Saison Journal,* April 20, 1990, p. 1.

80. *Saison Journal,* April 13, 1990, p. 3.

81. *Sezon no rekishi,* vol. 2, p. 600; *Sezon Gurūpu 1989–'90,* p. 49; *Saison Group 1992,* pp. 5–7.

82. *Sezon no rekishi,* vol. 2, p. 525; "Yoshinoya 'hatan chokugo kara zōshū zōeki' no himitsu," *Decide,* May 1987, p. 45.

83. *Sezon no rekishi,* vol. 2, p. 526; Hotta, p. 73.

84. Tsutsumi Seiji, *Hatsugen shirīzu,* vol. 20, p. 21 (1988).

85. *Sezon no rekishi,* vol. 2, p. 529; Asō, *Sezon,* p. 82; Graeme Marsh interview, July 30, 1986.

86. "Yoshinoya," p. 45; *Sezon no rekishi,* vol. 2, pp. 530–531.

87. *Sezon no rekishi,* vol. 2, p. 531.

88. *Saison Journal,* February 16, 1990, p. 2; *Sezon no rekishi,* vol. 2, p. 532; *Sezon Gurūpu 1989–'90,* expanded ed. (Tokyo, 1990), p. 135; *Saison Group 1992,* p. 8.

89. *Saison Journal,* January 12, 1990, p. 2, November 16, 1990, p. 2.

90. *Sezon no rekishi,* vol. 2, p. 435; Asō, *Seibu,* p. 106; "Sandaime shachō de tōsan 'Ōsawa Shōkai' wa sengo sanbanme no ōgata fusai," *Shūkan gendai,* March 17, 1984, p. 49.

91. Asō, *Seibu,* pp. 98–100, 110–111; Egashira interview, July 19, 1986; "Zig-zag Seibu Ryūtsū Gurūpu ga tōsanshita Ōsawa Shōkai no suponsā ni," *Shūkan hōseki,* May 25, 1984, p. 51.

92. Quoted in Esaka, "Tsutsumi Seiji keiei," p. 63.

93. *Sezon no rekishi,* vol. 2, p. 435; "Ōsawa Shōkai 'totsuzenshi' no nazo-toki," *Shūkan daiyamondo,* March 10, 1984, p. 9; "Aratanaru," p. 33. See *Sōgyō 100nenshi: Ōsawa Shōkai* (Tokyo, 1990), pp. 143–158; Tsutsumi Seiji, *Hatsugen shirīzu,* vol. 18, p. 3 (1986). In a 1986 interview, Tsutsumi said, "About two years before it collapsed, I was asked to take a look at Ōsawa Shōkai by Shirasu Jirō. At the time, I said the only thing to do was to be bold and close the overseas camera division; if this were not done, the company couldn't be straightened out." Tsutsumi Seiji, *Hatsugen shirīzu,* vol. 19, p. 8 (1987).

94. *Sezon no rekishi,* vol. 2, pp. 436–437.

95. Egashira interview, December 8, 1990.

96. *Sezon on rekishi,* vol. 2, pp. 437–438; *Ōsawa Shōkai kaisha gaiyō* (Tokyo, 1990), p. 23; Ikuno interview, August 1, 1986; *Saison Group 1992,* pp. 6–7; *Saison 1992* (Tokyo, 1992), p. 38. See Umemoto, p. 83.

CHAPTER EIGHT: INFORMATION FOR SALE

1. Tsutsumi Seiji, *Hatsugen shirīzu,* vol. 20, p. 2 (1988).

2. Tsutsumi Seiji, in *Riri ryūtsū sangyō* (August 1984), quoted in Esaka, "Tsutsumi Seiji: Risuku," p. 97.

3. The term is Tessa Morris-Suzuki's, in *Beyond Computopia: Information, Automation and Democracy in Japan* (New York: Kegan Paul International, 1988). See Manabe Shigeki, "Tsutsumi Seiji 'Seibu Sezon Gurūpu' no chi to yabō," *Gendai* (August 1986), p. 140.

4. Quoted in Asō, *Seibu,* p. 136.

5. *PHP Intersect,* March 1986, p. 16.

6. Morris-Suzuki, p. 134.

7. Estimates vary. "Shinka," p. 16; Gotō interview, December 6, 1990.

8. *Hyakkaten chōsa nenkan 1990* (Tokyo: Depāto Nyūsusha, 1990), p. 67. Five of the top six stores in sales of services were Seibu branches.

9. Nakamura Takafusa, p. 1; Keizai Koho Center, *Japan 1992: An International Comparison* (Tokyo, 1991), p. 46.

10. *Sezon no rekishi*, vol. 2, p. 379.

11. Keizai, *Japan 1992*, p. 11; Keizai, *Japan 1993*, p. 10.

12. Keizai, *Japan 1992*, p. 85; *Nippon: A Charted Survey of Japan 1990/91* (Tokyo: Kokuseisha, 1990), p. 296.

13. *Nippon: A Charted*, p. 295. Real household income for Americans decreased in the 1980s, except for the very rich. *Japan Times*, October 24, 1990, p. 21.

14. *Nippon: A Charted*, p. 108; *Japan Times*, October 27, 1990, p. 9; Nakamura Takafusa, p. 2.

15. *Japan Report*, May 1992, p. 8.

16. Tsūshō Sangyō Daijin Kanbō Chōsa Tōkeibu, *Shōgyō dōtai tōkei nenpō 1989* (Tokyo, 1990), p. 13. See Ogura, pp. 51–52; Nakamachi, p. 35.

17. *Saison Journal*, August 17, 1990, p. 5; Tsūshō, *Shōgyō*, p. 13.

18. Tsūshō, *Shōgyō*, p. 14.

19. Nihon Sen'i Keizai Kenkyūjo, *Nihon no hyakkaten 1991* (Tokyo, 1990), p. 9. See *Japan Update*, no. 13, pp. 9–10 (autumn 1989); *Quarterly Survey: Japanese Finance and Industry*, no. 75, p. 1 (fall 1988).

20. *Japan Times*, January 19, 1991, p.7; *Hyakkaten*, p. 30; *Intersect*, September 1993, p. 27.

21. Nihon Sen'i, p. 6; Nihon Hyakkaten Kyōkai, *Nihon Hyakkaten Kyōkai tōkei nenpō 1989* (Tokyo, 1990), p. 61; Tsūshō, *Shōgyō*, p. 17. See *Quarterly Survey: Japanese Finance and Industry*, no. 75, pp. 5, 8 (fall 1988); Matsunobu, pp. 90–91.

22. *USA Today*, October 27, 1989, p. 1B; *New York Times*, March 16, 1990, p. D1; *Japan Times*, March 19, 1991, p. 14.

23. Nakauchi, "Pursuit," p. 4.

24. See Morris-Suzuki, pp. 8–9.

25. *Asahi Evening News*, July 12, 1988, p. 3.

26. *Saison Group*, p. 3.

27. Katayama, p. 44; Eikawa, *Tsutsumi Seiji*, p. 191.

28. Tsutsumi Seiji, quoted in Esaka, "Tsutsumi Seiji keiei," p. 59. See Tsutsumi Seiji, *Hatsugen shirīzu*, vol. 19, p. 2 (1987).

29. *Saison Journal*, December 14, 1990, p. 5.

30. Seibu Department Stores, p. 2.

31. Yasuda, p. 14; Kishima, p. 217; *Sezon no rekishi*, vol. 2, p. 23.

32. Kishima, p. 217; Tanaka Kenji, *Depāto gyōkai zankoku monogatari* (Tokyo: Ēru Shuppansha, 1984), p. 143; Seibu Hyakkaten and Ryūtsū Sangyō, *Yūrakuchō*, p. 91.

33. Katayama, p. 86; *Sezon no rekishi*, vol.2, p. 422; Esaka, "Tsutsumi Seiji keiei," pp. 59–61; Uchimura Shun'ichirō, "Jōhō hasshin to jushin no kinō ga nai to kore kara no ryūtsū wa nobinai," *Dime*, January 1, 1988, pp. 53–54; Asō, *Seibu*, p. 93.

34. Quoted in Kaminogō Toshiaki, *Tsutsumi Seiji no ibento senryaku* (Tokyo: Taiyō Kikaku Shuppan, 1986), p. 151.

35. Koga Hiroyuki, *Tsutsumi Seiji no bunka o shōbai ni suru atama* (Tokyo: Besuto Serāzu, 1985), p. 19.

36. Seidensticker, p. 298. See Tsutsumi Seiji, *Hatsugen shirīzu*, vol. 18, pp. 29–31 (1986); Kizu interview, August 1, 1986; *Sezon no rekishi*, vol. 2, p. 27.

37. *Asahi Evening News*, July 12, 1988, p. 3. See Shiizuka, pp. 37, 132; Kishima, p. 219.

38. "Za raibaru," p. 23. See pp. 18–22; "Seibu Ryūtsū Gurūpu," p. 33; Esaka, "Tsutsumi Seiji keiei," p. 61; Shiizuka, p. 37.

39. Nakamachi, p. 34; "Seibu Ryūtsū Gurūpu," p. 39; Asō, *Seibu*, pp. 52–53; Eikawa, *Tsutsumi Seiji*, p. 81.

40. "Seibu Sezon Gurūpu daishakkin," p. 55; "Seibu Ryūtsū Gurūpu," p. 39.

41. *Sezon no rekishi*, vol. 2, p. 407.

42. Uchimura, p. 54.

43. *Saison Journal*, May 25, 1990, p. 2; *Sezon no rekishi*, vol. 2, p. 407.

44. Kikuchi, p. 50.

45. Yamanaka Tōru, president of Matsuya, quoted in Asō, *Seibu*, p. 68.

46. *Hyakkaten*, p. 46. See Matsueda, p. 169; Kaminogō, *Ginza*, p. 44; Nikkei Ryūtsū Shinbun, *Hyakkaten ni asu wa aru ka* (Tokyo, 1985), pp. 19–24; Kikuchi, pp. 72–73; Asō, *Seibu*, p. 68; Seibu Hyakkaten and Ryūtsū Sangyō, *Yūrakuchō*, pp. 91, 100.

47. Quoted in *Sezon no rekishi*, vol. 2, p. 402. See Tanaka, pp. 22, 25–26; Sakaguchi, *Tsutsumi*, p. 37.

48. *Sezon no rekishi,* vol. 2, p. 408.

49. "Shinka," p. 9. See Asō, *Sezon,* pp. 20–21.

50. *Sezon no rekishi,* vol. 2, p. 407; "Shinka," p. 9; *Saison Journal,* March 16, 1990, p. 1. See Eikawa, *Tsutsumi Seiji,* pp. 103–104; Kikuchi, p. 105; Tanaka, p. 189; Watanabe Kazuo, *Sogō no Seibu daihōi senryaku* (Tokyo: Kōbunsha, 1988), pp. 138–139.

51. "Shinka," pp. 8–9.

52. Asano Kyōhei, "Jitsubai mo agari, akarusa mo miehajimeta 'oka no kotō' Seibu Tsukashin," *Gekiryū,* April 1988, p.125. See p. 126; *Sezon no rekishi,* vol. 2, p. 412; *Best of Japan* (Tokyo: Kodansha International, 1987), pp. 252–253; Katayama, p. 70; Esaka, "Tsutsumi Seiji keiei," p. 61.

53. Tsutsumi Seiji, quoted in Eikawa, *Tsutsumi Seiji,* p. 115.

54. Quoted in *Sezon no rekishi,* vol. 2, p. 412.

55. Esaka, "Tsutsumi Seiji keiei," p. 63. See *Saison Journal,* August 17, 1990, p. 4–5; "Seibu Ryūtsū Gurūpu,' p. 34; Nishiyama, p. 146.

56. Asano, p. 124.

57. *Sezon no rekishi,* vol. 2, p. 412.

58. Quoted in "Shinka," p. 10. See Asano, p. 124.

59. *Sezon no rekishi,* vol. 2, p. 407.

60. Quoted in "Shinka," p. 10.

61. Asō, *Seibu,* p. 233.

62. *Saison Journal,* December 1, 1989, p. 1, September 28, 1990, p. 2; *Sezon no rekishi,* vol. 2, pp. 413–415; Noda and Koyama, pp. 74–75; Watanabe Kazuo, p. 13; *Japan Times,* October 25, 1990, p. 15.

63. *Tokyo Municipal News,* vol. 39, no. 4, p. 8 (winter 1989).

64. Quoted in *New York Times,* December 23, 1990, p. III:1.

65. *Japan Times,* June 1, 1988, p. 3.

66. *Tradescope,* vol. 6, no. 6, p. 7 (June 1986): Shiizuka, p. 157.

67. Shiizuka, pp. 14–15, 106; *Japan Company,* p. 992. See Hariki, *Netsujō,* p. 127; *Intersect,* vol. 6, no. 4, p. 6 (April 1990).

68. Seibu Department Stores, p. 8.

69. Seibu Hyakkaten Bunka, *SEED,* p. 144. See Ueno, p. 109; *Sezon no rekishi,* vol. 2, p. 417; Shiizuka, pp. 88, 103–104, 107–114; Miyashita and Shūdan, pp. 22–23; *Japan Times,* October 11, 1990, p. 15.

70. Shiizuka, *Kōkando,* p. 35; Seibu Hyakkaten Bunka, *SEED,* pp. 55, 144.

71. Seibu Department Stores, pp. 8–9; *Sezon no rekishi,* vol. 2, p. 418.

72. Mizuno interview, February 1, 1991.

73. *Saison Journal,* November 16, 1990, p. 1; *Hyakkaten,* p. 46.

74. *Sezon no rekishi,* vol. 2, pp. 404, 416; *Sezon Gurūpu 1989–'90,* expanded ed., p. 94; Asō, *Seibu,* pp. 22–24, 31; Shiizuka, pp. 84–86; Miyano, pp. 182–186.

75. *Mainichi Daily News,* July 10, 1990, p. 8.

76. *Saison Group,* p. 43; "Seibu Ryūtsū Gurūpu," p. 32; Miyano, pp. 190–91; Asō, *Seibu,* pp. 140–146.

77. *Saison Group,* p. 42; *Sezon Gurūpu 1989–'90,* expanded ed., p. 154; *Sankei shinbun,* July 11, 1986; *New York Times,* February 6, 1990, p. D20.

78. Egashira interview, July 19, 1986. See *Japan Report* (October 1992), p. 2.

79. Mizuno interview, February 1, 1991.

80. "Seibu Ryūtsū Gurūpu," p. 32. See *Saison Journal,* July 20, 1990, p. 2, December 7, 1990, p. 2; Sakaguchi, *Tsutsumi,* p. 167; Asō, *Seibu,* pp. 132–144.

81. Quoted in Asō, *Seibu,* p. 13.

82. *Sezon no rekishi,* vol. 2, pp. 371–372, 390.

83. "Shinka," p. 10.

84. Lee Smith, "Japan's Autocratic Managers," *Fortune,* January 7, 1985, p. 61; Shiizuka, p. 173; Niwa, pp. 32–33, 41–42. See *Sezon no rekishi,* vol. 2, pp. 426–427, 438–440.

85. Asō, *Sezon,* pp. 240–241; *Saison Journal,* March 9, 1990, p. 1; "Tsutsumi Seijishi ga otōto Yoshiakishi ni atama o sageta wake," *Shūkan gendai,* January 5–12, 1991, p. 42.

86. *Sezon no rekishi,* vol. 2, pp. 426–427.

87. Seibu Department Stores, p. 18; *Japan Times,* October 24, 1990, p. 12; *Saison Journal,* January 12, 1990, p. 1, November 16, 1990, p. 1; *Sezon no rekishi,* vol. 2, p. 427.

88. *Sezon Gurūpu 1989–'90,* p. 56. The figure for the year ending March 1989 was 31.4 percent. See Seibu Department Stores, data p. 2.

89. George Fields, "It's a New Generation," *Speaking of Japan,* no. 112, p. 11 (April 1990). See "Shinka," p. 11.

90. *Sezon Gurūpu 1989–'90,* expanded ed., p. 95. Sales in fiscal 1988 were $144 million.

91. Idem; *Saison Journal,* December 22, 1989, p. 2, March 9, 1990, p. 3; Asō, *Sezon,* pp. 246–247; *Saison Group 1992,* p. 5.

92. Mizuno interview, February 1, 1991. See Wada, *Chōsenteki,* pp. 67–68.

93. *Japan Times,* June 6, 1991, p. 15. See *Saison Journal,* September 21, 1990, p. 1.

94. *Japan Times,* January 12, 1991, p. 3, June 6, 1991, p. 15; *Saison Journal,* September 21, 1990, p. 1; *San Francisco Chronicle,* September 23, 1993, p. A18.

95. *Saison Journal,* January 12, 1990, p. 1, February 23, 1990, p. 1; *Japan Times,* August 9, 1990, p. 15.

96. *Japan Times,* August 9, 1990, p. 15; Mizuno interview, February 1, 1991.

97. *Hyakkaten,* p. 46.

98. Seibu Department Stores, p. 4.

99. *Sezon Gurūpu 1989–'90,* p. 57; *Hyakkaten,* p. 36; *Sezon no rekishi,* vol. 2, p. 426; *Saison Group 1992,* pp. 5–8.

100. Nihon Sen'i, p. V:2; *New York Times,* March 16, 1990, p. D1; *Japan Times,* March 19, 1991, p. 14. The figures for the American companies are for fiscal 1989.

101. Seibu Department Stores, data p. 2.

102. Niwa, p. 33.

103. *Sezon no rekishi,* vol. 2, p. 446.

104. *Hyakkaten,* p. 36.

105. Nihon Sen'i, p. V:2.

106. Ibid., p. V:4; *Hyakkaten,* pp. 69–70.

107. *Japan Times,* February 22, 1991, p. 10. Superstores like Wal-Mart and Kmart are excluded here.

108. *Sezon no rekishi,* vol. 2, p. 421.

109. *New York Times,* July 26, 1992, p. IV:4.

110. *Sezon Gurūpu 1989–'90,* p. 72.

111. Ichihara Iwao, "Seiyū Gurūpu zenten o musubu 'Smile netto shisutemu' ga 63nen haru ni kadō," *Gekiryū,* February 1988, p. 126. See *Saison Journal,* February 2, 1990, p. 1; *Saison Group,* p. 40; *Sezon no rekishi,* vol. 2, pp. 449–451; Hayashi, pp. 122–137; "Shōbai," p. 111.

112. *The Seiyu,* inside front cover.

113. *Saison Journal,* January 12, 1990, p. 1. See *Sezon no rekishi,* vol. 2, pp. 467, 471; Kawakami Seiji, "Mutenpo hanbai gyōkai seiha de Daiei Nakauchi Isao to Seibu Sezon Tsutsumi Seiji ga udekurabe," *Zaikai,* October 13, 1987, p. 32.

114. Egashira interview, July 19, 1986; *New York Times,* March 5, 1992, p. D4; *Saison Journal,* February 2, 1990, p. 2.

115. Asō, *Sezon,* p. 237. See pp. 82–83; *The Seiyu,* p. 24; *Sezon no rekishi,* vol. 2, pp. 456–457; *Saison Journal,* March 16, 1990, p. 3, May 25, 1990, p. 2.

116. *Sezon no rekishi*, vol. 2, pp. 460–461; *Saison Journal*, December 29, 1989, p. 1; Sakaguchi, *Tsutsumi*, pp. 28–30; *The Seiyu*, pp. 2–3, 11–12; *Saison 1992*, p. 17.

117. *The Seiyu*, p. 27. See *Yūka, Seiyū* (February 1990), p. 13.

118. *Yūka, Seiyū* (February 1990), p. 10; *The Seiyu*, p. 27.

119. *Sezon no rekishi*, vol. 2, pp. 479–480; *Hyakkaten*, p. 37.

120. *The Seiyu*, p. 26.

121. Ibid., p. 27.

122. *Sezon no rekishi*, vol. 2, pp. 500–501, 509.

123. Quoted in *Nikkei ryūtsū shinbun*, May 19, 1988. See *Saison Journal*, January 12, 1990, p. 1.

124. *Sezon no rekishi*, vol. 2, p. 508; "Paruko bunka senryaku o kirisuteta Tsutsumi Seiji no 'shihonka no kao,'" *Uwasa no shinsō*, July 1989, p. 42.

125. Quoted in *Saison Group*, p. 31.

126. *Sezon Gurūpu 1989–'90*, p. 72; *Paruko* (Tokyo: Paruko, 1990), pp. 8–9.

127. *Parco* (Tokyo: Parco, 1990), data sheet 11–12. See also sheet 3, 9–10; *Saison Journal*, December 22, 1989, p. 1.

128. *Parco*, data sheet 14; *Saison Journal*, January 12, 1990, p. 1.

129. *Paruko*, p. 38. See also data p. 16; *Sezon no rekishi*, vol. 2, pp. 508–509; *Saison Journal*, December 29, 1989, p. 1, May 11, 1990, p. 2; *New York Times*, June 21, 1993, p. B4.

130. *Saison Journal*, September 14, 1990, p. 1.

131. *Japan Company*, p. 991; *Sezon no rekishi*, vol. 2, p. 509; *Saison Group 1992*, p. 6.

132. *Japan Company*, p. 991; *Sezon no rekishi*, vol. 2, p. 215; *Kigyō keiretsu sōkan 1990* (Tokyo: Toyō Keizai Shinpōsha, 1990), p. 507.

133. Ikuno interview, August 1, 1986.

134. Kazuhiro Hiroe, "The Revolution in Japan's Consumer Credit Market," *Look Japan*, April 10, 1985, p. 10.

135. "Seibu Kurejitto," p. 40.

136. Quoted in *Sezon no rekishi*, vol. 2, p. 604.

137. Ibid., p. 611; "Seibu Kurejitto," p. 42. See Kawakami, "Seibu Sezon Gurūpu no," p. 27; "Seibu Sezon Gurūpu daishakkin," p. 52; *Sezon no rekishi*, vol. 2, p. 388; Watanabe Kazuo, p. 151.

138. *Credit Saison Co., Ltd. Annual Report 1990* (Tokyo, 1990), p. 3. See Imamatsu Eietsu interview, July 3, 1986; *Japan Times*, August 9, 1990, p. 15.

139. *Champaign-Urbana News-Gazette,* December 20, 1991, p. 13; Japan External Trade Organization, *Nippon 1990: Business Facts and Figures* (Tokyo, 1990), p. 55; Nara interview, June 22, 1988; Shiizuka, p. 175.

140. *Kuredei Sezon 1990–1991 kaisha gaikyō* (Tokyo: Kuredei Sezon, 1990), p. 22; *Credit Saison 1990,* p. 4; *Kuredei Sezon 1989 kaisha gaikyō* (Tokyo: Kuredei Sezon, 1989), p. 4; *Saison Journal,* November 24, 1989, p. 1.

141. *Credit Saison Co., Ltd. Annual Report 1991* (Tokyo, 1991), p. 5; *Japan Company,* p. 993; *Saison Group,* p. 23; *Saison Group 1992,* p. 5.

142. Harada Yōko interview, December 6, 1990.

143. Asō, *Sezon,* p. 92; *Saison Journal,* March 9, 1990, p. 1; Kishiro, p. 23.

144. *Credit Saison 1990,* pp. 15, 33. See *Kuredei Sezon 1990–1991,* p. 27; *Saison Journal,* February 23, 1990, p. 2.

145. *Credit Sasion 1990,* p. 33. See *Kuredei Sezon 1990–1991;* p. 27; Asō, *Seibu,* pp. 116, 175.

146. *Credit Saison 1990,* p. 33. See *Kuredei Sezon 1990–1991,* p. 28; *Sezon Gurūpu 1989–'90,* expanded ed., p. 74; Asō, *Seibu,* pp. 175–176.

147. *Ryūtsū shinbun,* June 5, 1986, p. 1; David Thornbrugh, "The Changing Exchange," *Japan Update,* winter 1987, p. 20; Kawakami, "Seibu Sezon Gurūpu no," pp. 30–31.

148. Tsutsumi Seiji, *Hatsugen shirīzu,* vol. 19, p. 15 (1987).

149. Quoted in Kawakami, "Seibu Sezon Gurūpu no," p. 30.

150. *Credit Saison 1990,* p. 33; *Saison Group 1992,* p. 7. See *Saison Journal,* April 6, 1990, p. 1.

151. *Sezon Gurūpu 1989–'90,* p. 51; *Japan Company,* p. 993. Calculations are affected by an irregular term in early 1990.

152. *Look Japan,* March 1992, p. 46.

153. *Sezon no rekishi,* vol. 2, p. 334.

154. Quoted ibid., p. 619. See pp. 332, 618.

155. *Sezon Gurūpu 1989–'90,* p. 54.

156. *Saison Group,* data p. 15.

157. *Saison Life Insurance Co., Ltd. Annual Report '90* (Tokyo, 1990), p. 17.

158. Hiroumi Kōichi, *Hoken gyōkai* (Tokyo: Kyōikusha, 1985), p. 209; *Sezon no rekishi,* vol. 2, pp. 334, 620; *Saison Life,* p. 17.

159. *Saison Life,* pp. 17–18.

160. *Saison Journal,* February 23, 1990, p. 2; *Saison Life,* p. 18; *Saison Group 1992,* p. 7.

161. *Look Japan,* March 1992, p. 42; *Intersect,* June 1992, p. 8.

162. *Yoke*, no. 33, p. 6 (January 1989). See *Sezon no rekishi*, vol. 2, pp. 614–616.

163. *Saison Group*, p. 32, data p. 15; *Sezon no rekishi*, vol. 2, pp. 617–618; *Saison Group 1992*, p. 5.

164. *Sezon Gurūpu 1989–'90*, p. 54.

165. Ibid., pp. 53–54; *Saison Group*, p. 32; *Daiyamondo kigyō*, p. 200.

166. *Saison Life*, pp. 1, 3.

CHAPTER NINE: JAPAN AT PLAY:
THE SEIBU RAILWAY GROUP IN THE 1980S

1. Quoted in Wakabayashi, p. 70.

2. *Nippon: A Charted*, pp. 270, 272; Un'yushō Un'yu Seisakukyoku Jōhō Kanribu, *Tetsudō yusō tōkei nenpō 1988* (Tokyo: Un'yushō, 1990), p. 1.

3. Fujii, pp. 40–41; Un'yushō Daijin Kanbō Kokuyū Tetsudō Kaikaku Suishinbu, *Tetsudō tōkei nenpō 1987* (Tokyo: Un'yushō, 1989), pp. 4–5, 6–7.

4. Un'yushō, *Tetsudō yusō*, pp. 10–11.

5. Dodwell Marketing Consultants, *Industrial Groupings in Japan*, rev. ed. (Tokyo, 1983), pp. 373, 460; *Japan Company*, p. 1186; *Japan Times*, November 29, 1990, p. 14. The figure for 1990 is annualized based on the interim report.

6. Dodwell, *Industrial*, pp. 373, 459–460; *Japan Company*, p. 1186; "Seibu Tetsudō Gurūpu 'LBO keiei,'" p. 38; Marsh interview, July 30, 1986.

7. "Seibu Tetsudō Gurūpu 'LBO keiei,'" p. 38; Asō, *Seibu*, 217–218.

8. "Seibu Tetsudō Gurūpu 'LBO keiei,'" pp. 41–42; Eikawa, *Jūnengo*, p. 207; *Japan Times*, November 29, 1990, p. 14; Doherty interview, July 30, 1986.

9. "Seibu Tetsudō Gurūpu 'LBO keiei,'" p. 38; *Yūka, Seibu* (March 1990), p. 4.

10. "Hadō," p. 38; Satō and Ōtemachi, p. 132; "Seibu teikoku," p. 64.

11. *Yūka, Seibu* (March 1990), p. 4. See Satō and Ōtemachi, pp. 137, 143–144.

12. Tsutsumi Yoshiaki, "Tochi wa koko made yasuku nara 'Tōkyō kaizō' shian," *Gendai*, January 1989, p. 254; "Hadō," p. 40; "Seibu teikoku," pp. 62–63; Narushima, p. 181.

13. "Hadō," p. 42.

14. *Nihon kaisharoku*, p. SA-526; "Hadō," pp. 41–42; Narushima, p. 187.

15. Yamaichi, p. 225; *Yūka, Seibu* (March 1990), p. 19.

16. Nihon Keizai Shinbunsha, *Kaisha sōkan mijōjō kaishaban* (Tokyo, 1990), p. 3791.

17. Dodwell, *Industrial*, pp. 373, 460; *Japan Company*, p. 1186; *Japan Times*, November 29, 1990, p. 14.

18. Daiyamondosha, *Daiyamondo kaisha yōran: hijōjō kaishaban* (Tokyo, 1990), p. 112. See Narushima, p. 202.

19. Nihon Keizai Shinbunsha, *Kaisha sōkan*, p. 3339.

20. *Yūka, Seibu* (March 1990), p. 17; Narushima, p. 174.

21. Yamaichi, p. 226; *Yūka, Seibu* (March 1990), p. 28.

22. *Japan Times*, November 29, 1990, p. 14; *Japan Company*, p. 1186; *New York Times*, September 23, 1993, p. D4.

23. *Yūka, Seibu* (March 1990), p. 18.

24. "Seibu Tetsudō Gurūpu 'LBO keiei,'" p. 43.

25. Tobit B. Morral, "Contemporary Entertainment in Japanese Society," B.A. thesis in Asian studies, Connecticut College (New London, 1986), p. 6.

26. Nishiyama Ikuo, "Seibu Sezon Gurūpu to Chichūkai Kurabu ni yoru rizōto kaihatsu," *Burēn*, July 1987, pp. 142–143.

27. *Tokyo Municipal News*, vol. 39, no. 4, p. 2 (1989).

28. *Nippon: A Charted*, p. 307; Yamaichi, p. 216.

29. *Mainichi Daily News*, July 14, 1990, p. 7; *Purinsu*, p. 307.

30. See *Japan Times*, July 3, 1990, p. 2, July 8, 1990, p. 2, August 1, 1990, p. 3.

31. Ibid., May 9, 1991, p. 2.

32. Yamaichi, p. 216.

33. Ibid., p. 218.

34. *Tokyo Business Today*, January 1991, p. 43.

35. Tsutsumi Yoshiaki, *Tsutsumi Yoshiaki wa*, p. 60.

36. Noda and Koyama, pp. 70–73; Eikawa, *Jūnengo*, p. 143. See Tsutsumi Yoshiaki and Esaka Akira, "Nihon no fūdo o ikasu ōja no kōsō," *Voice*, February 1987, p. 58.

37. Miyashita and Shūdan, *Tsutsumi Yoshiaki*, p. 97.

38. "Hadō," pp. 49–50; Noda and Koyama, p. 72.

39. Kosakai, "Tsutsumi Yoshiaki–tochi," p. 171.

40. Ibid., pp. 172–173; Miyashita and Shūdan, *Tsutsumi Yoshiaki*, pp. 100–102; Narushima, pp. 172–173.

41. Quoted in Hariki, "*Wakaki*," p. 50.

42. Ibid., p. 93. See Hara, Okamoto, and Inagaki, pp. 199–200; Narushima, p. 67; *Purinsu*, 180–181.

43. Tsutsumi Yoshiaki and Kaminogō, p. 37; "Hadō," p. 48.

44. *Purinsu,* pp. 476–482; *New York Times,* March 18, 1988, p. I:1.

45. Quoted in Hayakawa, *Tsutsumi Yoshiakishiki,* p. 142.

46. See "Kasokusuru Seibu Sezon no hoteru senryaku," *Zaikai,* January 6, 1987, p. 35; Hayakawa, *Tsutsumi Yoshiakishiki,* pp. 141–143; "Tsutsumi Yūji ga Sezon Gurūpu iri," *Shūkan posuto,* January 2–9, 1987, p. 46.

47. Tsutsumi Yoshiaki and Kawakami Seiji, "Seibu Tetsudō Gurūpu sōsui Tsutsumi Yoshiaki wa Purinsu Hoteru shachō o naze shirizoita ka," *Zaikai,* August 18, 1987, p. 36. See pp. 34–35.

48. Quoted in Kobayashi Kichiya, p. 152.

49. Eikawa, *Tsutsumi Seiji,* pp. 160–161; Hayakawa, *Tsutsumi Yoshiakishiki,* pp. 143, 176–177.

50. Tsutsumi Yoshiaki and Satō, p. 102. See Hariki, *Netsujō,* p. 177.

51. Tsutsumi Yoshiaki and Satō, p. 102; Noda and Koyama, p. 82; *Sankei kaisha nenkan,* 22nd ed. (Tokyo: Sankei Shinbun, 1990), p. Tokyo 378.

52. Tsutsumi Yoshiaki and Esaka, p. 54.

53. Takahashi, p. 174; Kosakai, "Nihon," p. 87; Atsuta, *Seibu,* p. 163.

54. Tsutsumi Yoshiaki and Kawakami, p. 38; Kosakai, "Nihon," pp. 80–81.

55. Takahashi, p. 176. See *Purinsu,* pp. 392–399; Kosakai, "Tsutsumi Yoshiaki ga," p. 182.

56. Yamane Ichigen, "Gekitotsu! Tsutsumi Seiji vs. Yoshiaki no rettō rizōto daisensō," *Gendai,* December 1988, pp. 112–113; "Hadō," p. 47.

57. *Purinsu,* pp. 404–408; Kusano, pp. 62–65.

58. Takahashi, pp. 171–178; Kosakai, "Gotō," p. 243.

59. *Purinsu,* pp. 360–369; Hayakawa, *Tsutsumi Yoshiakishiki,* pp. 173–174; "Tsuyosa," p. 28; Kosakai, "Gotō," p. 244; Ōtsuka, p. 139; Narushima, p. 58; *Japan Times,* December 6, 1990, p. 15; *New York Times,* February 18, 1993, p. B16.

60. *Purinsu,* pp. 282–285; Tateishi Yasunori, "Tochi shisan ō Tsutsumi Yoshiaki shachō no 'chiisa na zeikin,'" *Bungei shunjū,* March 1990, p. 199.

61. *Purinsu,* pp. 346–352; Narushima, pp. 60–61.

62. *Purinsu,* pp. 460–464; Yamane, p. 120.

63. Narushima, p. 70.

64. Miyashita and Shūdan, *Tsutsumi Yoshiaki,* p. 90; Honma Yoshito, "Dangers of the Resort-Building Drive," *Japan Echo,* vol. 17, no. 3, pp. 72–74 (1990); Eikawa, *Tsutsumi Seiji,* p. 141.

65. Honma, p. 72.

66. Yamane, p. 109.

67. Yamaichi, p. 245.

68. Yamane, p. 110.

69. Nakayama, pp. 74, 202–203, 206. See Inose, p. 139.

70. Quoted in Hayakawa, *Tsutsumi Yoshiakishiki*, p. 109.

71. Iwata Kaoru, "Tsutsumi Yoshiaki shachō ni watakushi wa katta," *Bungei shunjū*, June 1990, pp. 154–161; Narushima, p. 167; Hayakawa, *Tsutsumi Yoshiakishiki*, pp. 16, 103–109.

72. *Japan Times*, August 22, 1990, p. 2, September 11, 1990, p. 4.

73. Ibid., September 11, 1990, p. 4.

74. Quoted idem.

75. *New York Times*, April 16, 1990, p. A4; *Japan Times*, December 6, 1990, p. 3.

76. *Asahi shinbun*, April 13, 1990, p. 3; Hayakawa, *Tsutsumi Yoshiakishiki*, pp. 14–15, 109–114.

77. Quoted in Manabe, "Tsutsumi Yoshiaki 'boku,'" p. 112.

78. Quoted in "Hadō," p. 56. See Narushima, p. 111.

79. Quoted in "Hadō," p. 57.

80. Quoted ibid., p. 56.

81. Tsutsumi Yoshiaki and Kaminogō, p. 40.

82. Ibid., p. 74.

83. Ibid., p. 135.

84. Quoted in Matsueda, p. 107.

85. Tsutsumi Yoshiaki and Kaminogō, pp. 108–109.

86. *Asahi shinbun*, June 20, 1987. See "Tsutsumi Yoshiaki shachō ni 'yaku ni tatanai' to iwareta 'daisotsu shain,'" *Shūkan shinchō*, July 2, 1987, p. 146.

87. "Tsutsumi Yoshiaki shachō," p. 144; "Daisotsu fuyō 'Tsutsumi Yoshiaki Seibu' no shūshoku sensen," *Shūkan shinchō*, September 3, 1987, p. 134. See Tsutsumi Yoshiaki and Kaminogō, pp. 106–108.

88. Tsutsumi Yoshiaki and Kaminogō, p. 119.

89. Ibid., p. 120; Tsutsumi Yoshiaki, "Amaenaki," p. 15; Atsuta, *Seibu*, pp. 188–190; Wakabayashi, p. 70.

90. Tsutsumi Yoshiaki and Kaminogō, p. 47.

91. Ibid., pp. 48–49.

92. Quoted in Manabe, "Young," p. 29.

93. Tsutsumi Yoshiaki and Kaminogō, p. 80.

94. Ibid., p. 129.

95. Ibid., p. 77.

96. Ibid., pp. 55, 111, 114; *Yūka, Seibu* (March 1990), pp. 4–8; Hayakawa, *Tsutsumi Yoshiakishiki*, pp. 179–180.

97. Tsutsumi Yoshiaki and Kaminogō, pp. 64–100. See Hayakawa, *Tsutsumi Yoshiakishiki*, p. 180.

98. Tsutsumi Yoshiaki, *Tsutsumi Yoshiaki wa*, pp. 102–103.

99. Quoted in Tateishi, p. 100.

100. Quoted in Hayakawa, *Tsutsumi Yoshiakishiki*, p. 77.

101. "Tsuyosa," p. 31.

102. Ibid., pp. 34–36; Inose, p. 123.

103. "Seibu Tetsudō Gurūpu 'LBO keiei,'" p. 41. See "Tsuyosa," p. 29; Noda and Koyama, pp. 81–82; Tateishi, pp. 105–106; "Zeikin o harawanai Seibu 'Tsutsumi' ga sekaiichi no kanemochi," *Shūkan shinchō*, July 23, 1987, p. 130; Eikawa, *Jūnengo*, pp. 208–209.

104. "Seibu Tetsudō Gurūpu 'LBO keiei,'" p. 40. See Inose, p. 122.

105. "Seibu Tetsudō Gurūpu 'LBO keiei,'" p. 40; Noda and Koyama, p. 81; Atsuta, *Seibu*, p. 59.

106. Dodwell, *Industrial*, p. 468; "Tsutsumi Yoshiaki no," p. 30; "Seibu Tetsudō Gurūpu 'LBO keiei,'" p. 41.

107. "Seibu Tetsudō Gurūpu 'LBO keiei,'" p. 42.

108. Noda and Koyama, p. 81.

109. "Hadō," p. 38.

110. Eikawa, *Jūnengo*, p. 164.

111. "Seibu Tetsudō Gurūpu 'LBO keiei,'" p. 42.

112. Idem.

113. Kusano, pp. 58–61.

114. See "Seibu Tetsudō Gurūpu 'LBO keiei,'" pp. 39, 45.

115. Ibid., pp. 29–30. For slightly different calculations, see Tsumuji, p. 175.

116. Hariki, *Netsujō*, p. 132.

117. Miyashita and Shūdan, *Tsutsumi Yoshiaki*, p. 136; "Tsutsumi Yoshiakishi no," p. 28.

118. "Seibu Tetsudō Gurūpu 'LBO keiei,'" p. 44.

119. *Daiyamondo kigyō*, p. 16. The NTT figure is for fiscal year 1989.

120. "Seibu Tetsudō Gurūpu 'LBO keiei,'" p. 39.

121. Inose, p. 123.

122. Tateishi, p. 191.

123. "Tsutsumi Yoshiakishi no," p. 30.

124. *Japan Times,* July 11, 1990, p. 5, August 23, 1990, p. 4; *San Francisco Chronicle,* June 21, 1993, p. C2.

125. *Yūka, Seibu* (March 1990), p. 2. See "Tsutsumi Yoshiakishi no," p. 28; "Zeikin," p. 129; Hayakawa, *Tsutsumi Yoshiakishiki,* pp. 182–183; "Seibu teikoku," p. 60; "Seibu Tetsudō Gurūpu 'LBO keiei,'" p. 39.

126. *Kōgaku,* East Japan vol., p. 669. Tsutsumi's tax is for 1989. See Miyashita and Shūdan, *Tsutsumi Yoshiaki,* p. 134; *Japan Times,* May 2, 1991, p. 2.

CHAPTER TEN: LEISURE AS AMENITIES: THE SEIBU SAISON GROUP IN THE 1980S

1. Keizai, *Japan 1993,* p. 67; *Japan Report* (February 1992), p. 2; Robert Kuttner, review of Juliet B. Schor, *The Overworked American,* in *New York Times Book Review,* February 2, 1992, p. 1.

2. See Schor, *The Overworked American: The Unexpected Decline of Leisure* (New York: Basic Books, 1992).

3. *Japan Report,* February 1992, p. 2. On the transformation of foreign goods and services to suit Japanese culture, see Joseph J. Tobin, ed., *Re-Made in Japan: Everyday Life and Consumer Taste in a Changing Society* (New Haven: Yale University Press, 1992).

4. *Mainichi Daily News,* July 14, 1990, p. 7. The base figure is for fiscal year 1989.

5. *Japan Update,* May 1992, p. 25.

6. Egashira interview, December 8, 1990.

7. *Sezon no rekishi,* vol. 2, p. 389.

8. Tsutsumi Seiji, "Motomerareru shinri kankakuteki manzoku," *Asahi shinbun,* U.S. ed., October 21, 1991, p. 8.

9. Mizuno interview, February 1, 1991.

10. Idem.

11. Idem.

12. *Sezon Gurūpu 1989–'90,* p. 64.

13. Tsutsumi Seiji, ed., *Rejā no kagaku* (Tokyo: Jitsugyō no Nihonsha, 1962).

14. Quoted in Tawara, p. 213.

15. *The Seiyo Corporation: Environmental Planning and Development* (Tokyo, 1989), pp. 4, 6; Tawara, pp. 219–221.

16. Quoted in *Forbes,* July 24, 1989, p. 186.

17. *Sezon no rekishi*, vol. 2, p. 555; Asō, *Seibu*, p. 117; Noda and Koyama, p. 76.

18. *Sezon no rekishi*, vol. 2, p. 585; Asō, *Sezon*, p. 140. See Kawakami Seiji, "Seibu Sezon Gurūpu Tsutsumi Seiji ga yuitsu shachō o shite iru 'Sezon Kōporēshon' to iu kaisha," *Zaikai*, January 19, 1988, p. 18.

19. Quoted in Kosakai, "Nihon," p. 83. See Eikawa, *Jūnengo*, pp. 138, 141–142; Asō, *Seibu*, p. 85; Tawara, p. 218; Kaminogō, *Tsutsumi Seiji ga*, pp. 18–19.

20. Tawara, p. 218. See Noda and Koyama, p. 76.

21. Asō, *Seibu*, p. 221. See *Sezon no rekishi*, vol. 2, p. 564.

22. Asō, *Seibu*, p. 221; Kosakai, "Nihon," p. 83. See *Sezon no rekishi*, vol. 2, pp. 565–566; Esaka, "Tsutsumi Seiji: Risuku," pp. 93–94.

23. *Seiyo Corporation*, p. 12; *Sezon no rekishi*, vol. 2, pp. 574–575.

24. Quoted in Asō, *Sezon*, p. 135.

25. Matsueda, p. 184.

26. Kosakai, "Nihon," p. 88. See *Seiyo Corporation*, p. 13; Nishiyama, pp. 142, 146; *Sezon no rekishi*, vol. 2, pp. 561–562.

27. Asō, *Sezon*, p. 137.

28. Seibu Department Stores, p. 7.

29. Asō, *Seibu*, p. 122; Gotō interview, December 6, 1990. See Miyashita and Shūdan, *Tsutsumi Yoshiaki*, p. 105; *Saison Journal*, February 9, 1990, p. 1.

30. *Seiyo Corporation*, p. 3; *Saison Journal*, December 22, 1989, p. 1; *Japan Times*, January 24, 1991, p. 3.

31. *Sezon Gurūpu 1989–'90* p. 64. See *Saison Journal*, March 30, 1990, p. 1; *Seiyo Corporation*, p. 3.

32. *Sezon no rekishi*, vol. 2, p. 577. See also pp. 256–257, 560. See Satō and Ōtemachi, p. 135.

33. *Seiyo Corporation*, p. 16; Satō and Ōtemachi, p. 139; "Seibu Hyakkaten ga namae o kaeru hi," *Shūkan sankei*, June 19, 1986, p. 30; Kosakai, "Gotō," p. 261; Eikawa, *Jūnengo*, pp. 20, 139–141.

34. Miyashita and Shūdan, *Tsutsumi Yoshiaki*, p. 98; *Sezon no rekishi*, vol. 2, p. 558; "Kyōto hoteru sensō de honkakukasuru Purinsu vs. Sezon no kokutō kassen," *Keizaikai*, September 2, 1986, p. 26; Eikawa, *Jūnengo*, pp. 144–146; Miyashita Hiroyuki, "Sōgō rejā sangyō e koshitantan Seibu Sezon Gurūpu 'kai' shingeki no uragawa!," *Zaikai tenbō* (May 1987), p. 147.

35. "'Rosuchairudo' mo tomatta 'Hoteru Seiyō Ginza' no gōka kyakusuji," *Shūkan shinchō*, April 2, 1987, p. 38. See "Seibu Hyakkaten ga," p. 30; "Kyōto," p. 26.

36. Mizushima Aiichirō, "'Hoteru Seiyō Ginza' de roteishita Seibu Sezon Gurūpu Tsutsumi Seiji no ōki na gosan," *Keizaikai*, January 6, 1987, p. 46. See *Japan Times*, December 14, 1990, p. 14; Esaka, "Tsutsumi Seiji: Risuku," p. 93; "Hoteru Seiyō Ginza," *Seikai jānaru* (September 1987), pp. 4, 104.

37. "Kasokusuru," p. 34.

38. Mizushima, p. 45.

39. Miyashita, "Sōgō," p. 145.

40. Quoted in Eikawa, *Jūnengo*, p. 148. See "Rosuchairudo," p. 40; Kosakai Shōzō, "Josei no tame no raibaru sanpo Tōkyū vs. Seibu," *Fujin kōron*, July 1987, p. 377.

41. *Saison Journal*, May 11, 1990, p. 1. See also April 13, 1990, p. 1. See Miyashita, "Sōgō," p. 147; *Sezon no rekishi*, vol. 2, p. 578; "Kasokusuru," pp. 34–35; "Seibu Hyakkaten ga," p. 30; Miyashita and Shūdan, *Tsutsumi Yoshiaki*, p. 117.

42. "Seibu Sezon Gurūpu daishakkin," p. 52. See *Seiyo Corporation*, pp. 3, 8; *Sezon no rekishi*, vol. 2, pp. 567, 570–571; *Saison Group*, p. 6; Noda and Koyama, p. 73; Tamura, p. 228.

43. *Seiyo Corporation*, p. 10. See *Sezon no rekishi*, vol. 2, p. 568; *Saison Journal*, December 29, 1989, p. 1, February 16, 1990, p. 1.

44. *Saison Group*, data p. 19.

45. *Saison Journal*, October 5, 1990, p. 1; *Sezon no rekishi*, vol. 2, pp. 572–573.

46. *Sezon on rekishi*, vol. 2, pp. 243, 585; *Saison Group*, data p. 19; *Saison Journal*, May 25, 1990, p. 2; *Saison Group 1992*, pp. 5–7.

47. *Saison Journal*, June 15, 1990, p. 1, October 19, 1990, p. 1; *Sezon no rekishi*, vol. 2, p. 583; Peter J. Morgan interview, July 30, 1986.

48. *Sezon no rekishi*, vol. 2, p. 533.

49. Japan External, *Nippon 1990*, p. 141.

50. *Asahi Evening News*, March 31, 1992, p. 5.

51. *Seiyō Fūdo Shisutemuzu kaisha annai* (Tokyo, 1989), p. 11. See *Sezon no rekishi*, vol. 2, pp. 512–513, 519–524; *Seiyo Food Systems Inc. Annual Report 1990* (Tokyo, 1990), p. 3.

52. *Sezon Gurūpu 1989–'90*, pp. 67, 69.

53. Yamaichi, p. 215.

54. *Japan Company*, p. 957; *Seiyo Food*, p. 17; *Ryūtsū kaisha nenkan 90nenban* (Tokyo: Nihon Keizai Shinbunsha, 1989), p. 1266.

55. *Japan Times*, November 28, 1990, p. 12.

56. *Saison Group,* p. 27. See data p. 9; *New York Times,* March 6, 1992, p. D3; Asō, *Sezon,* p. 128.

57. *New York Times,* March 6, 1992, p. D3, May 2, 1992, p. I:37; *Saison Group 1992,* p. 6.

58. Gotō interview, December 6, 1990; *Saison Journal,* December 29, 1989, p. 1.

59. *Saison Journal,* January 19, 1990, p. 2; *Saison Group,* p. 27; Asō, *Sezon,* pp. 127–128.

60. *Sezon no rekishi,* vol. 2, p. 400.

61. Quoted in *Time,* November 21, 1988, p. 52.

62. *Saison Journal,* September 7, 1990, p. 1.

63. Egashira interview, December 8, 1990.

64. Idem.

65. *Saison Journal,* September 7, 1990, p. 1. See May 25, 1990, p. 1, November 9, 1990, p. 1; *Japan Times,* October 26, 1990, p. 14, January 17, 1991, p. 13; *Saison 1992,* p. 35.

66. Hotta, p. 21; *Sezon no rekishi,* vol. 2, p. 469; *Saison Group 1992,* p. 6.

67. *Saison Journal,* February 2, 1990, p. 3.

68. *Japan Times,* February 18, 1991, p. 8.

69. *Saison Journal,* May 18, 1990, p. 1.

70. Nikkei Ryūtsū, p. 138; Hotta, pp. 23–24, 66.

71. Nikkei Ryūtsū, p. 138. See Wada, *Chōsenteki,* p. 73. A thoughtful brief treatment of individualism is Kuniko Miyanaga, *The Creative Edge: Emerging Individualism in Japan* (New Brunswick, N.J.: Transaction Publications, 1991).

72. Tsutsumi Seiji, *Hatsugen shirīzu,* vol. 14, p. 14 (1982); Nikkei Ryūtsū, p. 138.

73. *Shūkan bunshun,* May 26, 1988, pp. 33–35; Eikawa, *Tsutsumi Seiji,* p. 183; Asō, *Seibu,* pp. 130–131.

74. Asō, *Sezon,* p. 177; *Saison Journal,* January 26, 1990, p. 2, September 28, 1990, p. 3; *The Seiyū,* p. 19. *Tea Master* won prizes at Venice and Chicago, *Shikibu* at Montreal.

75. Asō, *Sezon,* p. 177.

76. *Sezon no rekishi,* vol. 2, p. 470; "Shinka," p. 20. See *Saison Journal,* January 26, 1990, p. 2, February 23, 1990, p.3.

77. Katayama, p. 227; *Sezon no rekishi,* vol. 2, p. 397; *Saison Group,* p. 45.

78. *Saison Group,* p. 45.

79. Katayama, p. 227. See Atsuta, *Seibu*, p. 218.

80. Kaneko Kikuo interview, October 13, 1980.

81. Tsutsumi Seiji, *Hatsugen shirīzu*, vol. 20, p. 86 (1988).

82. Quoted in *Sezon no rekishi*, vol. 2, pp. 397–398. For another statement in the same vein, see Tsujii and Sakaki, p. 52.

83. Katayama, p. 216; Miura, pp. 416–419.

84. Tsutsumi Seiji, *Hatsugen shirīzu*, vol. 20, p. 86 (1988).

85. Quoted in *Japan Times*, August 30, 1990, p. 13.

86. See Miura, p. 417.

87. Quoted in Asō, *Seibu*, p. 127.

88. Katayama, p. 168. The Sezon Museum of Art's inaugural exhibition was a world-class show of fin-de-siècle Viennese art, October 7 to December 5, 1989. See *Sezon Gurūpu 1989–'90*, p. 1.

89. See Miura, pp. 413–416; Hotta, p. 20; *Shūkan bunshun*, May 19, 1988, p. 28.

90. *Saison Journal*, December 14, 1990, p. 1; Kinko Watanabe, "The Spirit of Ambivalence," *Look Japan*, July 1989, pp. 42–43.

91. Seibu Department Stores, pp. 22–23; Asō, *Sezon*, p.172; *Saison Group*, p. 12; *The Seiyu*, p. 20.

92. *Parco*, data sheet 20; Katayama, pp. 217–218; Asō, *Seibu*, pp. 128–129; *Asahi shinbun*, evening ed., August 22, 1986, p. 4; Yasuda, p. 138; Tsutsumi Seiji, *Hatsugen shirīzu*, vol. 20, pp. 4, 32 (1988); Tsujii and Sakaki, pp. 46–48; *The Seiyu*, p. 19; *Saison Journal*, January 19, 1990, p. 2; *Tokyo Journal*, March 1992, p. 59.

93. Rodney O'Brien, "Yenless: Artists Struggle as Society Thrives," *Intersect*, July 1989, pp. 31–32; Tsutsumi Seiji and Kometani, p. 25; *Sezon no rekishi*, vol. 2, p. 398; Seibu Department Stores, p. 23.

94. Tsutsumi Seiji interview, November 11, 1991.

95. *Japan Times*, September 13, 1990, p. 3. See also August 30, 1990, p. 13.

96. Egashira interview, December 8, 1990.

CHAPTER ELEVEN: ARCHITECTS OF AFFLUENCE

1. Wal-Mart's 1990 sales were $32.6 billion, Kmart's $32.1 billion, and Sears' retailing sales just under $32 billion. The Saison figure of $32.7 billion for the year ending March 1990 includes nonretailing sales. *Japan Times*, February 22, 1991, p. 10.

2. *Sezon no rekishi*, vol. 2, pp. 395–396; Niwa, pp. 46–48; Kawakami, "Seibu Sezon Gurūpu Tsutsumi," pp. 14–17; Egashira interview, December 8,

1990; Dodwell Marketing Consultants, *Retail Distribution in Japan,* 3d ed. (Tokyo, 1988), p. 112.

3. *Sezon no rekishi,* vol. 2, p. 394. See Niwa, p. 46.

4. Quoted in *Sezon no rekishi,* vol. 2, p. 387.

5. Ibid., vol. 2, pp. 372, 629; *Saison Group,* p. 17; Esaka, "Tsutsumi Seiji: Risuku," p. 99; Hashimoto Jurō, "Musenryaku no hyōryū kara," in Ueno et al., *Sezon no hassō: māketto e no sokyū* (Tokyo: Riburopōto, 1991), pp. 277–278; "Shinka," p. 16; Kawakami, "Seibu Sezon Gurūpu Tsutsumi," pp. 17–19; Mizuno interview, February 1, 1991; *Saison 1992,* p. 14.

6. *The Seiyu,* p. 4; *Sezon no rekishi,* vol. 2, pp. 398, 473.

7. *The Seiyu,* p. 4; *Saison Journal,* November 30, 1990, p. 1

8. *Saison Journal,* April 6, 1990.

9. *New York Times,* April 12, 1990, p. A22.

10. *Saison Group,* p. 3.

11. Tsutsumi Seiji interview, November 11, 1991.

12. Nakauchi, "Pursuit," p. 5. See Tobin passim; *Look Japan,* January 1993, p. 16.

13. *Look Japan,* March 1993, p. 23. See *New York Times,* February 8, 1993, p. D1.

14. *New York Times,* February 22, 1993, p. A1, April 14, 1993, p. D2, November 16, 1993, p. C11.

15. Ibid., March 3, 1993, p. A1; *Chicago Tribune,* February 28, 1993, business section, p. 5.

16. Quoted in *New York Times,* February 8, 1993, p. D1.

17. *Look Japan,* March 1993, p. 15. See *Saison 1992,* pp. 21, 37–38.

18. *Asahi Evening News,* June 4, 1992, p. 4.

19. Quoted in Hayakawa, *Tsutsumi Yoshiakishiki,* p. 154. See *Saison Journal,* August 17, 1990, p. 4.

20. Tsutsumi Yoshiaki and Kaminogō, p. 102.

21. Egashira interview, December 8, 1990. Egashira adds about Tsutsumi Seiji: "His is a very unassuming lifestyle."

22. Shuichi Yamamoto [pseud.], "Economics: Young Turks," *PHP Intersect,* March 1986, p. 12.

23. Eikawa, *Jūnengo,* p. 33; Matsueda, p. 133. See "Shinka," p. 11; Esaka, "Tsutsumi Seiji: Risuku," p. 99; Niwa, p. 35.

24. See Johannes Hirschmeier and Tsunehiko Yui, *The Development of Jap-*

anese Business, 1600–1973 (Cambridge: Harvard University Press, 1975), pp. 253–254, 257.

25. Quoted in Eikawa, *Tsutsumi Seiji,* p. 217.

26. "Seibu Tetsudō Gurūpu 'LBO keiei,'" p. 42.

27. Niwa, p. 33; *The Seiyu,* p. 27. See *Sezon Gurūpu 1989–'90,* p. 29. *New York Times,* December 23, 1990, p. III:1, gives the figure as $9.4 billion.

28. Egashira interview, December 8, 1990.

29. Idem.

Sources Cited

INTERVIEWS

Doherty, James A. Manager, Research Department, Jardine Fleming, Ltd., Tokyo Branch. Tokyo, July 30, 1986.

Egashira Keisuke. President, Seibu International, Ltd. Tokyo, July 19, 1986.

———. President, J. Osawa & Co., Ltd. Tokyo, December 8, 1990.

Gotō Ryūichi. Manager, Public Relations Office, Saison Group. Tokyo, December 6, 1990.

Harada Yōko. Public Relations Officer, Saison Group. Tokyo, November 16, 1990; December 6, 1990.

Ikuno Shigeo. President and CEO, Seibu Allstate Life Insurance Company, Ltd. Tokyo, August 1, 1986.

Imamatsu Eietsu. Staff Writer, Mainichi Shinbunsha. Tokyo, July 3, 1986.

Kaneko Kikuo. Head, Planning Department, Seibu Museum of Art. Tokyo, October 13, 1980.

Kizu Haruhiko. Secretary, Seibu Saison Group. Tokyo, August 1, 1986.

Marsh, Graeme. Analyst, Jardine Fleming, Ltd., Tokyo Branch. Tokyo, July 30, 1986.

Mizuno Seiichi. President and CEO, Seibu Department Stores, Ltd. Tokyo, February 1, 1991.

Morgan, Peter J. Economist, Research Department, Jardine Fleming, Ltd., Tokyo Branch. Tokyo, July 30, 1986.

Murai Hajime. Director, Public Relations, Kokudo Keikaku. Tokyo, May 8, 1991.

Nagai Michio. Adviser, United Nations University. Tokyo, July 23, 1986.

———. Director, International House of Japan, Inc. Tokyo, December 4, 1990 (by telephone).

Nara Chizuko. Vice President, Japanese Equity Research, Salomon Brothers Asia, Ltd. Tokyo, June 22, 1988.

Noda Kazuo. Chair, Japan Research Institute; Professor of Business Administration, Rikkyo University. Tokyo, July 11, 1986.

Sakai Toshiyuki. Ice Hockey Division, Kokudo Keikaku. Tokyo, May 8, 1991.

Sugiyama Katsuhiko. Senior Analyst, Credit Suisse, Tokyo Branch. Tokyo, August 6, 1986.

Tada Chiyoko. Associate, Landor Associates International, Ltd. Tokyo, July 17, 1986.

Takabatake Michitoshi. Professor of Political Science, Rikkyo University. Tokyo, July 1, 1986.

Tsutsumi Seiji. Chair, Saison Corporation. Tokyo, November 11, 1991.

Yamada Naohiro. Economic News Editor, Mainichi Shinbunsha. Tokyo, July 3, 1986.

Yui Tsunehiko. Director, Japan Business History Institute. Tokyo, July 1, 1986.

PRINTED SOURCES

Andō Masasuke. "Igyōshū to no teikei de gyōtai henshin," *Zaikai*, December 20, 1987, pp. 32–35.

"'Aratanaru gurūpu senryaku' no kagi Tsutsumi Seiji no saiken tetsugaku," *Decide*, May 1987, pp. 30–34.

Asahi Industries Co., Ltd. Tokyo: Asahi Industries, 1985.

Asahi Kōgyō kaisha annai. Tokyo: Asahi Kōgyō, 1990.

Asahi Kōyō Kabushiki Kaisha. *Keirekisho.* Tokyo: Asahi Kōyō, 1989.

Asano Kyōhei. "Jitsubai mo agari, akarusa mo miehajimeta 'oka no kotō' Seibu Tsukashin," *Gekiryū*, April 1988, pp. 124–129.

Asō Kunio. *Seibu Sezon Gurūpu.* Tokyo: Nihon Jitsugyō Shuppansha, 1985.

———. *Sezon Gurūpu no subete.* Tokyo: Nihon Jitsugyō Shuppansha, 1991.

"At Your Service," *Look Japan*, December 10, 1985, p. 28.

Atsuta Masanori. *Seibu Gurūpu Tsutsumike no hassō.* Tokyo: Tokuma Shoten, 1979.

———. *Tsutsumi Yoshiaki no 10nengo hassō.* Tokyo: Yumanite, 1983.

Best of Japan. Tokyo: Kodansha International, 1987.

"Commercial Activities in Tokyo," *Tokyo Municipal News*, vol. 22, no. 4, pp. 1–4, 8 (June 1972).

Credit Saison Co., Ltd. Annual Report 1990. Tokyo: Credit Saison, 1990.

Credit Saison Co., Ltd. Annual Report 1991. Tokyo: Credit Saison, 1991.

Creighton, Millie R. "Department Store *Hina* Dolls and Japan's Equal Employment Opportunity Law," Seminar Paper, New England Japan Seminar, University of Massachusetts, Boston, February 7, 1989.

"Curbing Land Prices in Tokyo: Causes and Effects of the New Land Tax," *Tokyo Business Today*, January 1991, pp. 10–16.

"Daisotsu fuyō 'Tsutsumi Yoshiaki Seibu' no shūshoku sensen," *Shūkan shinchō*, September 3, 1987, pp. 134–137.

Daiyamondo kigyō rankingu '90. Tokyo: Daiyamondosha, 1990.

Daiyamondosha. *Daiyamondo kaisha yōran: Hijōjō kaishaban*. Tokyo: Daiyamondosha, 1990.

"Distribution Moves Toward the Information Age," *KKC Brief*, no. 34, pp. 1–7 (April 1986).

Dodwell Marketing Consultants. *Industrial Groupings in Japan*. Revised ed. Tokyo: Dodwell Marketing Consultants, 1983.

———. *Retail Distribution in Japan*. 3rd ed. Tokyo: Dodwell Marketing Consultants, 1988.

Ebisawa Yasuhisa. *Seibu Raionzu: Puro yakyū gurafuitei*. Tokyo: Shinchōsha, 1983.

Eikawa Kōki. *Jūnengo no Tsutsumi Seiji to Tsutsumi Yoshiaki*. Tokyo: Daiichi Kikaku Shuppan, 1987.

———. *Tsutsumi Seiji: Keiei wa eikyū kakumei da*. Tokyo: Daiichi Kikaku Shuppan, 1988.

———. *Tsutsumi Yoshiaki to iu otoko no yomikata*. Tokyo: Besuto Serāzu, 1984.

———. *Tsutsumike no gokui*. Tokyo: Besuto Serāzu, 1984.

———. *Yabō to kyōki*. Tokyo: Keizaikai, 1988.

Esaka Akira. "Tsutsumi Seiji keiei to wa 'eikyū kakumei' de aru," *Purejidento*, vol. 24, no. 7, pp. 54–63 (July 1986).

———. "Tsutsumi Seiji: Risuku o osorenu 'keiei wa eikyū kakumei' shugi," *Purejidento*, vol. 26, no. 1, pp. 90–101 (January 1988).

FamilyMart Co., Ltd. Annual Report 1990. Tokyo: FamilyMart, 1990.

Fields, George. "It's a New Generation," *Speaking of Japan*, no. 112, pp. 9–12 (April 1990).

FuamirīMāto anyuaru ripōto '90. Tokyo: FuamirīMāto, 1990.

Fujii Yatarō, ed. *Shitetsu gyōkai*. Tokyo: Kyōikusha, 1985.

Fujioka Wakao. *Sayōnara, taishū*. Kyoto: PHP Kenkyūjo, 1984.

Fujiya Yōetsu. "Mejiro Bunkamura," in Yamaguchi Hiroshi, ed., *Kōgai jūtakuchi no keifu*. Tokyo: Kajima Shuppankai, 1987. Pp. 153–174.

Gendai Kigyō Kenkyūkai. *Seibu*. Tokyo: Gendai Kigyō Kenkyūkai, 1964.

Goto, Fusako, and Hideo Inohara. *From Salary to Quality of Working Life— CASE: Seibu Department Stores*. Sophia University, Institute of Comparative Culture, Business Series no. 88. Tokyo, 1982.

"Hadō kara ōdō e," *Heisei gijuku*, September 1990, pp. 36–57.

"Hanayakasa no uragawa de aikawarazu no futōmeiburi o hakkisuru Seibu Hyakkaten," *Gekiryū*, pp. 62–65 (April 1979).

Hara Tsutomu, Okamoto Nobuyuki, and Inagaki Tsutomu. *Hoteru sangyōkai*. Tokyo: Kyōikusha, 1988.

Hariki Yasuo. *Netsujō no kenjitsu keiei: Tsutsumi Yoshiaki*. Tokyo: Kōdansha, 1987.

———. *"Wakaki teiō" Tsutsumi Yoshiaki ga yuku*. Tokyo: Kou Shobō, 1984.

Hashimoto Jurō. "Musenryaku no hyōryū kara," in Ueno Chizuko, Nakamura Tatsuya, Tamura Akira, Hashimoto Jurō, and Miura Masashi, *Sezon no hassō: māketto e no sokyū*. Tokyo: Riburopōto, 1991. Pp. 277–338.

Hashimoto Ryūgō. "Kokunai no saidai Seiyū shokuchūdoku jiken yonenme no shinjijitsu," *Seikai jānaru*, February 1987, pp. 74–80.

Hayabusa, Nagaharu. "The Tsutsumi Brothers, Feuding Magnates," *Japan Quarterly*, vol. 35, no. 2, pp. 192–195 (1988).

Hayakawa Kazuhiro. *Tsutsumi Yoshiaki: Aku no teiōgaku*. Tokyo: Ēru Shuppansha, 1981.

———. *Tsutsumi Yoshiakishiki keiei no shippai*. Tokyo: Ēru Shuppansha, 1990.

Hayashi Fumiko. *Ukigumo*. Tokyo: Shinchōsha, 1951. Translated as *Floating Clouds* by Yoshiyuki Koitabayashi and Martin C. Collcutt. Tokyo: Hara Shobō, 1965.

Hayashi Kaoru. *Ryūtsū biggu san no gyōmu kaikaku*. Tokyo: Paru Shuppan, 1986.

"Henka no jidai ni shinayaka ni taiō seyo," *Hōseki*, March 1985, pp. 333–340.

Hiroe, Kazuhiro. "The Revolution in Japan's Consumer Credit Market," *Look Japan*, April 10, 1985, pp. 10–11.

Hirose Yoshinori. "Tsutsumi Seiji Yoshiaki kyōdai—Seibu ōkoku 'bunkatsu tōchi' no uchigawa," *Hōseki*, December 1978, pp. 72–87.

Hiroumi Kōichi. *Hoken gyōkai*. Tokyo: Kyōikusha, 1985.

Hirschmeier, Johannes, and Tsunehiko Yui. *The Development of Japanese Business, 1600–1973*. Cambridge: Harvard University Press, 1975.

Hongō Kan'ichirō. *Mokka funtōchū*. Tokyo: Tokuma Shoten, 1963.

Honma Yoshito. "Dangers of the Resort-Building Drive," *Japan Echo*, vol. 17, no. 3, pp. 72–76 (1990).

"Hoteru Seiyō Ginza," *Seikai jānaru*, September 1987, pp. 4–5, 104–105.

Hotta Masayuki. *Seibu Ryūtsū Gurūpu*. Tokyo: Asahi Sonorama, 1981.

Hyakkaten chōsa nenkan 1990. Tokyo: Depāto Nyūsusha, 1990.

Ichihara Iwao. "Seiyū Gurūpu zenten o musubu 'Smile netto shisutemu' ga 63nen haru ni kadō," *Gekiryū*, February 1988, pp. 126–129.

Imaoka Kazuhiko. *Konnichi o kowase*. Tokyo: Parusu Shuppan, 1977.

———. *Tsutsumi Seiji no kigyōka seishin*. Kyoto: PHP Kenkyūjo, 1985.

Inose Naoki. *Mikado no shōzō*. Tokyo: Shōgakkan, 1986.

Ishikawa Tatsuzō. *Kizudarake no sanga*. Tokyo: Shinchō Bunko, 1964.

Iwata Kaoru. "Tsutsumi Yoshiaki shachō ni watakushi wa katta," *Bungei shunjū*, June 1990, pp. 154–162.

Japan Company Handbook, first section, spring 1991. Tokyo: Tōyō Keizai Shinpōsha, 1991.

Japan External Trade Organization. *Nippon 1990: Business Facts and Figures*. Tokyo: Japan External Trade Organization, 1990.

———. *Retailing in the Japanese Consumer Market*. Revised ed. Tokyo, 1979.

Japan Report. Consul General, New York.

"Japan's Service Industry and Service Trade: An Overview," *Japan Economic Institute Report*, November 8, 1985. Washington, D.C.

Kajiyama Toshiyuki. *Akunin shigan*, vol. 11 of *Kajiyama Toshiyuki jisen sakuhinshū*. Tokyo: Shūeisha, 1972.

Kamibayashi Kunio. "Waga Tsutsumi ichizoku chi no himitsu," *Bungei shunjū*, August 1987, pp. 156–176.

Kaminogō Toshiaki. *Ginza ryūtsū sensō*. Tokyo: Kōdansha, 1985.

——. *Seibu ōkoku.* Tokyo: Kōdansha, 1982.

——. *Tsutsumi Seiji ga Yoshiaki ni atama ga agaranai riyū.* Tokyo: Kōbunsha, 1985.

——. *Tsutsumi Seiji no ibento senryaku.* Tokyo: Taiyō Kikaku Shuppan, 1986.

——. *Tsutsumi Yoshiaki hisokanaru ketsudan.* Tokyo: Ushio Shuppansha, 1984.

——, ed. *Tsutsumi Yoshiaki wa kataru.* Tokyo: Kōdansha, 1984.

Kamiya Yūji. *Tsutsumi Yoshiaki to Kokudo Keikaku.* Tokyo: Paru Shuppan, 1987.

Karuizawa-machi. *Ko Tsutsumi Yasujirō sensei o shinobu.* Karuizawa-machi, 1964.

"Kasokusuru Seibu Sezon no hoteru senryaku," *Zaikai,* January 6, 1987, pp. 34–35.

Katayama Mataichirō. *Tsutsumi Seiji chōjōshiki no keiei.* Tokyo: Keirin Shobō, 1987.

Kawakami Seiji. "Mutenpo hanbai gyōkai seiha de Daiei Nakauchi Isao to Seibu Sezon Tsutsumi Seiji ga udekurabe," *Zaikai,* October 13, 1987, pp. 28–33.

——. "Seibu Sezon Gurūpu no kin'yū senryaku no zenbō," *Zaikai,* July 1, 1986, pp. 24–33.

——. "Seibu Sezon Gurūpu Tsutsumi Seiji ga yuitsu shachō o shite iru 'Sezon Kōporēshon' to iu kaisha," *Zaikai,* January 19, 1988, pp. 14–19.

Keizai Koho Center. *Japan 1991: An International Comparison.* Tokyo: Keizai Koho Center, 1990.

——. *Japan 1992: An International Comparison.* Tokyo: Keizai Koho Center, 1991.

——. *Japan 1993: An International Comparison.* Tokyo: Keizei Koho Center, 1992.

Kigyō keiretsu sōkan 1990. Tokyo: Tōyō Keizai Shinpōsha, 1990.

Kikuchi Hisashi. *Shura no gun'yū.* Tokyo: Besuto Bukku, 1985.

Kishima Akihiko. "Tsutsumi Seiji to 'Yūrakuchō Seibu,'" *Purejidento,* January 1985, pp. 216–225.

Kishiro Yasuyuki. "Tsutsumi Seiji Yoshiaki no ikon keiei," *Shūkan asahi,* June 13, 1986, pp. 20–23.

Kobayashi Kazunari. *Tsutsumi Yoshiaki.* Tokyo: Paru Shuppan, 1985.

Kobayashi Kichiya. *Tsutsumi Yoshiaki no keieijutsu zenmanyuaru.* Tokyo: Paru Shuppan, 1988.

Koga Hiroyuki. *Tsutsumi Seiji no bunka o shōbai ni suru atama.* Tokyo: Besuto Serāzu, 1985.

Kōgaku nōzeisha meibo 1990. Tokyo: Teikoku Dēta Banku, 1990.

Koren, Leonard. *Success Stories: How Eleven of Japan's Most Interesting Businesses Came to Be.* San Francisco: Chronicle Books, 1990.

Kosai, Yutaka. *The Era of High-Speed Growth: Notes on the Postwar Japanese Economy.* Translated by Jacqueline Kaminski. Tokyo: University of Tokyo Press, 1986.

Kosakai Shōzō. "Gotō Noboru, Tsutsumi Seiji, Tsutsumi Yoshiaki: Mitsudomoe no seizetsu osero gemu," *Gendai,* March 1987, pp. 242–262.

———. "Josei no tame no raibaru sanpo Tōkyū vs. Seibu," *Fujin kōron,* July 1987, pp. 376–383.

———. "Nihon rettō seiha sensō," *Hōseki,* September 1987, pp. 80–91.

———. "Tsutsumi Yoshiaki ga nerau!," *Hōseki,* January 1987, pp. 172–188.

———. "Tsutsumi Yoshiaki–tochi o seishi, seikai o ugokasu," *Hōseki,* April 1988, pp. 164–173.

Koyama, Shuzo. "The Japanese Distribution System: 'Complex and Incomprehensible'?," *Look Japan,* December 10, 1984, pp. 10–11.

Kuredei Sezon 1989 kaisha gaikyō. Tokyo: Kuredei Sezon, 1989.

Kuredei Sezon 1990–1991 kaisha gaikyō. Tokyo: Kuredei Sezon, 1990.

Kusaka Kimindo. *Hapuningu abenyū "246."* Tokyo: Taiyō Kigyō Shuppan, 1984.

Kusano Hiroshi. *Seibu shōhō–aku no kōzu.* Tokyo: Ēru Shuppansha, 1983.

"Kyōto hoteru sensō de honkakukasuru Purinsu vs. Sezon no kokutō kassen," *Keizaikai,* September 2, 1986, p. 26.

Lam, Alice C. L. *Women and Japanese Management: Discrimination and Reform.* London: Routledge, 1992.

Lufty, Carol. "Changing Expectations," *Tokyo Business Today,* June 1988, pp. 14–17.

Maeda, Kazutoshi. "The Evolution of Retailing Industries in Japan," in Akio Okochi and Koichi Shimokawa, eds., *Development of Mass Marketing: The Automobile and Retailing Industries.* Tokyo: University of Tokyo Press, 1981. Pp. 265–289.

Manabe Shigeki. "Tsutsumi Seiji 'Seibu Sezon Gurūpu' no chi to yabō," *Gendai,* August 1986, pp. 134–145.

——. "Tsutsumi Yoshiaki 'boku wa bushi, Seijisan wa shōnin,'" *Gendai*, April 1986, pp. 104–115.

——. *Tsutsumi Yoshiaki no keiei tama: "Jūnen saki ni katsu."* Tokyo: Kōdansha, 1986.

——. *Tsutsumi Yoshiaki no 21seiki senryaku.* Tokyo: Kōdansha, 1984.

——. "Young Dictator Hidden in Veil," *Tokyo Business Today*, July 1986, pp. 26–29.

Masuda Tsūji. *Paruko no senden senryaku.* Tokyo: Paruko Shuppan, 1984.

Matsueda Fumiaki. *Tsutsumi Seiji no kenkyū.* Tokyo: Tōkyō Keizai, 1982.

Matsui Haruko. "Hakone Tochi no Ōizumi, Kodaira, Kunitachi no kōgai jūtakuchi kaihatsu," in Yamaguchi Hiroshi, ed., *Kōgai jūtakuchi no keifu.* Tokyo: Kajima Shuppankai, 1987. Pp. 221–236.

Matsunobu Hiromasa. *Dainiji ryūtsū kakumei.* Tokyo: Kyōikusha, 1986.

McCraw, Thomas K. and Patricia A. O'Brien. "Production and Distribution: Competition Policy and Industry Structure," in Thomas K. McCraw, ed., *America Versus Japan.* Boston: Harvard Business School Press, 1986. Pp. 77–116.

Miki Yōnosuke. *Gekidōki no keieisha.* Tokyo: Sekkasha, 1965.

——. "Zaikai saigo no kaibutsu no shi," *Zaikai*, June 1, 1964, pp. 8–13.

Mimura, Yohei. "Expert Consumers: Trends in Japanese Purchasing and Lifestyles," *Speaking of Japan*, no. 96, pp. 6–9 (December 1988).

Miura Masashi. "Ikeru gyakusetsu," in Ueno Chizuko, Nakamura Tatsuya, Tamura Akira, Hashimoto Jurō, and Miura Masashi, *Sezon no hassō: Māketto e no sokyū.* Tokyo: Riburopōto, 1991. Pp. 341–447.

Miyanaga, Kuniko. *The Creative Edge: Emerging Individualism in Japan.* New Brunswick, N.J.: Transaction Publications, 1991.

Miyano Tōru. *Onnatachi no chōsen.* Tokyo: Kōdansha, 1985.

Miyashita Hiroyuki. "Sōgō rejā sangyō e koshitantan Seibu Sezon Gurūpu 'kai' shingeki no uragawa!," *Zaikai tenbō*, May 1987, pp. 144–149.

—— and Shūdan Topura. *Seibu Sezon zankoku monogatari.* Tokyo: Ēru Bukkusu, 1987.

——. *Tsutsumi Yoshiaki no gekirin ni fureta Seiji no yabō.* Tokyo: Appuru Shuppansha, 1988.

Miyata, Mitsuru. "Problem Points in a Services-Oriented Economy." *Economic Eye*, vol. 4, no. 4, pp. 14–18 (1983).

Miyauchi, Yoshihiko. "Sunrise, Sunset: Japan's Transformation into a Service Economy," *Speaking of Japan*, October 1987, pp. 16–24.

Miyazaki Yoshikazu. *Sengo Nihon no kigyō shūdan.* Tokyo: Nihon Keizai Shinbunsha, 1976.

Mizushima Aiichirō. "'Hoteru Seiyō Ginza' de roteishita Seibu Sezon Gurūpu Tsutsumi Seiji no ōki na gosan," *Keizaikai,* January 6, 1987, pp. 44–47.

"Mono no ryūtsū kara bunka no ryūtsū e: Tsutsumi Seiji," *Rekishi tokuhon,* autumn 1987, pp. 56–57.

Morral, Tobit B. "Contemporary Entertainment in Japanese Society," B.A. thesis in Asian Studies, Connecticut College. New London, 1986.

Morris-Suzuki, Tessa. *Beyond Computopia: Information, Automation and Democracy in Japan.* New York: Kegan Paul International, 1988.

Nagatomi, Yuichiro. "The Dynamics of Service-Sector Growth." *Economic Eye,* vol. 4, no. 4, pp. 4–7 (1983).

Nakamachi, Hiroshi. "Ginza Store Wars," *Japan Quarterly,* vol. 33, no. 1, pp. 32–36 (1986).

Nakamura Kōhei. "Seibu Gurūpu o meguru sōkoku no kōzu," *Rekishi tokuhon,* pp. 130–139 (summer 1987).

Nakamura Takafusa. "What the Strong Yen Wrought: The Japanese Economy Yesterday and Today," *Japan Foundation Newsletter,* May 1990, pp. 1–7.

Nakamura Tatsuya. "Togisumasareta Don Kihōte," in Ueno Chizuko, Nakamura Tatsuya, Tamura Akira, Hashimoto Jurō, and Miura Masashi, *Sezon no hassō: Māketto e no sokyū.* Tokyo: Riburopōto, 1991. Pp. 139–187.

Nakata, Shin'ya. "Retailing: Variety of Means and the Conglo-merchants," *Japan Update,* no. 8, pp. 18–20 (summer 1988).

Nakauchi, Isao. "The Pursuit of 'Real' Affluence," *Look Japan,* December 10, 1986, pp. 4–5.

———. "The Yoke of Regulation Weighs Down on Distribution," *Economic Eye,* vol. 10, no. 2, pp. 17–19 (summer 1989).

Nakayama Hiroto. *Rejā sangyōkai.* Revised ed. Tokyo: Kyōikusha, 1988.

Narushima Tadaaki. *Seibu no subete.* Revised ed. Tokyo: Nihon Jitsugyō Shuppansha, 1989.

Natsubori Seigen. "Tsutsumi Yasujirō," *Purejidento,* February 1989, pp. 112–119.

Nihon chimei daijiten, 7 vols. Tokyo: Asakura Shoten, 1968.

Nihon Hyakkaten Kyōkai. *Nihon Hyakkaten Kyōkai tōkei nenpō 1989*. To-kyo, 1990.

Nihon kaisharoku. 17th ed. Tokyo: Kōjunsha, 1989.

Nihon Keizai Shimbun. *Nikkei Placement/International 1990*. Tokyo: Nihon Keizai Shimbun, 1989.

Nihon Keizai Shinbunsha. *Kaisha sōkan mijōjō kaishaban 1990*. Tokyo: Nihon Keizai Shinbunsha, 1990.

Nihon Sen'i Keizai Kenkyūjo. *Nihon no hyakkaten 1991*. Tokyo: Nihon Sen'i Keizai Kenkyūjo, 1990.

Nijūisseiki Kigyō Kenkyū Gurūpu. *Shin Seibu vs. Tōkyū aratanaru kōsō*. Tokyo: Yamanote Shobō, 1984.

Nikkei Ryūtsū Shinbun. *Hyakkaten ni asu wa aru ka*. Tokyo: Nikkei Ryūtsū Shinbun, 1985.

Nippon: A Charted Survey of Japan 1990/91. Tokyo: Kokuseisha, 1990.

Nishio Keisuke and Inoue Hirokazu. *Nihon no shitetsu 2 Seibu*. Osaka: Hoi-kusha, 1980.

Nishiyama Ikuo. "Seibu Sezon Gurūpu to Chichūkai Kurabu ni yoru rizōto kaihatsu," *Burēn*, July 1987, pp. 142–147.

Niwa Tetsuo. *Godai kigyō gurūpu no senryaku kakushin*. Tokyo: Tōyō Keizai Shinpōsha, 1992.

Noda Mineo and Koyama Tadashi. "Futatsu no Seibu o eguru!," *Hōseki*, October 1986, pp. 70–85.

O'Brien, Rodney. "Yenless: Artists Struggle as Society Thrives," *Intersect*, July 1989, pp. 31–32.

Oda Susumu. "Kenryokusha no seishin byōri (14) Tsutsumi Yoshiaki," *Hōseki*, September 1982, pp. 106–115.

Ogura, M. "Japan's Retail Industry in Trouble," *Tokyo Business Today*, February 1986, pp. 50–53.

Okada Yasushi. *Hyakkaten gyōkai*. Tokyo: Kyōikusha, 1985.

Orihashi Seisuke. *Sūpā gyōkai*. Revised ed. Tokyo: Kyōikusha, 1988.

Ōsawa Shōkai kaisha gaiyō. Tokyo: Ōsawa Shōkai, 1990.

"Ōsawa Shōkai 'totsuzenshi' no nazotoki," *Shūkan daiyamondo*, March 10, 1984, pp. 8–10.

Ōtsuka Hideki. "Tsutsumi Yoshiaki: waga 'jūnen senryaku,'" *Hōseki*, February 1987, pp. 134–145.

Parco. Tokyo: Parco, 1990.

Paruko. Tokyo: Paruko, 1990.

"Paruko bunka senryaku o kirisuteta Tsutsumi Seiji no 'shihonka no kao,'" *Uwasa no shinsō,* July 1989, pp. 42–45.

"Paruko 'ryūtsū bunka' o kaeta Masuda Tsūji to iu otoko," *Decide,* May 1987, pp. 35–38.

Pictorial Encyclopedia of Modern Japan. Tokyo: Gakken, 1986.

Purinsu Hoteru rejā katarogu. Tokyo: Purinsu Hoteru, 1991.

"'Rosuchairudo' mo tomatta 'Hoteru Seiyō Ginza' no gōka kyakusuji," *Shūkan shinchō,* April 2, 1987, pp. 37–41.

Ryūtsū kaisha nenkan 90nenban. Tokyo: Nihon Keizai Shinbunsha, 1989.

Saison Group. Tokyo: Saison Group, 1990.

Saison Group 1992. Tokyo: Saison Group, 1992.

Saison Life Insurance Co., Ltd. Annual Report '90. Tokyo 1990.

Saison 1992. Tokyo: Saison Group, 1992.

Sakaguchi Yoshihiro. *Seibu zankoku monogatari.* Tokyo: Ēru Shuppansha, 1979.

———. *Tsutsumi Seiji no sōdai na yabō.* Tokyo: Seinen Shokan, 1990.

"Sandaime shachō de tōsan 'Ōsawa Shōkai' wa sengo sanbanme no ōgata fusai," *Shūkan gendai,* March 17, 1984, p. 49.

Sankei kaisha nenkan, 22nd ed. Tokyo: Sankei Shinbun, 1990.

Sasaki Fumie. *Depāto sensō.* Tokyo: Keirin Shobō, 1985.

Sataka Makoto. "Seibu Tetsudō Gurūpu—hadaka no ōsama." *Asahi jānaru,* May 2, 1986, pp. 100–104.

Satō Ichidan. *Biggu sutoa doko ga tsuyokute doko ga yowai ka.* Tokyo: Nihon Jitsugyō Shuppansha, 1982.

Satō Tatsuya and Ōtemachi Tadashi. "Kokutetsu hyakuchōen riken kara shimedasareta Tsutsumi Yoshiaki no tai Nakasone, Gotō, soshite ani Seiji e no daihangeki," *Hōseki,* August 1986, pp. 130–147.

Saxonhouse, Gary R. "Services in the Japanese Economy," in Robert P. Inman, ed., *Managing the Service Economy: Prospects and Problems.* New York: Cambridge University Press, 1985. Pp. 53–83.

Sazanami, Yoko. "Japan's Trade and Investment in Finance, Information, Communications, and Business Services," in Chung H. Lee and Seiji Naya, eds., *Trade and Investment in the Asia Pacific Region.* Boulder, Colo.: Westview, 1988. Pp. 153–179.

Seibu Department Stores, Ltd., *Seibu Department Stores Group 1990–91.* Tokyo, 1990.

Seibu Hyakkaten. *Kurashi no yume no furonteia.* Tokyo: Fuji Intānashonaru Konsarutanto Shuppanbu, 1962.

Seibu Hyakkaten Bunka Kyōiku Jigyōbu. *SEED reboryūshon.* Tokyo: Daiyamondosha, 1987.

"Seibu Hyakkaten ga namae o kaeru hi," *Shūkan sankei,* June 19, 1986, pp. 28–31.

Seibu Hyakkaten Ikebukuro Komyunitei Karejji and Ryūtsū Sangyō Kenkyūjo. *Hōshoku jidai no shokuhin māketeingu senryaku.* Tokyo: Daiyamondosha, 1983.

———. *Kansei jidai no jinji senryaku.* Tokyo: Daiyamondosha, 1985.

———. *Yūrakuchō "Marion genshō" o toku.* Tokyo: Daiyamondosha, 1985.

"Seibu Kurejitto Marui ni yabureta geppu hyakkaten no tettei henshin," *Decide,* May 1987, pp. 39–44.

"Seibu Ryūtsū Gurūpu—yume to risuku no 'shingata shōsha' e sōdai no chōsen," *Nikkei bijinesu,* December 24, 1984, pp. 30–42.

"Seibu Sezon Gurūpu daishakkin hensai sakusen no shingan," *Shūkan daiyamondo,* October 26, 1985, pp. 50–55.

"Seibu teikoku," *Shūkan hōseki,* November 13, 1987, pp. 60–64.

Seibu Tetsudō. *Tsutsumi Yasujirō kaichō no shōgai.* Tokyo: Seibu Tetsudō, 1973.

"Seibu Tetsudō Gurūpu 'LBO keiei' no kakushin," *Shūkan daiyamondo,* July 21, 1990, pp. 38–46.

Seidensticker, Edward. *Tokyo Rising: The City Since the Great Earthquake.* New York: Knopf, 1990.

The Seiyo Corporation: Environmental Planning and Development. Tokyo: The Seiyo Corporation, 1989.

Seiyo Food Systems Inc. Annual Report 1990. Tokyo: Seiyo Food Systems, 1990.

Seiyō Fūdo Shisutemuzu kaisha annai. Tokyo: Seiyō Fūdo Shisutemuzu, 1989.

The Seiyu, Ltd. 1990 Annual Report. Tokyo: Seiyū, 1990.

Sezon Gurūpu. *O.E.S.* Tokyo: Sezon Gurūpu, 1989.

Sezon Gurūpu Gesuto Hausu. *Tsutsumi Yasujirō.* Tokyo: Sezon Gurūpu, 1991.

Sezon Gurūpu 1989–'90. Tokyo: Sezon Gurūpu, 1990.

Sezon Gurūpu 1989–'90. Expanded ed. Tokyo: Sezon Gurūpu, 1990.

Sezon no rekishi. Yui Tsunehiko, gen. ed. 2 vols. Tokyo: Riburopōto, 1991.

Shiizuka Takeshi. *Kōkando shōnin shūdan: Marui, Seibu ni miru "datsuryūtsū" senryaku.* Tokyo: Jatekku Shuppan, 1986.

"Shinka no kenkyū: Seibu Sezon Gurūpu," *Nikkei bijinesu,* September 28, 1987, pp. 8–23.

"Shōbai wa aruku koto kara—Seiyū," *Chūō kōron,* September 1987, pp. 111–113.

Smith, Lee. "Japan's Autocratic Managers," *Fortune,* January 7, 1985, pp. 56–65.

Sōgyō 100nenshi: Ōsawa Shōkai. Tokyo: Ōsawa Shōkai, 1990.

Suzuki Tōichi. "Misshitsu 'Takeshita' saiteigeki o kimeta Tsutsumi Yoshiaki 'gokuhi jōhō' no iryoku," *Sandē mainichi,* November 8, 1987, pp. 28–31.

Takabatake Michitoshi. *Chihō no ōkoku.* Tokyo: Ushio Shuppansha, 1986.

Takahashi Kenji. "Tōkyū Gotō Noboru no 'fuzai' de funshutsushita Osano Kenji Tsutsumi Yoshiaki," *Hōseki,* February 1986, pp. 165–179.

Takaoka Sueaki. *Seiyū Sutoā no ryūtsū shihai senryaku.* Tokyo: Nihon Jitsugyō Shuppansha, 1970.

Tamura Akira. "'Kabe' e no chōsen," in Ueno Chizuko, Nakamura Tatsuya, Tamura Akira, Hashimoto Jurō, and Miura Masashi, *Sezon no hassō: Māketto e no sokyū.* Tokyo: Riburopōto, 1991, pp. 191–274.

Tanaka Kenji. *Depāto gyōkai zankoku monogatari.* Tokyo: Ēru Shuppansha, 1984.

Tateishi Yasunori. "Tochi shisan ō Tsutsumi Yoshiaki shachō no 'chiisa na zeikin,'" *Bungei shunjū,* March 1990, pp. 190–206.

Tawara Sōichirō. "'Shinsōgyō' jidai," *Purejidento,* January 1987, pp. 208–222.

Thornbrugh, David. "The Changing Exchange," *Japan Update,* winter 1987, pp. 18–21.

Toba Kin'ichirō. *Nihon no ryūtsū kakushin.* Tokyo: Nihon Keizai Shinbunsha, 1979.

Tobin, Jospeh J., ed. *Re-Made in Japan: Everyday Life and Consumer Taste in a Changing Society.* New Haven: Yale University Press, 1992.

Tōkyōto. *Tokyō hyakunenshi.* 7 vols. Tokyo: Gyōsei, 1972–1979.

Tominaga Masabumi. *Seiyū Sutoā no keiei.* Tokyo: Nihon Jitsugyō Shuppansha, 1978.

Tomizawa Uio. *Raitei Tsutsumi Yasujirō.* Tokyo: Arupusu, 1962.

Toshimakushi. 7 vols. Tokyo: Toshimaku, 1975–1983.

Tsujii Takashi [Tsutsumi Seiji]. *Hōkō no kisetsu no naka de.* Tokyo: Shinchōsha, 1969.

———. *Itsumo to onaji haru.* Tokyo: Kawade Shobō Shinsha, 1983. Translated as *A Spring Like Any Other* by Beth Cary. Tokyo: Kodansha International, 1992.

———. *A Stone Monument on a Fine Day: Selected Poems.* Hisao Kanaseki and Timothy Harris, trs. Tokyo: Libro Port Publishing Company, 1990.

———. "Yoshida Shigeru to chichi Tsutsumi Yasujirō no tegami," *Shinchō*, no. 45, pp. 92–106 (August 1987).

——— and Sakaki Jirō. "'Kashiburu' yori mo 'gekijō' o tsukure," *Voice*, March 1987, pp. 46–55.

Tsukui Masayoshi. *Tstusumi Yasujirōden.* Tokyo: Tōyō Shokan, 1955.

Tsumuji Takao. "Itan no tōshō: Seibu ōkoku Tsutsumi Yoshiaki no henshin," *Shūkan asahi*, January 18, 1985, pp. 174–179.

Tsūshō Sangyō Daijin Kanbō Chōsa Tōkeibu. *Shōgyō dōtai tōkei nenpō 1989.* Tokyo: Tsūshō Sangyō Daijin Kanbō Chōsa Tōkeibu, 1990.

Tsutsumi Seiji. *Hatsugen shirīzu*, vols. 14–20. Tokyo: Seibu Ryūtsū Gurūpu, 1982–1988.

———. *Henkaku no tōshizu.* Tokyo: Torebiru, 1986.

———. "Motomerareru shinri kankakuteki manzoku," *Asahi shinbun*, U.S. ed., October 21, 1991, p. 8.

———. "Shinkeiei no shikon shōken," *Jitsugyō no Nihon.* 14-part series, January 1–July 15, 1970.

———. *Tsutsumi Seiji Tsujii Takashi fuīrudo nōto.* Tokyo: Bungei Shunjū, 1986.

———, ed. *Rejā no kagaku.* Tokyo: Jitsugyō no Nihonsha, 1962.

——— and Foumiko Kometani. "The Conversation," *Tokyo Journal*, January 1991, pp. 22–25.

"Tsutsumi Seiji vs. Tawara Sōichirō," *Hōseki*, January 1986, pp. 95–107.

"Tsutsumi Seijishi ga otōto Yoshiakishi ni atama o sageta wake," *Shūkan gendai*, January 5–12, 1991, pp. 40–43.

Tsutsumi, Yasujiro. *Bridge Across the Pacific.* Tokyo: Sanko Cultural Research Institute, 1963.

Tsutsumi Yasujirō. *Kutō sanjūnen.* Tokyo: Sankō Bunka Kenkyūjo, 1962.

———. *Shikaru.* Tokyo: Yūki Shobō, 1964.

———. "Watakushi no keiei tetsugaku," in Ōya Sōichi et al., eds., *Watakushi no keiei tetsugaku.* Tokyo: Chikuma Shobō, 1964. Pp. 163–177.

———. "Watakushi no rirekisho," in Nihon Keizai Shinbunsha, ed., *Watakushi no rirekisho, keizaijin 1.* Tokyo: Nihon Keizai Shinbunsha, 1980. Pp. 53–78.

——— and Tsutsumi Seiji. "Jigyō wa hōshi nari," *Chūō kōron*, December 1961, pp. 154–160.

Tsutsumi Yoshiaki. "Amaenaki kyōiku: Seisaku aru seiji o," in *Matsushita sei-keijuku kōwaroku*, vol. 7. Kyoto: PHP Kenkyūjo, 1984. Pp. 9–42.

———. "Tochi wa koko made yasuku nara 'Tōkyō kaizō' shian," *Gendai*, January 1989, pp. 246–256.

———. *Tsutsumi Yoshiaki wa kataru—Kyūjitsu ga hoshikereba kanrishoku o yamero*. Ed. Kaminogō Toshiaki. Tokyo: Kōdansha, 1984.

——— and Esaka Akira. "Nihon no fūdo o ikasu ōja no kōsō," *Voice*, February 1987, pp. 48–59.

——— and Kaminogō Toshiaki. *Tsutsumi Yoshiaki no ichinichi ikkun*. Tokyo: Rongu Serāzu, 1985.

——— and Kawakami Seiji. "Seibu Tetsudō Gurūpu sōsui Tsutsumi Yoshiaki wa Purinsu Hoteru shachō o naze shirizoita ka," *Zaikai*, August 18, 1987, pp. 34–39.

——— and Satō Masatada. "Kokudo Keikaku Tsutsumi Yoshiaki shachō ga akasu 'rizōto kaihatsu de seikōsuru hō,'" *Keizaikai*, December 13, 1988, pp. 100–103.

"Tsutsumi Yoshiaki, ani Seiji to no ketsubetsu no shinsō o kataru," *Keizaikai*, August 19, 1986, pp. 18–22.

"Tsutsumi Yoshiaki no 12chōen 'shisan' to 'ketsuzoku' kōsō no akirakasarenai bubun," *Shūkan gendai*, August 1, 1987, pp. 26–30.

"Tsutsumi Yoshiaki shachō ni 'yaku ni tatanai' to iwareta 'daisotsu shain,'" *Shūkan shinchō*, July 2, 1987, pp. 144–147.

"Tsutsumi Yūji ga Sezon Gurūpu iri," *Shūkan posuto*, January 2–9, 1987, pp. 46–47.

"Tsuyosa no kenkyū: Seibu Tetsudō Gurūpu," *Nikkei bijinesu*, June 25, 1984, pp. 22–39.

Uchimura Shun'ichirō. "Jōhō hasshin to jushin no kinō ga nai to kore kara no ryūtsū wa nobinai," *Dime*, January 1, 1988, pp. 52–54.

Ueno Chizuko. "Imēji no shijō," in Ueno Chizuko, Nakamura Tatsuya, Tamura Akira, Hashimoto Jurō, and Miura Masashi, *Sezon no hassō: Māketto e no sokyū*. Tokyo: Riburopōto, 1991. Pp. 3–136.

Ukaji Kiyoshi, ed. *Nihon no kaisha 100nenshi*. 2 vols. Tokyo: Tōyō Keizai Shinpōsha, 1975.

Umemoto Katsushi. "Gekitotsu! Sakakura Mitsukoshi vs. Tsutsumi Seibu," *Hōseki*, June 1986, pp. 70–85.

Un'yushō Daijin Kanbō Kokuyū Tetsudō Kaikaku Suishinbu. *Tetsudō tōkei nenpō 1987*. Tokyo: Un'yushō, 1989.

Un'yushō Un'yu Seisakukyoku Jōhō Kanribu. *Tetsudō yusō tōkei nenpō 1988.* Tokyo: Un'yushō, 1990.

Wada Shigeaki. *Chōsenteki keiei no himitsu.* Tokyo: Jōhō Sentā Shuppankyoku, 1981.

——. "Seibu Hyakkaten no hassō," in Seibu Hyakkaten Ikebukuro Komyunitei Karejji and Ryūtsū Sangyō Kenkyūjo, *Sentan shōgyō no hassō to senryaku.* Tokyo: Daiyamondosha, 1982. Pp. 119–132.

Wakabayashi Terumitsu. "Shafū wa 'chikara' nari—Tsutsumi Yoshiaki to Kokudo Keikaku," *Will,* December 1983, pp. 69–72.

Watanabe Kazuo. *Sogō no Seibu daihōi senryaku.* Tokyo: Kōbunsha, 1988.

Watanabe, Kinko. "The Spirit of Ambivalence," *Look Japan,* July 1989, pp. 42–43.

Whiting, Robert. *You Gotta Have Wa: When Two Cultures Collide on the Baseball Diamond.* New York: Macmillan, 1989.

"Yahari motsurehajimeta Tsutsumi 'shichi kyōdai' shusshō no innen," *Shūkan shinchō,* July 12, 1986, pp. 36–40.

Yamaguchi Hiroshi. "Kaisetsu," in Yamaguchi Hiroshi, ed., *Kōgai jutakuchi no keifu.* Tokyo: Kajima Shuppankai, 1987. Pp. 45–55.

——, ed. *Kōgai jutakuchi no keifu.* Tokyo: Kajima Shuppankai, 1987.

Yamaichi Shōken Keizai Kenkyūjo. *Sangyō no subete, 1990.* Tokyo: Yamaichi Shōken Keizai Kenkyūjo, 1990.

Yamakawa Sanpei. *Gotō Tsutsumi fūunroku.* Tokyo: Zaikai Tsūshinsha, 1959.

Yamamoto, Shuichi [pseud.]. "Economics: Young Turks." *PHP Intersect,* March 1986, pp. 11–13.

Yamane Ichigen. "Gekitotsu! Tsutsumi Seiji vs. Yoshiaki no rettō rizōto daisensō," *Gendai,* December 1988, pp. 108–124.

Yamashita Takeshi. *FuamirīMāto—yakushin no himitsu.* Tokyo: TBS Buritanika, 1990.

——. *Seibu Ryūtsū Gurūpu no subete.* Tokyo: Kokusai Shōgyō Shuppan, 1980.

Yamazaki Masakazu. *Yawarakai kojinshugi no tanjō.* Tokyo: Chūō Kōronsha, 1984.

Yasuda Shinji. *Tsutsumi Seiji.* Tokyo: Paru Shuppan, 1985.

Yonekawa, Shin-ichi. "Recent Writing on Japanese Economic and Social History," *Economic History Review,* 2nd ser., vol. 38, no. 1, pp. 107–123 (February 1985).

Yoshida Sadao, ed. *Kimi wa eien no teki da.* Tokyo: Chūkei Shuppan, 1984.

"Yoshinoya 'hatan chokugo kara zōshū zōeki' no himitsu," *Decide,* May 1987, pp. 45–47.

Yūka shōken hōkokusho sōran. Semiannual. Tokyo: Ōkurashō Insatsukyoku.

"Za raibaru: Seibu Hyakkaten vs. Isetan." *Gekiryū,* December 1987, pp. 18–23.

Zaikai kakushin no shidōsha. Tokyo: TBS Buritanika, 1983.

"Zeikin o harawanai Seibu '"Tsutsumi' ga sekaiichi no kanemochi," *Shūkan shinchō,* July 23, 1987, pp. 128–131.

"Zig-zag Seibu Ryūtsū Gurūpu ga tōsanshita Ōsawa Shōkai no suponsā ni," *Shūkan hōseki,* May 25, 1984, p. 51.

Index

Harvard East Asian Monographs
Subseries on the History of
Japanese Business and Industry